Edwin Abbott Abbott

Thomas of Canterbury

His Death and Miracles

Edwin Abbott Abbott

Thomas of Canterbury
His Death and Miracles

ISBN/EAN: 9783743350557

Manufactured in Europe, USA, Canada, Australia, Japa

Cover: Foto ©ninafisch / pixelio.de

Manufactured and distributed by brebook publishing software (www.brebook.com)

Edwin Abbott Abbott

Thomas of Canterbury

St. Thomas of Canterbury

HIS DEATH AND MIRACLES

BY

EDWIN A. ABBOTT, M.A., D.D.

FORMERLY FELLOW OF ST. JOHN'S COLLEGE, CAMBRIDGE
AND HULSEAN LECTURER
AUTHOR OF 'PHILOCHRISTUS' 'ONESIMUS' ETC.

IN TWO VOLUMES

VOL. I

LONDON
ADAM AND CHARLES BLACK
1898

TO THE MEMORY OF

THOMAS

ONCE ARCHBISHOP OF CANTERBURY

NOW VENERATED BY SOME AS SAINT AND MARTYR

BY OTHERS ADMIRED AS A HERO

BY SOME FEW VILIFIED AS A NARROW ECCLESIASTIC

BUT DESERVING TO BE STUDIED BY ALL

WHETHER FRIENDS CRITICS OR ENEMIES

AS A CONSPICUOUS PROOF

THAT THE SPIRIT

MAY BE THEN FIRST MANIFESTED IN ITS FULL POWER

WHEN DEFEAT AND CORRUPTION

HAVE TRIUMPHED OVER THE FLESH

PREFACE

IN the course of preparing a critical commentary on the Four Gospels, it became necessary to consider other instances of documents relating the same fact in different language, as the Gospels relate in different language the acts and words of Christ.

A brief glance at the *Materials for the History of Thomas Becket* published under the direction of the Master of the Rolls, at once suggested extracts likely to afford useful illustrations. But afterwards, when more closely studied, those volumes seemed to present parallelisms to problems of New Testament criticism so exact and so helpful that, instead of forming a few paragraphs in the proposed work, the extracts and notes grew, first into a chapter, and then into a separate section.

Up to this point, the audience in view being mainly students of theology, all extracts had been kept in their original Latin. But when it became needful to quote passages from the two books composed by Benedict and William of Canterbury on the *Miracles of St. Thomas*, many of the narratives seemed so fresh and interesting, so full of touches of perennial human nature, and often so instructive as to a past in danger of being forgotten, yet not to be forgotten without danger—that a change of front was made, so as to give the text in English as well as in Latin, thus throwing everything open to the general reader while retaining all that was of use for the student.

The result has been that the "few paragraphs" have grown into a book of considerable size, and probably a book in which several blemishes of detail may be detected, owing, partly to the method of its evolution, and still more to the want of leisure for doing full justice to the subject. But on this last point there was no alternative. The claims of the main object did not allow time for more than this incidental excursion. Errors and imperfections in this somewhat hasty translation of ecclesiastical Latin will not (it is hoped) prevent the unlearned reader from deriving from it a fairly accurate notion of Becket's Miracles; and learned critics may forgive much to one who has given them, in almost every case of doubt or difficulty, the means of judging for themselves—by setting before them the original documents so classified as to save them a great deal of trouble, and so annotated as never to pass over any point that appeared open to question.

It will be readily understood that, in this enlarged and separate form, the work rarely touches on New Testament criticism. Nevertheless the author is not without hope that it may be of some indirect service to theologians of all schools, in so far as all are, or ought to be, students of evidence. One reason why the criticism of the Gospels oscillates much, and progresses little, is that there has been little systematic study of other similar documents such as may be called Synoptic (like our first three Gospels) or Supplementary (like our fourth). On this subject, a vast superfluity of opinions coexists with a paucity of arranged materials for forming opinions, and with an almost complete absence of recognized rules of criticism. The object of this treatise, so far as it bears on theology, is to supply a store of classified facts that no reasonable critic can afford to despise.

The translations of the extracts from Garnier's *Vie de Saint Thomas le Martir* have been revised by Mr. H. Symons, B.A., formerly Scholar of Wadham College, Oxford, Assistant in the Department of Printed Books in the British Museum. To him I am also indebted for the quotations from Godefroy bearing on points of difficulty; and without his aid I should not have ventured on publishing my attempts at a literal rendering of the original. The *Étude Historique* on Garnier by E. Étienne (Paris, 1883) did not come to my notice till the first volume of this work was in type. Its value on philological subjects seemed greater than on the question of Garnier's relation to the Latin biographies. On the latter point students would find great help in the very full and able Introduction to *Thomas Saga Erkibyskups* by Mr. Eirikr Magnusson, Sub-Librarian of University Library, Cambridge (Rolls Series, London, 1875).

CONTENTS

INTRODUCTION . . . . Page 1

PART I

ST. THOMAS'S DEATH

CHAPTER I

THE NARRATORS

§ 1. The five eye-witnesses. § 2. The absent friend. § 3. Anonymous writers. § 4. Garnier, and the Saga 11

CHAPTER II

THE BREAKING OPEN OF THE PALACE

§ 1. Introduction. § 2. The different accounts. § 3. The "extraordinary timidity" imputed by Stanley to the monks 27

CHAPTER III

THE CONVEYANCE OF THE ARCHBISHOP TO THE CATHEDRAL

§ 1. The different accounts. § 2. The carrying of the cross. § 3. The bolt that came off "as though it had been fastened by glue." § 4. Another door that "opened as if spontaneously." § 5. The "carrying" of the Archbishop
45

CHAPTER IV

THE ENTRANCE OF THE ARCHBISHOP INTO THE CATHEDRAL

§ 1. The different accounts. § 2. The *Saga's* regard for the Fitness of Things. § 3. Different points of view . . . . . Page 58

CHAPTER V

THE APPROACH OF THE KNIGHTS

§ 1. The different accounts. § 2. Omissions and errors .   64

CHAPTER VI

THE ENTRANCE OF THE KNIGHTS INTO THE CATHEDRAL

§ 1. The different accounts. § 2. The flight of the Archbishop's friends   77

CHAPTER VII

THE MEETING OF THE ARCHBISHOP AND THE KNIGHTS

§ 1. The different accounts. § 2. What did the Archbishop say? § 3. The Martyr's last footsteps. § 4. Stanley and Tennyson . . . 87

CHAPTER VIII

THE STRUGGLE

§ 1. The different accounts. § 2. The words of the dialogue. § 3. Has Grim omitted any of the Archbishop's words? § 4. Striking off "the cap." § 5. Who, if any one, was "shaken off" by the Archbishop? § 6. Hugh of Morville. § 7. Stanley and Tennyson 100

CHAPTER IX

THE FIRST BLOW

§ 1. The different accounts. § 2. Who struck the first blow? § 3. Garnier's testimony. § 4. The Archbishop's words. § 5. Stanley and Tennyson

127

CHAPTER X

THE DEATH AND OUTRAGE

§ 1. The different accounts. § 2. Details of the death. § 3. The Archbishop's last words . . . . Page 149

CHAPTER XI

AFTER DEATH

§ 1. The different accounts. § 2. Was the body "entirely deserted"? § 3. Was there "a tremendous storm"? § 4. The date . . . 175

CHAPTER XII

INFERENCES

§ 1. A general inference. § 2. An early narrative, if not from an eye-witness, mostly contains "lies." § 3. The evidence of one eye-witness is of more value than the concurrent testimony of many non-eye-witnesses. § 4. The evidence of non-eye-witnesses is only so far valuable as it preserves the evidence of eye-witnesses, distinct from inferences and corrections made by the former. § 5. The evidence of a late non-eye-witness is particularly liable to the inferential taint. § 6. Errors of word. § 7. Misarrangement of statements. § 8. Misapplication of statements. § 9. Misjudgment of statements. § 10. Omissions or alterations for edification. § 11. Floating Tradition. § 12. The importance of internal evidence 192

APPENDIX I

GERVASE OF CANTERBURY

APPENDIX II

HOW THOMAS WAS SAVED FROM DROWNING

§ 1. Garnier. § 2. Anon I. § 3. Grim. § 4. The *Saga*   216

PART II

ST. THOMAS'S MIRACLES

SECTION I

THE BEGINNING OF THE MIRACLES

§ 1. Miracles, at first, unfashionable, and even dangerous. § 2. The nature of the first miracles. § 3. Benedict's description of the night and day after the Martyrdom. § 4. Benedict's account of the first miracle. § 5. John of Salisbury. § 6. William's Preface. § 7. Apparent allusions to Benedict. § 8. William acts on the principle "Choose what thou wilt." § 9. Grim's account of the first miracle, and of the burial. § 10. Anon. I. on the burial. § 11. Fitzstephen's account of the burial. § 12. Fitzstephen's account of the first miracles. § 13. Fitzstephen on the hostility to the miracles. § 14. Herbert on the burial. § 15. Herbert's silence on the miracles. § 16. Anon. II. on the miracles. § 17. Anon. III. and Anon. IV. on the miracles. § 18. Anon. V. reports legends. § 19. Anon. X. on the burial and miracles; "redness in the sky." § 20. Garnier on the burial and miracles. § 21. The *Saga*; St. Thomas's Well. § 22. Origin of the *Saga's* legends. § 23. Contrast between the *Saga* and a contemporary letter. § 24. The singular value of Benedict's testimony . . . . . Page 223

SECTION II

THE GROWTH OF THE MIRACLES, OR BENEDICT'S EARLIEST RECORDS

§ 1. Benedict's list compared with William's. § 2. Miracles of January, 1171. § 3. Lent, 1171. § 4. Easter, 1171. § 5. Two disappointments. § 6. The Water of Canterbury. § 7. Danger from the enemies of St. Thomas. § 8. Increase of miracles after Easter, 1171. § 9. Influence of neighbourhood; the worm; the cherry-stone. § 10. Two peaceful deaths. § 11. A boy blind from birth. § 12. Whitsuntide; candle-miracles. § 13. The moral effect of the miracles. § 14. Dream? self-deception? or lie? § 15. Benedict is scolded for scepticism. § 16. Welsh miracles. § 17. St. Thomas or St. Ithamar? An enemy convinced. § 18. Offerings of money. § 19. The stories of Edric. § 20. The testimony of Henry of Houghton. § 21. Miracles at Newington. § 22. The thirteen "candles" . . 249

SECTION III

THE LATER MIRACLES, OR BENEDICT ASSISTED BY WILLIAM

§ 1. William's attitude to Benedict. § 2. The new Prologue. § 3. Leprosy. § 4. The chronicler seeks variety. § 5. Foreign cures; miraculous chastisements. § 6. The son of William of Banwell; Matilda from the region of Cologne. § 7. The Saint's "merry jests." § 8. Miracles for mariners; an imposture works a cure. § 9. The Water; imperfect cures; Benedict's miracle. § 10. Restoration after drowning. § 11. Leprosy again. § 12. Trial by ordeal. § 13. Dropsy; beer that will not ferment. § 14. End of the Fourth Book; the Fifth Book; confusion in arrangement. § 15. The Sixth Book . . . . . Page 302

INTRODUCTION

[1][1] Thomas, Archbishop of Canterbury, was murdered on Tuesday, 29th December 1170. Three days later, Emma, wife of a knight in Sussex, wept for him as a martyr, and, while weeping and praying, recovered from a temporary attack of blindness. On the Sunday afterwards, Huelina, in Gloucestershire, recovered from a terrible complaint in the head that had troubled her for years (taking away all

---

[1] [1a] *Black Arabic numbers* refer to subsections, indicated by black numbers, in this volume : **1**a, **2**a, etc., mean footnotes on subsections **1**, **2**, etc. An ordinary Arabic number, following a black one, refers to a paragraph in a subsection in the Parallel Miracles : *e.g.* **679** (2) = subsection **679**, paragraph (2).

Anon. I. means the author commonly called "Roger of Pontigny." As there is practically no evidence for the latter title, Anon. I. has been adopted as being less misleading, and also as indicating that this writer is superior in authority to all the other anonymous writers.

Garnier means Garnier's *Vie de Saint Thomas*, ed. Hippeau, Paris, 1859, referred to by the line in that edition.

Lupus, see *Quadrilogus* below.

Mat. means *Materials for the History of Thomas Becket Archbishop of Canterbury,* vols. i.-vii., edited by the Rev. J. C. Robertson, Canon of Canterbury, Rolls Series, London, 1875-1885. Thus *Mat.* iii. 51 means p. 51 of vol. iii. of the *Materials.* In Part II. *Mat.* is often omitted for brevity, where the reference is to William's or Benedict's works on St. Thomas's Miracles, which are, severally, in vols. i. and ii. of the *Materials.*

Quadrilogus, or the *Early Quadrilogus,* means the early form of that work (**21**), sometimes called by the misleading name of the *Second Quadrilogus* because it was not printed till 1682. A later (**23**) and ampler edition, printed in 1495, is sometimes called by the misleading name of the *First Quadrilogus.* In this work it is called the *Late Quadrilogus.*

The *Early Quadrilogus* is sometimes referred to as "Lupus," or "Wolf," the name of its editor.

Saga means *Thomas Saga Erkibyskups*, edited by Mr. Eirikr Magnusson,

power of motion for days together)—and this, immediately after her mother Aaliza, of London, had professed faith in Thomas as a martyr and had pledged her daughter to a pilgrimage to the place of his death.

[2] So says Benedict, the author of the earliest treatise on St. Thomas's miracles, and few will dispute that his statements are correct. Of course, it may be said about these two cases that, in each, the recovery was a mere coincidence, or a sequel, not a result. But a glance at Benedict's book will shew that the coincidence-theory soon breaks down. There are too many of such "coincidences," or "sequels," to be explained under' either heading. In a large number of these cases probably, and in some certainly, men and women were instantaneously or rapidly healed, in a way in which an ordinary physician could not have healed them; and the most reasonable statement of the cause is that it was a strong emotional shock conveyed to them through faith in the late Archbishop whom people now called Saint and Martyr.

[3] Facts like these are more helpful than volumes of vague generalities, or even acute discussions of political questions, in bringing before us the attitude of the poorer classes in England in the great contest between Henry II. and his former Chancellor. They were for the Archbishop, as the champion of the poor and of righteousness—or, perhaps, more negatively, their defender against brutalizing encroachments of rapacity, violence, and lust. It does not seem to have been with them, primarily, a national question,

---

Sub-Librarian of University Library, Cambridge (Rolls Series, London, 1875). It is referred to by vol. and page.

Stanley means Stanley's *Memorials of Canterbury*, 10th edition, London, 1883.

N.B.—In the spelling of names it has not been thought necessary to aim at uniformity. For example, by calling Reginald Fitzurse, Reginald in translations from William of Canterbury, but Reynald, Rainald, or Renald in translations from other authors, there is gained the advantage of distinguishing an author using the Latin from those using the French form.

English against French,—though in a few of the miracles, and especially the notable one of Eilward of Westoning,[2] there appears in the burgesses a sense of resentment against the law of mutilation for theft and its hard administration. Fundamentally, their zeal for the Martyr was a zeal for him as the representative of the oppressed in either nation, French or English, and strongest among the English simply because the English were most oppressed.

[4] Thomas himself did not put forth the poor, but "his order," or "the liberties of the Church," as the good cause for which he was ready to die. But still the poor felt that their cause was bound up in his. His "order," besides including as it did the great mass of those who could read and write, might at any time include the child of a common labourer. A "villain" might become Archbishop, or even Pope. It was a "clerk" of Picardy who expressed the feelings of the English poor in verses of which the following is a literal translation:—

> "Kings, Counts, and Dukes, seldom we see them holy,
> These God refuseth oft as loth to serve Him,
> Oft do they swerve from right through covetousness,
> Naught do they, save what falleth with their pleasure,
> Laws make they at their will; to lie they fear not.
> Kings God doth not elect, nor choose, nor take,
> Nor Dukes, nor other lords of high degree;
> But whoso cry to Him and lead just lives,
> Whether of high estate or from low folk,
> God doth exalt, if they intend His service.
>
> . . . . .
>
> The humble doth God love, the poor as well,
> For from their toil they live, in torment ever,
> And Holy Church they love, and clerks, and poor folk,
> And righteous alms they give, and lead clean lives,
> And such as these will God exalt for ever.

---

[2] See below, **710**.

> Peter and Andrew, brothers brotherly,
> With boat and net were toiling, fishermen,
> When they were called by God from that poor labour.
> Then for His love they both were crucified,
> Apostles now in heaven and glorious lords."³

[5] "Apostle now in heaven" hardly exaggerates the feeling of the English for their new Martyr. William of Canterbury⁴ gives us a vision, seen soon after the Archbishop's death, and before the arrival of the papal letter authorizing his canonization. Two priests are seen by the sleeper, or seer, clothed in full vestments, one of whom beckons to the other to begin a mass in honour of the new Saint. The other replies that this must not be, because the canonizing letter has not yet arrived from the Successor of the Apostles. Upon this, the first rejoins, "Then if it

---

³   Reis et cuntes et ducx, poi les véum saintir :
       Deus les refuse mult, car ne l'voelent servir.
       Koveitise les feit sovent del dreit guenchir ;
       Ne funt rien se ço nun ke lur veint à pleisir.
       Leis funt à lur talent, n'ont poür de mentir.
         Les Reis n'eslist pas Deus, ne ne koisist, ne prent,
       Ne les Ducx, ne les hautes persones ensement.
       Mès chascun qui Deu crient et qui vit léument,
       U il seit de haut liu, u seit de basse gent,
       Deus le munte et eshauce, s'à lui servir entent.

           .   .   .   .   .

         Les humles aime Deus, les povres ensement,
       Kar de lur travail vivent ; tut dis sunt en torment,
       Et aiment sainte Eglise et clers et povre gent,
       Et dreites dimes dunent, et vivent nettement ;
       Et teus eshaucera Deus parmeinnablement.
         Et Pères et Andreus furent frère frarur ;
       A batel et à reiz esteient péchéur,
       Quant Deus les apella de cel povre labur ;
       Puis furent mis en cruiz et mort pur sue amur,
       Apostles sunt el Cel et glorius Seignur !

This extract is from Garnier's *La Vie de Saint Thomas* (ll. 81-115, ed. Hippeau, Paris, 1859), written (*ib.* 5825) in the fourth year after the Archbishop's death (**39**).

⁴ See below, **594**.

cannot be in Latin, let us have it in English," and strikes up an Anglican antiphon that hails Thomas as—

> " Hali Thomas of hevenriche (heaven-kingdom)
> Alle postles eve[n]liche,"

—that is to say, " equal to all the apostles."

[6] From these and many other stories to be found in the following pages, it is manifest that the memory of the murdered Archbishop had a great power in shaping political results, and still more in moulding the character of the people, during that memorable generation which witnessed the signing of Magna Charta.

[7] In time, it is true, he became the fashionable Saint, and then his influence degenerated. He was supposed to have brought about the defeat and captivity of William, King of Scotland, on the very day on which Henry did penance at his Memorial in Canterbury. After that, it was natural that courtiers, and great people, and fine ladies, should visit his tomb, and that they and others should associate his name with degenerate miracles about the finding of falcons, the recovery of lost coins and rings, and other petty coincidences. But even then, and for a long time afterwards, he was associated, in the hearts of the masses, with the helpful Providence that watches over men's stumblings, dangers, and afflictions. Sailors saw St. Thomas pushing their vessel off a sunken reef, or bringing them safe into port in spite of tempest. Travellers by land or water attributed to him their most marvellous escapes. But, above all, among the sick and suffering, his face, with the blood-streak of Martyrdom sloping from the forehead across the cheek, made him known through visions, as well as pictures and poems, throughout the huts and workshops of England, not only as the household saint among the poor, but also as the special patron of those afflicted with disease.

[8] Some may assert that Becket had no right thus to

bless and be blessed. He was no saint, they may say, but a man of uncontrolled and uncontrollable disposition. Having passed—perhaps reluctantly, perhaps with the appearance of reluctance—from the position of Chancellor to that of Archbishop, he transferred to the service of the Church the imperious temper that he had been able to indulge without restraint in the service of the King. It was, they may urge, the circumstances of his death, and not the spirit of the man, that caused him to be identified with justice and righteousness.

[9] Fully to judge this question would need an examination of the life of the Archbishop, with which this treatise does not deal. Yet the miracles by themselves go far to prove that those who see in Thomas Becket nothing more than a hot-tempered ecclesiastic, jealous for the exclusive privileges of his order, are virtually drawing an indictment not only against a nation but also against the very laws of human nature. And, so far as I have studied the records of his life, it seems more consistent with them also to believe that not till his consecration as Archbishop did the former Chancellor realize the abominable badness of the forces that were at work among the secular rulers, and the pitiable condition of the lower classes who lived, as Garnier says, " all their days in torment " and for whom each oppressor " made laws to his liking." Even when the existing laws were observed, yet how oppressively they may have worked, the reader may perceive by a glance at the story of the famous restoration of the mutilated Eilward of Westoning (**710**).

That afterwards the secular courts improved, and the ecclesiastical courts degenerated, does not shew that the former were at that time fitted to encroach, if Henry II. wished them to encroach, on the jurisdiction of the latter, without injury to the prospects of national liberty. And this the Archbishop may have felt, and thousands of poor folk, too, with a keenness not easily intelligible now.

Gradually, but with all sincerity, he may have grown into the conviction that he was called to contend for "his order," and that in fighting this battle he was championing the cause of the Universal Church, the spiritual Commonweal of mankind. For this, in his last moments, he professed his readiness to die; and, dying for this, unarmed against arms, with faith in invisible against visible forces, and attesting his faith with his blood, he seems fairly entitled to the name of Martyr.

[10] Be this as it may, all those who are interested in the shaping of religions, the foundation of churches, and generally in the moulding of the human mind by emotional and imaginative forces, may here find much that may throw light on these fascinating subjects. Indeed, from one point of view, the less saintly and the more imperfect St. Thomas was, the more interesting becomes the study of his influence. For if a very imperfect and wholly unsaintly person could be placed by death in a position to work such wonders, how much more mighty works might be expected, after death, from one who was a real Saint, a Saint of Saints, identified also with the cause of righteousness at a time when, to the eyes of the Christian seer in Patmos, a Beast seemed seated on the throne of the civilized world!

The preceding remarks refer only to Part II., which deals with the miracles.

[11] Part I. deals with the Martyr's death, and attempts to shew from a classification of several narratives how even eye-witnesses may have been misled, and may have misled others, as to important details, and also how easy and natural it was for the miraculous element to intrude, even within five years of the Martyrdom, as soon as a writer, quitting documents, began to quote what he called (**31**) "veracious report."

PART I
ST. THOMAS'S DEATH

CHAPTER I

THE NARRATORS

§ 1. *The five eye-witnesses*[1]

[12] AMONG a large number of accounts of the murder of Archbishop Becket in 1170, five were written (wholly or in part) from ocular testimony, viz. those by (1) Edward Grim, (2) William Fitzstephen, (3) John of Salisbury, afterwards Bishop of Chartres, (4) William of Canterbury, and (5) Benedict, afterwards Prior of Canterbury. (6) A sixth writer, Herbert of Bosham, was with the Archbishop almost to the day of his death, and had been on intimate terms with him during his archiepiscopal career. Some account of these writers will enable the reader to understand their several points of view and to appreciate the explanations of their divergences.

[13] (1) The place of honour is due to Edward Grim, "an Englishman by birth," who had but recently come to the Archbishop. Newcomer though he was, he stood by his patron's side, when the rest of his clerks (except Fitzstephen) abandoned him, and almost lost an arm in the attempt to save him from being dragged out of the church. He is mentioned as dead by Herbert of Bosham in his list of Becket's "Eruditi," a list[2] compiled before the death of Pope Urban III. Hence Grim must have written before,

---

[1] For the abbreviations of references, see 1*a*.
[2] He refers in it to Pope Urban III. ("hodie totius ecclesiae rector"), who died 20th October 1187, *Saga*, ii. p. xcii.

and probably several years before, 1187. His work concludes with a description of the king's penance at St. Thomas's Tomb (1174). He mentions Benedict as Prior of Canterbury (1175-77), and probably wrote about, or before, 1177.[3]

[14] (2) William Fitzstephen, one of the Archbishop's "clerks," was an inmate of his household, remembrancer in his chancery, and sub-deacon in his chapel, occasionally acting as advocate in the archiepiscopal court. Both he and John of Salisbury were with the Archbishop just before the murder; but he claims that, when John and the rest of the "clerks" ran away, he remained, along with Edward Grim and Robert of Merton (of whom mention will be made below). Fitzstephen, like Becket, was a native of London, and he gives a glowing description of the city. The editor of his biography notes the enthusiasm with which he writes of the good points of a horse: and, in general, he takes a less monastic view of things than Herbert of Bosham, Benedict, and William. He will be found the only one to tell us concerning the knights, as they enter the Cathedral, that they had their visors down.

[15] On a memorable occasion at Northampton, when Herbert advised the Archbishop to excommunicate any one that might lay hands on him, Fitzstephen dissuaded his patron from following this advice. Perhaps there was no love lost between him and his fellow "clerks"—John of Salisbury, in particular, whom he singles out for unfavourable mention, tacitly contrasting his flight with the courage of a few. Herbert of Bosham says that John "remained with our martyr in his trial strenuously and manfully to the end," while he excludes Fitzstephen from his long list of the Archbishop's faithful and learned companions. Fitzstephen did not accompany the Archbishop into exile, and he himself tells us that he made his peace with the King by presenting

---
[3] If Grim, as is probable, borrowed from Garnier, the former must have written after the latter, *i.e.* after the beginning of the year 1175 (39).

to him a form of prayer fit for the King's use composed in rhyming Latin verse. There is nothing of the flatterer in it, and he makes the King accuse himself of a multitude of sins. And the Archbishop himself does not seem to have blamed his follower. But the exiles may naturally have felt bitter against the man who could keep on terms both with their banisher and with their leader. He probably began to write some time before 1177, and before the publication of William of Canterbury's book of Miracles.[4]

[16] (3) John of Salisbury, one of the Archbishop's most familiar friends and counsellors, is known, from the testimony of Benedict, to have been with the Archbishop in his palace and to have expostulated with him for his bitter and contumelious language to the four knights; and he is expressly mentioned (somewhat unkindly) by Fitzstephen as abandoning the Archbishop in the Cathedral. Yet his account of the murder is most meagre—being little more than a repetition of a letter actually written soon after its occurrence.[5] For this, several probable reasons may be assigned. He was a man of temperate disposition, favouring moderate courses, and he may have thought that no good could be done by mentioning the names of the murderers in detail and heaping execrations on them; he was a man of affairs (not long afterwards Bishop of Chartres) and may have felt that detailed reminiscences and reproaches, while doing no one any good, might injure his own prospects of useful work; and widen the breach between the King and the Church. He *makes no mention of Edward Grim.* It is probable that he wrote his biography before 1176 when he was made Bishop of Chartres: but in any case he seems to have taken no trouble to revise and amplify his account of the Martyrdom, which he leaves as he first wrote it. For

---

[4] [15*a*] There appear to have been two editions of Fitzstephen's biography. The briefer (and probably earlier) is now found only in one MS., called *J.*

[5] *Mat.* ii., Introd. p. xlii., vii. 465 *sq.*

our purposes, therefore, he wrote immediately after the events that he describes (29th December 1170).

[17] (4) William, a monk of Canterbury—subsequently author of a book on St. Thomas's miracles dedicated to Henry II.—describes himself as present at the time of the murder, and admits with contrition that he fled to a neighbouring altar just before the fatal blow. In his book on the miracles he makes no attempt to arrange them chronologically; and his account of the Martyrdom is confused, partly, perhaps, because it combines an original narrative written shortly after the act with what seems an appendix of later date. It is only in the appendix that Grim is mentioned, and there somewhat grudgingly. William began to compile the Book of Miracles seventeen months (May 1172) after the Martyrdom (1170). After Henry II. had done penance at the tomb of St. Thomas (1174) there was no reason why eulogies of the Martyr should not be freely published. Most of the important miracles toward the end of William's book took place in 1174. He was probably sent to King Henry with his book shortly after Benedict was removed from the Priorate of Canterbury to the Abbacy of Peterborough (1177). In its present form, William's work contains very severe censures on the Irish War,[6] and there are other passages that King Henry might have disliked to read. But there is no necessity to suppose that the dedication copy presented to the King included everything that appeared in later copies. In describing Henry's cruelty to Becket's relations,[7] William prudently copies the exact words of John of Salisbury (Bishop of Chartres in 1176). His book on Miracles must have been published before 1189 (the year of Henry's death). His biography, at all events in part, was probably written much earlier than that date; at all events, long before 1199, in which year it

---

[6] E.g. *Mat.* i. 507, see also 600.   [7] *Mat.* i. 47.

was incorporated in a Harmony of four lives of Becket, called *Quadrilogus*.

[18] (5) Benedict, a monk of Canterbury (Prior from 1175 to 1177), is said[8] to have been "among the Archbishop's familiar friends, in specially familiar attendance, on the day of his death." At the time of the murder, he would naturally be in the Cathedral at vespers, or else in attendance on the Archbishop. Probably the latter was the case. He does not speak of himself as an eye-witness; but neither does Grim until he casually reveals the fact when speaking of the wound he receives. From the very first, Benedict began to collect accounts of the miracles performed in the name of the Martyr, and it is reasonably supposed that his narrative of the death was intended to be prefixed to his Book of Miracles. But in later times the latter was published by itself, and the former fell into such oblivion that it is now preserved nowhere but in a Harmony of four biographies (called *Quadrilogus*), and there only in a fragmentary shape. In reading his evidence, therefore, we have to bear in mind that, so far as concerns the Martyrdom, we do not have it completely before us. He describes clearly and sometimes vividly, so far as his knowledge goes; and he alone, of our Latin writers, gives the year of the Martyrdom correctly.[9] He probably wrote the present narrative in 1171, but revised it when he prefixed it to his Book of Miracles which was probably completed, in its first form, before 1175.

§ 2. *The absent friend*

[19] (6) Herbert of Bosham is said by Fitzstephen to have been Becket's "teacher in the (sacred) page," *i.e.* in Scripture. Though one of the Archbishop's staunchest

---

[8] *Quadrilogus, Mat.* iv. 371 "inter familiares illius familiarius illi assistens."
[9] Of the writers quoted below, four give it wrongly; one implies the right year; the rest omit it. Garnier agrees with Benedict (348).

friends and adherents, both at home and in his exile abroad, he happened to be absent on the day of the murder, having been sent away by the Archbishop on a confidential mission. He is described by Fitzstephen as a man of striking presence and high spirit, well able to answer an angry king, and prone to advise violent courses. "Now you will see a proud man," said King Henry to his Council, when Herbert was summoned before them.[1] That there is no trace of violence or abruptness in his style is perhaps due to the softening influence of old age. He wrote after almost all the companions with whom he had enjoyed the Archbishop's friendship had passed away. His narrative of facts, his comments on his own narrative, his defences of his own prolixity, carry prolixity to its height.

[20] He is generally fair and accurate, where he testifies —as he is fond of saying—to what he has "seen and heard" from the Archbishop himself. Unfortunately, in describing Becket's death, he had to rely on the testimony of others. This testimony he does not mention as written. "Accepimus," he says, not "legimus." Hence he makes many mistakes. On the stormy interview between Becket and the four knights just before the murder—when the Archbishop refused at first to notice their presence, continuing his conversation with a monk, and afterwards following them to the door with reproaches—Herbert says little more than that he "made a mild answer." The villain who scattered the Martyr's brains about the pavement is described by him as Robert de Broc, though all the English world knew it was Hugh Mauclerc. Benedict and Fitzstephen expressly say that the body was *not* washed before burial ; Herbert says it *was* washed.[2] This

---

[1] *Mat.* iii. 99, one of the very interesting passages not found in the earliest text of Fitzstephen (15*a*).

[2] Herbert might easily misunderstand Grim's words (*Mat.* ii. 442) "ut moris est, corpus . . . *lavandum* exspoliantes." It was stripped *in order to be* washed, but was *not* washed.

[20*a*] The *Quadrilogus*, in quoting Herbert's "postquam exutum fuit, *postquam*

inaccuracy was perhaps in part the result of long residence abroad (though he came to England for a time while writing his biography). Old age, weakness of memory, a disposition to trust to oral tradition, and a desire to find parallelisms between the Passion of our Lord and the Martyrdom of Becket, may account for much inaccuracy even in a scrupulous lover of truth. His work was dedicated to Baldwin (who was consecrated Archbishop of Canterbury in 1185, elected in 1184). It contains a passage referring to the death of Henry II. If this is (as I believe it to be) genuine, his book was not completed till after 1189. In any case, he refers to the death of the King's son, Geoffrey (Aug. 1186). He describes himself as engaged in the work in the fourteenth year after the Martyrdom (1184-85).[3]

§ 3. *Anonymous writers*

[21] Though writing very soon after Becket's death, John of Salisbury speaks of "great volumes" already written "by him and about him,"[1] and of the Martyrdom as "already known and popularized almost throughout the Latin-speaking world."[2] For this cause, perhaps, it seemed desirable to compose a Harmony of the most authoritative Lives. This was done about 1199 A.D. by a monk of Evesham and Henry, Abbot of Croyland. The work was called *Quadrilogus*, from the "four" authors from whose works it was compiled.

[22] In selecting their authors, the compilers would be influenced by two considerations, (1) intimacy with the late

---

lotum, acceperunt . . . ," modifies the whole, and omits "postquam lotum," *so as to harmonize Herbert with Benedict*, who expressly denies that the body was washed. This is parallel to omissions in the Diatessaron, made for the sake of harmonizing incompatibilities. [3] *Mat.* iii., Introd. xxii.

[1] *Mat.* ii. 302 "epistolae eius et *scripta* aliorum, fide plena et digna relatu." These words show that he does not mean "letters" but "writings," or biographies. Garnier wrote the first draft of his biography as early as 1172.

[2] *Ib.* 316 "fere per orbem Latinum."

Archbishop, (2) connection with the Abbey of Canterbury, the natural repository for records of his life. They accordingly chose Herbert of Bosham, who had instructed the Archbishop in Scripture; John of Salisbury, his confidential adviser and companion in exile; and William of Canterbury, who had been requested by the monks to compile a book about the Saint's miracles and to present it to Henry II. But John's sketch was recognized by all his contemporaries to be inadequate, and had been supplemented by Alan (Prior of Canterbury from 1179 to 1188), who prefixed the biography, thus supplemented, to a volume of the Archbishop's correspondence. Alan, therefore, was recognized by the compilers of the *Quadrilogus* as their fourth author. When describing the Martyrdom, they call in Benedict as a fifth witness. But, as Alan does not describe the death, the witnesses practically remain four.

[23] A later version of the *Quadrilogus* (printed in 1495, before the printing of the earlier one) inserts passages from Grim and Fitzstephen. This also contains the legend of the Syrian origin of Becket's mother, and an account of the sudden withering of a tree under which the conspirators plotted his death.[3]

[24] All this indicates that "The Passion of St. Thomas of Canterbury" would be a common subject for clerical discourses and sermons abroad, as well as popular in England, where the poor, and the "English by birth," regarded him as their special champion and miraculous healer. Hence would spring a great number of anonymous "Passions," from some of which extracts are given below. The first two are portions of complete Lives.

---

[3] The early *Quadrilogus* (Magnusson, *Saga*, ii. p. xcv.) was recast by Roger, a monk of Croyland, by desire of the same Abbot Henry, in 1212-13: "The method adopted in this edition was to let the correspondence tell the tale." In its narrative parts, it "agrees substantially with Elias's story, but the arrangement of the chapters differs considerably. This edition, preserved in 'MS. e Museo 133,' in the Bodleian Library, has never been printed."

[25] (7) The author of Anon. I. (*Mat.* iv. 1 *sq.*)—commonly, but on no evidence, called Roger of Pontigny—says that he ministered to Becket in his exile and was ordained priest by him.[4] Of many events in the Archbishop's life he gives a most vivid and apparently faithful record, and in his account of the death, he is superior even to Grim and other eye-witnesses. The only men who stood by the Archbishop, almost up to the last, are said by Fitzstephen to have been Fitzstephen himself, Grim, and "brother Robert,

---

[4] *Mat.* iv. 2. He writes to record "ea *quae de ipso minus dicta sunt* ne temporis vetustate penitus pereant a memoria." This implies that imperfect or inadequate accounts had been already published; but accounts (like Garnier's first poem) may have been published so early that this gives little indication of date.

[25*a*] Magnusson (*Saga*, vol. ii. p. lxxxiv.) has pointed out that in a passage describing Becket's boyhood, closely resembling Garnier, the author (*Mat.* iv. 8) makes a slip in his Latin ("Lundrensis," for "Londoniensis"; Garnier (l. 241), "Lundreis"). It might be added that shortly afterwards, where Garnier (l. 217) has "*tut* enchaperunez," "*quite* hooded," Anon. I. has "*tutus* capucciatus" (401).

In another passage, Garnier has—

"Kar en *Engleterre* ad une kustume mise,
Ke l'Aide al Veskunte est par les kuntez prise:
Si est par dubles soud par les *hides* assise."

In the corresponding passage, Anon. I. has (*Mat.* iv. 23) "Erat consuetudo in *partibus illis* . . . duos solidos de singulis dimensionibus terrae suae, quas *patrio nomine hydas* vocant." At first sight it is difficult, as Mr. Magnusson says, to suppose that a native Englishman would call England "those parts," and "think it necessary to explain that 'hides' was a thing so called 'patrio nomine.'" But is it not possible that the author, having communicated these facts to Garnier (when the latter came to Canterbury to write the second draft of his poem), and having found that Garnier's terse statement bewildered readers in "transmarine regions," may have thought it desirable to enter into explanations specially adapted for them, so as to make it clear to a man of Picardy what a "hide" was, explaining also that the custom prevailed only in "those parts" of the king's dominion, and not in the French regions? It is possible that the author, though English, may have been residing abroad when he wrote, and may have written for foreigners. If he misunderstood Garnier's "tut," would not this shew that he was not a Frenchman? But "tutus" may be a scribal error for "totus."

The relation of Anon. I. to Garnier would well repay a full and careful investigation. See **184***a*, **253, 401**.

priest and canon of the religious house of Merton, a worthy man, who had held fast to him (the Archbishop) from the first day of his ordination as his chaplain and companion," and whom he also describes as his confessor.[5]

[26] Now Robert of Merton "ministered" to Becket "in his exile." This we know from Grim, who, after speaking of the Archbishop's habits of self-mortification at Sens, says, "For these facts we have the evidence of (testis et relator) the venerable Robert of Merton, chaplain of the sainted Archbishop, who learned all facts from the Archbishop himself, or saw them with his own eyes."[6] Whoever the author may have been, it appears probable that he was inspired by Robert of Merton, if he was not Robert himself.

---

[5] *Mat.* iii. 147.

[6] [26a] See the context, *Mat.* ii. 417-8. It seems strange that Robert of Merton is not included in Herbert of Bosham's list of the Archbishop's faithful and learned friends (whom he calls "Eruditi"). Fitzstephen may have been excluded, because he did not follow Becket into exile; but why exclude the chaplain who did follow him? Was it because, according to Herbert's standard, he was not "eruditus"—being indeed a model of accuracy, clearness, terseness, and good sense, never moralizing and rarely commenting or indulging in classical quotations, being wholly absorbed in the scene he is describing?

[26b] The evidence in favour of Roger of Pontigny as author amounts to no more than this (Magnusson, *Saga*, vol. ii. p. lxxxiii.) :—(1) the author says he ministered to the Archbishop during his exile; (2) a composite Life of the Archbishop (by Thomas of Froimont) states that a monk named Roger was the Archbishop's minister at Pontigny.

The two years at Pontigny were but a small part of the exile; and the words, "during his exile," appearing to cover the whole period, seem more applicable to Robert of Merton than to this unknown Roger. In describing Becket's life at Pontigny, the author says that he refrains from details " ne et fratribus nostris nota(m) ingeramus " (reading "nota" with Magnusson, "lest we should inflict on our brethren what they know already"): and it has been suggested by Magnusson that it may mean "our brethren at Pontigny," implying that he himself was one of those brethren. But may not the words mean simply "our readers," or the monks of Canterbury, or any others for whom he was writing and to whom these details were already known in the extremely full account given by Grim, probably from information supplied by Robert of Merton? On the very same page there is a sentence in which the author speaks of the monks of Pontigny as "them" (instead of "us"), which indicates that, at all events when Becket came to Pontigny, the author was not one of the monks there.

His regard for accuracy of fact appears equal to his praiseworthy dislike for commenting and moralizing. His account is generally in agreement with those of Grim, Garnier, and Fitzstephen.

[27] (8) Anon. II. (*Mat.* iv. 80 *sq.*), sometimes called Lambethiensis, claims, in its Preface, to proceed from an eye-witness. But in the body of the work no such claim is made: and the same Preface is found prefixed *to a fragment of an altogether different biography.*[7] It is probably of French origin, describing Becket's father as from Rouen and his mother (whom it calls Roesa,[8] instead of Matilda) as coming from Caen. The author follows John of Salisbury, the Bishop of Chartres, in his description of the Council of Clarendon and elsewhere. He occasionally touches on censures passed on Becket's "rashness," makes no mention of the King's words that practically caused the murder, but only of "the mad fury of his persecutors," and gives a totally false description of the Archbishop's reception of the four knights in the palace.[9] This will prepare us for an inaccurate account of the Martyrdom itself, in which the Archbishop is represented as bidding Grim desist from attempting to defend him.[10]

[28] It must have been a very early work; for it contains the remarkable confession that the writer *had once thought Becket's conduct that of a madman.*[11] Moreover, its mention of the King's self-purgation at Avranches (1172), but not of his penance at Canterbury, leads to the con-

---

[7] *Mat.* iv. p. xiv.

[8] *Mat.* iv. p. xiv. "probably the same with *Rohesia*, the name borne by one of her daughters." Hence John Fox, the author of the *Acts and Monuments*, is said to have derived his statement that the Saint's mother was "named Rose."

[9] *Ib.* 128 "a quo benigne digneque suscepti, postquam de viae suae prosperitate dominique regis salute requisiti responderunt."

[10] *Ib.* 130 "Desine, frater, non hanc defensionem vult dominus." This appears to be suggested by a desire to draw a parallel between Christ's rebuke of Peter and Becket's rebuke of Grim.

[11] *Mat.* i. 140 "et nos quidem vitam ejus putaveramus insaniam."

clusion that it was written before the latter event, *i.e.* before 1174.[12]

[29] (9) Anon. IV.[13] (*Mat.* iv. 186 *sq.*) is a sermon preached on the day set apart for St. Thomas who was canonized in 1173. It speaks of "innumerable miracles in divers nations and kingdoms"; but such language is used by other writers within five years of the Martyrdom. The author mentions the Englishman Grim (though not by name), and his first paragraph calls St. Thomas "our father and the protector of his country." He falls into the error of supposing that the man who thrust out the Martyr's brains was one of the four knights. The preacher's careful attitude toward the King, and the general tone of the discourse, suggest that it is an early composition proceeding from some one who had not read an accurate account, but had received merely the popular tradition with emphasis laid on the final outrage and on the "red" and "white" of the Archbishop's wounds (**331, 334**). The date was probably soon after 1173.

[30] (10) Anon. V. (*Mat.* iv. 196 *sq.*) concludes with the words "Some one came in, after I had written what is written above, asserting that one of the Archbishop's murderers had turned mad and killed his own son." A tradition of this kind, current for a time but not substantiated, and not adopted by later writers, indicates a very early date. All the murderers were (wrongly) believed by Herbert[14] to have died within three years from the Martyr-

---

[12] One passage in this life seems to speak of Henry II. as no longer living, "regi restitit in faciem, cui, praeter Angliam, pars major regni Gallicani *parebat*, ad cujus etiam nomen reges . . . *tremebant*, cui quoque prope subditum *ibat* quicquid *impetebat*." But the meaning may be that the Archbishop resisted Henry when the latter was at the height of his power, and before the calamities that befell him in 1173 when his own son revolted against him.

[13] Anon. III., as printed in the *Materials*, gives no account of the Martyrdom.

[14] [30*a*] *Mat.* iii. 536 *sq*. A similar assertion is made by the so-called Matthew of Westminster. He says "four years" instead of "three"; but he places the Martyrdom in 1170 whereas Herbert places it in 1171.

dom. If this belief prevailed in the region where the writer lived, we are justified in inferring—even after allowing a year or two for the spread of the rumour that they had died abroad—that this Passio was written about 1174–75, or earlier, before the popular belief had reached or persuaded him.

[31] It appends to the Martyrdom an account of a miracle, perhaps suggested by the historical account of the dignity with which the Archbishop fell "like one praying." The germ of it appears in Anon. II., which added that he fell, "fortifying himself with the sign of the Cross." The present writer goes further: "Also, as I have learned from men's veracious report, the body, long dead, arose, and signed itself, and those who stood by, with the sign of the life-giving cross, and again fell to the ground." As a whole, the narrative is of little value except as proof that a short and early tradition may sometimes be both vague and tame, yet more inaccurate, and more given to legend, than much later compositions.

[32] (11) Anon. X. (*Mat.* iv. 431 *sq.*) is a composite work, being apparently a discourse on the day of St. Thomas of Canterbury, together with an appendix on his miracles. In the discourse, the words describing the facts are mostly borrowed; but the commentary, in which he draws a moral from the facts, is (so far as we know) the preacher's own. It refers to the history "of that wise Englishman who has related all these things in order," meaning John of Salisbury. By its mention of English men and writings, and its contrast between "Anglici regis furorem" and "gloriosissimum Ludovicum regem Francorum," it would seem to be the work of a foreigner. It borrows from Grim and others, and sometimes spoils in the borrowing, altering, for example, Grim's "them that kill the *body* (interfectores *carnis*)" into "murderous *dogs* (interfectores *canes*),"[15] and William's

---

[15] See 44a. It must be admitted, however, that Grim himself, when previously describing the landing of the four knights at "the port of *Dogs*," had

"praecurrere" into "percurrere," and elsewhere injuring the sense in the attempt to abridge.

[33] But if the writer is a foreigner, he must have included, without acknowledgment, and without altering the first person plural, a statement apparently made by the monks of Canterbury about a redness in the sky on the night of the Martyrdom : " However, a few days afterwards, came the prior of Ely *from the other side of the sea* (transmarinis partibus)[16] asking whether the air had appeared blood-red to *us* on the day of the Passion, asserting that *when he was at Rouen* he had seen an excessive redness in the air, in company with other witnesses innumerable, who wondered greatly and believed it to be a miracle (signum)." [17]

[34] It uses the Archbishop's death to point a moral on the power of the priests : " Learn thou that the priests shut heaven and open it for thee, and that they are above, not below, the power of man." In transcribing some of the Miracles of Benedict's book, it inserts, beside other slight alterations, a passage extolling the power of the Virgin Mary.[18] Its close verbal imitation of Grim, Benedict, and others, indicates a comparatively late date.

---

used the expression (*Mat.* ii. 429) "*canes* ipsi, ex tunc, et miseri (non milites) appellandi."

[16] So the four knights are said to come to Canterbury "ex transmarinis partibus."

[17] Fitzstephen also mentions this "redness" in a high-flown passage (*Mat.* iii. 142) "avertit sol oculos," etc. But as the murder took place (*Mat.* ii. 19) about 5 P.M. on 29th December, when the sun sets about 4 P.M., it is hard to see how the sun could be said to "turn aside his eyes, hide his rays, darken the day, lest he should look on this sin." Stanley (p. 98) suggests that it was the aurora borealis lighting up the midnight sky. But if this had been the case, would not more writers have referred to it ? More probably, it is an instance of error, arising from metaphorical language drawing a parallel between the martyrdom of Thomas and the crucifixion of Christ (439*a*).

[18] *Mat.* iv. 440.

§ 4. *Garnier, and the Saga*

[35] (12) Garnier, a clerk of Pont Sainte Maxence in Picardy, says, in his Prologue, that whoever wishes to hear the truth about the life of the Holy Martyr without fault or falsehood will find it in his poem about which he has "spent *four years in composing and perfecting.*"

[36] At first, he wrote in the fervour caused by the fresh news of the Martyrdom. Consequently, he says, he "often lied." But, in this imperfect state, his poem was stolen from him by a scrivener, and copies were bought by many rich people—before he had time to "temper the bitter and the sweet," or to complete and correct it—"with lies in some places, and lacking in fullness." So he went to Canterbury. There he heard the truth, and "culled it from the friends of St. Thomas and from those who had served him from childhood." Now, he says, people will be able to find in his book the truth, and the full truth.

[37] From what point is the period of "four years" to date? So far, in the context as given above, it dates most naturally from the commencement of his first and uncorrected draft, and not from the visit to Canterbury, *which is mentioned afterwards, and as to which he gives no date here.* In that case, the poem would be finished early in 1175.

[38] In his Epilogue, the poet says that he often read his poem at the tomb in Canterbury: "At Canterbury it was both composed and corrected." Then, as to the date: "In the *second* year from *the killing of the Saint in the church* I began this story . . . and in the *fourth* I finished it."

[39] This will harmonize with the Prologue, *if the "four years" there mentioned include the whole time spent on the poem* including the first draft of it begun immediately after the Martyrdom: and thus the view above suggested will be confirmed—namely, that the poem was completed in the early part of 1175. It must certainly have been completed

after the summer of 1174, as it describes Henry's penitential visit to the Martyr's tomb: but no internal evidence is alleged, of such a nature as to require a later date.[1]

[40] (13) The *Saga* is of much later date than any of the non-anonymous compositions above mentioned. It shews acquaintance with the early *Quadrilogus*, published in 1199. But it also borrows from other traditions not now extant, and that these may have been very early is shewn by the fact that before the end of the twelfth century, the life of the Archbishop was eagerly studied in Iceland, and poems on the subject were current, "either in Latin or in Icelandic."[2]

---

[1] [39a] Magnusson says (*Saga*, ii. p. lxxxvii.) "he went to Canterbury, in 1172, ... After four years' labour, he had, in 1176, finished his 'Sermun.'. . ." This takes "the fourth year" to mean "the fourth from *beginning the poem at Canterbury*." But the context appears to be against this, and to support the earlier date, 1175. The full context in Prologue and Epilogue will enable readers to judge for themselves.

PROLOGUE.

Se vuleiz escuter la vie al saint martyr,
Ci la purreiz par mei plenèrement oïr.
N'i voil rien trespasser, ne rien n'i voil mentir.
Quatre aunz i ai bien mis, al fère et al furnir,
D'oster de remettre poi la peine soffrir.
Primes treitai de joie, et suvent i menti ;
A Chantorbire alai ; la verité oï ;
Des amis saint Toma la verité cuilli,
Et de cels ki l'aveint dès l'enfance servi.
D'oster et de remettre le travail en suffri.
Mès cel primer romaunz m'unt escrivein emblé,
Ainceis ke jo l'éusse parfet et amendé,
Et l'amer et le duz adulci et tempré.
Et là ù j'oi trop mis, ne l'oi encor osté,
Ne le plus ne le meins, esrés ne ajusté.
Par lius est menchunges et saunz plenèreté,
Et ne por quant i ad le plus de verité.
Et maint riche hume l'unt acquis et akaté.
Mès cil l'en deivent estre, qui l'emblèrent, blamé.
Mès cestui ai del tut amendé et finé.
Tut cil autre romaunz, c'un ad fet del martyr,
Clerc u lai, muine u dame, mult les i oi mentir ;
Ne le veir, ne le plein, ne les i oi furnir.
Mes ci porreiz le veir et tut le plein oïr,
N'istrai de verité, pur perdre u pur murir !
ll. 141-165.

EPILOGUE.

Guarniers li clers del Punt fine-ci sun SERMUN
Del martir saint Thomas et de sa passiun ;
Et mainte feiz le list à la tumbe al barun :
Ci n'a mis un sul mot, se la verité non.
De ses mesfez li face Jhesu li pius pardon !
Ainc mès mieldre romanz ne fu fez, ne trovez ;
A Cantorbire fu et fet et amendez ;
N'i a mis un sul mot qui ne seit veritez.
Li vers est d'une rime en cinc clauses coplez.
Mis languages est buens ; car en France fui nez.
L'an secund que li Sainz fu en l'iglise ocis
Comenchai cest roman, et mult m'en entremis ;
Des privez saint Thomas la verité apris ;
Meinte fez en ostai ço que jo ains escris,
Pur oster la mençunge, et al quart, fin i mis.
Iço sachent tut cil ki ceste vie orrunt
Que pure verité par tut oïr purrunt ;
E ço sachent tut cil qui del Seint treitié unt,
Ou Romanz ou Latin, et cest chemin ne vunt,
Ou el dient que jo, cuntre verité sunt.
Or priun Jhésu Crist le fil seinte Marie,
Pur amur seint Thomas, nus doinst la sue aïe ;
Ke rien ne nus suffraigne à la corporal vie,
Et si nus esneium de séculer folie
K'al moriant aium la sue conpaignie !
ll. 5811-5835.

[2] *Saga*, ii. p. xxii.

CHAPTER II

THE BREAKING OPEN OF THE PALACE

§ 1. *Introduction*

[41] THE murder in the Cathedral was preceded by an interview between the Archbishop and the four murderers in the adjacent archiepiscopal Palace. This has been omitted by John of Salisbury, and passed over most briefly by the prolix Herbert of Bosham. But the most trustworthy authorities tell us that Becket received the knights discourteously and contemptuously, not deigning at first to notice their presence or to discontinue his conversation with a monk to whom he happened to be talking at the moment of their entrance. His discourtesy was only a return for theirs: but still, this, and the violence of word and gesture with which the Archbishop followed them to the door on their retirement, brought upon him the expostulations of John of Salisbury, which are recorded by Benedict, Anon. I., and Garnier.[1]

---

[1] [41*a*] Possibly some of the Archbishop's chaplains differed from John. At all events, Fitzstephen, recounting the gross provocations that he received from the knights, says that he followed them to the door "asking them in temperate language (satis modeste) to release his knight," whom they were forcing to accompany them. There was certainly strong language on both sides. The knights proclaimed the Archbishop a traitor, and made the monks responsible for his safe keeping. This exasperated him. Benedict thus reports his reply: "What do you mean? Do you think I want to sneak away (fuga labi)? I will not run away for the king or for any man living. I did not come here to run away but to face the fury of cut-throats (grassantium rabiem) and the malice of impiety." "Good sooth," replied the knights, "by God's will, you shall not run away."

[42] The Archbishop's last word to the knights had been, "You will find me here," which he uttered pointing to his throat, anticipating their murderous intentions.[2] Not unnaturally, therefore, when he returned to his seat, encouraging his friends and attendants, he refused at first to leave the Palace. Meantime the retinue of the knights had been making their way into the outer courtyard. But the hall-doors, closed behind the knights after their retirement, prevented them from re-entering and would not yield to their assault. Then Robert de Broc, who had been custodian of the Palace during the Archbishop's exile, undertook to lead the knights in by another way through a window, breaking down a partywall. It is at this point that the following narratives begin.[3]

§ 2. *The different accounts*

[43] (1) (Grim) Without delay the murderers return, with hauberks, swords, hatchets and axes, and other implements suitable for the accomplishment of the crime. And finding the doors barred, and not opened at their knocking, they turn aside by a less public way through an orchard to a wooden barrier, hacking, and cleaving, and crashing it away. Frightened by the uproar and terrible crashing, the servants, and almost all the clerks, like sheep before wolves, scattered in every direction.

---

[43] (1) (Grim) Nec mora, redeunt carnifices in loricis, cum gladiis securibusque et bisacutis, et caeteris utensilibus commodis ad scelus quod animo conceperant peragendum. Cumque obserata ostia reperissent, nec pulsantibus aperiretur, secretiori quodam aditu per pomerium ad ligneum obstaculum divertentes, scindunt, caedunt, et diruunt. Quo fragore terribili ac tumultuoso tremefacti servientes ac clerici fere omnes velut oves ante faciem luporum, hac illacque dispersi sunt.

[2] *Mat.* ii. 433, iv. 73.

[3] In these extracts, words describing fact are given fully. But moral inferences and comments are mostly omitted, the omissions being, in each case, indicated in the usual way.

Those comments are inserted which reveal a bias that may modify narration of fact, *e.g.* comparisons between the Martyrdom and the Crucifixion.

In the translation, the English is sometimes sacrificed to the Latin where it is necessary to bring out minute differences of expression in the several accounts.

[44] Those who remained cried to him to fly to the church. But he, mindful of his former promise—namely, that he would not through fear of death flee from these mere killers of the flesh [1]—rejected flight. . . . But the monks still pressed him, urging that it was not seemly that he should absent himself from vespers which were just at that time going on in the church. Still he remained unmoveable, deliberately determining to await in a less sacred spot [2] that blessed hour of consummation which he had craved with many sighs and sought with fervent prayers: [fearing] lest, as has been said, reverence for the sanctity of the sacred building might both restrain the impious from effecting their purpose and also cheat the Saint himself of the fulfilment of his heart's desire. For being confident that after martyrdom he would pass out of this miserable existence, he is reported [3] to have said in the hearing of many, after his return from exile, " Ye have already here a martyr, Elphegus, well-beloved of God, and a true Saint. Another will the Divine compassion provide for you. It will not delay . . ."

[44] Acclamantibus autem qui remanserant ut in ecclesiam fugeret, memor ille promissi prioris, metu videlicet mortis non se fugiturum carnis [1] interfectores, fugam renuit. . . . Insistunt monachi, dicentes non decere ipsum vespertinis deesse laudibus, quae jam tunc celebrabantur in ecclesia. Mansit ille immobilis, minoris reverentiae loco, [2] felicem illam ac multis praeoptatam suspiriis, multa devotione quaesitam, consummationis suae horam exspectare deliberans ; ne, sicut dictum est, aedis sacrae reverentia et impios arceret a proposito et sanctum cordis sui desiderio defraudaret. Certus namque quod ab hac miseria migraret post martyrium, postquam ab exsilio reversus est, multis audientibus dixisse fertur [3] " Habetis hic dilectum Deo ac vere sanctum martyrem Elfegum ; alium vobis divina miseratio providebit ; non morabitur . . ."

[1] [44a] Anon. X. (55) has "*canes* interfectores, those murderous dogs "—a very graphic expression. But Grim is probably alluding to Matt. x. 28 " Be not afraid of them which *kill the body*."

[2] " Minoris reverentiae loco," *i.e.* in the palace as being less sacred than the cathedral and less likely to deter his enemies and to delay his martyrdom. The words are explained by what follows, "lest reverence for the sacred building should hinder them from their purpose."

[3] [44a] " He is reported." According to Fitzstephen, the Archbishop (*Mat.*

[45] (2) (Fitzstephen) *Before this, Fitzstephen has described in detail the prearrangements of the knights. Their men had been collected in a great house just opposite the gate of the Archbishop's courtyard. They had already contrived quietly to introduce a few of these into the courtyard and had placed a gate-keeper of their own, Simon de Croil, removing the Archbishop's servant.*[4] *William son of Nigel, the Archbishop's steward, is described before as carried off by the four knights from his presence, and as now aiding them. Reginald Fitzurse arms himself in the forecourt, and compels Robert Tibias the Archbishop's trencherman to assist him. This Reginald also took a hatchet from a carpenter repairing some steps there. Meanwhile, in the Archbishop's room, some declared there was no cause for fear. The knights, they said, must have been drunk, it was Christmas time, they had the pledge of the King's peace—and so on. Others said that there was good cause for alarm, and that there were many visible tokens of murderous intent. Meanwhile, they hear, from the side of the Cathedral, the lamentable outcries of the multitude, who knew what was going on, and who felt for the Archbishop's people, " as sheep for the slaughter." On the other side, they could hear the servants in the palace going down the steps at a run towards the Cathedral, flying through the midst of the hall from the face of the armed men who were entering into the courtyard. The writer now continues as follows :—*

[46] Osbert, and Algar, and certain other servants of the Archbishop, seeing that the armed men were rushing in,

---

[45] See *Mat.* iii. 136, 137.
[46] (2) (Fitzstephen) Osbertus et Algarus et quidam alii servientes archi-

iii. 130) uttered these words in a sermon four days previously (Christmas day). Grim, who had "newly come" to the Archbishop, may not have heard the sermon. Describing it above, he mentions merely that part in which the Archbishop published excommunications. Garnier appears to attribute the saying (58) to "one of his clerks."

[4] [45a] Note, throughout, Fitzstephen's frequent mention of the Archbishop's servants, from whom he seems to have derived much of his information.

closed the hall door and barred it firmly. Seeing this, Robert de Broc began to hew away a kind of party-wall, and, getting in that way, threw open the hall door to those parricides, inflicting severe blows and wounds on those who had barred it.

[47] We, too, we clerks, seated inside with the Archbishop, we heard these blows of Robert de Broc as he hewed away the party-wall. What but fear and trembling came on us, monks, and clerks, and companions of the Archbishop! . . . But the good Thomas despised death. . . . Moreover also the holy man behaved as one free from all care, as though rejoicing that he had found an honourable cause to die for, [dying for] justice and liberty and the cause of his Church, and as though desiring to be dissolved and to be with Christ. . . . Then said the monks, a good many of whom were attending on him, "My lord, go into the church." "Never," said he; "fear not! Most monks are too timorous and fainthearted."

(3) (John) Omits this.

[48] (4) (William) So having planned to break into[5] the house, going out into the court, and letting in those whom

---

episcopo, viso quod irruerent armati, ostium aulae clauserunt, et repaguli obice firmaverunt. Quod videns Robertus de Broch coepit securi diruere parietem quendam, et illac ingressus per interiora domus, aulae ostium illis parricidis aperuit, et illos qui ostium aulae obfirmaverant, gravissime cecidit et vulneravit.

[47] Audivimus etiam, nos clerici, introrsus cum archiepiscopo, ictus illos Roberti de Broc parietem diruentis. Quid nisi timor et tremor venerunt super nos, monachos, clericos, et socios archiepiscopi? . . . Sed bonus ille Thomas contemptor mortis erat. . . . Insuper et securum se sanctus homo gerebat, quasi gaudens se nactum honestam causam moriendi pro justitia et libertate et causa ecclesiae suae; et quasi cupiens dissolvi et esse cum Christo. . . . Tunc monachi, qui plurimi aderant, dicunt ei, "Domine, intrate in ecclesiam." Ille: "Absit; ne timeatis; plerique monachi plus justo timidi sunt et pusillanimes."

(3) (John) Omits this.

[48] (4) (William) Igitur considerata imminutione[5] domus, exeuntes in curtim, et immitentes quos in facinus acciverant, sub moro ramosa loricis super-

---

[5] "Imminutione" seems to mean a violation of the sanctity of the house. "Curtim," soon afterwards, appears to mean a "courtyard."

they had summoned for their enterprise, they cast aside under a branching mulberry tree the surcoats that had covered their hauberks, and with drawn swords assault the doors of the outer building which the servants, taking alarm, had barred.

[49] Seeing themselves repelled there, under the guidance of that most wretched of clerks, Robert, who knew the passages, they rushed in by way of a shrubbery and found some steps, broken half-way, leading up to a postern door, where the workmen (after their manner) had left their tools, when they went away for their meal. Thence they found means for breaking open locks; and, climbing up by ladders instead of steps, with none to resist them, they force an entrance. And that excellent Champion of God awaited the hour of his Passion. [*Here William inserts an account of a vision of his future martyrdom supposed to have been seen by the Archbishop during his exile at Pontigny*] . . . Consequently no exhortations, no prayers, no, nor the tears of his friends could move him from the spot,

[50] (5) (Benedict). But some ran to warn the Archbishop, shouting, "My lord, my lord, they are arming." "Why care for that?" replied he: "let them arm." Along with their detestable crew was that son of perdition, Robert de Broc [6] . . . Under the guidance of the aforesaid Robert,

indutas vestes abjiciunt, gladiisque exsertis in ostia domus exterioris quam pueri metuentes obseraverant, impingunt.

[49] Ubi videntes se repelli, duce miserrimo clericorum Roberto, scito diverticulorum, irruentes a virgulto posticii gradus interruptos inveniunt ubi architecti (sicut fit) ad necessaria digressi ferramenta sua reliquerant. Hinc ad infringendas seras occasione sumpta, scalis pro gradibus nitentes, nemine resistente, aditus irrumpunt. Et egregius athleta Dei securus horam suae passionis exspectabat. . . . Igitur non hortatu, non prece, non lachrymis suorum, loci (*sic*, ? loco) moveri poterat,

[50] (5) (Benedict) Praecurrentes vero aliqui ad archiepiscopum clamabant : "Domine, domine, armant se." At ille, "Quae cura? sinite armare." Erat in detestanda illorum societate perditionis ille filius, Robertus de Broc [6] . . . ducatu

---

[6] [50*a*] Benedict here inserts, in effect, "whom he had excommunicated." The Early *Quadrilogus*, having previously described the excommunication, from

they speedily turned off to a less public flight of steps, by which there was a way of getting down from an outer chamber into an orchard; and, having broken down a window, they also unbarred the door. And [7] when the brave Champion of God was warned to flee by the cries of his servants who came running from all sides, he—counting nothing more contemptible than to fear death in fighting for Christ's cause—would neither change place nor purpose. Even when the clerks urged him, as well as the monks, and with all their power exhorted flight, he [*mindful of his former promise, namely, that he would not, through fear of death, flee from these mere killers of the flesh* [8]] sat none the less intrepid, not knowing what it was—with those who "believe for a time"—to "fall away in time of temptation." [9]

[51] (6) (Herbert) So the knights having now armed, and having collected a cohort with swords and staves,[10] began

---

praefati Roberti ad gradus quosdam secretiores, per quos de thalamo exteriori in pomerium erat descensus, quantocius diverterunt, proximaque fenestra demolita, ostium etiam reserarunt. Quumque [7] fortissimo Dei athletae a praecurrentibus famulis undique acclamatum esset ut fugeret, ille, cui nihil vilius erat quam mortem timere pro Christo, nec loco nec animo motus est. Instantibus etiam tam clericis quam monachis, et oppido illum ad fugam hortantibus, [*memor ille promissi prioris, metu videlicet mortis se non fugiturum carnis interfectores* [8]], nihilominus sedebat intrepidus, nesciens, cum his qui "ad tempus credunt in tempore tentationis recedere." [9]

[51] (6) (Herbert) Militibus itaque armatis, et collecta cohorte cum gladiis et fustibus,[10] per fenestras palatii coacervatim jam coeperunt irruere. . . . Illi

---

Herbert, now, quoting *Benedict*, has "whom, *as we have said*, he had excommunicated." Hence, some have inferred that Benedict wrote a life, now lost, in which he described the excommunication. But it is more probable that the composers of the *Quadrilogus* inserted the phrase in reference to their extract from Herbert, *appropriating, as it were, both extracts as their own work*. The editor who first printed the Early *Quadrilogus* (Lupus by name) omits "as we have said." See *Mat.* ii. 10, iv. 393.

[7] [50*b*] "And when." We should have expected "But when . . ." But this Hebraic use of "and" is frequent in Benedict's writings.

[8] These bracketed words are probably an interpolation from Grim. They are not inserted by Lupus, nor by two other MSS.   [9] Luke viii. 13.

[10] "Cohort," and "swords and staves," are used by Herbert in order to suggest a comparison with the arrest of Christ.

to rush into the palace in crowds through the windows. . . . But those who sat in the chamber with the Archbishop, hearing the uproar and the crashing outside, and by this time understanding what it all meant, were not unreasonably terrified ; and they now began to advise the Archbishop to betake himself to a more sacred and secure place, meaning the church. Again and again did he refuse, in his fearlessness of death,

[52] (7) (Anon. I.) Meanwhile the knights, having come out [of the palace], put on their armour to attack an unarmed man. For the rest of the knights (or, soldiers), who had waited outside while these (*i.e.* the four knights) were talking with the man of God, had come with hauberks on, under their surcoats.[11] When word of this was brought to the Archbishop, the monks said to him, "My lord, come into the church: for these men are making themselves ready to take or kill you." "I do not fear them," he replied, "I will await here God's pleasure." But the knights, being now made ready, with terrible shouts and noise approached the hall doors. Finding them barred, they tried with all their force to break them from their hinges, but could not succeed.

vero qui in thalamo cum archipraesule consederunt, audientes tumultum exterius et fragorem, et jam advertentes quid hoc, non sine causa exterriti sunt, monentes jam archipraesulem ut in locum sanctiorem et tutiorem, ecclesiam videlicet, se reciperet. Quo iterum et iterum renuente, tanquam mortis intrepido,

[52] (7) (Anon. I.) Interim egressi armis se munierunt inermem aggressuri. Caeteri enim milites qui foris expectaverant dum illi cum viro Dei loquerentur, sub tunicis suis loricati venerant.[11] Quod cum nuntiatum fuisset ei, dixerunt monachi ad eum, "Domine, veni in ecclesiam ; nam homines isti vel ad captionem vel ad interfectionem tuam se praeparant." Et ille ait "Non timeo eos : hic exspectabo quicquid Deo placuerit." Milites vero jam parati cum terrore et strepitu ad januas aulae accesserunt : quas, obseratas reperientes, nulla vi, quanquam id totis nixibus tentaverint, effringere potuerunt. Erat autem cum eis

[11] [52*a*] Garnier makes a similar statement (56*a*) about "the knights without." Perhaps he intends a distinction between (56*a*) "chevalier" and (56*b*) "bacheler." Anon. I., differing from William (48), implies that the four knights had not their armour on in the palace. Gervase's statement (396), "apparuerunt loricati," may apply to the four knights, or to those "without." There may be some confusion between the four knights and their attendant knights or soldiers.

Now they had with them one Robert de Broc, who knew all the entrances and side-passages of the building. . . . So under his guidance they came through the orchard [12] and as far as the (arched) chamber.[13] But when even there they could not find ingress, the above-mentioned Robert mounted up through a portico (which was being repaired) in order to open the doors. Perceiving them to be close at hand, those who were within, [sitting] with the man of God, all fled, except some monks, and a clerk named Master Edward.

[53] (8) (Anon. II.) Meantime there was a great rush of the king's knights [14] into his courtyard, and no small din of armed men, so that the Archbishop's door-keepers, in just alarm, closed the doors and barred them against the onrush and assault. . . . Disturbed and terrified by the uproar and noise, the crowd of clerks and monks that surrounded the

---

quidam Robertus de Broc, qui omnes aditus et diverticula domus noverat. . . . Eo igitur ducente, venerunt per pomerium [12] et usque ad cameram [13] pervenerunt. Sed cum nec ibi ingressum invenirent (subj. "milites"), ascendit praedictus Robertus per deambulatorium quod ibi de veteri renovabatur ut aperiret ostia. Quos adesse sentientes qui intus cum viro Dei erant, omnes fugerunt praeter aliquot monachos et unum clericum, cui nomen magister Edwardus.

[53] (8) (Anon. II.) Factus est interim satellitum [14] in atrium ejus concursus, et armatorum fragor non minimus, ita ut, justo timore percussi, domus archiepiscopalis custodes januas ad concurrentium impetum clauserint et obstruxerint. . . . Tumultu vero strepituque motus ac territus clericorum monachorumque circum-

---

[12] "Orchard (pomerium)" should be "pomarium" (as one MS. reads here). "Pomerium" is properly a "verge round a city wall." But "pomerium" means "orchard" in *Mat.* ii. 110, "in pomerio amoenissimo."

[13] [52*b*] "The chamber," or "a chamber." But it looks as though the writer (see 56*b*) had a special chamber in his mind. Anon. I. seems to have received these details from some servant of the Archbishop's, forced to accompany the knights; and hence the attempts to enter *from without* are placed before us more vividly than the noise of breaking through "windows," or "barriers," or "party-walls," which would be heard *from within*. The hearing of the noise is implied, rather than expressed, in the following words ("*perceiving* them to be close at hand").

[14] "Satellitum," lit. the attendants, here the King's attendants, is used by several writers to denote the four knights. Compare "count," *i.e.* "comes," meaning originally "companion."

Archbishop could scarcely persuade him, nay, could scarcely even compel him, to betake himself to the church.

(9) (Anon. IV.) Omits this.

[54] (10) (Anon. V.) Then they . . . departed, retiring no great way from the door of the palace. Nay, in the episcopal court itself, donning their armour, they prepared themselves for returning. Seeing this, those who were round the Bishop (*sic*)[15] besought him to seek the safer refuge of the monastery. But he replied, "It is not fitting, my brethren, that the church should be polluted with the blood of sinners. It is better to wait here. Whatever is in store must be patiently endured."

[55] (11) (Anon. X.) Without delay they return with hauberks, and swords, and hatchets, and axes, and other implements suitable for breaking open bolts and doors, and for the perpetration of the crime they had planned. But as the servants had taken precautions and (without the Archbishop's knowledge) had shut them out of the palace, they turn aside to a wooden barrier, and hack, and cleave, and crash it away. [Twice, yea,] thrice, did his

---

fusorum archiepiscopo coetus vix ei suadere potuerunt, immo vix impulerunt, ut in ecclesiam se conferret.

(9) (Anon. IV.) Omits this.

[54] (10) (Anon. V.) Illi vero . . . abierunt, non longe ab ostio domus recedentes. Immo in ipsa episcopali curia se armantes redire paraverunt. Quod videntes qui circa episcopum (*sic*)[15] erant, quatenus tutiora loca monasterii peteret oraverunt. At ille "Non decet," inquit, "fratres mei, ecclesiam peccatorum sanguine pollui, sed potius exspectandum hic ; quicquid imminet, patienter ferendum est."

[55] (11) (Anon. X.) Nec mora ; redeunt in loricis cum gladiis et securibus et bisacutis et aliis utensilibus commodis ad seras et ostia confringenda, et ad scelus quod in animo conceperant perpetrandum. Sed praecaventibus famulis et eos, ignorante archipraesule, excludentibus, ad ligneum obstaculum divertentes, caedunt, scindunt et diruunt. Cumque a suis undique et ter acclamatum ut in

---

[15] Both here and below (chap. vi.) this writer uses "bishop" for "archbishop." Here, "*circa archi*episcopum" might have caused a scribal omission. It is not so easy to explain (in chap. vi.) "iisque ad episcopum" for "ad archiepiscopum." In French, "arcevesque" might be more easily taken for "al evesque."

friends cry to him from all sides to fly to the Minster; but he, having formerly promised that he would not fly from those murderous dogs,[16] now kept his word in manly fashion.

[56] (12) (Garnier) Meanwhile the knights armed themselves there without, And stripped their coats,[17] and girt on their swords of steel, For all came armed, each on his steed of war, Quickly were they prepared to begin great evil; Very quick was he that went to tell the Archbishop. "Sire," said the monks, "go to the Minster, Now are they singing vespers; you should not be absent, These knights desire to take or slay you." "No whit for that," replied he, "will ye see me dismayed. Here will I await all that God shall judge [best] for me."

When they had armed themselves, those four young knights, They come to the doors of the hall, but could not enter: For they had been well barred beforehand, after

---

monasterium fugeret, ille, qui se ante non fugiturum canes [16] interfectores promiserat, virilius implet promissum.

[56] En dementiers s'armèrent là hors li chevalier,
Et ostèrent les cotes,[17] ceinstrent les branz d'acier;
Kar tut vindrent armé, chascuns sur sun destrier,
Tost furent apresté de grant mal commencier.
Assez fu ki l'ala l'arcevesque nuncier.
"Sire," funt-li li moine, "alez en cel mustier,

Il chauntent ore vespres, n'es déussez leissier;
Cil chevaler vus voelent u prendre u detrenchier,"
—"Ne me verrez pur ço," fet-il, "rien esmaier;
Ci attendrai tut ço que Deus m'i volt jugier."
Quant se furent armé li quatre bacheler,
Vunt ad us de la sale; mès n'i porent entrer,
Kar un les out ainz fet, après els, bien barrer.

[16] Probably (44a) the writer has misread Grim's "carnis" as "canes." But Theobald, Count of Blois, calls the four murderers (*Mat.* vii. 434) "those courtier dogs (*canes* aulici)."

[17] [56a] See Anon. I. above, who makes a similar statement about *other attendant* knights—but not about the four, whom he appears to describe as having come without their armour on, into the palace. Perhaps Garnier, too, implies a distinction between the "knights there without" (who had their armour on already, under their "coats," so that they had nothing to do except strip off their "coats" and gird on their swords) and the four knights who now came out and armed themselves. In any case Anon. I. is probably right. Fitzurse would not have needed the enforced assistance of Robertus Tibias (see Fitzstephen, above, 45) to help him to gird on his sword. But to put on a hauberk was a more difficult matter.

"Assez" (three lines below) seems to require the repetition of "tost apresté," so as to mean "very [quickly prepared]." Or is it an error for "assi," *i.e.* "also"?

them. Then began they violently to beat upon the doors: For they wished to take the Saint and wound him to the death. When they could not by force break down the doors, Robert de Broc, who knew how to devise all the evil,[18] said " Follow me now, my lords and noble knights, I will let you in there by another way." By the way of the kitchen did they enter, in the orchard.[19] At the door of the chamber [20] was an oriel closed, (Right over against the garden) which had been [so] for many a day. To renew this, the steps had been just then taken down, And the carpenters had gone to their dinner. To this oriel did the knights turn. By this way enters Robert de Broc to the [inner] chambers; By ladders did the knights mount up. The tools of the workmen who made the steps,—An axe and hatchets— did they carry with them, To break down the door if they found it shut.

[57] When the people of St. Thomas heard them come, As sheep before wolves they made haste to flee: Even as the Apostles when they saw Jesus seized By Pilate's band —Jesus, who, in order to die, Had come into the world, to found His Church. There was not one left of all his servants, Save a few of his clerks, of whom he had many

Dunc commencent as us durement à buter:
Kar il voleient prendre le saint et decolper.
 Quant ne porent les us par force depescier,
Roberz del Broc, qui sot tut le mal enginger [18]:
"Or ni'en siwez," fet-il, "seignur franc chevalier;
Jo vus mettrai laenz par un altre sentier."
Par de vers la cuisine sunt entré el vergier [19].
Al us de la chaumbre [20] out un oriol fermé,
Dreit devers le gardin, qui out maint jur esté;
Pur refere èrent dunc abatu li degré,
E li charpentier èrent à lur disner alé.
A cel oriol sunt li chevalier turné.

Par iluec est as chaumbres Roberz del Broc entrez,
A eschieles i ad les chevaliers muntez;
Les ustilz as ovrers qui firent les degrez,
Besagüe et cuingnies en unt od els portez,
Pur depescier les us, s'es trovassent fermez.
 [57] Quant la gent saint Thomas les oïrent venir,
Come berbiz pur lous s'enpristrent à fuïr:
Si come li apostre, quant il virent saisir
La meisnie Pilate Jhesu, qui pur murir
Esteit venuz el mund, pur s'Iglise establir.
Ne remist là un sul de trestus ses serganz,

---

[18] "All the evil," *i.e.* this evil plot. Or (?) "all evil"? "Laenz" is a variant of "laiens," *i.e.* là, ici.

[19] "Vergier." Perhaps this French word, with its double meaning, induced William to use "virgultum." The others have "orchard."

[20] [56*b*] "The chamber." The writer does not say *what* "chamber." Does this confirm the view that "camera," above, (52*b*) means "*the* chamber"?

and brave there, And only Master Grim, and monks I know not how many, These seized[20a] St. Thomas, who still kept sitting, And waiting for death and the end of his years.

[58] For since he had come back from exile across the sea, He said, in the hearing of many whom I have heard relate it, That he would die in that year; he could well affirm it. Now were there but two days of the year to pass. The third was almost gone, whereon he was to end [his life]. But on Christmas day men heard him avow, in the hearing of many who were there to hear his discourse: "Here am I," said he, "come among you to suffer death." Now was come the day that was ordained for his consummation, And both his life and death made him a holy martyr. Nay also, at the end of his discoursing, One of his clerks said, in prophesying,—Alexander of Wales, in the hearing of many of the [Archbishop's] people—"Canterbury has one martyr, St. Elphege, in truth; Another will it have, if God will, and that, presently." [21]

Fors un poi de ses clers, dunt i out mult vaillanz,
Et sul mestre Edwart Grim, et moines ne sai quanz,
Qui pristrent saint Thomas, qui uncore ert seianz,
Et atendeit iluec mort et fin de ses anz.
[58] Car puis k'il repeira d'issil d'ultre la mer,
Dist-il, oianz plusurs, cui l'ai oï cunter,
Qu'il moreit en cel an, buen le sout afermer;
Or n'i ot mès de l'an que dous jurs à passer;

Li tierz est près alez, où il deveit finer.
Mès le jur de Noel li oï-l'un gehir,
Oiant plusurs, qui èrent pur sun sermun oïr:
"Ci sui," fet-il, "venus entre vus mort suffrir";
Or ert venuz li jurs ke l'covint accomplir,
E sa vie et sa mort l'unt fet mult halt martir.
Nis idunc à la fin de sun sermonement
Ad dit uns de ses clers, en profetisement,
Alisandre de Guales, oiant mult de la gent:
"Chaienz a un martir, saint Elphe, veirement;
Un autre en i aurez, se Deu plest, à présent." [21]

[20a] "Seized." Garnier uses this word twice (ll. 5570-1) for "seize." So above in l. 5322 "enpristrent" seems to be from "emprendre" (like "entreprendre"), and to mean literally "took in hand." See Étienne, p. 220.

[21] The meaning seems to be that *Alexander* was inspired to say this. Grim, above (44*a*), perhaps referring to Garnier's account, says, "It is said that he (i.e. *the Archbishop*)" uttered the prophecy. Fitzstephen, after stating that the Archbishop preached on Christmas day, says (*Mat.* iii. 130) "And when he spoke about the holy Fathers of the church of Canterbury, who are [buried] there as confessors, he said that they had one martyr archbishop, St. Elphege, [and] that it was possible that they would shortly have a second also there."

[59] For this cause waited he there and would not flee. For he was resolute[22] and quite ready to die. He thought that men would not dare to assail him in the Minster. For this cause he waited there and would not shrink from death. But God would have him die in a better place.

[60] (13) (The *Saga*) When the knights come to their followers, they put on armour as if they were about to enter the brunt of a battle, declaring in clear words to all their accomplices that they are minded to set on the archbishop; "for we deem he is a doomed man, by reason of that folly which is manifestly in him." Of the armour of the four knights it is told that they bore both bole-axes and swords, but one of them carried a halberd and a sword,—bole-axes for the purpose of breaking or cutting open chambers, wheresoever they should come upon them,—and besides these, other instruments of war, hard and two-edged, for breaking down walls or timber-work, in order that their wickedness should meet with all the less delay. And thus equipped they proceed up to the archbishop's court.

[61] But when the servants of the holy Thomas see this, they put strong bolts on the court gate, but the others set on it in fury, beating and bellowing, cutting doors open and smashing whatever cometh across their path, so that from their tumult and noise, their egging and whooping, most people were filled with fright, outtaken the archbishop alone. He comforteth the sorrowing, and becometh as blithe as if the visitors had come to ask him to a bridal feast. Now when the hardihood of the knights may not prevail in bringing them into the palace, they get them for guide the clerk Robert of Brock, who by reason of his long sojourn there knew all passages within the court.

---

[59] Pur ç'atendi iluec et ne volt pas fuïr;
Car il ert aséur[22] et tut près de morir;
Cuida k'un ne l'osast el mustier assaillir.

Pur ç'atendeit iluec, ne volt la mort guenchir.
Mès Deus le voleit fère en plus bel liu chaïr.
ll. 5291-5350.

[22] Godefroy gives "asseur" (var. "aseur") = "sur," "assuré."

[62] But the yelling and tumult, crashing and knocking with which they go on, is heard throughout all the chambers within the court. And even those who are now singing in the church at the first vespers blend their voices therewith in fear and awe. For this reason we mentioned first vespers, that the church of Canterbury has two services sung every day, that is to say, that of the monks and that of the clerks.[23]

These are the facts as stated by eye-witnesses and others nearest to the event. The reader may be interested in comparing with these the description of the scene in (1) Stanley's *Memorials of Canterbury*, and (2) Tennyson's *Becket*. Italics call attention to the passages where the modern writers differ from most of the ancient ones, or appear to have misinterpreted something in them.

[63] (i.) (Stanley) The dialogue was interrupted by one of the monks rushing in to announce that the knights were arming. "Let them arm," said Becket. But in a few minutes the violent assault on the door of the hall, and the crash of a wooden partition in the passage from the orchard, announced that danger was close at hand. *The monks, with that extraordinary timidity which they always seem to have displayed, instantly fled*, leaving only a small body of his intimate friends or faithful attendants. They united in entreating him to take refuge in the cathedral. "No," he said, "fear not ; *all monks are cowards.*"

[64] (ii.) (Tennyson)

GRIM (*re-entering*). My lord, the knights are arming in the garden
Beneath the sycamore.
    BECKET.   Good ! let them arm.
    GRIM. And one of the De Brocs is with them, Robert,
The apostate monk that was with Randulf here.
He knows the twists and turnings of the place.
    BECKET. No fear !

---

[23] Apparently the object of the writer was to shew that the Archbishop was not late for vespers (**98**). There was first a service of vespers for the monks, and a second, immediately afterwards, for the clerks. The first was now going on. The Archbishop was presently conducted by his friends to the second.

GRIM.   No fear, my lord.
         [*Crashes on the hall-doors. The* MONKS *flee.*
BECKET (*rising*). Our dovecot flown!
I cannot tell why monks should all be cowards.
JOHN OF SALISBURY. Take refuge in your own cathedral, Thomas.
BECKET. Do they not fight the Great Fiend day by day?
Valour and holy life should go together.
Why should all monks be cowards?
JOHN OF SALISBURY.   Are they so?
I say, take refuge in your own cathedral.
BECKET. Ay, but I told them I would wait them here.
GRIM. May they not say you dared not shew yourself
In your old place? and vespers are beginning.
         [*Bell rings for vespers till end of scene.*
You should attend the office, give them heart.
They fear you slain : they dread they know not what.
BECKET. Ay, monks, not men.
GRIM.   *I am a monk, my lord.*

§ 3. *The "extraordinary timidity" imputed by Stanley to the monks*

[65] Both Stanley and Tennyson assert that the monks fled. Tennyson adds that John of Salisbury remained; and that Grim himself was "a monk."

First, as to the monks, Garnier (to whom Stanley refers in proof of his statement [1]) says that it was the *servants* that all fled. Those who remained were "a few" clerks, and *monks* "*I know not how many*," which means more than "a few." Grim, in his description of those who ran away, mentions "the *servants*, and *almost all the clerks*," but *no* "*monks.*" Even Fitzstephen says that "a *good many* (plurimi) monks" were in attendance on the Archbishop to the last, in the palace. Anon. I. says that "all fled except *several* (aliquot) *monks* and *one clerk*, *i.e.* Grim." There is difference of

---

[1] Stanley's reference is to "Garnier 70 b. 16." He mentions (p. 60) an edition published in 1838-44, and another in 1843, but not Hippeau (1859).

opinion as to the "clerks,"[2] but concerning the "monks" there is no room for doubt at all.

[66] *Those whom Stanley and Tennyson describe as flying, and on whose cowardice they comment, are just those who did not fly, when the rest did.* No doubt, Fitzstephen quotes, as the Archbishop's words,[3] "Most monks"—Stanley and Tennyson, "all monks"—"are too timid and fainthearted." But this was addressed to "*the monks,*" *the men who stood by him, when all others had fled.* He was reproaching them for advising him to go to the Cathedral. If that was "cowardice," it was, at all events, not what Stanley, or Tennyson, or any ordinarily brave man, ought to have called "extraordinary timidity." Relatively to Becket, the monks may be called, by some, "cowards," — by others, prudent ;— relatively to all the rest, they were brave.

[67] Next, it is very doubtful whether John of Salisbury remained with the Archbishop when most of his clerks fled. It is also certain that Grim was not a monk.[4]

[68] The differences in the accounts of the forcible entry may arise, in part, from the fact that some give the view from without, some from within. Fitzstephen is ampler than the rest on the preliminary rush into the courtyard, and on the seduction or constraint of the Archbishop's servants by the knights. On this point, there were

---

[2] Did Fitzstephen and John (the Archbishop's "clerks") run away, or are they both included in the term "monks"? "Monks" or not, they do not appear to have been monks of the Canterbury Minster, who seem to be generally intended, throughout, under the term "monks." Once, describing the vespers, Fitzstephen uses the phrase (*Mat.* iii. 138) "monks of the church," *i.e.* of the Canterbury Monastery or Abbey.

[3] See **47**. Stanley gives also a reference for this to Anon. I. I can find no such words.

[4] Of course, also, Grim, a stranger in Canterbury, would not have known the De Brocs, and would not have been the messenger sent to inspect what was going on in the courtyard. But in a drama, the character needed to be utilized.

probably jealousies and heartburnings, which, if we knew them, would explain his diffuseness.[5]

---

[5] [68a] For example, Garnier says that the Archbishop's seneschal, William Fitz-Nigel, on seeing the four knights in the hall, advanced to salute them with the greatest courtesy. Then, hastily returning to the Archbishop, without mentioning the arrival, he requested to be relieved from service, on the plea that he did not wish to incur the hatred of the King: and he then and there received permission to retire.

Fitzstephen says that William Fitz-Nigel was compelled by the knights to accompany them from the Archbishop's presence, and that he appealed to Becket, "My lord, you see what they are doing with me." Possibly the seneschal felt himself aggrieved by Garnier's account, and the Archbishop's servants may have felt with him. Benedict, William, and Fitzstephen make no mention of the "servants" running *away*. But Benedict describes them as running *into the room* to bid him fly; and Fitzstephen, as running *through the hall* from the men in the courtyard.

CHAPTER III

THE CONVEYANCE OF THE ARCHBISHOP TO THE CATHEDRAL

§ 1. *The different accounts*

[69] (1) (Grim) But when neither arguments nor prayers could force him to take refuge in the church, the monks seized him in spite of his reluctance, and, between dragging, carrying, and pushing (without heeding his opposition and reproachful commands to let him go), they brought him as far as into the church. But the door, by which one passed into the cloister of the monks, happened to have been, several days before this, carefully barred up: and this fact [coming to mind just] when the torturers were pressing on their heels, utterly banished all hope of getting out. However, one [of them] ran [on before], and as soon as he touched the bolt, to the intense astonishment of all, he drew it out as if it had been attached by [nothing stronger than] glue.

[70] (2) (Fitzstephen) They (the monks) would not acquiesce. Some cast hands on him and raise him from

---

[69] (1) (Grim) At ubi nec ratione nec precibus persuaderi potuit ut in ecclesiam refugeret, invitum ac renitentem arripiunt monachi, trahunt, portant, et impellunt, nec attendentes quanta convitiando opponeret, ut ipsum dimitterent, in ecclesiam usque perducunt. Ostium vero, per quod iter erat in claustrum monachorum, multis ante diebus diligentius obseratum, cum jam tortores a tergo insisterent, omnem prorsus evadendi fiduciam abstulit ; currens tamen unus, ubi primum seram contigit, non sine multa omnium admiratione tanta facilitate extraxit ac si glutino cohaesisset.

[70] (2) (Fitzstephen) Illi non acquiescunt. Alii eum injectis manibus

[his feet] and force him [onwards]. Others try to persuade him that he ought to go because he was to attend nones and vespers, and the monks were now saying vespers. So he orders the cross of the Lord to be carried before him.[1] It was borne by a clerk of his, named Henry of Auxerre.[2] When we had reached the monks' cloister, the monks wished to shut fast the door behind him. But he was displeased and would not allow it; and he walked on slowly, last of all, driving all before him, like a good shepherd [driving] his sheep. For indeed fear was so cast out of him by love of God that there was no trace of it in his gesture or gait: it was as far off from all his outer region, so to speak, as from the inner citadel of his soul. Once, indeed, he turned his eyes back over his right shoulder, perchance in case he might see the King's men following his footsteps, perchance lest some one should bar the door.[3]

(3) (John) Omits this.

[71] (4) (William)—until, suggesting that the service of vespers must be sung, they applied violence to him, and,

erigunt, et vim ei faciunt. Alii persuadent eundum esse, quia monachi jam vesperas dicerent, et ille horam nonam et vesperas esset auditurus. Jubet ergo crucem Domini proferri.[1] Quidam clericus ejus, Henricus Autissiodorensis, eam bajulat.[2] In claustrum monachorum cum venissemus, voluerunt monachi ostium post eum accludere. Ille aegre ferens non sustinuit, et lento passu postremus vadit, omnes agens ante se, quasi oves pastor bonus. Equidem timor, quem caritas Dei foras miserat, ejus nec in gestu nec in incessu poterat notari : tam procul aberat ab omni ejus continentia exteriori, quam a mentis arce interiori. Semel quidem super dexteram oculos restorsit, forte si videret illos regales vestigio ejus imminentes, forte ne aliquis pessulum ostii obderet.[3]

(3) (John) Omits this.

[71] (4) (William) . . ., donec de vespertina synaxi decantanda suggerentes

---

[1] " Proferri " ought rather to mean "to be brought forward," but seems used here for "praeferri." Benedict (72) has " praeferri."

[2] [70a] In spite of this express assertion, several traditions, followed by Tennyson, make Grim the cross-bearer.

[3] Fitzstephen alone mentions Becket's refusal to allow the door that led from the palace to the cloister to be barred. Is he confusing it with the door that led from the cloister into the Cathedral? Probably not. The remark that the Archbishop "looked back over the right shoulder" implies a keen observer of fact.

breaking (?)[4] the barred door that leads into the cloister, forced him on in spite of his resistance. Then step by step, and at a slow pace, he moved forward as though he voluntarily awaited death.[5]

[72] (5) (Benedict) But the monks, a few of whom happened to be present,[6] breaking the bolt of the door that led to the church through the cloister, did their best to draw forth their father [in God], in spite of his unwillingness, by setting before him a very honourable reason for departing, namely, that it was the hour when he was bound to pay God due praises at vespers in the church. *Others cast hands on him and raise him from [his seat], and force him [onwards].*[7] Then the Saint, not unmindful of the observance, even to the letter, of that command of the Lord, "Whoso will come after me, let him deny himself and take up his cross and follow me," gave command that his cross should be borne before him. But having come out [of the palace], when

---

vim inferrent ei, et ostium obseratam [4] (*sic*) quod in claustrum ducit infringentes (?), reluctantem propellerent. Inde pedetentim et lento gressu progressus est tanquam ultroneus mortem expectaret.[5]

[72] (5) (Benedict) Monachi vero, qui forte pauci aderant,[6] seram ostii, quod ad ecclesiam per claustrum ducebat, confringentes, patrem suum, licet invitum, educere satagebant, honestiorem ei discedendi causam proponentes, horam videlicet esse qua eum in ecclesia vespertinas Deo laudes oporteret exsolvere. *Alii eum injectis manibus erigunt, et vim ei faciunt.*[7] Tunc sanctus, Dominicum illud praeceptum etiam ad litteram non immemor observare, Qui vult venire post me, abneget semetipsum, et tollat crucem suam et sequatur me," crucem suam

---

[4] "Obseratam ... infringentes." The wrong gender might be a misprint, as the Editor gives eight or nine other confusions of -um and -am in his *Corrigenda*. But "infringere,"—which often means "snap off"—is better applied to "snapping" a "bolt (seram)" than to "breaking down," or "breaking open," a door. Also Benedict and others speak of the "bolt." Probably therefore the text is corrupt, for "*ostii obserati seram* ... infringentes."

[5] The brevity of this and of the preceding section suggests that William was by this time in the Cathedral, perhaps at vespers.

[6] Most of the monks of Canterbury would be in the Cathedral at vespers.

[7] [72*a*] The italicized words are, almost certainly, an interpolation from Fitzstephen. They are omitted by two MSS. and by Lupus.

those who were conveying him were compelling him to quicken his pace, he stopped, as though he were ashamed [8] of flight. Then, since the monks none the less persisted, and absolutely compelled him to go on—whether because they did not treat him with their usual reverence, or because he wished to strengthen and comfort their hearts—he kept saying to them "What means this, sirs? What is your fear?"

[73] (6) (Herbert), they at last with difficulty constrained him to go to the church. Even in this moment of peril, the calm grace of his countenance remained absolutely unchanged. Neither in feature nor in gesture was there any trace of alarm. But when he had advanced some little distance and did not see the cross, which he had been wont to have borne before him, he had the cross-bearer summoned, and halted, waiting for the cross to precede him:—in truth (as I take it) not unmindful of his Lord, who, with the cross, hastened to the cross.[9]

[74] (7) (Anon. I.) These, catching hold of the venerable man (for he still remained sitting), began—in spite of

praeferri sibi praecepit. Egressus autem, cum a commeantibus accelerare cogeretur, quasi fugam erubescens,[8] gradum fixit. Instantibus autem nihilominus monachis, et ut procederet oppido compellentibus, sive quia irreverentius solito se haberent, sive ut suos confirmaret et consolaretur, haec eis verba saepius replicabat: "Quid est hoc, domini, quid formidatis?"

[73] (6) (Herbert), vix tandem coegerunt ut ad ecclesiam pergeret, gratia vultus ejus, etiam in articulo hoc, nec vel in modico immutata; adeo, sicut nec in vultu, sic nec in gestu ullum parebat trepidationis vestigium. Cum vero paullulum processisset, nec crucem videret quam ante se bajulare consueverat, accito crucis bajulo substitit, crucem exspectans ut praecederet; revera, ni fallor, Domini sui non immemor, qui cum cruce properavit ad crucem.[9]

[74] (7) (Anon. I.) Hi apprehendentes venerabilem virum (adhuc enim sedebat) coeperunt eum reluctantem et renitentem atque contradicentem inter manus

---

[8] Not (as Stanley) "changing colour."

[9] Herbert improves on Benedict, who above ("not unmindful" etc.) quoted Christ's words "Let him *take up* his cross." Now the Archbishop did not "*take up* his cross"; for some one else carried it before him. Hence, Herbert likens the Martyr to the Saviour, who, though not bearing the cross (for Simon of Cyrene bore it), nevertheless went "*with* the cross *to* the cross," *i.e.* to the place of Martyrdom or Crucifixion.

his resisting, and struggling, and refusing—to carry him, by force of hand, to the church. But, on looking about, they saw the court full of armed men, and the orchard, and the customary ways to the church, blocked by soldiers. Then they were at their wits' end. Presently, they turned aside to another door, a private one, which had been long closed and barred so that none had passed through it. However, one of the monks ran on before the rest to try if by main force he could wrest the bar out of the socket. But as soon as he touched it, it slipped out altogether into his hands— by Divine will, to the astonishment of himself and all present —just as if it had not been fastened to the door. Then said the monk, " Catch hold of him and carry him this way." So they took him, and began to carry him, and did not let him go till they brought him to the church, within the walls. However, they had some halts before they came to the church, two in the cloister, and one in the chapter-house: for he kept angrily resisting and slipping out of their hands, not wishing them to carry him.

[75] (8) (Anon. II.) He, however, was in nothing terrified, but like one utterly free from trouble, nay, carrying himself as though he counted the delaying of martyrdom to be a diminution of his reward.

---

suas ad ecclesiam portare. Circumspicientes autem viderunt curiam plenam armatis, et pomerium, viasque quibus ad ecclesiam pergebatur, praeoccupatas militibus, et obstupuerunt. Tunc diverterunt ad aliud ostium secretius, quod multo tempore clausum et obseratum nulli transitum praebuerat. Praecucurrit autem unus ex monachis, volens tentare si forte seram viribus effringere posset ; sed mox ut eam tetigit, divino nutu, mirante ipso et omnibus qui aderant, ita in manus ejus collapsa est ac si ostio minime adhaesisset. Tunc monachus, "Apprehendite," inquit, "eum et apportate." Qui accipientes eum coeperunt portare, nec dimiserunt donec in ecclesiam eum introduxerunt. Substiterunt tamen antequam in ecclesiam venirent, bis in claustro, et semel in capitulo ; nam ipse irascens eis reluctabatur et elabebatur de manibus eorum, nolens se portari ab eis.

[75] (8) (Anon. II.) In nullo tamen territus erat, sed velut omnino securus, immo sic agens quasi martyrii dilationem remunerationis suae diminutionem reputarit.

(9) (Anon. IV.) , they (*i.e.* the knights) burst into the cloister of the monks, with a following of armed men, armed also themselves. By this time the Archbishop had gone before them, with all dignity and calmness, to the house of prayer, by the advice, or rather by the compulsion, of the monks, because of the solemn season, to perform the service of vespers—when he looked back and saw them behind him, in the middle of the cloister, in arms.

(10) (Anon. V.) Omits this.

[76] (11) (Anon. X.) However, as the monks present constrained and impelled him,[10] he at last unwillingly arose, and, hastening to the cross [of martyrdom], commanded them to bring his cross.[11]

[77] (12) (Garnier) Then began they to lead him to the Minster[12]; But needful it was for them to carry him almost by main force: Some you might have seen dragging, others pushing him; But they [would have] had to go by the whole length of the wall Or through the doors that had been closed [against the knights], if they had wished to pass

---

(9) (Anon. IV.) . . . claustrum monachorum irruperunt cum multa armatorum sequela, et ipsi armati. Iam praecesserat eos praesul cum modestia. et gravitate in oratorium, suadentibus monachis, immo compellentibus propter diem solennem, ad peragendam vespertinam synaxin, cum eos a tergo respiceret in medio claustri armatos. . . .

(10) (Anon. V.) Omits this.

[76] (11) (Anon. X.) Cogentibus tamen monachis qui affuerunt et impellentibus,[10] tandem invitus surrexit, et ad crucem maturans crucem sibi suam afferre praecepit.[11]

[77] Idunc le commencièrent al mustier à   Les uns véissiez treire et les autres buter;
mener;[12]   Mès par mi l'entier mur lur estoueit aler,
Mès proef par vive force lur estoueit porter;   U par les us fermez, s'il volsissent passer.

---

[10] "Impellentibus," in Grim's context, clearly means "pushed." Anon. X., who perhaps borrows this word from Grim and the rest from Herbert, may use it metaphorically.

[11] This is probably borrowed from Herbert above, "cum cruce properavit ad crucem."

[12] [77*a*] No mention of vespers (such as Fitzstephen, William, and Benedict make) is made here, as a reason for going. " Par mi," three lines below, should = " au milieu de," but seems here to mean "along."

[that way]. Adjoining the other chambers there was one
By which the way to the cloister was more private. But at
that time it was shut with a great bolt. Sorely dismayed
were the hooded folk (*i.e.* the monks) When they saw their
way thus barred on every side. To the door of that chamber
went one of the monks, Took the bolt in his two hands:
then did God do a mighty work: When he would have
wrenched the bolt out, at that moment it fell, As though it
had been fastened with a little glue.[13] The monk opened
the door, then gave them passage through.

[78] So, will he or nill he, they led him to the Minster,
Even as though he willingly waited for his death. Some of
them pulled him and the others pushed him, So that at a
great pace they entered the cloister. Yet twice in that cloister
did they make a stay. For as soon as the Saint could
touch the ground And was able on the ground to set his
two feet, He pushed them all from him, [and] began to
accuse [them]: "What mean you with me," said he, "to
drag and pull? Let me be!" Then took they him, and
carried him, [and placed him] in the Minster.

[79] (13) (*Saga*) Now when the vespers of the brethren
wear on, they having their service always first, the learned
men go to the Archbishop, whereas he sitteth in the same
place still, and with them his familiar friends, all praying
together that he save himself into the monastery. But the

As autres chaumbres out une chambre
ajustée,
Par où la veie esteit al cloistre plus privée ;
Mès à cel ore esteit à un grand loc fermée.
Mult en fu esbaïe la gent chaperunée,
Quand virent si lur veie totes parz estopée.
A l'us de la chambre est un des moines venuz ;
Le loc prist à dous mains; là ad Deus feit
    vertuz ;
Quant le loc volt estuerdre, el puinz li est
    chaûz,
Cum se il fust aers à un petit de gluz.[13]
L'us a overz li moines, puis les ad esmeûz.

[78] Dunc l'en unt al mustier, ou voille ou
    nun, mené,
Ensement cum la mort atendist de sun gré ;
Li un i unt sachié et li autre buté,
Tant qu'il sunt le grant pas dedenz le cloistre
    entré.
Mais il se sunt dous feiz enz el cloistre aresté.
  Car si tost cum li sainz pout la terre atuchier,
Et il pout à la terre ses dous piez afichier,
Tuz les enpainst de sei, commença à pleidier :
"Que me volez," fet-il, "de trère et de sachier ?
Leissiez mei !" Dunc l'unt pris et porté el
    mustier.   ll. 5351-75.

---

[13] "Cum se il fust aers à un petit de gluz," Grim, "ac si glutino cohaesisset,"
Anon. I., "ac si ostio minime adhaesisset."

blessed Archbishop abhorreth all flight, and sitteth still as before.

So, when this availeth naught, they tell him that the brethren have now finished their vespers, and that it behoveth themselves to go to church, and to do their duty to God on so great a high day. For this reason he at last standeth up and ordereth the cross to be borne before him. Now against custom the mode of procession was changed, inasmuch as the Archbishop, who had always been wont to go first, now goeth last. Others, from fear natural to man, walked with haste whilst he walked quietly, and slower than was his wont. But when they wanted to quicken more the pace, in order that he might save himself into the church, he spoke: "Why behave ye so, or what fear ye?" They say that armed men have entered the cloister already. He answereth, "Why should that change your reverence? They may do naught more than God permitteth."

[80] (i.) (Stanley, pp. 83-5) Partly forced, partly persuaded by the argument, partly feeling that his doom called him thither, he rose and moved, but *seeing that his cross-staff was not, as usual, borne before him, he stopped and called for it.* He remembered, perhaps, the memorable day at the Council of Northampton, when he had himself borne the cross through the royal Hall to the dismay and fury of his opponents. His ordinary cross-bearer, Alexander Llewellyn, had, as we have seen, left him for France two days before, and the cross-staff was, therefore, borne by one of his clerks, Henry of Auxerre.

They first *attempted* to pass along the usual passage to the cathedral, through the orchard, to the western front of the church. But both court and orchard being by this time thronged with armed men, they turned through a room which conducted to a private door that was rarely used, and which led from the palace to the cloisters of the monastery. One of the monks ran before to force it, for the key was lost. Suddenly the door flew open as if of itself, and in the confusion of the moment, when none had leisure or inclination to ask how so opportune a deliverance occurred, it was natural for the story to arise which is related, with one exception, in all the narratives of the period—that the bolt came off as though it had merely been fastened on by glue, and left their passage free.

[81] *This one exception is the account by Benedict*, then a monk of the monastery, and afterwards Abbot of Peterborough, and his version, compared with that of all the other historians, is an instructive commentary on a thousand fables of a similar kind. Two cellarmen, he says, of the monastery, Richard and William, whose lodgings were in that part of the building, hearing the tumult and clash of arms, flew to the cloister, drew back the bolt from the other side, and opened the door to the party from the palace. Benedict knew nothing of the seeming miracle, as his brethren were ignorant of the timely interference of the cellarmen.

[82] But both miracle and explanation would at the moment be alike disregarded. Every monk in that terrified band had but a single thought—to reach the church with their master in safety. The whole march was a struggle between the obstinate attempt of the Primate to preserve his dignity, and the frantic eagerness of his attendants to gain the sanctuary. As they urged him forward, he *coloured*[14] and paused, and repeatedly asked them what they feared. The instant they had passed through the door which led to the cloister, the subordinates flew to bar it behind them, which he as peremptorily forbade. For a few steps he walked firmly on, with the cross-bearer and the monks before him ; halting once, and looking over his right

---

[14] This seems to be based upon Benedict's "quasi fugam *erubescens* gradum fixit," "stopped, *as though ashamed* of flight." But no literal "change of colour" is implied in the Latin.

shoulder, either to see whether the gate was locked, or else if his enemies were pursuing.

[83] Then the same ecclesiastic who had hastened forward to break open the door, called out, "Seize him and carry him." Vehemently he resisted, but in vain. Some pulled him from before, others pushed from behind; half carried, half drawn, he was borne along the northern and eastern cloister, crying out, "Let me go, do not drag me." Thrice they were delayed, even in that short passage, for thrice he broke loose from them—twice in the cloister itself, and once in the chapter-house, which opened out of its eastern side. At last they reached the door of the lower north transept of the cathedral, and here was presented a new scene.

[84] (ii.) Tennyson represents the Archbishop as accompanied by none but Grim and John of Salisbury, and Grim as bearing the cross.

§ 2. *The carrying of the Cross*

[85] Grim, William, Anon. I., and Garnier, make no mention of the carrying of the cross, no doubt because they assumed it as a matter of course. Benedict and Fitzstephen mention it to shew that the Archbishop, in that crisis, did everything that was seemly, and especially this seemly and typical act. It is the latest writer alone, Herbert, who gives us the impression that the Archbishop had gone a little way through the cloister before he noticed the absence of the cross. This emphasizes the matter. But had it been so, it would surely have been stated by earlier writers.

[86] There was no such "attempt" as Stanley mentions to pass along the usual passage. The monks knew that to be hopeless. They simply "looked round," or "cast about" (circumspexerunt), as Anon. I. says, for some other way.

§ 3. *The bolt that came off " as though it had been fastened by glue "*

[87] As regards the explanation of the wonderful opening of the bolted door that led from the Palace into the cloister, Stanley has been misled by confusing *two doors* mentioned by Benedict. Both of these might be called "cloister doors." But the first is, as described by Benedict above, "the door that led *to the church through the cloister*," *i.e.* a door *in the Palace*. The second, which will be mentioned in the next chapter, is "the door of the cloister *that opens from the cloister into the church*."

It is this latter that is unbarred by the two cellarers. As to the former, Benedict says briefly that the monks led the Archbishop through it, "breaking the bolt of the door (seram ostii confringentes)." Undoubtedly Benedict sees no miracle in the opening of the door now in question; but he regards it as opened, not by the two cellarers, but by the monk who broke the bolt.

§ 4. *Another door that " opened as if spontaneously "*

[88] When the Archbishop, surrounded by a hostile crowd, was leaving the royal castle at Northampton, a similar miracle was thought to have occurred by some writers, but not by all.

(*a*) William says that the Archbishop (*Mat.* i. 40) "burst out (erupit)," while the porter was beating some one and neglecting his duty. John of Salisbury (alluding to Luke iv. 30, John viii. 59) says, in a brief summary, "but he, passing through the midst of them, went his way." Grim omits it, and says (*Mat.* ii. 399) that a command was given from the King that the Archbishop should be allowed to leave. Fitzstephen has (*Mat.* iii. 68) "the door, which had been carefully barred ("obseratum," al. "watched (observatum)") all that day, was opened for him, as if spontaneously." Herbert — who writes as a companion of the Archbishop, and says that he "alone followed him outside the inner buildings until *we* entered the hall"—makes no mention of any difficulty as to the door. Anon. I. says (*Mat.* iv. 52) that, when the Archbishop (on horseback) had reached the castle gate, he was terrified at finding it closed, but Peter of Mortorium, one of his servants, got hold of a bundle of keys, and at once chose the right key, "which *seemed to some as it were* a miracle," and the gate was opened quickly. Garnier says the same thing, only calls the servant a squire, named Trunchez. The *Saga* (i. 223) curiously minimizes the miracle by saying "And soon this hindrance becometh lighter through the will of God, for they see many keys somewhere on the wall, of which they bore to the lock one after the other until the very one was found which fitted the gate."

What are we to infer as to the Northampton gate? Unquestionably this, that some servant of the Archbishop's did get hold of the porter's keys so as to open the gate in the manner described, and that the opening of the gate in the nick of time was regarded variously as (1) fortunate but not worthy of mention in history, (2) a quasi-miracle, (3) a miracle.

(*b*) So, too, as regards this cloister-door, the bolt, bar, or lock of a door, long disused and closed, came off at once in the hands of some monk, say Robert of Merton, the chaplain. To him it seemed little short of a miracle, just as to Peter (or Trunchez) at Northampton. As Peter, the opener of the door, seems to have inspired Anon. I. then, so the unknown monk that opened this door (if he is not himself Anon. I.) may have inspired Anon. I. now, and also Garnier, and Grim. Benedict and William simply say that the bolt (or door) was broken. Herbert omits the whole of this feature, perhaps as distracting the reader from the scene of the Christ-like progress "with the cross to the cross": and so does the *Saga*.

§ 5. *The carrying of the Archbishop*

[89] The statement of Grim and Anon. I. that the Archbishop was "carried" by the monks cannot be literally reconciled with that of Fitzstephen, that he "drove them all before him as a shepherd drives sheep." But we may suppose that, even when carried by force, he insisted on being carried in the rear. Yet some of his attendants appear (so it is stated below) to have been left outside the Cathedral door. How could this be, if he was carried last? The explanation may be that, when the procession, or crowd, reached the Cathedral, the foremost waited, to allow the Archbishop to enter first. Or others may have fled into the cloister afterwards, chased by the armed knights. The worst inaccuracy is that of Anon. IV., which represents the Archbishop as seeing the armed men behind him in the cloister, even before he had entered the Cathedral.

CHAPTER IV

THE ENTRANCE OF THE ARCHBISHOP INTO THE CATHEDRAL

§ 1. *The different accounts*

[90] (1) (Grim) When the monks had got inside the doors of the church, the four knights already mentioned followed at the top of their speed behind their backs. Among them came a sub-deacon, Hugo by name, as bent on mischief as the knights, known for his villainy by the appropriate appellation of Mauclerk (bad clerk), one that reverenced neither God nor saints [or, holy things], as he shewed in his subsequent action. But as soon as the holy Archbishop entered the Minster, the monks, breaking off the vespers which they had begun to offer to God, come hastily to meet him, glorifying God because they saw living and unharmed their father [in God] who had been reported dead.

[91] (2) (Fitzstephen) They entered the church itself.[1]

---

[90] (1) (Grim) Postquam autem intra fores ecclesiae monachi se receperant, jam dicti milites quattuor cursu rapidissimo post terga secuti sunt. Affuit inter illos subdiaconus quidam, eadem qua milites armatus malitia, Hugo Malus-clericus merito suae nequitiae cognominatus, qui nec Deo nec sanctis reverentiam exhiberet ; quod sequens factum probavit. Intranti vero monasterium sancto archiepiscopo, omissis vesperis quas Deo libare inceperant, occurrunt monachi, glorificantes Deum quod patrem suum, quem exstinctum audierant, vivum cernerent et incolumem.

[91] (2) (Fitzstephen) Intratum est in ecclesiam ipsam.[1] Monachi ecclesiae,

---

[1] All the words from "Monachi" onwards are omitted in one MS. called J. (see 15*a*).

The monks of the church, trembling and astounded at so strange and vast a tumult, left their vespers without singing them through, and came out of the choir to meet the Archbishop as soon as he entered the church, rejoicing and thanking God that they saw and welcomed him alive after he had been reported to them as slain with the sword.

(3) (John) Omits this.

[92] (4) (William) As the brethren were duly at vespers, there had run [up the choir], through the midst of them, two servant lads, before the rest, announcing (rather by gestures of terror than in articulate speech) that the enemy was upon them. Some of the brethren persisted still in their prayers, some made for passages of outlet, some wished to help [the Archbishop]; but one of the brethren went out, saying, "Hither, father, hither: enter and abide with us, that, if need be, we may at one stroke suffer together and be glorified together. Sorely have we been distracted by your absence: now let us be consoled by your presence."[2]

[93] (5) (Benedict) And when they had come near to the cloister door [opening into the church[3]]—it being im-

---

pro tali et tanto tumultu tam pavidi quam attoniti, relictis et non percantatis vesperis, Domino archiepiscopo in ecclesiam intrante, a choro exeunt ei obviam, gaudentes et Deo gratiam habentes quod eum vivum cernunt et recipiunt, quem jam detruncatum audierant.

(3) (John) Omits this.

[92] (4) (William) Praecurrerant per medium fratrum vespertinae synaxeos debita prosequentium pueri duo, plus terrore quam voce hostilem invasionem nuntiantes. Quibusdam ergo ex fratribus ad orationem adhuc persistentibus, quibusdam diverticula petentibus, quibusdam subvenire volentibus, exivit quidam ex fratribus dicens, "Ingredere, pater, ingredere, manens nobiscum, ut, si necesse est, una compatiamur et conglorificemur. Exanimatos absentia tua, praesentia consoletur.[2]

[93] (5) (Benedict) Cumque ad ostium claustri[3] appropinquassent, et neque

---

[2] This section, with its full details about the monks at vespers, confirms the view that William was in the Cathedral with them.

[3] "Ostium claustri," *i.e.* the door leading (a) *from the cloister* into the Cathedral. This must be distinguished from the door mentioned in the last chapter by Benedict ("ostii quod ad ecclesiam *per claustrum* ducebat"), *i.e.* the

possible for them either to break it down or to open it with a key (for they had none at hand)⁴—lo, two cellarers of the Canterbury church, Richard and William by name (who, hearing the uproar and the clatter of arms, began to hasten thither by the way of the cloister⁵), tore away the bolt and threw open the above-mentioned door for the Archbishop as he came [up].⁶

[94] (6) (Herbert) When he entered the church, all that belonged to him were presently scattered in fear. They fled on this side, and they fled on that side, and through the crypts of the church, and under the altars, they "hid themselves from him."⁷

[95] (7) (Anon. I.) So when the man of God had stepped into the church, the monks looked back and saw that the knights were by this time stepping into the cloister.

illud confringere possent, neque clavem prae manibus haberent,⁴ ecce cellerarii duo Cantuariensis ecclesiae, Ricardus et Willelmus — qui, audito tumultu et collisione armorum, per viam claustri⁵ illo properabant—ostium idem, avulsa sera, venienti archiepiscopo patefecerunt.⁶

[94] (6) (Herbert) Cum autem intrasset ecclesiam, quotquot sui prae timore mox dispersi sunt : fugerunt ·hi, fugerunt et illi, et per cryptas ecclesiae et sub altaribus absconderunt se ab eo.⁷

[95] (7) (Anon. I.) Ingresso igitur viro Dei in ecclesiam, respicientes monachi viderunt milites jam ingredi claustrum :

door leading (*b*) *from the Palace*, through the cloister, toward the Cathedral. Stanley (87 and 88) has confused the two. Taking Benedict's statement about (*a*), he bases on it an attempt to explain the quasi-miraculous opening of (*b*).

⁴ Lit. "and could neither break it down nor had a key at hand," a curious order of words.

⁵ "By way of the cloister" may grammatically be taken with (1) "clatter of arms," or (2) "hastening." But the sense requires the latter. The cellarers ran round the cloister, by the way leading past their chambers, and thus got to the Cathedral ahead of the Archbishop's procession. The Archbishop went by two sides of the square, the cellarers by the other two.

⁶ After this, they appear to have rushed into the choir, announcing the "invasio," as William says above.

⁷ We should have expected "hid themselves from *the enemy*"; but Herbert apparently discerns here a fulfilment of Isaiah liii. 3 "And we *hid* as it were our faces *from him*." In the context, Herbert, who places the flight of Becket's companions somewhat earlier than the others do, comments here on this providential flight as securing the glory of martyrdom for the Archbishop alone.

(8) (Anon. II.) Omits this.

(9) (Anon. IV.) Omits this.

(10) (Anon. V.) But they hurried him forcibly away and carried him to the Minster.

(11) (Anon. X.) When he entered the Minster, the vespers were broken off, and some of the monks came to meet him, astounded by the clamour of those who (?) ran [8] through [the church].

(12) (Garnier) Omits this.

[96] (13) (The *Saga*) Now when he cometh into the church, even as the vespers had come to an end, they came running to meet him, weeping from joy, and thanking God that they saw him alive; for they thought he was already reft of life by then.

[97] (i.) (Stanley, p. 85) The vespers had already begun, and the monks were singing the service in the choir, when two boys [9] rushed up the nave, announcing, more by their terrified gestures than by their words, that the soldiers were bursting into the palace and monastery. Instantly the service was thrown into the utmost confusion; part remained at prayer—part fled into the numerous hiding-places the vast fabric affords; and part went down the steps of the choir into the transept to meet the little band at the door. "Come in, come in!" exclaimed one of them, "come in, and let us die together."

---

(8) (Anon. II.) Omits this.

(9) (Anon. IV.) Omits this.

(10) (Anon. V.) At illi vi eum rapientes monasterio intulerunt.

(11) (Anon. X.) Intranti monasterium, omissis vesperis, quidam monachorum occurrunt, clamore percurrentium [8] attoniti.

---

[8] "Ran through." The Editor suggests "praecurrentium," "those who ran up first," either (*a*) to announce the Archbishop's approach, or (*b*) to hide from the knights. William (92), who mentions two "lads" as "running before the rest (praecurrentes)," rather implies that they did not shout ("plus terrore quam voce").

[9] "Boys (92, pueri)." Better, "lads," or "servants."

(ii.) (Tennyson)

[*Service stops.* MONKS *come down from the stairs that lead to the choir.*

MONKS. Here is the great Archbishop! He lives! he lives!
Die with him, and be glorified together.

§ 2. *The* Saga's *regard for the Fitness of Things*

[98] The solitary assertion of the *Saga* that "the vespers had come to an end," when the monks flocked to meet the Archbishop, is more seemly, but less probable, than the versions that represent the monks as "breaking off vespers." It is characteristic of the Icelandic poet that he should take this decorous view. Above (**62**), he frees the Archbishop from the blame of going to vespers late, by explaining (alone of all our writers) that there were *two* services, and that he was going to the *second*.

§ 3. *Different points of view*

[99] There is no error in either of the two modern writers; and the differences between the original authorities can be easily explained.

Benedict's point of view is in the front of the procession, which passes along the northern and eastern sides of the cloisters. Before they reach the door opening from the cloister into the Cathedral, two cellarers, whom he knows and mentions by name, having come round the cloisters by the other two sides (the western and southern), and having reached the door first, manage to wrench out the bolt, and throw the door open for them. William, on the other hand, sees things from the interior of the Cathedral, where he was probably engaged at vespers. Two "lads," he says,—probably Benedict's two "cellarers," who had first opened the door for the Archbishop—had run into the choir during vespers, and had announced the approach of the enemy. Many of the monks now rush towards the entrance. "A brother," says William, goes out and welcomes the Archbishop in the name of all the monks. The other narrators speak of no single "brother" but of "the monks" as a body. Anon. I. has his point of view in the rear of the Archbishop's procession. The Archbishop enters first. Anon. I., still outside, looks back, and sees the knights in pursuit, just entering the cloister as the Archbishop enters the Cathedral.

CHAPTER V

THE APPROACH OF THE KNIGHTS

§ 1. *The different accounts*

[100] (1) (Grim) They also hasten to keep off the foe from the slaughter of their Shepherd by barring the folding-doors of the church. But the admirable Champion [of God] turned to them and commanded the doors to be opened, saying, " It is not seemly to make into a tower the house of prayer, the church of Christ, which, even though it be not closed, suffices its children for a stronghold ; and by suffering, rather than by fighting, shall we triumph over the foe ; for indeed we have come to suffer [violence], not to fight against it."

[101] (2) (Fitzstephen)[1] And whereas some were weeping for joy or fear, and some advising this, others that (like Peter saying to our Lord, " That be far from thee "[2]), he himself, " not timorous to die "[3] for the liberty and interests of the Church of God, bade them depart and stand back from

---

[100] (1) (Grim) Valvas etiam ecclesiae repagulando hostes a nece pastoris arcere festinant. Ad quos conversus athleta mirabilis imperat ecclesiae januas aperiri, "Non decet," inquiens, "orationis domum, ecclesiam Christi, turrem facere, quae, etsi non claudatur, suis sufficit ad munimen ; et nos patiendo potius quam pugnando triumphabimus hostem, qui et pati venimus, non repugnare."

[101] (2) (Fitzstephen)[1] Et cum alii prae gaudio vel timore flerent, alii hoc, alii illud suaderent (ut Petrus Domino dicens " Propitius esto tibi "[2]), ille, pro ecclesiae Dei libertate et causa "non timidus mori,"[3] jussit eos abire et a se

---

[1] The MS. (called J) (15*a*) that omitted part of the last section, omits " Et cum . . . videbat."   [2] Matthew xvi. 22.

[3] From Horace, *Odes*, iii. 19. 2 " pro patria *non timidus mori.*"

him, that they might by no means hinder his Passion, which he had predicted as destined to come, and now saw on the point of coming.

[102] On his way to the altar up above,[4] where he was wont to hear "familiar mass" and "hours," he had already ascended four[5] steps, when lo, at the cloister door, by which we had come [out of the Palace],[6] there came up first Reginald Fitzurse, in hauberk, with sword unsheathed, exclaiming, "Now! This way! King's men!" A few moments afterwards he was joined by his three companions above mentioned, in hauberks too, head and body in full armour, all but the eyes, and with naked swords [in their hands].

[103] There were a great many besides, without hauberks, but armed, from their own retinue and friends, and some from the city of Canterbury, whom they had compelled to come along with them.[7] . . . On the sight, I say, of these men in arms, the monks wished[8] to close and bar the door

---

recedere : utique ne impedirent passionem ejus, quam futurum (*sic*) praedixerat et imminere videbat.

[102] Iturus ad aram [4] superius, ubi missas familiares et horas solebat audire, jam quatuor [5] gradus ascenderat, cum ecce ad ostium claustri,[6] quo veneramus, primus adest Raginaldus (*sic*) Ursonis loricatus, ense evaginato, et vociferans, "Nunc huc ad me, homines regis!" Nec multo post adduntur ei tres praedicti socii ejus, similiter loricis contecti corpora et capita, praeterquam oculos solos, et ensibus nudatis.

[103] Plurimi etiam alii, sine loricis, armati, de sequela et sociis suis, et aliqui de urbe Cantuariae, quos coactos secum illi venire compulerant.[7] . . . Visis, inquam, illis armatis, voluerunt monachi [8] ostium ecclesiae obfirmare : sed

---

[4] Does Fitzwilliam distinguish this "ara" from the "high altar (altare majus)"?

[5] Herbert says "seven or eight," see 163.

[6] It is important to distinguish this (1) "cloister-door," leading *out* of the *Palace*, from (2) the "cloister door" leading *into* the *Cathedral*. If the knights had reached (2), there would have been no time for the monks to attempt to bar (2). But the knights were seen emerging from (1), just before the monks began to bar (2). See 87.

[7] Here the writer digresses to say that Dover, Hastings, and other ports, had been guarded to prevent the Archbishop's escape.

[8] "Voluerunt monachi" om. by the MS. called J. This would make "obfirmare" historical infinitive (or perf. used for "obfirmavere").

of the church. But the good man, having his trust fixed in the Lord, and not being carried away by the sudden panic at the onrush of these powers of the wicked, turned back and came down from the steps, forbidding the closing of the church door, and saying, " Far be it from us to make a castle out of the church of God.[9]   Let all come into the church of God that wish to come in.   God's will be done."

(3) (John) Omits this.

[104] (4) (William) He replied, " Go, complete divine service as is due." And standing back, near the door, he said, "As long as you hold the entrance, I will not enter in." On their retiring, he stepped inside the Minster, but [again] stood back on the threshold, and driving back the common folk, who crowded round him as though to see some spectacle, " What is it," he asked, " that these folk fear ? " Answer was made, " The armed men in the cloister." " I am going forth," he said, " to meet them." But when the brethren hindered his going forth, he stood fronting them,[10] round about the

---

bonus homo, fiduciam habens in Domino, et non expavescens repentino terrore irruentes potentias impiorum, e gradibus descendit regressus, prohibens ne ostium ecclesiae clauderetur, et dicens "Absit ut de ecclesia Dei castellum faciamus;[9] permittite intrare omnes ecclesiam Dei intrare volentes : fiat voluntas Dei."

(3) (John) Omits this.

[104] (4) (William) Respondit, "Ite, pensum Divinae servitutis explentes." Et subsistens ad ostium inquit "Quamdiu tenebitis introitum, non introibo." Cedentibus illis introgressus monasterium substitit in limine, repellensque populares quasi ad spectaculum circa se constipatos, "Quidnam," inquit, "metuit gens ista?" Responsum est, "Armatos in claustro." "Ad ipsos," ait, "exeo." Prohibentibus autem fratribus eum exire, coepit circa limen obversari;[10] et cum

---

[9] [103a] "Absit . . . faciamus" om. by the MS. called J. The saying is assigned to the Archbishop, in some form, by Garnier, Grim, Anon. I., and Herbert. William (129) has an echo of them in some remarks of his own. If they were here originally, there is no reason why a scribe should omit them. But there is good reason why a later edition, or a scribe of the first edition, should insert them. Probably therefore these words were not in the first edition (15a).

[10] "Coepit obversari." The meaning seems to be that the monks stood with their backs to the door, and the Archbishop, fronting them, tried to pass through them.

threshold; and, though he was advised to go further on and betake himself to the Holy of Holies [*i.e.* the altar], so that reverence for the place might secure deference for his person, he would not listen. Meanwhile, as the clerks were making a great confusion, and some of the brethren were setting up an iron bar against [the door], " Away," cried he, " faint of heart! Let these blind wretches work their mad will! On your duty of obedience we bid you not to close fast the door."

[105] (5) (Benedict) [11[*Meanwhile, as the clerks were making a great confusion, and some of the brethren were setting up an iron bar against* [*the door*], *he cried, " Away, faint of heart! Let these blind wretches work their mad will. On your duty of obedience, I bid you not to close the door.*] *For it is not seemly that a church should be turned into a castle.*" 12] Some of the monks, therefore,[13] breaking off vespers, run towards him, and, bringing their Shepherd inside in spite of his resistance, they hasten to shut the folding-doors of the church so as to shut out the enemy.

procedere moneretur, et ad sancta sanctorum se conferre, ut ei deferretur ex reverentia loci, non acquievit. Tumultuantibus interea clericis, quibusdamque fratribus vectem ferreum obducentibus, "Abite," inquit, "pusillanimes, sinite miseros et caecos delirare. Praecipimus in virtute obedientiae ne ostium accludatis."

[105] (5) (Benedict) [11] [*Tumultuantibus interea clericis, quibusdamque fratribus vectem ferreum obducentibus, inquit,* "*Abite, pusillanimes, sinite miseros et caecos delirare: praecipimus in virtute obedientiae ne ostium claudatis;*] *non enim decet ecclesiam incastellari.*" 12] Omissis igitur [13] vesperis accurrunt quidam monachorum, pastoremque suum, licet renitentem, introducentes, clausis ecclesiae valvis hostes festinant excludere.

[11] The Editor (*Mat.* ii. 11) says that the passage, "Tumultuantibus . . . claudatis," here ascribed in the *Quadrilogus* to Benedict, "is really by William of Canterbury." If so, the position of "inquit" here, a violation of Latin usage, is an interesting instance of a scribe erroneously altering the original. Probably (see 105*a* below) the rest of the sentence is interpolated from Herbert.

[12] Al. "incastellare." Comp. Herbert below, "decere minime *incastellari* ecclesiam."

[13] [105*a*] "Therefore" is inexplicable, if the context is correct. How could Benedict write, in effect, "The Archbishop said, 'Go away.' Some of the monks *therefore* run towards him"? Probably *the whole* of the italicized passage is an interpolation (slightly varied) from William and Herbert. The genuine Benedict

[106] But the holy Father stepped back, and began speedily to rebuke them, saying, " Suffer my people to enter." And he went to meet them, and, thrusting away now this one now that one from the folding-doors, he with his own most sacred hands began to drag his people into the church—for they had been left outside the doors to the jaws of the wolves—saying, " Come inside, come inside, with all speed " :—[which came to pass] that he might be able to say with the Lord, " Those whom thou hast given me, I have not lost one of them."[14]

[107] But at last, torn violently from the spot by the urgency of his sons, he left the doors thrown open to the enemy (who were now near at hand), lest, by impeding their way, he should impede his martyrdom, wherewith he had known and declared aforetime that he was destined to be blessed. For while still in the parts beyond the seas, he had foretold—and that in clear terms—to two Abbots, those of Pontigny and Val-luisant, as we wrote above,[15] that he must suffer martyrdom and be slain in a church. . . .

---

[106] Regressus autem pater sanctus quantocius increpabat eos, dicens, "Dimittite meos intrare." Et occurrens ostium aperuit, et hos et illos a valvis removens, suos, qui de foris luporum morsibus relicti fuerant, sacratissimis manibus suis trahebat in ecclesiam, dicens, "Introite, introite citius " : ut dicere posset cum Domino, "Quos dedisti mihi, non perdidi ex eis quenquam."[14]

[107] Tandem vero, filiorum suorum instantia inde violenter abstractus, hostibus jam prope positis ostia patefacta reliquit, ne impedito illorum itinere ejus impediretur martyrium, quo se scierat et praedixerat futurum esse beatum. In finibus enim transmarinis adhuc positus, duobus abbatibus, Pontiniaci scilicet et Vallis-lucentis, sicut praescripsimus,[15] passurum se esse martyrium et in ecclesia occidendum manifeste praedixerat. . . .

---

continues from the last section thus : " . . . they opened the door for the Archbishop as he came up. Some of the monks, *therefore*, run towards him."

[14] John xviii. 9. In what precedes, "citius " may mean " faster " (so Stanley, " faster, faster "). But the comparative is so seldom thus used in this kind of Latin (without quam) that I prefer " with all speed."

[15] [107a] " As we wrote above." No extant words of Benedict describe this vision. Two explanations of the phrase are open : (1) Benedict wrote a life of Becket, and it is lost ; (2) the phrase comes from the compiler of the *Quadrilogus*, who interpolates it in order to refer the reader to the previous mention of this

[108] (6) (Herbert) However, a certain one [16] of them that were with him, when the Archbishop had entered the church, presently closed the church doors and barred them. But those murderous knights with their cohort, with arms, and swords, and staves, following the Archbishop hard at his heels, and by this time coming up to the church doors, with terrible noise and loud shouts thundered to some one to open the doors to them with all speed. Then, as there was some delay about it, they attempted to batter the doors down with certain iron implements they had prepared for that purpose, and to force a passage in that way. Presently the din and shouting near the folding-doors of the church were overheard by the future Sacrifice of Christ,—[himself] a Christ [17] of the Lord—and he gave orders that they should be immediately

---

[108] (6) (Herbert) Quidam [10] tamen de suis, cum ecclesiam intrasset ipse, ecclesiae fores clausit mox et seravit. Illi vero carnifices milites cum cohorte, cum armis, et gladiis, et fustibus, archipraesulem pedatim sequentes, et jam ad ecclesiae fores venientes, terribiliter et clamose intonabant ut cito sibi aperirentur fores. Quod quia aliquantisper dilatum, quibusdam praeparatis ferreis machinis fores dejicere et irruere sic intentabant. Quorum fragorem et clamorem ad ecclesiae valvas mox futura Christi victima christus [17] Domini

---

prediction in his compilation (*Mat.* iv. 353). The latter is almost certainly to be adopted. (*a*) The two Abbots are mentioned by the *Quadrilogus* above, in an extract from Herbert, and the vision is given at great length. Moreover, (*b*) the *Quadrilogus* does not shrink from even altering the text for the purpose of harmonizing it (20*a*), so that we may reasonably suppose it would not scruple at such a comparatively slight matter as this insertion. (*c*) There is strong evidence to shew that Benedict was known by his contemporaries Anon. I., Grim, and Elias of Evesham (*i.e.* the Early *Quadrilogus*) to have written *only* about the Passion and the Miracles, and Elias distinctly *asserts* this (*Mat.* ii. 448, iv. 2, 425).

[16] [108*a*] "A certain one." These words seem inserted by Herbert because he has previously said that, on the Archbishop's entrance, *all that were with him* deserted him. Now he has to admit that some one remained, and barred the door. But he makes this *the act of one man alone*. That is improbable, and is contradicted by the evidence. Herbert cannot be trusted, when biassed by the desire to find analogies between the Martyr and the Saviour. Note his repetition of the "cohort" in the next sentence, because Christ was arrested by a "cohort."

[17] "Christ of the Lord," *i.e.* as being "Anointed of the Lord," anointed Archbishop.

opened, adding that it was by no means seemly that a church should be turned into a castle.[18]

[109] (7) (Anon. I.) They (the monks) closed against them (the knights) the doors of the church. But seeing that the doors were being closed, the man of God said to them, "By your holy obedience I order that they be opened without delay. For we ought not to make a castle of the house of God." A second time did the monks [now] seize the man of God and began to escort him by the steps into the choir. "Let me be," he said to them, "and go back. You have naught to do here. Suffer God, according to His will, to arrange concerning His own business."

[110] (8) (Anon. II.) They barred the folding-doors behind him. But he presently had them opened, saying, "Far be it that we should make the church of God a castle."

(9) (Anon. IV.) Omits this.

(10) (Anon. V.) But he himself, [going up] by some steps, betook himself to the altar of St. Benedict,[19] which was at the entrance of the church.

---

exaudiens, praecepit ut confestim aperirentur, addens decere minime incastellari ecclesiam.[18]

[109] (7) (Anon. I.) Clauserunt contra eos januas ecclesiae. Videns autem vir Dei claudi januas, dixit, "Per sanctam obedientiam praecipio ut sine mora aperiantur. Non enim debemus facere castellum de domo Dei." Iterum arripuerunt monachi virum Dei, et coeperunt eum per gradus in chorum deducere. Quibus ipse ait, "Dimittite me, et recedite; nihil hic habetis facere; permittite Deum secundum voluntatem suam disponere de suo negotio."

[110] (8) (Anon. II.) Post quem cum valvas obserassent, mox eas aperiri fecit, dicens, "Absit ut ecclesiam Dei castellum faciamus."

(9) (Anon. IV.) Omits this.

(10) (Anon. V.) Ipse vero ad altare beati Benedicti,[19] quod erat in introitu ecclesiae, per gradus quosdam se contulit.

---

[18] [108*b*] No other writer says that the knights found the church door closed and attempted to force it open. Fitzstephen (see 128 below) says that the knights, "contrary to their expectation," found the door open. Herbert is perhaps confusing the entry into the Cathedral with the entry into the palace.

[19] The consent of the authorities is that he went up the steps leading to the choir on the way to the High Altar. See however 102.

(11) (Anon. X.), and they hasten to keep off the foe from the slaughter of their Shepherd by barring the folding-doors of the church. But the holy Father turned back and thrust away, now this one, now that one, from the folding-doors; lest, by impeding the way of the enemy, his martyrdom should be impeded.[20]

[111] (12) (Garnier) When the monks had thus carried him to the Minster, Then had the knights entered inside the cloister, Sword in hand, and armed with hauberks, And one, Hugh Malclerk (so was he named); Clerk he was of Robert de Broc, very full of iniquity. These four came in front, to begin the evil, But from afar there followed four other knights: This Hugh went with them [the former four] and entered the Minster. They [the latter four] entered not, for that son of the Adversary Had met them in the cloister (?) to turn them back.[21]

[112] Some of the monks closed the doors against them; "Open," said St. Thomas; and himself went unclosing them. "By [your] holy obedience," said he, "I command you; Let them do their will, these who have come forward.[22] As long as ye close these doors, I will not go a step forward.

---

(11) (Anon. X.), et valvas ecclesiae repagulando hostes a nece sui pastoris arcere festinant. Revertens autem pater sanctus hos et illos a valvis removet, ne, impedito itinere hostium, ejus impediretur martyrium.[20]

[111] Quand l'orent el mustier li moine issi porté,	Cil n'i entrèrent pas, car li fil l'aversier Encuntrez les aveit el cloistre al repcirier.[21]
Dunc sunt li chevalier dedenz le cloistre entré,	[112] Cuntr'els tindrent les us des moines li alquant;
Les espées es puinz, et des haubers armé,	—"Ovrez," fet saint Thomas; qui's ala atendant.
E uns Huge malclers (issi la-un nummé); Clers ert Robert del Broc, mult pleins d'iniquité.	
Avant vindrent li quatre, pur le mal commencier.	"Par sainte obedience!" fet-il, "le vus commant;
Mès de luing l'en siwirent quatre autre chevalier;	Lur voil lur leissiez fere, qui sunt *venus*(?) *avant*.[22]
Cil Huge ala od els et entra el mustier.	Tant cum tendrez les us, n'irai un pas avant.

[20] The first sentence is from Grim. The second (with omissions) from Benedict.

[21] None of our writers mention these four knights. See below (116a). I have not found authority for the transitive use of " repeirier."

[22] "Avant." Can this mean the knights "in front," as distinct from those who remained *behind*, in the cloister? If it does, how could the Archbishop know of

No man must make a castle, or fortress, or tower, Of the house of God, the true Lord, But we clerks, who are ministers and servitors thereof, Are bound to be evermore thereof defenders, [And] to make of our body a shield against the evil-doer."

[113] The doors himself he opens and unbars, [And] pushed back the common folk [23] that was there assembled To see the issue. "What fear ye?" said he. "See yonder," they replied, "the knights in arms." "I will go to them," he said. They reply, "You shall not do it." As soon as they had caused him to come on the steps of the North, They wished to lead him for safety to the Holy Body.[24] "Sirs," said he to the monks, "I tell you, let me be! You have naught to do here; let God take thought for it. Go yonder, up to the choir, to sing your vespers."

[114] (13) (The *Saga*) But others run straightway to bolt the church. But when the man of God seeth this, he turneth back and throweth open the church, saying: "It beseemeth Christians in no wise to turn the church into a

---

Nuls hum ne deit chastel ne fermeté ne tur
Fère de la meisun Deu, le verai Seigneur;
Mès nus clercs qui en sumes menistre et servitur
En devrium adès estre defendéur;
Fère del cors escu cuntre le malfaitur!"
[113] Les us a-il méesmes overs et desbarez;
Buta le peuple [23] arère, ki là ert assemblez
Pur véer l'aventure. Fet lur il: "Ke cremez?"
Funt-li il: "Véez-ci les chevaliers armés!"

"G'irai," fet-il, "à els." Funt-li il, "ne l'ferez."
Très que sur les degrez del Nort l'unt fet aller;
A guarant al cors sainz [24] le voleient mener.
"Seigneurs," fet-il as moines, "kar me laissiez ester;
Vus n'avez ci ke fère, Deu en leissiez penser:
Alez là sùs el cuer, a vos vespres chanter."
ll. 5376-5405.

---

the latter, so as to make such a distinction? And does Garnier often elsewhere use *the same disyllabic word* to end two consecutive lines ("avant . . . avant")?

The context, in other writers, suggests something about madness (William, above, "delirare"). Some phrase with "ment," signifying "these men who are out of their mind" (like the Latin "amens"), would make good sense instead of "avant."

[23] "Peuple," (**104**) "populares."

[24] "Al cors sainz": William has, "when he was advised to betake himself to the *Holy of Holies*." This favours the view that "holy body" means the sacred bread on the altar. This seems more probable than "for the [Saint's] holy body."

castle." So the learned men endeavour to push him on up the church, and into the sanctuary, but he goeth with them unwilling away from the door.

[115] (i.) (Stanley, pp. 85-6) The Archbishop continued to stand outside, and said, "Go and finish the service. So long as you keep in the entrance, I shall not come in." They fell back a few paces, and he stepped within the door, but, finding the whole place thronged with people, he paused on the threshold and asked, "What is it that these people fear?" One general answer broke forth, "The armed men in the cloister."

[116] As he turned and said, "I shall go out to them," he heard the clash of arms behind. The knights had just forced their way into the cloister, and were now (as would appear from their being thus seen through the open door) advancing along its southern side. They were in mail, which covered their faces up to their eyes, and carried their swords drawn. With them was Hugh of Horsea, surnamed Mauclerc, a subdeacon, chaplain of Robert de Broc. Three had hatchets. Fitzurse, with the axe he had taken from the carpenters, was foremost, shouting as he came, "Here, here, king's men!" Immediately behind him followed Robert Fitzranulph,[25] with three other knights, whose names are not preserved; and a motley group—some their own followers, some from the town—with weapons, though not in armour, brought up the rear.

[117] At this sight, so unwonted in the peaceful cloisters of Canterbury, not probably beheld since the time when the monastery had been sacked by the Danes, the monks within, regardless of all remonstrances, shut the door of the cathedral, and proceeded to barricade it with iron bars. A loud knocking was heard from the terrified band without, who, having

---

[25] [116a] "Fitzranulph." Stanley refers only to "Foss's Judges, i. 243." No one else mentions Fitzranulph. Is it a confused tradition about (296) Ranulph de Broc? Garnier alone, among our narrators, mentions four knights waiting in the cloister, distinct from the four knights who enter the Cathedral.

vainly endeavoured to prevent the entrance of the knights into the cloister, now rushed before them to take refuge in the church. Becket, who had stepped some paces into the Cathedral, but was resisting the solicitations of those immediately about him to move up into the choir for safety, darted back, calling aloud as he went, "Away, you cowards! By virtue of your obedience I command you not to shut the door—the church must not be turned into a castle." With his own hands he thrust them away from the door, opened it himself, and catching hold of the excluded monks, dragged them into the building, exclaiming, "Come in, come in—faster, faster!"

[118] (ii.) (Tennyson)

BECKET. Together? . . . get you back! go on with the office.
MONKS. Come, then, with us to vespers.
BECKET. How can I come
When you so block the entry? Back, I say!
Go on with the office. Shall not Heaven be served
Tho' earth's last earthquake clash'd the minster-bells,
And the great deeps were broken up again,
And hiss'd against the sun? [*Noise in the cloisters.*
MONKS. The murderers, hark!
Let us hide! let us hide!
BECKET. What do these people fear?
MONKS. Those arm'd men in the cloister.
BECKET. Be not such cravens!
I will go out and meet them.
GRIM *and others.* Shut the doors!
We will not have him slain before our face.
[*They close the doors of the transept. Knocking.*
Fly, fly, my lord, before they burst the doors. [*Knocking.*
[119] BECKET. Why, these are our own monks who follow'd us!
And will you bolt them out, and have *them* slain?
Undo the doors: the church is not a castle:
Knock, and it shall be open'd. Are you deaf?
What, have I lost authority among you?
Stand by, make way!
[*Opens the doors. Enter* MONKS *from cloister.*

Come in, my friends, come in!
Nay, faster, faster!
MONKS.   Oh, my lord Archbishop,
A score of knights, all arm'd with swords and axes—
To the choir, to the choir!

> [MONKS *divide, part flying by the stairs on the right, part by those on the left. The rush of these last bears* BECKET *along with them some way up the steps, where he is left standing alone.*

[120] BECKET.   Shall I too pass to the choir,
And die upon the Patriarchal throne
Of all my predecessors?
JOHN OF SALISBURY. No, to the crypt!
Twenty steps down. Stumble not in the darkness,
Lest they should seize thee.
GRIM.   To the crypt? no—no,
To the chapel of St. Blaise beneath the roof!
JOHN OF SALISBURY (*pointing upward and downward*). That way, or this! Save thyself either way.
BECKET. Oh no, not either way, nor any way
Save by that way which leads thro' night to light.
Not twenty steps, but one.
And fear not I should stumble in the darkness,
Not tho' it be their hour, the power of darkness,
But my hour too, the power of light in darkness!
I am not in the darkness but the light,
Seen by the Church in Heaven, the Church on earth—
The power of life in death to make her free!

§ 2. *Omissions and errors*

[121] Why does Benedict alone insert the interesting description of the Archbishop's pulling his friends inside? Possibly, Herbert thought it beneath the archiepiscopal dignity, and the others may not have known of it. It was suggested in the last chapter that Benedict's point of view was the front of the procession. If he was there, and was shut out, the doors being closed as soon as the Archbishop had stepped inside, he might well remember, and

record, his being pulled into the Cathedral by the Archbishop himself. Anon. I. at the rear of the procession, and William and Grim, inside the Cathedral, may have known nothing of what was going on at the door, except that the Archbishop was insisting that it should be unbarred.[1]

[122] The prohibition to "turn the church into a castle" is omitted by William,[2] by the MS. representing the earliest text of Fitzstephen, and probably by the correct text of Benedict. It was no doubt uttered by the Archbishop; for Grim, Anon. I., and Garnier all have it, and Herbert has adopted it. Grim has "tower"; Anon. I. "castle"; Garnier, "castle, or fortress, or tower." A fine epigram like this, uttered at such a moment, was naturally interpolated, or added, in other narratives.

[123] Not one of our authorities, except Garnier, mentions the four knights who wait as a reserve in the cloister, and it is possible that this detail is an instance of (**368**) the Error of Duplication. See however **324**.

[124] The two modern writers have been misled by Herbert into supposing that the doors were opened in consequence of a "knocking" from the outside. Tennyson, however, so far deviates from Herbert as to make the "knocking" proceed from the Archbishop's own friends. But there seems to have been no "knocking" at all. There was no time to allow of it, because the Archbishop had the doors unbarred almost before the process of barring was completed.

---

[1] [121*a*] Fitzstephen, alone, inserts some words (**103**) "permit all to enter," which may proceed from an imperfect hearing of the words recorded by Benedict alone (**106**) "let my people enter."

[2] [122*a*] But William, *speaking in his own person*, inserts in this place some remarks containing words that resemble those of Garnier (*Mat.* i. 132) "Ye have not here a fortified castle (castrum) . . . or walled or towered city. . . ."

CHAPTER VI

THE ENTRANCE OF THE KNIGHTS INTO THE CATHEDRAL

§ 1. *The different accounts*

[125] (1) (Grim) Without delay these desecrators, with swords unsheathed, advanced into the house of peace and reconcilement, even by their mere aspect and the clatter of their armour causing no little dread to those who caught sight of them.

[126] (2) (Fitzstephen) Just when he was in the act of coming down from the steps toward the door, lest it should be closed, John of Salisbury and all his other clerks—except Robert the Canon, and William Fitzstephen, and Edward Grim (who had newly come to him)—seeking some protection, and making it their [only] care to place themselves in safety, left the Archbishop, and made away, some for altars, some for hiding-places.[1]

---

[125] (1) (Grim) Nec mora, sacrilegi gladiis evaginatis ingrediuntur domum pacis ac reconciliationis, solo quidem aspectu et armorum strepitu non modicum horroris cernentibus ingerentes.

[126] (2) (Fitzstephen) Eo tunc a gradibus descendente versus ostium, ne clauderetur, Johannes Saresberiensis et alii ejus clerici omnes, praeter Robertum canonicum, et Willelmum filium Stephani, et Edwardum Grim, qui novus ad eum venerat, praesidia captantes, et se in tuto collocare curantes, relicto ipso, petiverunt alii altaria, alii latibula.[1]

---

[1] The emphatic position of "hiding-places," and the emphasis laid on the motives of John and the rest, indicate some contempt.

[127] And indeed had the Archbishop been willing to turn [a little] aside, and to free himself with the protection of flight,[2] he might right well have availed himself of opportunities, both of time and place, not needing to be sought but offering themselves to be used. It was evening. The long night of the winter solstice was at hand. The crypt was near, full of winding passages, mostly very dark. Another door, too, was near, through which he might have gone up by a spiral staircase to the arched chambers in the roof of the church. Perchance he would not have been found: or meantime some change of circumstances might have arisen.[3]

[128] But he would do none of these things. He neither turned aside, nor stooped to conciliate his murderers, nor uttered a murmur or complaint in the whole of his agony[4]: but in patient endurance for Christ, and for the cause of the Church, awaiting his extreme hour, which was now almost upon him, he manifested such a strength and steadfastness of mind, body, and speech, as we have never heard exceeded [in the history] of any other martyr—until

---

[127] Et quidem si vellet archiepiscopus declinare, et se fugae praesidio[2] liberare, optime uti posset, non quaesita, sed oblata occasione temporis et loci. Vespera erat, nox longissima instabat; crypta erat prope, in qua multa et pleraque tenebrosa diverticula. Item erat ibi aliud ostium prope, quo per cochleam ascenderet ad cameras [et] testudines ecclesiae superiores; forte non inveniretur vel interim aliud[3] fieret.

[128] Sed nihil horum voluit. Non declinavit, non percussoribus supplicavit, non murmur edidit, non querimoniam in tota sua agonia[4]: sed extremam horam, quae imminebat, pro Christo et causa ecclesiae patienter expectans, fortitudine et constantia mentis, corporis, et sermonis, qualem de aliquo martyrum majorem

---

[2] In this twofold use of "protection," Fitzstephen seems to contrast the Martyr, who looked to the sole protection of God, with John and the rest who "anxiously sought other kinds of protection (praesidia captantes)."

[3] The MS. called J reads "aliquid," which was perhaps corrected by the author in a later edition to the more definite "aliud."

[4] "Agony," probably in the Greek sense, a "(martyr's) struggle, or conflict," Luke xxii. 44 "being in an *agony*."

the total consummation.⁵ [But] lo, by this time those executioners,⁶ in furious haste, enter the church door at a running pace, seeing it unexpectedly open,

(3) (John) Omits this.

[129] (4) (William) While he was still speaking, behold the lictors,⁷ after searching through the Cathedral palace,⁸ rush through the cloisters. Three of them brought⁹ hatchets in their left hands, one a two-edged chopper or axe. All brandished drawn swords in their right hands. Whither rush ye, O men of Belial? . . . ye have not here to storm a castle . . . or a city . . . fortified. . . .¹⁰

[130] When they burst into the open doorway, they separated from one another at the central door-post on which rests the burden of the arch. Fitzurse takes the right side; the three others the left.

---

nunquam audivimus, usus est, donec totum consummaretur.⁵ Ecce jam illi spiculatores,⁶ furia invecti, praeter spem apertum cernentes, cursim ostium intrant ecclesiae. . . .

(3) (John) Omits this.

[129] (4) (William) Adhuc eo loquente, ecce lictores⁷ perscrutato palatio ecclesiae⁸ conglobati per claustra ruunt. Ex quibus tres in laevis secures, unus bipennem vel bisacutam deferebant,⁹ omnes vero in dextris strictos gladios vibrabant. Quo ruitis, viri Belial? . . . non expugnandum est *castrum* . . . non *civitas* . . . circumvallata. . . . ¹⁰

[130] Postquam patens ostium irruperunt, divisi sunt ab invicem ad medium postem cui testudinis onus innititur. Ursides dexteram partem, tres alii sinistram occupant.

---

⁵ See 315-30.

⁶ "Spiculatores," a form of "speculatores," a Greek word used in Mark vi. 27 of the "executioner" sent by Herod to behead John the Baptist. It suggests that they came from the King.

⁷ "Lictors," the servants who preceded a Roman Consul, and whose business it was, among other things, to execute consular sentences of death. It is a strange word here, but is perhaps used for variety. Herbert also has it (277). Is it intended to suggest that they acted as the King's servants?

⁸ "Cathedral palace" (lit. "palace of the church") is a strange expression, but seems the rendering demanded by the order of the words.

⁹ "Deferebat" seems to require explanation.

¹⁰ This apostrophe continues for some ten lines of wonderfully florid style. The remarks about a "castle" and "fortified city" may be an echo of the

[131] (5) (Benedict) And, although the man of the Lord might have quite [11] avoided that hour of death, if he had been willing, when the aforesaid knights of the King were entering into the Minster,

(6) (Herbert) But when the folding-doors were opened, the murderers presently rushing in,

(7) (Anon. I.) Meanwhile the knights rushed into the church,

[132] (8) (Anon. II.) And he might quite [11] have turned aside, had he wished, and might have escaped the hands of the impious. But he deemed it too unseemly, and indeed full fraught with danger, to retreat any further, especially since he had by this time publicly proclaimed as with a trumpet that he had come to give his head for the Church.[12]

[133] He therefore passed on to take his stand before the High Altar,[13] and to consummate the contest, if need should be, in his own peculiar place, and to pour forth his own blood for Christ in the very spot where he had also been

---

[131] (5) (Benedict) Et quum vir Domini illam mortis horam satis [11] declinasse potuisset, si vellet, intrantibus in monasterium praedictis satellitibus,

(6) (Herbert) Valvis vero apertis, mox irruentes carnifices,

(7) (Anon. I.) Interim irruerunt milites in ecclesiam,

[132] (8) (Anon. II.) Et utique satis [11] poterat divertisse si vellet, et manus impiorum evasisse; sed nimis indecens planeque periculosum censuit ulterius cedere, praesertim cum publice jam insonuisset quod venerat pro ecclesia caput dare. . . .[12]

[133] Transibat igitur ut subsisteret ante altare majus,[13] et in ipsa sede sua certamen, si necesse foret, consummaret, ibique suum pro Christo funderet sangui-

---

words—assigned to the Archbishop by Garnier, Anon. I., and Herbert, but not by William—about "turning a church into a castle." See 122*a*.

[11] "Satis (quite)." This ill-sounding rendering is adopted to express the curious construction in Benedict and Anon. II. If it did not occur in both, we might have supposed that some word like "facile" had dropped out.

[12] The writer here declares that on that same day the Archbishop had confessed himself to two of the more religious monks of the Cathedral and had made satisfaction according to their decision; and that this was in accordance with his practice for some time past. This explains the following "therefore." He was prepared, by (1) confession and (2) penance, to be a sacrifice.

[13] This writer, insisting on the sacrificial aspect of Becket's death, represents that he goes up to stand and to die before "the *high altar.*"

wont to offer up Christ for the salvation of himself and of the world. But the malefactors, having collected a band—not being able at first to seize him (as they had desired) in his own Palace, no, nor so much as to set foot in the Palace—found a guide in that son of Belial, Robert de Broc, (who had always been inflamed by a special fury and malignity against the Archbishop's fortunes and followers, and had for this cause been excommunicated); and so, breaking open a window, they burst in, and [passing] through the monks' cloister, they [now]—in spite of the prohibitions and struggles [of the monks]—entered [the church].[14]

(9) (Anon. IV.) So in headlong haste and madly blind[15] pursuit of the Archbishop, they enter the church with drawn swords,

(10) (Anon. V.) Meanwhile the knights, close behind him, bursting into (*sic*) the doors of the cloister, came with drawn swords right up to the Bishop (*sic*).[16]

---

nem, ubi et Christum immolare consuerat ad sui mundique salutem. Agmine vero coacto malefactores, cum non eum in domo propria comprehendere sicut optaverant, immo nec domum ingredi possent, duce quodam filio Belial Roberto de Broc, qui nequius et ardentius in eum et ejus res fidelesque semper debacchaverat et ob hoc anathema erat, rupta fenestra quadam irruperunt, et per claustrum monachorum, quamvis iis prohibentibus et reluctantibus, ingressi sunt.[14]

(9) (Anon. IV.) Praecipites ergo et stupidi[15] insequentes archiepiscopum, extractis gladiis intrant ecclesiam,

(10) (Anon. V.) Interea milites, post tergum illius ostia claustri irrumpentes, extractis gladiis usque ad episcopum (*sic*) pervenerunt.[16]

---

[14] This astonishing sentence appears to go back to describe the forcible entry into the palace: and the words "in spite of the prohibition and resistance of the monks" agree with nothing in the other narratives. The word "reluctans" is applied by others to the Archbishop resisting the efforts of the monks to drag him to the Cathedral. It looks as though the writer, attempting to make up for a previous omission by a brief misplaced parenthesis, has confused, in the attempt to condense, some passage from which he has borrowed.

[15] "Stupidi (madly blind)," because they had no eyes for the foulness of their sacrilege.

[16] This seems loose. (1) They did not burst "*into* the doors," but "*through* the *door*." Most of the writers, when they use the pl. "doors," use it for folding-doors, either in the Palace hall, or in the Cathedral. (2) They burst *into* the

(11) (Anon. X.) So on the entrance of the aforesaid King's knights and their accomplices,

[134] (12) (Garnier) The train of Satan is come to the Minster; In his right hand each bore his naked sword; In the other, the hatchets [above mentioned], and the fourth a two-edged axe. A pillar by that place held up the arched roof. And this took from them the sight of the holy Archbishop. The three went on one side of the pillar.

[135] (13) (The *Saga*) Now all these things befall at once: that he steppeth unto the grades before the choir, while the foes of God enter the church with mad crying,

[136] (i.) (Stanley, pp. 86-9) At this moment the ecclesiastics who had hitherto clung round him fled in every direction; some to the altars in the numerous side chapels, some to the secret chambers with which the walls and roof of the cathedral are filled. One of them has had the rashness[17] to leave on record his own excessive terror. Even John of Salisbury, his tried and faithful counsellor, escaped with the rest. Three only remained—Robert, canon of Merton, his old instructor; William Fitzstephen (if we may believe his own account), his lively and worldly-minded chaplain; and Edward Grim, the Saxon monk. William,

---

(11) (Anon. X.) Intrantibus ergo praedictis satellitibus et complicibus eorum. . . .

[134] La meisnie al Satan est el muster venue;
En sa destre main tint chascuns s'espée nue;
En l'autre les cuingnies, et li quarz besagüe.
Un piler ot iluec la volte ad sostenue,
Ki del saint arcevesque lur toli la veüe.
D'une part del piler en sunt li trei alé.
ll. 5406-11.

---

cloister. (3) They did not come "right up to the Archbishop" at all, in a body. They separated at the entrance of the Cathedral. Fitzurse was the first to be confronted by the Archbishop. Possibly, however, the writer may be condensing William's "*patens ostium* irruperunt" (where the meaning seems to be "doorway") and may mean "the cloister doors that *open into the Cathedral*."

[17] See 142.

one of the monks of Canterbury, who has recorded his impressions of the scene, confesses that he fled with the rest. He was not ready to confront martyrdom, and, with clasped hands,[18] ran as fast as he could up the steps.

[137] Two hiding-places had been specially pointed out to the Archbishop.[19] One was the venerable crypt of the church, with its many dark recesses and chapels, to which a door then as now opened immediately from the spot where he stood, the other was the chapel of St. Blaise in the roof, itself communicating by a gallery with the triforium of the cathedral, to which there was a ready access through a staircase cut in the thickness of the wall at the corner of the transept. But he positively refused. One last resource remained to the staunch companions who stood by him. They urged him to ascend to the choir, and hurried him, still resisting, up one of the two flights of steps which led thither. They no doubt considered that the greater sacredness of that portion of the church would form their best protection. Becket seems to have given way, as in leaving the palace, from the thought flashing across his mind that he would die at his post. He would go (such at least was the impression left on their minds) to the high altar, and perish in the Patriarchal Chair, in which he and all his predecessors from time immemorial had been enthroned. But this was not to be.

[138] What has taken long to describe must have been compressed in action within a few minutes. The knights who had been checked for a moment by the sight of the closed door, on seeing it unexpectedly thrown open, rushed into the church. It was, we must remember, about five

---

[18] "Clasped." Better "striking my hands together (complodens manus)," a "scenic action," says Quintilian.

[19] None of our writers say this. But Fitzstephen mentions the crypt and the roof as possible hiding-places, and Tennyson, above, dramatically puts the suggestion into the mouths of Grim and John.

o'clock in a winter evening[20]; the shades of night were gathering, and were deepened into a still darker gloom within the high and massive walls of the vast cathedral, which was only illuminated here and there by the solitary lamps burning before the altars. The twilight, lengthening from the shortest day a fortnight before, was but just sufficient to reveal the outline of objects.

[139] The transept in which the knights found themselves is the same as that which—though with considerable changes in its arrangements—is still known by its ancient name of "The Martyrdom." Two staircases led from it, one from the east to the northern aisle, one on the west to the entrance of the choir. At its south-west corner, where it joined the nave, was the little chapel and altar of the Virgin, the especial patroness of the Archbishop. Its eastern apse was formed by two chapels, raised one above the other; the upper in the roof, containing the relics of St. Blaise, the first martyr whose bones had been brought into the church, and which gave to the chapel a peculiar sanctity; the lower containing the altar of St. Benedict, under whose rule from the time of Dunstan the monastery had been placed. Before and around this altar were the tombs of four Saxons and two Norman archbishops. In the centre of the transept was a pillar, supporting a gallery leading to the chapel of St. Blaise, and hung at great festivals with curtains and draperies. Such was the outward aspect, and such the associations, of the scene which now, perhaps, opened for the first time on the four soldiers.

[140] But the darkness, coupled with the eagerness to find their victim, would have prevented them from noticing anything more than its prominent features. At the moment

---

[20] [138a] There is practically no light at 5 P.M. on 4th Jan., which (according to Stanley) corresponds now to 29th Dec. then. Still less would there have been light inside the Cathedral. What was seen must have been seen by artificial light.

of their entrance the central pillar exactly intercepted their view of the Archbishop ascending (as would appear from this circumstance) the eastern staircase. Fitzurse, with his drawn sword in one hand, and the carpenter's axe in the other, sprang in first, and turned at once to the right of the pillar. The other three went round it to the left. In the dim twilight they could just discern a group of figures mounting the steps.

(ii.) (Tennyson) [*Enter the four* KNIGHTS. JOHN OF SALISBURY *flies to the altar of St. Benedict.*]

§ 2. *The flight of the Archbishop's friends*

[141] The flight of Becket's "clerks" or "clergy" is placed here by Fitzstephen. Herbert, a little before, says that he was abandoned by "all his friends (quotquot sui)." William, a little later, describes a general panic and flight, in which he himself shared. If some hung back when the Archbishop descended to meet his enemies, that might be called by Fitzstephen the beginning of the flight. It is remarkable that Fitzstephen should single out John of Salisbury by name among those who fled. Anon. I. above, says that—in the alarm caused by the soldiers breaking into the palace—all fled "except some monks and a clerk called Edward Grim by name," where Fitzstephen admits that he was afraid, but not that he fled. It is not unnatural that Fitzstephen, if he stood by the Archbishop here, with Grim, should mention the fact; but his mention of John of Salisbury seems to indicate some animosity against the latter. John himself is silent about all that occurred in the Cathedral till the murder was on the point of being perpetrated. If Anon. I. is to be taken as exactly correct, both John and Fitzstephen must have fled from the Archbishop in the Palace: but the flight may have been brief. They may have returned for a time.

[142] William's candour in confessing (272) that he fled, would contrast favourably with John's absolute silence, if we did not bear in mind that the latter is, in effect, writing a letter with the view of urging vengeance for the murder, rather than a narrative of the murder itself and its circumstances. But it seems strange that Stanley (136) should call William's candour " rashness," and have nothing to say about John's silence—especially as William was but a recent acquaintance of the Archbishop's while John was (as Stanley says) his " tried and faithful counsellor."

CHAPTER VII

THE MEETING OF THE ARCHBISHOP AND THE KNIGHTS

§ 1. *The different accounts*

[143] (1) (Grim) Now by this time those who had been attending vespers had run up to the fatal spectacle;[1] and, as the crowd made some confusion and uproar, the knights exclaimed in a spirit of mad fury, " Where is Thomas Becket, traitor to King and realm ? " Then, as he made no answer, they called aloud more urgently, saying " Where is the Archbishop ? " At this utterance—without a touch of fear, and fulfilling the Scripture that saith " the righteous man will be as bold as a lion without fear "—he comes to meet them from the flight of steps[2] whither he had been carried[3] by the monks in their fear of the knights; and in

---

[143] (1) (Grim) Turbatisque qui aderant ac tumultuantibus (jam enim qui vespertinis intenderant laudibus ad lethale spectaculum[1] accurrerant), in spiritu furoris milites exclamaverunt, " Ubi est Thomas Beketh, proditor regis et regni ? " Quo non respondente, instantius vociferati sunt, dicentes, "Ubi est archiepiscopus?" Ad hanc vocem (intrepidus quidem et, ut scriptum est, "Justus quasi leo confidens absque terrore erit") occurrit e gradu[2] quo delatus fuerat[3] a monachis

---

[1] Comp. William (104) "as to a spectacle." There it was used of the "people (populares)," not of the clerks or monks. And this seems to be the meaning here. Grim seems to suggest that the knights were incensed still further by the fear of a rescue.

[2] Grim and John seem to use "gradus" sing. for "altar stairs" collectively. Comp. Grim (*Mat.* ii. 441), "altaris conscendens *gradum.*"

[3] "Delatus (carried)." Comp. Anon. I. (109), "the monks again seized the man of God and began to escort (deducere) him by the steps into the choir." Probably Grim does not mean, "carried in a rush of fugitives seeking their own safety."

a perfectly audible voice he answered, " Here I am, no traitor to the King, but a Priest. What do you seek of me ? " [4]

[144] (2) (Fitzstephen) One of them said to the monks [5] that stood by with the Archbishop, " Do not you move ! " [And indeed, as though ashamed and astounded, and abashed by his countenance, these cut-throats at first drew back on seeing the Archbishop.[6]] Afterwards some one shouted, " Where is the traitor ? " To that the Archbishop, possessing his soul in patience, made no reply. Then said some one, " Where is the Archbishop ? " to which he answered, " Here am I, no traitor, but priest of God : and I wonder that in such attire you have entered into the church of God. What is your pleasure ? "

[145] (3) (John) But when he was on the point of enduring his Passion in the church, as has been said, before the altar,[7] the Martyr of Christ, before receiving the [fatal]

metu militum, et satis audibili sermone respondit : " Ecce adsum, non regis proditor, sed sacerdos ; quid me quaeritis ? " [4]

[144] (2) (Fitzstephen) . . . Quidam autem illorum monachis [5] dixit, qui cum eo astabant, " Ne vos moveatis." [Et quidem quasi confusi et attoniti, a reverentia vultu ejus, illi grassatores primo retulerunt pedem, viso archiepiscopo.[6]] Postea clamavit aliquis, " Ubi est ille proditor ? " Archiepiscopus, suam in patientia animam possidens, ad verbum illud non respondit. Aliquis item : " Ubi est archiepiscopus ? " Ille : " Ecce ego, non proditor, sed presbyter Dei ; et miror, quod in tali habitu ecclesiam Dei ingressi estis. Quid placet vobis ? "

[145] (3) (John) Passurus autem in ecclesia, ut dictum est, coram altari,[7] Christi martyr, antequam feriretur, cum se audisset inquiri a militibus qui ad hoc

---

[4] The Latin 2nd pers. pl., in these writers, often expresses the French 2nd pers. pl., so that the words might be addressed to one man. But when the Archbishop addresses Reginald separately, he uses the 2nd pers. *sing.* (153). So we must regard him here as meaning "you and your accomplices."

[5] This, and F.'s subsequent remarks, indicate that the "monks" remained when the "clerks" fled. The sentence implies that the knights saw a group of monks, but could not, in the dimly lighted cathedral, distinguish the Archbishop among them. So they first called out "Do not you stir !" and then bade them say where was the traitor, or the Archbishop. The next sentence is almost certainly an interpolation.

[6] The bracketed passage is omitted by J. It does not seem probable that, *after they had seen* the Archbishop, some one should ask where he was.

[7] Strictly speaking, Becket did not die " before the altar " (162).

blow, on hearing inquiry made by the knights, who had
come for this purpose, and who were calling aloud in the
crowd of the bystanders, "Where is the Archbishop?" goes
to meet them from the flight of steps⁸ which he had in
part ascended, saying, with a fearless countenance, "Here
am I : what is your will?"

[146] (4) (William) But the president of the games of
God⁹ planted his footsteps¹⁰ over against them in a place
where long ago in a dream he had seen himself crucified,¹¹
as it is asserted—having, on the left, the cross that was
wont to precede him ; on the rear, the party-wall ; before
him, the eicon of the blessed Virgin Mary ; on all sides, the
memorials and relics of the Saints. In rushes Fitzurse, and,
coming suddenly on some one,¹² asks him, "Where is the
Archbishop?" He (*i.e.* the Archbishop), forestalling the

---

venerant, in turba circum astantium vociferantibus "Ubi est archiepiscopus?"
occurrit iis ex gradu⁸ quem pro parte ascenderat, vultu intrepido dicens, "Ecce
ego : quid vultis?"

[146] (4) (William) Perstans autem mente et corpore agonotheta⁹ Dei fixit
ex adverso gradum¹⁰ ubi pridem per somnium viderat se crucifixum,¹¹ sicut
asseritur ; habens a laeva praeviam crucem suam, a tergo parietem, prae se beatae
Mariae virginis iconiam, circumquaque memorias et reliquias sanctorum. Irruit
Ursides, et quaerit a quodam quem offendit,¹² "Ubi est archiepiscopus?"

---

⁸ "Flight of steps," see **143**.

⁹ "Agonotheta (president of the games)" is wrongly used by William as a
variation for "athleta (champion)." He is fond of using—with the result of
frequently misusing—Greek terms (**611***a*), *e.g.* "iconiam" in this section.

¹⁰ "Footsteps" are mentioned by William where Grim, John, and others,
mention a "flight of steps."

¹¹ Fitzstephen (iii. 150) mentions a vision of *Jesus* crucified in the *crypt*, in
the place where St. Thomas was *buried*. There seem to have been different
versions of this tradition (**162***a*, **426***a*).

¹² Stanley (**155**) says, "stumbling against one of the monks, on the lower
step." But "offendere aliquem" frequently means "come suddenly on," "catch."
Garnier has simply "encuntré." It is perhaps because of this notion of "stumbling" that Stanley supposes Fitzurse to have advanced as far as the *step*. Then,
in consequence of that, the Archbishop (in order to be brought to the place
where he falls) is supposed by Stanley (**155**) to "pass" Fitzurse. But all this
is highly improbable, and not supported by evidence.

answer of any one but himself,[13] answered with a slight motion of the head, "See, I am here."[14]

[147] (5) (Benedict) And, when some cried aloud, "Where is the traitor?" others, "Where is the Archbishop?" the Saint, knowing in the spirit all things that were to come to pass concerning himself,[15] goes to meet them from the steps, some of which he had by this time ascended, saying, with a fearless countenance, "Here am I, no traitor, but Archbishop"—imitating the Lord, who, when the Jews sought him, went to meet them, saying, "I am he."

[148] (6) (Herbert), one called out and said, "Where is the rebel?" But the Lord's Christ (or Anointed) said nothing to this. But a second voice afterwards called out and said, "Where is the Archbishop?" And the Lord's Christ replied, "I am he. What is your will?"[16]

Praeveniens ille omnium responsiones,[13] respondit cum levi motu capitis, "En ego."[14]

[147] (5) (Benedict) Et aliis "Ubi est ille proditor?" aliis "Ubi est archiepiscopus" vociferantibus, sciens sanctus in spiritu omnia quae ventura erant super eum,[15] occurrit iis e gradibus, quorum aliquos jam conscenderat, vultu intrepido dicens, "Ecce ego, non proditor, sed archiepiscopus": Dominum videlicet imitatus, qui quaerentibus se Judaeis processit obviam, dicens, "Ego sum."

[148] (6) (Herbert), clamabat unus, "Ubi est," inquiens, "seductor ille?" Sed christus Domini ad hoc nihil. Alter vero subsequenter clamans, "Ubi est," inquit, "archiepiscopus?" Et christus Domini, "Ego sum; quid vultis?"[16]

---

[13] Lit. "the answers of all." The Archbishop would not permit *any* of his monks or flock to be coerced into giving information; he saved not only *this* man, but every other, from such a risk.

[14] According to William, the Archbishop neither ascends "steps," nor descends them again to meet the knights, but simply *plants his "footsteps"* near the entrance, in the place where he is destined to fall. This throws William into complete confusion, for he first represents the Archbishop as being in a place where Fitzurse could see him, and then Fitzurse as calling out, "Where is the Archbishop?"

Stanley (155) has been misled by following William at this point, attempting to combine his details with those of other writers.

[15] John xviii. 4.

[16] Below (176) he says that the Archbishop had previously ascended "seven or eight steps towards the choir."

[149] (7) (Anon. I.), shouting terribly and crying aloud, " Where is Thomas, traitor to the King ? " But to this the man of God made no reply. So they shouted again, and said, " Where is the Archbishop ? " Then said the holy man, " Priest I am, and Archbishop I am : and if you seek me, you have found me." Saying these words he came down to meet them from the steps he had ascended ; and, turning aside to the northern part of the church, took up his stand there, by the wall, close to the altar of St. Benedict.

[150] (8) (Anon. II.) But when they called out " Where is the Archbishop ? "—for as it was evening [17] the place was very dark so that they could not quickly discern him—he came to meet them from the steps that he had in part ascended, saying to them, " Here am I. What is your will ? "

[151] (9) (Anon. IV.) —shouting in mad fury, " Where is the traitor ? " But as no one replied, they repeated [their shouts, saying], " Where is the Archbishop ? " Now he— blessed Confessor of Christ and soon to be Christ's Martyr —knew that it was false to assail him with that former name,

---

[149] (7) (Anon. I.), terribiliter clamantes, et vociferantes, "Ubi est Thomas proditor regis?" Vir autem Domini ad ista nihil respondit. Clamaverunt igitur iterum, et dixerunt, "Ubi est archiepiscopus?" Tunc vir sanctus, "Et sacerdos," inquit, "et archiepiscopus sum; et si me quaeritis, ecce, invenistis." Haec dicens descendit obviam eis de gradibus quos ascenderat; divertensque in partem ecclesiae aquilonarem, ibi ad murum prope altare beati Benedicti substitit.

[150] (8) (Anon. II.) Cum autem vociferarentur, "Ubi est archiepiscopus?" (erat enim ex vespera [17] locus obscurior ut ipsum secernere non mox possent), occurrit iis ex gradibus, quos partim ascenderat, dicens, "Ecce ego; quid vultis?"

[151] (9) (Anon. IV.) furiose clamantes, "Ubi est proditor ille?" Nemine vero respondente, ingeminant illi, "Ubi est archiepiscopus?" Sciens itaque beatus Christi confessor, et mox futurus martyr, priore nomine se falso impeti,

---

[17] The "evening" would probably make no difference, as at that hour, nothing could be seen in the Cathedral without lights ; see above (138*a*). Garnier (134) explains the reason why they could not see the Archbishop: a "pillar took away their view of him."

but the latter appertained to him in respect of his office. So he went forward, away from the steps, to meet them, saying, " Here I am." Now so steadfastly did he bear himself that there was no trace of fear in mind nor of trembling in body.

[152] (10) (Anon. V.) But the Archbishop going to meet them by some steps,[18]

(11) (Anon. X.), and when they called aloud, " Where is the traitor ? " he went to meet them with fearless countenance, saying, " Here am I, no traitor, but Priest of God."

[153] (12) (Garnier) " The traitor to the King ! " they sought and demanded. Renald, on the other side,[19] met a monk ; He [*i.e.* Reginald] asked [the monk] for " the Archbishop." Then did the Saint speak, " Renald, if you seek me," said he, " see, here, you have found me." The name of " traitor " St. Thomas did not understand : But at the name of " Archbishop " he stayed and gave heed : And he meets Renald, having come down from the flight of steps : " Renald, if you seek me, you have found me," he said, " see, here."

[154] (13) (The *Saga*), saying : " Where is the traitor and betrayer of the realm ? " But when the blessed Thomas

---

alterum vero sibi pro officio competere, a gradibus obviam illis procedens, " Ecce," inquit, " adsum." In tanta autem se exhibebat constantia, ut nec animus ejus pavore nec corpus horrore concuti videretur.

[152] (10) (Anon. V.) Archiepiscopus vero, per aliquot gradus [18] iis occurrens,

(11) (Anon. X.), et vociferantibus " Ubi est ille proditor ? " occurrit eis vultu intrepido, dicens, " Ecce ego, non proditor sed Dei sacerdos."

[153] "—Le traïtur le Rei" unt quis et demandé. Renalz, de l'autre part,[19] un moine a encuntré ; Demanda "l'arcevesque." Dunc a li sainz parlé : "Renalz, se tu me quiers," fet-il, "ci m'as trové."	Le nun de traïtur saint Thomas n'entendi ; Mès al nun d'arcevesque restut et atendi, E encuntre Renalt del degré descendi : "Renalz, se tu me quiers, trové," fet-il, "m'as ci." ll. 5412-5419.

---

[18] The writer probably means " stairs " (not " steps ") ; but the expression is curious.

[19] *i.e.* on the other side of "the pillar" mentioned in the last chapter.

heareth the knights, he turneth on the grades,[20] and goeth straightway down the church to meet them with a fearless heart and a blithe countenance, speaking thus: "Here am I," said he, "no traitor, but an archbishop; whom seek ye, or what will ye?"

[155] (i.) (Stanley, pp. 89-90) One of the knights called out to them "Stay." Another, "Where is Thomas Becket, traitor to the King?" No answer was returned. None could have been expected by any who remembered the indignant silence with which Becket had swept by when the same word had been applied by Randulf of Broc at Northampton. Fitzurse rushed forward, and, *stumbling against one of the monks*, on the lower step, still not able to distinguish clearly in the darkness, exclaimed, "Where is the Archbishop?" Instantly the answer came,—"Reginald, here I am, no traitor, but the Archbishop and Priest of God; what do you wish?"—and from *the fourth step*, which he had reached in his ascent, with a slight motion of his head—noticed apparently as his peculiar manner in moments of excitement—Becket descended to the transept. Attired, we are told, in his white rochet, with a cloak and hood thrown over his shoulders, he thus suddenly confronted his assailants. *Fitzurse sprang back two or three paces*, and Becket passing by him took up his station between the central pillar and the massive wall which still forms the southwest corner of what was then the chapel of St. Benedict.

[156] (ii.) (Tennyson)

> [*Enter the four Knights. John of Salisbury flies to the altar of St. Benedict.*
> FITZURSE. Here, here, King's men!
> [*Catches hold of the last flying Monk.*
> Where is the traitor Becket?

---

[20] [154a] "Grades." The text has "steps." But the Icelandic, which is the word rendered "grades" in the previous sentence, differs from the Icelandic word rendered "steps" (in the sense of "foot-steps") later on.

MONK. I am not he! I am not he, my lord.
I am not he indeed!
    FITZURSE.   Hence to the fiend!
[Pushes him away.
Where is this treble traitor to the King?
    DE TRACY. Where is the Archbishop, Thomas Becket?
    BECKET.   Here.
No traitor to the King, but Priest of God,
Primate of England.
[Descending into the transept.
I am he ye seek.
What would ye have of me?

§ 2. *What did the Archbishop say?*

[157] We may regard it as certain that, when the knights entered, the cry was raised, "Where is the traitor?" It is omitted by William, John, Anon. II., and Anon V. alone; by the last three perhaps (partly) for brevity; by all perhaps (partly) because nothing came of it at once. The Archbishop, as Garnier says, "did not understand," *i.e.* ignored it.

[158] But the omission may have influenced the omitters in what follows: for, if they did not insert "traitor" in the cry of the knights, *they could not insert "no traitor" in the reply of the Archbishop*, and they accordingly omit it.

[159] Herbert omits "no traitor" for a different reason, probably because he wishes to assimilate (as Anon. IV. also does) the Archbishop's answer to the answer of Christ in John xviii. 5 "I am he." The *Saga* goes further still towards John xviii. 4-5, by giving the reply as "*Here am I . . . Whom seek ye?*" and, for this purpose, *actually omits the previous question*, "Where is the Archbishop?" Thus, by making the knights ask *nothing but* "Where is the traitor?" it is able to represent St. Thomas as saying, in effect, "I do not know who is meant by traitor, but *here am I*, no traitor, but Archbishop. *Whom seek ye?* And what

will ye?" And the italicized words are like those in John xviii. 4-5.

[160] Garnier may have omitted the words "no traitor" because he felt them a little inconsistent with his statement that the Saint "*did not understand*" *the word* "*traitor*": and, having gone so far, he allows himself to express the Archbishop's *words* in a poetic comment on what the Archbishop *thought*, so that he omits all reply, except the rather contemptuous " Renald, if you seek me, you have found me!" For the same reason, Anon. I., having declared that "the man of God said nothing" in answer to the cry of "traitor," gives his reply to the cry of "Archbishop," in full, "I am both Priest and Archbishop."

[161] Again, did the Archbishop say (as Benedict declares) "No traitor, but Archbishop"? or (as Grim (copied by Anon. X.) and Fitzstephen) "No traitor, but Priest (of God)"? or (as Anon. I.) "I am both Priest and Archbishop"? On this point, the testimony of Grim (an ear-witness) and of Fitzstephen (according to his own statement, an ear-witness) must rank very high. They might not have heard all: but they could be sure of what they did hear: and we may feel fairly certain that they heard these words. There is also no reason why they should invent them. They correspond to nothing in Scripture. Indeed, Scripture might suggest reason for omitting them, as Herbert does. But it is also quite possible that they did not catch the last words of the sentence, which may have been less easy to hear owing to the noise of the by-standers or a dropping of the speaker's voice. The last words may well have been added as an after-thought, "No traitor, but Priest of God, in the church of God,—and, if you seek the Archbishop, why, then, Archbishop too." Having regard to these considerations, and to the very high authority of Anon. I., we are justified in concluding that he, if we add the words "no traitor," will give us the substance of what was really said: "Here! No

traitor, but Priest of God and Archbishop. And if ye seek me, ye have found me."

§ 3. *The Martyr's last footsteps*

[162] William, and Anon. I., here—and, in the next chapter, Grim and Garnier—note the place where the Martyr took his stand. It was *not*—as John of Salisbury says, and as it came to be believed and recorded in pictures and books —" in front of (coram) the altar." It was, as Anon. I. says, "*near* an altar of St. Benedict," the Martyr having "turned aside to the northern part of the church." William is still more definite: " He took his stand in the place where he had long ago beheld himself crucified in a dream (so it is asserted), having on his left the Cross that went before him; at his back, a wall; before him, an image of the blessed Mary; on all sides, memorials and relics of the Saints." Probably Benedict — himself, like William, a monk of Canterbury—specified the place in his narrative also: but as the *Quadrilogus* has used William's words, it has not preserved Benedict's. Grim's description is (168): "Saying this, he turned aside to the right under a column, having on one side an altar of the blessed and ever Virgin Mother of God, on the other side that of the Confessor Saint Benedict."[1] Garnier (185) says that it was " towards the aisle of the North," by a pillar, between two altars, of which the one below was consecrated to the Mother of God, the other to St. Benedict.

[163] As in later times the pilgrims are said[2] to have been in the habit of kissing the stone where St. Thomas

---

[1] [162a] Shortly afterwards, Grim has "following whose example he [the Archbishop] . . . was *crucified to the world.*" This is quite different, in meaning, from William's statement here, that St. Thomas, in a vision, had *seen himself* "*crucified*" *in this place.* But the two may be different versions of one tradition (146, 426a). [2] *Saga*, i. 541.

fell, it is worth while noting the various phrases bearing on the Martyr's last movements:

(1) (Grim) . . . occurrit *e gradu* quo delatus fuerat.
(2) (Fitzstephen) (**102**) jam *quatuor gradus* ascenderat.
(3) (John) occurrit *iis ex gradu* quem pro parte ascenderat.
(4) (William) *fixit ex adverso gradum* ubi . . .
(5) (Benedict) occurrit *iis e gradibus* quorum aliquos jam conscenderat.
(6) (Herbert) (**176**) *septem octove gradus* conscenderat.
(7) (Anon. I.) descendit obviam *eis de gradibus* quos ascenderat, and (**177**) stabat in gradu suo.
(8) (Anon. II.) occurrit *iis ex gradibus* quos partim ascenderat.
(9) (Anon. IV.) *a gradibus* obviam illis procedens.
(10) (Anon. V.) *per aliquot gradus iis* occurrens.
(11) (Anon. X.) occurrit *eis vultu intrepido.*
(12) (Garnier [**113, 153**]) Très que *sur les degrez del Nort* l'unt fet aller (l. 5401). E encuntre Renalt *del degré descendi* (l. 5418).
(13) (The *Saga*) He steppeth unto *the grades before the choir* . . . he turneth on *the grades.* . . . That knight of God, the Archbishop, *is so firmly planted by the Holy Ghost*, that he moveth nowhere from *his steps*. . . . He turneth to the East, towards that altar of our Lady . . . whereat he had stood in *those steps of the Holy Ghost* which we mentioned before.

It should be added that the *Saga* connects a miracle with these "steps." For it adds, "But the church of Canterbury beareth witness, ever since, to what Lord God the Holy Ghost did in this case, according to what is written, inasmuch as *the very marble rendered itself soft to the footsteps of the Archbishop*, as if he had stood on snow, or some other yielding matter. As an everlasting testimony of this, *these footsteps may still be seen*, and now receive many a kiss amid the devotion of kneeling pilgrims."

[164] Are we to suppose that Fitzstephen was so keen an observer that he noted the exact number of steps to be "four," and thought it worth recording, simply as a statistical fact? and that Herbert, who was not present, knew of Fitzstephen's tradition, and thought it worth contradicting? Even if we grant both these suppositions, why does William, omitting all mention of "ascending steps," say "planting *his steps,*" while Anon. X. omits all mention of the word, alone among the eleven narrators?

[165] It is possible that we have here an instance of literary corruption. If William had a version of John's tradition "fit ex adverso (for "fit obviam") e gradu," it might be corrupted to "fixit ex adverso gradū (*i.e.* gradum)." Anon. X. may have wholly omitted the phrase because it was obscure.[3] Be this as it may, led by the *Saga*, and by antecedent likelihood, we may infer with probability that, although some of the earliest traditions laid stress on the ascending and descending of the steps by the Archbishop, the later traditions found it better to concentrate the devotion of pilgrims on the place where he had finally taken his stand and fallen.[4]

§ 4. *Stanley and Tennyson*

[166] In the two modern accounts, Tennyson is remarkably faithful to the best authorities. He represents

---

[3] If it did not seem probable that Anon. X. borrowed "intrepido vultu" from Benedict or John, it might be worth considering whether some confusion originated from Garnier's French. "Degré" might have been taken by the writer as two words "de [bon] gré," *i.e.* "voluntarily."

[4] Garnier, speaking of the Apostle St. Thomas and the Martyr St. Thomas, says (ll. 5773·4) "El servise Deu unt tuz les cinc sens mis, E tuz *les cinc degréz* unt muntez et purpris." Stanley (p. 228) quotes, from the hymn repeated by St. Thomas's pilgrims, as they mounted the steps leading to the grave to which he was ultimately transferred, " Fac nos Christo *scandere* Quo Thomas *ascendit.*" It is possible that a few traditions saw a mystical meaning in the Saint's "ascending and descending," but could not agree as to the best mystical number.

Fitzurse as "*catching hold of* the last flying monk," immediately upon entering the Cathedral, not as (Stanley) "stumbling upon" him on "the lower step" of the northern staircase. Also, Stanley's version of the reply to "Where is the Archbishop?" though following Garnier pretty closely, does not express the contempt that breathes in the latter. "Reginald, here I am, no traitor," sounds expostulatory. But, in the French second person singular— naturally used by a *lord* addressing a *vassal*—" Renald [thou 'man' of mine], if thou seekest me, thou hast found me" is a very different thing. Tennyson's version agrees with that of the ear-witnesses, and is shorter, sharper, and better every way. It is a pity, however, that the poet inserted "I am he ye seek." Moreover the rather magniloquent "Primate of England" is not so good as the repeated "Archbishop" in the original. For the meaning is "You seek the Archbishop? Then you have found the Archbishop."

[167] Stanley's notion that Fitzurse "sprang back two or three paces" and that Becket "passed by him" into the corner of the chapel of St. Benedict is not supported by the evidence. The only support for it, at this stage, is a passage of Fitzstephen, omitted by the MS. that represents the earliest text.

CHAPTER VIII

THE STRUGGLE

§ 1. *The different accounts*

[168] (1) (Grim) He had told them before that he had no fear of them, and now he added, "I am ready to suffer in the name of Him who redeemed me by His blood. Far be it from me to flee for your swords, or to quit the path of righteousness." Saying this, he turned aside to the right under a pillar, having on one side the altar of the blessed Mother of God and ever Virgin Mary, on the other, that of the Confessor St. Benedict—under whose protection, and [by] whose example, he was [presently] crucified to the world and to the lusts thereof, and endured with such a steadfast courage every penalty inflicted by the executioner of the flesh,[1] that you might have thought he was not in the flesh.

---

[168] (1) (Grim) Et qui se eos non timere jam antea dixerat, adjunxit, "Praesto sum in nomine Ejus pati qui me sanguine suo redemit ; absit ut propter gladios vestros fugiam, aut a justitia recedam." Quo dicto divertit in dextram sub columna, hinc habens altare beatae Dei genetricis et perpetuae virginis Mariae, illinc vero sancti confessoris Benedicti ; quorum exemplo et suffragiis crucifixus mundo et concupiscentiis ejus, tanta animi constantia ac si in carne non esset, quicquid carnifex[1] inferebat, sustinuit ac superavit.

---

[1] "Carnifex (executioner)" here rendered "executioner of the flesh" to keep up the apparent play on "carne." Elsewhere (69) the knights are called "torturers (tortores)." For "crucified," applied to St. Thomas, see 146. John elsewhere (*Mat.* ii. 317) speaks of him as "crucifying his flesh" by asceticism.

[169] He was followed by his torturers. "Absolve," said they, "and restore to communion, those whom you have excommunicated, and restore the right of office to those who are suspended." "No satisfaction," he replied, "has been given to prepare the way [for their restoration], and I will not absolve them." "You, too,"[2] said they, "shall [suffer and] die this instant, receiving your desert." "I, too," said he, "am ready to suffer for my Lord, that in my blood the Church may obtain liberty and peace: but I interdict you, in the name of God, from harming in any wise those who are mine, whether clerks or laymen...."[3] Most fit was it that the true soldier of the Captain of Salvation should walk in the footsteps of his Saviour, who, when he was sought by the wicked, said, "If ye seek me, let these go their way."[4]

[170] So they made assault on him, and cast on him sacrilegious hands, dragging him on roughly and violently that, having him outside the church, they might either cut his throat there, or bind him and carry him off—as they

---

[169] Quem insecuti carnifices, "Absolve," inquiunt, "et communioni restitue quos excommunicasti, et caeteris officium redde qui suspensi sunt." Quibus ille, "Nulla," ait, "satisfactio praecessit, nec eos absolvam." "Et[2] tu," inquiunt, "modo morieris, suscipiens quod meruisti." "Et ego," ait, "pro Domino meo paratus sum mori, ut in meo sanguine ecclesia libertatem consequatur et pacem; sed meis, sive clerico, sive laico, in nomine Dei omnipotentis interdico ne in aliquo noceatis."[3] . . . Decuit plane Ducis sui militem martyrem Salvatoris inhaerere vestigiis, qui, quum quaereretur ab impiis, "Si me," inquit, "quaeritis, sinite hos abire."[4]

[170] Igitur, facto impetu, manus sacrilegas injecerunt in eum, durius illum contrectantes et trahentes, ut extra fores ecclesiae aut jugularent, aut vinctum inde

---

[2] [169a] "Et . . ." apparently means "you, *too, as well as those whom you have caused to suffer*, shall suffer—and shall suffer something worse." "Et ego" plays on this first use of "et." If the punctuation were "Et 'tu,' inquiunt," the meaning would be "And they replied, 'You shall die at once.'"

[3] Here Grim inserts a remark that the Martyr herein provided not only for the safety of his followers but also for his own glory, which would have been shadowed by "any *very serious mischance* befalling one that stood by his side (*proximi casus tristior*)." This comes very gracefully from Grim, whose arm was almost cut in two in the attempt to protect the Martyr. Presumably Grim did not regard this as "very serious." [4] John xviii. 8.

afterwards confessed. But besides that they could not easily move him from the pillar, he also, when one of them pressed rather too vigorously on him and came too close, shook him right away, calling him a pander, and saying, "You must not lay finger on me, Reinald. You owe me fealty and obedience. You act like a madman, you and your accomplices."

[171] (2) (Fitzstephen) One cutthroat made reply,[5] "Your death. It is impossible that you should live [a minute] longer." " I accept death," replied the Archbishop, "in the name of the Lord, and I commend my soul and the cause of the Church to God and St. Mary and the Patron Saints of this church. Far be it from me to flee for your swords! But, by the authority of God, I interdict you from touching any one of those who are mine."—One of them had a two-edged axe and a sword too, that in (?) [the strength of][6] the hatchet (?) and two-edged axe, they might batter down the door of the church if barred against them; but, keeping his sword, he set down the two-edged axe; and it is there to this day.—A certain one struck him with the flat of his sword between the shoulders, saying, "Fly! you are a dead man." But the Archbishop stood on unmoved, and

---

asportarent, sicut postmodum confessi sunt. Sed cum facile non posset a columna moveri, unum ex ipsis acrius insistentem et accedentem propius a se repulit, lenonem appellans, dicensque "Non me contingas, Reinalde, qui fidem ex jure debes et subjectionem; insipienter agis cum tuis complicibus."

[171] (2) (Fitzstephen) Unus grassator:[5] "Ut moriaris; impossibile est ut vivas ulterius." At ille: "Et ego in nomine Domini mortem suscipio, et animam meam et ecclesiae causam Deo et beatae Mariae et sanctis hujus ecclesiae patronis commendo. Absit ut propter gladios vestros fugiam: sed, auctoritate Dei interdico, ne quempiam meorum tangatis." Aliquis eorum bisacutam et gladium simul habuit, ut in[6] securi et bisacuta, si eis obfirmaretur, ostium dejicerent ecclesiae; sed retento gladio, bisacutam, quae adhuc ibi est, deposuit. Quidam eum cum plano ense caedebat inter scapulas, dicens, "Fuge, mortuus es." Ille immotus perstitit, et cervicem praebens, se Domino commendabat; et sanctos

---

[5] "Made reply," in answer to the Archbishop's question, "What is your will?"
[6] "In," though intelligible in Hebraic Greek, is unintelligible here. There is probably some corruption.

presenting his neck [to the blow] commended himself to God; and his lips repeated the names of the holy Archbishops who were martyrs [before him], St. Denis, and St. Elphege of Canterbury.

[172] Some,[7] saying "You are [our] prisoner, you will come with us," laid hands on him, and would fain have dragged him out of the church. [And perhaps they would have persisted] had they not feared that the people would rescue him. The Archbishop replied, "I will go nowhere hence. Here shall you work your will and obey your orders." And with all his force he struggled against them.

[173] (3) (John) To this,[8] one of the knights, those ministers of death, in a spirit of mad fury, rejoined, "Your instant death : for it is impossible that you should live [one minute] longer." Then the Archbishop answered, steadfast in voice as in heart—for, with all reverence for the Martyrs, I venture boldly to say that in my judgment none surpassed him in steadfastness—" I, too,[9] am ready to die for my God, and for the assertion of righteousness and the liberty of the Church. But if you seek my life, I forbid you, in the name

---

archiepiscopos martyres in ore habebat, beatum Dionysium et sanctum Aelfegum Cantuariensem.

[172] Aliqui[7] dicentes, "Captus es; venies nobiscum," injectis manibus, eum ab ecclesia extrahere volebant; nisi timerent, quod populus eum esset erepturus de manibus eorum. Ille, respondens, "Nusquam ibo; hic facietis quod facere vultis et quod vobis praeceptum est," quod poterat, renitebatur.

[173] (3) (John) Cui[8] unus funestorum militum in spiritu furoris intulit, "Ut modo moriaris; impossibile enim est ut ulterius vivas." Respondit autem archiepiscopus non minori constantia verbi quam animi—quia, quod (omnium martyrum pace) ex animi mei sententia fidenter dixerim, nullus videtur isto fuisse constantior —" Et[9] ego pro Deo meo mori paratus sum et pro assertione justitiae et ecclesiae libertate. Sed si caput meum quaeritis, prohibeo ex parte omnipotentis Dei, et

---

[7] The absence of names is noticeable. Fitzstephen tells us that (102) the knights had their visors down : and apparently he could not distinguish them with certainty.

[8] In answer to the question "What is your will?"

[9] [173a] Here "et" seems to mean, "I as well as you." "You wish not to delay my death *ulterius*. I too wish the same" (169a).

of Almighty God, and under penalty of anathema, to harm in any wise any other, be he monk, clerk, or layman, high or low:[10] but let them be as exempt from penalty as they have been from action to deserve it. For not to them, but to me, must be imputed the charge, if any of them have undertaken the cause of the suffering Church.[11] Willingly do I embrace death, if, through the shedding of my blood, the Church can obtain peace and liberty. . . ." Do not his words seem to set forth an image of Christ, saying in His Passion, " If ye seek me, let these go their way "?[12]

[174] (4) (William) " Reginald, Reginald, I have bestowed many benefits on you. Do you come armed to me ?" He replied, " You shall know. Are you that traitor to the King? You will come this way,"[13] and struck off his cap with the point of his sword. "I am no traitor," rejoined the Archbishop, " I will not go out [of the church], abominable man "— and shook free from the knight's hand the border of his pallium. Then the knight thundered in reply " Fly !" " I

sub anathemate, ne cuiquam alii, sive monacho sive clerico vel laico, majori vel minori,[10] in aliquo noceatis, sed sint immunes a poena sicut extiterunt a causa ; non enim illis, sed mihi imputandum est, si qui eorum causam laborantis ecclesiae susceperunt :[11] mortem libenter amplector, dummodo ecclesia in effusione sanguinis mei pacem consequatur et libertatem." . . . Verba ejus nonne Christum exprimere videntur in Passione dicentem, " Si me quaeritis, sinite hos abire "?[12]

[174] (4) (William) "Reginalde, Reginalde, multa tibi contuli beneficia. Ingrederis armatus ad me ?" "Scies," ait, "tune ille regis proditor ? Huc abscedes,"[13] pileumque mucrone decussit. "Non," inquit, "proditor sum ; non egrediar, vir abominabilis," palliique sui laciniam de manu excussit. Ergo subin-

[10] So the *Saga* has it (191) : and this makes better sense than " old or young."
[11] This seems written rather for the Pope and for partisans of the Church, than for those who wanted to know what the Archbishop really said. It must be remembered that the writer probably ran away before this.
[12] The omitted words comment on the Archbishop's anxiety "lest those who were *nearest* (proximi) to him should be hurt." In this, and what follows, Grim (169) agrees with John. As it is comment, not fact, Grim probably borrowed from John.
[13] "Huc abscedes," if not an error for " huc accedes" (comp. Benedict "veni huc "), would seem to mean " This way! You must leave," *i.e.* leave the Cathedral.

will not fly," said the Martyr: "here you shall glut your malice." [As though] smitten by these words the assassin recoiled two or three paces. He was all but striking; but he hesitated, either because he was gathering his strength, or because, for the time, mindful of past [benefits] he was disposed to spare his lord, through whom he had obtained promotion and an introduction to the King. Meanwhile, the three others attack him with insults, saying, "You shall die this instant." To these he replied, "If you seek my life, I prohibit you under the interdiction of anathema from harming any of those who stand round [me]. Willingly do I embrace death, provided that the Church, through my blood, may obtain liberty and peace."

[175] (5) (Benedict) Then the first of them came up to the Saint, and said, "Fly! You are a dead man." "In no wise," said the Saint, "will I fly." So the sacrilegious King's knight, laying hands on him, and casting down his cap with the point of his sword, said, "Come this way! You are my prisoner." "I will not come," replied the Saint: "here shall you do to me what you will"—and shook free from the knight's hand the border of his pallium.

[176] (6) (Herbert) The other, in tones of thunder, replied,[14] "That you should die. Nor shall you live any

---

tonat "Fuge." Subjunxit "Non fugiam; hic tuam explebis malitiam." Quibus verbis sicarius repercussus duos passus vel tres resiliit. Percussurus quidem erat, sed haerebat, aut quia vires suas colligebat, vel quia interim domino suo memor praeteritorum parcebat, per quem promotus regiam familiaritatem adeptus fuerat. Interea tres alii insurgunt insultantes, "Inpraesentiarum morieris." "Si caput," inquit, "meum quaeritis, prohibeo sub interminatione anathematis ne cuiquam circumstantium noceatis. Mortem libens amplector, dummodo ecclesia in sanguine meo libertatem consequatur et pacem."

[175] (5) (Benedict) Accedens autem primus illorum dixit sancto "Fuge, mortuus es." Ait sanctus, "Nequaquam fugiam." Sacrilegus autem satelles, manu in eum conjecta, pileumque mucrone dejiciens, "Veni huc," inquit, "captus es." At sanctus "Non veniam," inquit; "hic mihi facietis quae facere vultis": palliique sui laciniam de manu ejus excussit.

[176] (6) (Herbert) Et ille, intonando, "Ut moriaris," inquit,[14] "nec

---

[14] In answer to the question "What is your will?"

longer." And the Archbishop said, "And I, too,[15] am ready to lay down my life for my God and for the liberty of the Church." But, wonderful to relate, this brave president of the games of God,[16] singularly great and greatly singular, whereas (before those butchers had entered the church) he had already gone up seven or eight steps on his way towards the church choir (to which one goes up by steps), now, as soon as he saw swords in the church, [and] drawn, hastened to confront them. And . . . he reproved those gladiators with all authority for entering the Church, their mother, in a manner so disorderly and profane. And as for one of them—who had first come up close to him and then tried to seize him—the Archbishop, [taking him] by his hauberk, shook him off with a force that almost prostrated the man on the pavement. This was William de Traci, as [Traci] himself afterwards confessed.

[177] (7) (Anon. I.) So the four knights above mentioned, coming up to him together with a certain clerk whom they had brought with them (Hugo Mauclerc by name), said to him, "Absolve with all speed the King's Bishops, whom you have

---

ullatenus vives." Et ille, "Et[15] ego," inquit, "pro Deo meo et pro ecclesiae libertate paratus animam ponere." Sed, quod mirum dictu, iste tam fortis Domini agonotheta,[16] singulariter magnus et magnifice singularis, qui antequam lanistae illi intrassent ecclesiam, versus chorum ecclesiae pergens, ad quem per gradus ascenditur, septem octove gradus jam conscenderat, mox ut gladios in ecclesia exsertos vidit, festinanter occurrit. . . . Et . . . gladiatores cum omni imperio arguens, quod tam inordinate, tam profane, matrem suam ecclesiam introissent, unum eorum, qui prius appropinquaverat, manu mox apprehendens, per loricam tam valide excussit, quod ipsum fere ad pavimentum usque prostravit. Willelmus de Traci hic erat, sicut ipsemet postea de se confessus est. . . .

[177] (7) (Anon. I.) Accedentes igitur ad eum quatuor milites memorati, et quidam clericus quem secum adduxerant, cui nomen Hugo Malus-clericus, dixerunt ei, "Absolve celeriter episcopos regis, quos excommunicasti." Quibus

---

[15] "I, too." See 169a and 173a.
[16] "Agonotheta." See William's use of this word (146). But one MS. has "agoniteta." Herbert may have used "agonista" (*i.e.* "champion"), and it may have been perverted into conformity with William's form.

excommunicated!" "I will do nothing," said he, "other than what I have said and done." Then began they to threaten him with death. But he answered, "I fear not your threats, for I am ready to die for God: but let my men go, and lay not a finger on them." Then they cast hands on him, and began to drag him on by force, striving to set him on the shoulders of William [de Tracy], and to cast him forth from the church. But the holy man stood firmly in the place of his footsteps, and could not be moved from the spot. For Master Edward, who, alone of all his [clerks], had remained with him, held him back stoutly against all their efforts. And when Rainald Fitzurse, who had first cast hands on him, pressed on him very forcibly, the man of God shook him off and dashed him away from himself with such force that he almost fell flat on the pavement, saying to him, "Back! Away! You are my man. You may not so much as lay a finger on me."

[178] (8) (Anon. II.) And when one of the knights shouted aloud, "Your death;[17] for you cannot possibly live a minute longer," he courageously answered, "I, too,[18] am ready to die for God and my Church." Now they had come with hauberks, helmets, and naked swords. Frightened

---

ille, "Non faciam," inquit, "aliud nisi quod jam dixi et feci." Tunc coeperunt ei minari mortem. Quibus ille respondit "Minas vestras non timeo, nam mori pro Deo paratus sum; verumtamen homines meos dimittite, neque contingatis eos." Injecerunt igitur manus in eum, coeperuntque eum fortiter trahere, nitentes eum imponere humeris Guillelmi et de ecclesia ejicere. Sed vir sanctus firmiter stabat in gradu suo, nec loco moveri potuit; magister namque Edwardus, qui solus ex omnibus suis cum eo remanserat, validissime eum contra eos retinebat. Cumque Rainaldus filius Ursionis, qui primus injecerat manus in eum, vehementius instaret, excutiens se vir Dei impegit eum a se, ita quod fere corruit super pavimentum, dicens illi "Recede hinc; homo meus es, contingere me non debes."

[178] (8) (Anon. II.) Unoque proclamante militum, "Ut moriaris;[17] nec enim esse potest ut ulterius vivas," constanter respondit, "Et[18] ego pro Deo et ecclesia mea paratus sum mori." Venerant autem in loricis et galeis ensibusque

---

[17] In answer to the question "What is your will?"
[18] "I, too." See 169*a*, 173*a*, 176.

by these, the monks and clerks scattered and fled away in all directions [19]—as though fulfilling here a second time the Scripture " I will smite the shepherd and the sheep shall be scattered." Now at first they strove to seize him in their arms and carry him away [from the church]. But presently they gave up the hope of this, because he, disdaining to follow, struggled against them—though only in word ; [20] then they feared that rescuers might come in and snatch him from their hands, so that he might escape once more from the realm : and so at last they were inflamed to madness against him, as though the devil were urging them headlong to their act of murder.

[179] (9) (Anon. IV.) The knights immediately cast their hands on him and held him, [hoping] to drag him outside the church, to execute their purpose [there]. But they were alarmed by the vast concourse of men and women and feared that he might be rescued before their object was attained. This made them hasten their crime.

[180] (10) (Anon. V.), and demanding life for his [friends and attendants],and praying for his murderers,[21] he said," Willingly, so far as my frail flesh suffers, will I undergo death."

nudatis, quibus perterriti subito dilapsi sunt huc illucque cum cleris monachi,[19] tanquam et hic iterum impleto quod scriptum est " Percutiam pastorem et dispergentur oves." Nisi sunt autem primo comprehensum eum abducere. Quod fieri posse desperantes, cum sequi dedignans solo tamen verbo reluctaretur,[20] timentesque ne supervenientibus auxiliis ereptus denuo regnum exiret, velut ad facinus praecipitante diabolo caedis in ipsum furia mox exarserunt.

[179] (9) (Anon. IV.) Cui statim injicientes manus milites eum tenuerunt, ut extra ecclesiam ad peragendum propositum traherent. Sed timentes undique concurrentium utriusque sexus multitudinem, ne forte voto infecto eriperetur, facinus acceleraverunt.

[180] (10) (Anon. V.) , suisque vitam postulans, et pro suis occisoribus [21] orans, " Libenter," inquit, "quantum mea fragilitas patitur, mortem suscipiam."

---

[10] This author (like Herbert) represents the flight of Becket's followers as being universal, like that of our Lord's disciples.

[20] This directly contradicts the statement of the earlier writers that St. Thomas shook off Fitzurse (or Tracy) with great violence.

[21] [180a] An extraordinary mistake. To explain it as arising from Herbert's

[181] (11) (Anon. X.) And, turning to one, he said, "What is [this], Reginald? Do you come to me, [and] into a church, in arms?" "You shall presently know,"[22] he replied, "you are a dead man." The Archbishop answered, steadfast in voice as in heart, "Willingly,[23] too, do I undergo death for the sake of righteousness. But, on the part of God, I forbid you from harming any other man":—imitating Christ, who said in His Passion, "If ye seek me let these go their way."[24] While he was uttering these words, they cast their sacrilegious hands on him, with all speed dragging him on that they might accomplish their sacrilegious enterprise outside the church. But, being held by one[25] of his clerks, he could not easily be moved.

---

[181] (11) (Anon. X.) Et ad unum conversus dixit, "Quid est, Reginalde? Ad me in ecclesiam armatus accedis?" Cui ille, "Jam scies;[22] mortuus es." Respondit archiepiscopus non minori constantia verbi quam animi, "Et libens[23] mortem suscipio pro justitia. Sed ex parte Dei prohibeo ne cuiquam alii noceatis": Christum imitans, in Passione dicentem, "Si me quaeritis, sinite hos abire."[24] Haec eo dicente ipsi manus sacrilegas injecerunt in eum, quantocius trahentes eum ut extra ecclesiam inceptum sacrilegium adimplerent. Sed tentus ab uno[25] clericorum suorum facile moveri non poterat.

---

statement that the Saint "prayed *for his own*, pro *suis*," would necessitate the improbable conclusion that this author wrote after Herbert. More probably it is to be explained by the fact that the Archbishop of Sens, in a letter (*Mat.* vii. 431) written to the Pope, from imperfect information, immediately after the murder, has a similar phrase, "pro occisoribus suis exoravit." This belief may have, for some time, influenced French writers. Besides, errors of this sort are common in ecclesiastical writings: "What *ought* to have happened *must* have happened. St. Stephen, the first martyr, prayed for his murderers: therefore St. Thomas, the last, *must* have done the same."

[22] These words, assigned by *Quadrilogus* to Beñedict, occur also (without "jam") in William. The author appears to take them from Benedict, or from a version of *Quadrilogus*.

[23] "Willingly, too." This author retains, but misplaces, the traditional "et," 169*a*, 173*a*, etc.

[24] "Go their way." The words "The Archbishop . . . go their way" are condensed from John.

[25] "One." This implies, though it does not mention, Grim. This confirms Grim—against Fitzstephen, who says (219) that the monks held him, and Grim with them.

[182] (12) (Garnier) By the corner of his mantle had Renald seized him: "Renald," said the good Priest, "so many benefits have I done thee,[26] And what seekest thou of me in holy church, in arms?" Said Renald Fitzurse to him, "Certainly you shall know." (He had pulled him toward himself, so that he (*i.e.* the Martyr) was all shaken.) "Traitor to the King are you," said he, "Here! You must come forth!"

[183] So forth from the holy Minster he thought to drag him. One may well suppose that St. Thomas was wroth at that deed, Because this Renald roughly pulled and pushed him. So strongly did he smite Renald that he recoiled backward, And the corner of his mantle he shook free from his hands.

[184] "Fly hence, evil man,"[27] said the holy Priest, "I am no traitor, nor ought to be accused."[28] "Fly," said

---

[182] Par le corn del mantel l'aveit Renalz saisi;
"Renalz, tanz biens t'ai fez,"[26] fet-li buens ordenez,
"E que quiers-tu sur mei en sainte Eglise armez?"
Fet Renalz li fils Urs: "Certes vus le saurez!" (Sachei l'aveit à sei, que tut fu remuez;)
"Traïtùr le Rei estes," fet-il, "chà en vendrez!"

[183] Kar hors del saint mustier trainer le quida;
Bien crei que saint Thomas à cele feiz s'ira
De ço que cil Renalz le detrest et buta.
Si ad enpeint Renalt k'arrère rebusa,
E la corn del mantel hors des mains li sacha.
[184] "Fui, malveis hum[27] d'ici," fet li sainz ordenez.
"Jo ne sui pas traïtres, n'en dei estre retez."[28]
—"Fuiez," fet li Renalz, quant se fu purpensez.

---

[20] "Thee." The Archbishop addresses Fitzurse in the 2nd pers. sing. as a lord might address a vassal. Fitzurse addresses the Archbishop here in the 2nd pers. plural.

[27] [184a] "Fui, malveis hum d'ici." Anon. I. represents St. Thomas as saying to Rainald "You are my *man*." Did he understand "hum d'ici" to mean "*man* of this person"? or did Garnier (25a) misunderstand "You are my *man*"? Could "fui" be a form of "fi," *i.e.* "fie!", which, in Latin, is spelt "phui"? More probably "fui" represents Anon. I. "*Recede hinc!* homo meus es." The *Saga* represents Tracy as saying to St. Thomas, "Flee, thou art death's man." William represents the Archbishop as saying to Fitzurse, "I will not go out, *abominable man.*"

[28] "Nor ought to be accused." This is extremely weak. What is needed is "I am no traitor, but *priest of God*," "dei presbyter," "prestre deu" (instead of "dei estre retez"). In the next line, "purpensez" is, literally, "had taken thought."

Renald, when he had recovered himself. "I will not," said the Saint; "here shall ye find me, And here accomplish your great felonies."

[185] Toward the aisle of the North went the [noble] man, And held himself by a pillar close beside it. Between two altars is that pillar placed. To the Mother of God is the one below [28a] hallowed, In the name of St. Benedict is the other consecrated. There did they drag and draw him, these servants [of the King] in their fury: "Absolve," said they, "those who have been excommunicated, And those who have been by you suspended and inhibited." "I will not do," he replied, "anything else than I began to do." Then they all together began to threaten to kill him.

[186] Said he, "Of your threats I am not afraid; To suffer martyrdom I am wholly prepared; But my friends let go, touch them not. And do with me alone that which you are to do." In death the good shepherd did not forget his own [flock]. So it happened with God, when He went to pray Upon Mount Olivet, during the night. . . . [28b] And those who sought him began to cry out, "Where is the Nazarene?" "Here can ye find me," Said God unto them, "but let my [friends] all go."

—"Ne l'ferai," dit li sainz, "ici me troverez,
E voz granz felunies ici accomplirez."
  [185] Devers l'ele del Nort s'en est li bers alez,
E à un piler s'est tenuz et acostez.
Entre dous altels ert cil pilers mesurez;
A la mère Deu est cil de desuz [28a] sacrez;
El non seint Beneit est li autres ordenez.
  La l'unt tret et mené li ministre enragié:
"Assolez," funt-il, "cels qui sunt escummingié,
E cels ki sunt par vus suspendu et lacié!"
— "N'en ferai," fet-il, "plus que je n'ai commencié."
A ocire l'unt dunc ensemble manacié.

[186] Fet-il: "De vos manaces ne sui espoantez:
Del martire suffrir sui del tut aprestez,
Mès les miens en leissiez aler, n'es adesez;
E fètes de mei sul ço que fère devez."
N'a les suens li buens pastre à la mort obliez.
  Eissi avint de Deu, quant il ala orer,
Desur munt d'Olivet, la noit à l'avesprer: [28b]
E cil li commencièrent qui l'quistrent, à crier:
"U est li Nazareus?"—"Cí me poez trover,"
Fit lur Deus, "mès les miens en leissiez tuz aler."

[28a] "Desuz," according to Roget (*Old French*, p. 342), a form of "desoz," *i.e.* "*dessous*," not "*dessus*."

[28b] "À l'avesprer" often = "au soir," but seems tautological here unless it means "on the evening [*before the Passion*]."

[187] Then did they seize him in their hands, those sons of Satan, So did they begin with all their might to drag and draw him, And on the shoulder of William [de Tracy] they would fain have placed him; For outside did they wish either to slay or to bind him. But from the pillar could they not thrust nor move him away. Even as St. Thomas leant on the pillar, [Namely, Him] who suffered death on the cross to establish His Church, None could move him away nor thrust him therefrom. But now it was fitting to deliver one man alone to death At the pillar of the Minster, to save the people.[29]

[188] For those who should rather have held by the Church, Would fain have altogether crushed both her and her members, [And] cast down to earth the pillar, and the head that sustained her. Meet it was to wash this blood of sin with blood [of the sinless]; In order to raise up the head, [it was meet] to give the Head of the head.[30] It was not God's will that he should be shamefully treated; Thus did he prove those evil-working people, Whether they could dare in the Minster to do so cruel a sin, For there is none such a felon from here to the East That would hear tell thereof, and not feel shame for the deed.

---

[187] Dunc l'unt saisi as puinz li fil à l'aversier,
Si l'commencent forment à trère et à sachier,
E sur le col Willams le voldrent enchargier;
Kar là hors le voleient ou occire ou lier.
Mès del piler ne l'porent oster, ne esluingnier.
  Cum seint Thomas s'esteit apuiez al piler,
Ki suffri mort en croiz pur s'iglisle estorer,
Ne l'en poeit nuls huem esluignier ne oster.
Mès ore en coveneit un sul à mort livier,
Al piler del mustier, pur le pueple sauver.[29]

[188] Car cil qui mielz déussent sainte Eglise tenser
La voldrent et ses menbres del tut agraventer,
Le piler et le chief ki l'sustint aterrer.
Icel sanc de péchié covint par sanc lavere,
Pur relever le chief, le chief del chief doner.[30]
Ne Deus ne voleit pas k'il fust traitiez vilment:
Si l'fist pur espruver cele malveise gent,
S'osassent el mustier errer si cruelment.
Car il n'a si felun, entrès k'en Orient,
Qui en oï parler, qui ne s'en espoent.

---

[29] John xi. 50. The "pillar" is Christ: and the Saint cannot be moved because he leans on Christ.

[30] The general meaning is clear, that the Archbishop must fall as a sacrifice. But what is meant by "the head of the head"? Comp. 132, "give his head for the Church." Is there any allusion to the Pauline doctrine about the "head"?

[189] Master Edward Grim had seized him with all his might, And had clasped him from behind when they had attacked him; [And] held him fast against them all, by naught dismayed, Nor, for all the knights did, had he abandoned him, Though clerks, though servants, had all fled from him. Master Edward held him for all that they dragged him: "What will ye do?" said he, "Are ye mad? Consider where ye are, and to whom belong [30a] the holy places! To lay hand on your Archbishop is great sin." But neither for thought of holy places nor for the Minster do they let him go.

[190] (13) (The *Saga*) But the knight that goeth first is the knight William de Traci. He strideth forward to the Archbishop, saying, "Flee," he said, "thou art death's man." The Archbishop answereth, "I flee nowhither." Then the knight seizeth the mantle with one hand, and with the other [31] smiteth the mitre from off the Archbishop's head, saying, "Go hence, thou art a prisoner. It is not to be endured that thou shouldst live any longer." The Archbishop pulleth to him the skirt of the mantle, speaking thus: "Hence I go nowhither, and here you shall do to me whatever you please. I am now ready to give my life for the freedom of Holy Church, in the name of Him who purchased her peace in His blood. Think never that I shall yield God's right to your swords."

[191] The lord Archbishop, seeing that, next to William, Reginald sweepeth forward towards him with a

[189] E mestre Edward Grim l'aveit forment saisi,
Enbrascié par de sus, quant l'orent envaï;
Cuntr'els tuz le retint, de rien ne s'esbahi,
Ne pur les chevaliers ne l'aveit pas guerpi;
Si clerc et si sergant s'en èrent tuz fuï.

Mestre Edward le tint kan k'il l'unt desachié:
"Que volez," fet-il, "fère? Estes-vus enragié?
Esguardez ù vus estes et qui sunt li feirié! [30a]
Main sur vostre arcevesque metez à grant pecchié!"
Mès pur feirié ne l'unt, ne pur musticr lessié.
ll. 5420-85.

[30a] "Qui" is for "cui." "Feirié" is (Godefroy) "lieu ensacré."
[31] The *Saga* alone represents the "mitre" as struck off with the *hand*. The evidence of early pictures, and the Latin "pileus," indicate rather "skull-cap" than "mitre." For "mitre" William uses "mitra" (**698***a*).

drawn sword, speaketh thus: "To thee, Reginald, I have done many good things, and yet thou comest armed to my church"[32]—words resembling those of our Lord the Son of God, when the Jews laid hands on him.[33] But Reginald answereth the Archbishop: "Thou shalt surely know, now that I am come,[34] for thou art a man of doomed life." The blessed Thomas answereth, "If you are minded to have my life, I forbid you on behalf of God, under penalty of excommunication, that you do no hurt to any of my men, higher or lower. Let them be as exempt from pain as they are free from guilt."

[192] And when the holy Archbishop Thomas had thus shewn this episcopal steadiness, God's enemies seize him for the purpose of dragging him out of the temple, in order that they may do their deed of shame rather without the church than within. But this is not to be done; for that knight of God, the Archbishop, is so firmly planted by the Holy Ghost that he moveth nowhere from his steps: and yet in that tug he hath no more aid of man than one monk and a clerk hight Edward who bore the cross.[35] But the church of Canterbury beareth witness ever since to what Lord God the Holy Ghost did in this case, according as it is written, inasmuch as the very marble rendered itself soft to the footsteps of the Archbishop, as if he had stood in snow or some other yielding matter. As an everlasting testimony of this,

---

[32] So Magnusson, rendering "At í kirkju til mín." The other writers say, or imply, "into *the* church, against me." But Stanley has "my church."

[33] The reference probably is to John x. 32 "Many good works have I shewed you ... For which of those works do ye stone me?"

[34] The words "now that I am come" appear to be inserted in order to explain "Thou shalt know," — which is misplaced and ought to have come immediately after the Archbishop's question "What will ye?" The *Saga* takes it to mean "Thou shalt know [*the difference*] now that I have come."

[35] [192*a*] According to Fitzstephen, (1) the cross was borne by (*Mat.* iii. 138) Henry of Auxerre, and (2) Fitzstephen himself remained with the Archbishop, as well as Robert of Merton and Edward Grim.

these footprints may still be seen, and now receive many a kiss amid the devotion of kneeling pilgrims.[86]

[193] (i.) (Stanley, pp. 90-91) ["Reginald, you have received many favours at my hands; why do you come into my church armed?"[87]] Fitzurse *planted the axe against his breast*, and returned for answer, "You shall die—*I will tear out your heart.*"[88] Another, perhaps in kindness, striking him between the shoulders with the flat of his sword, exclaimed, "Fly, you are a dead man." "I am ready to die," replied the Primate, "for God and the Church; but I warn you, I curse you in the name of God Almighty, if you do not let my men escape."

[194] The well-known horror which in that age was felt at an act of sacrilege, together with the sight of the crowds who were rushing in from the town through the nave, turned their efforts for the next few moments to carry him out of the church. Fitzurse threw down the axe, and tried to drag him out by the collar of his long cloak, calling "Come with us—you are our prisoner." "I will not fly, you detestable

---

[36] [192*b*] Many miracles were performed on the place where the Archbishop stood in his last moments. It is probable that some marks in the stone were made by the monks to indicate the exact spot. These (perhaps under the influence of some poetic tradition how "the very stones were softer than the hearts of his murderers and received the imprint of his feet") may have led to the conclusion that St. Thomas's feet actually left miraculous footprints on the Cathedral pavement.

A similar story is told about the baptism of St. Francis, that a stranger who attended it "disappeared after the ceremony, leaving the print of his knees on the stone upon which he had knelt"; on which the comment made by a recent biographer is that "There is nothing incredible in them" [*i.e.* traditions of this kind] "to those who believe in the constant and consistent action of a good God."

But is it not "the constant and consistent action of a good God" to make such traditions depend (as on this occasion) on evidence that is always weak, and mostly worthless? And ought not believers in God to be influenced by *this* "action of a good God"?

[37] Repeated from last section. No authority except the *Saga* (191) has the words "*my* church."

[38] These details are not mentioned in any of our authorities. Stanley quotes for them "Grim 79, Anon., Passio Quinta, 176."

fellow," was Becket's reply, roused to his usual vehemence, and wrenching the cloak out of Fitzurse's grasp. The three knights, to whom was now added Hugh Mauclerc, chaplain of Robert de Broc, struggled violently to put him on Tracy's shoulders. Becket set his back against the pillar, and resisted with all his might, whilst Grim, vehemently remonstrating, threw his arms around him to aid his efforts. In the scuffle Becket *fastened upon Tracy, shook him by his coat of mail, and exerting his great strength, flung him down on the pavement.*[39]

[195] It was hopeless to carry on the attempt to remove him. And in *the final struggle*[40] *which now began*, Fitzurse, as before, took the lead. But, as he approached with his drawn sword, the sight of him kindled afresh the Archbishop's anger, now heated by the fray ; the spirit of the chancellor rose within him, and with a coarse epithet, not calculated to turn away his adversary's wrath, he exclaimed, " You profligate wretch, you are my man—you have done me fealty—you ought not to touch me."[41]

---

[39] "Flung him down." For this, Stanley refers to Benedict, Anon.I., Herbert, and Garnier (as well as Gervase). But none of these writers say that any one was "flung down" : and two expressly say that he "*almost* fell down." The others use "shook off," "recoiled," etc. Stanley adds, "All but Herbert and Garnier believe this to have been Fitzurse." This is a mistake, for Garnier says it was Fitzurse. It is important to note that the only one who says Tracy was "shaken off" is Herbert, the latest of the authoritative writers, relying (as will be seen hereafter) on hearsay evidence.

Dramatically, the error is of some importance. By adopting it, Stanley and Tennyson are enabled to make a pause, during which, according to Stanley, Tracy gets up and takes off his hauberk. According to Tennyson (**242**), while Tracy is rising from the ground, Fitzurse strikes the Archbishop, and the latter utters his prayer of commendation.

[40] "Struggle" is hardly the right word. There is no more "struggle." What "now began" was butchery.

[41] This is Stanley's worst mistake. When the Archbishop saw his end thus approaching, he committed his soul to God. The Archbishop's hard words to Fitzurse were uttered when the latter was trying to drag him out of the church. The knightly Martyr would not be pushed and pulled about by his vassal, like a sheep by a butcher, but he was ready to abide the stroke of the sword.

[196] (ii.) (Tennyson)

FITZURSE. Your life.
DE TRACY. Your life.
DE MORVILLE. Save that you will absolve the bishops.
BECKET. Never,—
Except they make submission to the Church.
You had my answer to that cry before.
  DE MORVILLE. Why, then you are a dead man; flee!
  [197] BECKET. I will not.
I am readier to be slain, than thou to slay.
Hugh, I know well thou hast but half a heart
To bathe this sacred pavement with my blood.
God pardon thee and these, but God's full curse
Shatter you all to pieces if ye harm
One of my flock!
  FITZURSE. Was not the great gate shut?
They are thronging in to vespers—half the town.
We shall be overwhelm'd. Seize him and carry him!
Come with us—nay—thou art our prisoner—come!
  [198] DE MORVILLE. Ay, make him prisoner, do not harm the man.
    [FITZURSE *lays hold of the* ARCHBISHOP'S *pall.*
  BECKET. Touch me not!
  DE BRITO. How the good priest gods himself!
He is not yet ascended to the Father.
  FITZURSE. I will not only touch, but drag thee hence.
  BECKET. Thou art my man, thou art my vassal. Away!
    [*Flings him off till he reels, almost to falling.*
  DE TRACY (*lays hold of the pall*). Come; as he said, thou art our prisoner.
  BECKET. Down!
    [*Throws him headlong.*

§ 2. *The words of the dialogue*

[199] Grim, having the advantages of proximity and steadfastness (which implies presence of mind and ability to note and remember) is our best authority here. Then why does he omit the words of the knights, (1) (in answer to the

question, "What is your will?") "Your death," and (2) "Flee!"

The reason appears to be that he concentrates his attention on *the words of the Martyr*. But these, as he gives them, harmonize well with these utterances of the knights, as will be seen by inserting them in italics, as follows, in the passage of Grim (*Mat.* iii. 435) "Why do ye seek me? [THE KNIGHTS. *That ye may die.*] . . . " Behold, I am ready to suffer in the name of Him who redeemed me by His blood." [THE KNIGHTS. *Fly! Come this way!* etc.] "Far be it from me to fly, or move a step from the straight course of righteousness!" The Archbishop then passes into the place of martyrdom, near a "pillar," and here the demand is made that the Bishops shall be absolved. He refuses. The knights repeat their threats. "Thou shalt die," they cry: to which he replies that he is ready to die for the liberty of the Church, but prohibits the knights, on pain of excommunication, from harming those with him.

[200] Not till now do the knights, fearing a rescue, seek to place him on Tracy's shoulders and to haul him out of the church: and not till now does the Archbishop, loathing such treatment, and perhaps preferring the sword to such handling, shake off Fitzurse, almost dashing him on the floor, calling him "pander," and saying in effect, "You are my 'man,' you act like a blind fool. Every knight knows his lord. You do not, for you are no knight."

§ 3. *Has Grim omitted any of the Archbishop's words?*

[201] (1) Garnier and Anon. I. agree in saying that the Archbishop said to Fitzurse (Garnier) "Fly, bad man, hence (Fui, malveis hum d'ici)!" or (Anon I.) "Recede hinc, homo meus es." This is confirmed by an interesting letter written to the Pope anonymously by one who says that, though not present at the murder, he came to Canterbury

the same day. His account is as follows: "They pursue him with drawn swords before the altar accosting him thus, 'Fly, traitor! A cruel death awaits you.' [I should have said that] they had first asked, owing to the great number of monks and clerks present, 'Where is the Archbishop?' To this, he, in a low but perfectly audible tone, replied,[1] 'I am he;[2] and as for you, Reginald, and your accomplices,[3] get you back,[4] for ye know not what ye do.[5] But if ye seek me for slaughter, lay no finger on the rest.[6] I am ready to receive death in the name of Him who deigned to die for me His servant.'"[7]

[202] Although in every phrase of this letter there is apparent a bias that conforms the Martyr's words to those of Scripture, yet it furnishes important confirmation of the view that the first attempt of the knights was to scare the Archbishop out of the church, and that he said to Fitzurse, "Back!" or "Fly [yourself, instead of bidding me fly]!"

Did Grim, then, omit these words? He probably did, and for this reason, that, when the Archbishop sent Fitzurse staggering back so that he almost "fell in a crash upon the pavement," this was a practical way of expressing "Back!" which might well seem to render the word itself superfluous.

[203] (2) Did the Archbishop say to Fitzurse, and Grim omit, the words, "I have bestowed many benefits on you"?

---

[1] *Mat.* vii. 436 "demisso quidem sed *audibili valde sermone respondit.*" Comp. Grim (143) "satis *audibili sermone respondit.*"

[2] "I am he (ego sum)" approaches more closely than our writers to John xviii. 5.

[3] "Cum tuis complicibus." Comp. Grim (170) "insipienter agis cum tuis complicibus."

[4] "Vade retro," probably an allusion to the words of Christ (Matth. xvi. 23), "Get thee behind me, Satan."

[5] Probably an allusion to Luke xxiii. 34, "they know not what they do."

[6] "Lay no finger (contingatis)," the word used by Anon. I. The rest use 'tangere,' "nocere," etc.

[7] Grim has two versions, (1) "to suffer for Him who redeemed me with His blood," (2) "to die that in my blood the Church may obtain liberty." William has (2). The others do not mention "blood."

It is antecedently improbable. Yet William and Benedict (**222**) (if the *Quadrilogus* is right), besides Garnier, assign these words to the Archbishop. William, however, makes the appeal a merely personal one, being, in effect, " I have been very kind to you, and do you come to me in arms ? "—an absolutely impossible utterance for any man of spirit. And how impossible for such a man as this—an Archbishop, too, absorbed in the cause of the Church, and seeing the sanctity of the Church violated by the entrance of armed men ! The tradition may have found favour as indicating the mildness of the Saint,—for the same reason that induced almost all the writers to drop the word " pander ! " which Grim alone describes as applied by the Archbishop to Fitzurse. The *Saga* may have retained the erroneous tradition because it presented a likeness to some words of Christ (John x. 32 " many good works ") which the poet quotes in the context. Possibly the originator may have confused something that meant " I am your lord, and benefactor," with the words now extant about " benefits."

In any case, the probable conclusion is that the Martyr did not utter the words in their present context.[8] Antecedent improbability would not suffice to condemn them : but their omission by Grim, Anon. I., and Fitzstephen, is almost conclusive. For at least two of these writers must have heard the words if they were uttered : and there is no reason why they should have omitted them.

---

[8] [**203***a*] The words, " I have bestowed benefits on you and you come to me in arms," are somewhat like a saying of the Archbishop's to the knights in the Palace (*Mat.* iii. 135), " You know what there is betwixt you and me " [*i.e.*, as Fitzstephen explains, Fitzurse, Tracy, and Morville, had " become his men "], " and hence I the more wonder that you dare to threaten the Archbishop in his own house."

To those who transferred this saying from the Palace to the Church, three courses would be open, (1) to omit "in his own house," (2) to substitute "a church," (3) to substitute "his church." William does (1), Benedict and Garnier (2), the *Saga* (3). See above (**108***b*) for another error probably caused by confusing the Cathedral with the Palace.

[204] (3) As regards William's words, "Do you come armed *to me?*" it is scarcely possible that they were uttered thus. But the Archbishop may very well have reproached Fitzurse with his blind sacrilege, when he told him that he was "acting like a fool." Placed at that point, and with the addition of the words "into holy church," or "into a church," they may well have been uttered, and yet omitted by Grim as implied in the brief statement of "folly."

§ 4. *Striking off the cap*

[205] William and Benedict, alone among our authorities, represent a knight as striking off the Archbishop's cap with the point of his sword, not apparently as the result of a blow aimed at his head, but in order to terrify him into flight. The *Saga* modifies the detail so as to shew more distinctly that it had this object, saying that Fitzurse smote "the mitre" off with his *hand*.

In the parallel passage, Fitzstephen says that some one struck the Archbishop "with the flat of his sword on the shoulder." No one else mentions this: and the question arises whether he may not be describing the same act as that mentioned by William and Benedict, seen from a different point of view.

This supposition will be found confirmed in the next chapter by Anon. I., who says that Fitzurse struck a blow that (1) cast the cap to the ground, (2) lighted on the Archbishop's left shoulder, yet (3) did not strike down, or even move, the Archbishop himself, though it was really the first blow that drew blood. But this will be discussed below. Meantime, it may be taken provisionally that William, Benedict, and the *Saga*, are wrong. Fitzstephen's blow on the shoulder might possibly be part of the "rough handling" mentioned by Grim; but it so well corresponds with the first blow, as described by Anon. I., and as mis-described by William and Benedict, that we may provisionally regard him also as in error.

§ 5. *Who, if any one, was "shaken off" by the Archbishop?*

[206] Fitzstephen and John mention no one as "shaken off." John's silence counts for nothing, on account of his general brevity; but the omission of the former requires a different explanation. It is probably this, that he wished to represent St. Thomas as dying, like most martyrs, in a lamb-like manner. The same motive leads Anon. II. to say that "he resisted *in word alone*": and we have seen above that Anon. V. actually represents him as "praying for his murderers," which is hardly compatible with "shaking them off" so as to make them "almost fall to the earth."

Without going so far as this, Benedict (if correctly represented by the *Quadrilogus*) supports William in saying that the Archbishop "shook off" the corner of his mantle from Fitzurse's hand. William then adds a word or two between the Archbishop and Fitzurse, and then says, "Smitten by *these words*, the assassin recoiled two or three paces."

[207] This ought to suffice any reasonable man, to shew that the Archbishop *did*, as Grim says, "cast back," or as Anon. I. says, "dash away, shaking himself free (se excutiens)"—somebody. Ecclesiastical notions suppressed, or softened, what seemed to be a "scandal." But the scandal was there. The Archbishop did, in a very emphatic way, "dash," or "cast," or "shake," some one. And the only question is, whom did he treat thus?

[208] Herbert expressly tells us that Tracy was the knight here "shaken off." But, beside being the latest of the writers, he himself tells us that his statement is based on a subsequent confession of Tracy to others, not on testimony collected from eye-witnesses. Now in the struggle between

the Archbishop and the knights it is possible that more than one may have been "shaken off" by him at different times; and Tennyson accordingly represents *both Fitzurse and Tracy* as thus shaken off, and the former first. For many reasons, therefore, Herbert's testimony cannot weigh heavily against that of Grim supported by Anon. I. and Garnier.[1]

[209] William says that the Archbishop "shook off" the corner of his mantle from Fitzurse's hand, and then, when the latter said "Fly," replied, "I will not fly. Glut thy malice here." "*Smitten by these words,*" adds William, "the assassin recoiled two or three paces."[2] Absurd though this is, it shews that Fitzurse, at all events, did recoil (whether Tracy did, too, or did not) according to William himself; so that the latter indirectly confirms Grim.

[210] We may conclude with certainty that Fitzurse, and not Tracy, was the knight who was (pre-eminently) "dashed back," and almost fell to the ground. Very probably, this was simultaneous with the "shaking free" of the mantle. Herbert's words "shook him off by the hauberk (per loricam tam valide excussit)" may possibly be another version of the tradition "shook the corner of his mantle free (laciniam e manu excussit)."

[211] It is interesting to see, reproduced here, the same contrast between Fitzstephen and Herbert that appeared at the Council of Northampton. There, Herbert advised excommunication; Fitzstephen, prayer. Here Fitzstephen suppresses the fact that St. Thomas was a fighting Saint.

---

[1] [208a] Herbert elsewhere (*Mat.* iii. 513) quotes Tracy as saying in confession that (whereas, before the deed, he had walked lightly and easily) in retiring after the deed he felt as if he should at any moment fall into the earth which seemed opening to receive him. Such a confession might be easily confused with a statement of fact, that he did *actually*, in his sacrilegious attempt, recoil and almost fall to the earth.

[2] William goes on to express a doubt whether the consequent hesitation to strike arose from physical causes or from remorse. The *Quadrilogus* omits all this, and adds—*ascribing the addition to William*—"Like those who, in our Lord's Passion, when the Lord said, 'I am he,' went backward and fell to the ground."

Herbert on the contrary glories in it. For Scriptural reasons, no doubt, he would have liked to adopt the view of William and the *Quadrilogus*, that the Martyr simply said "I am he," and that the murderers, "struck by *these words*," as in the Gospel (John xviii. 6), "went backward and fell to the ground." But the fighting spirit is so strong in him that he not only inserts the fact, but takes pains perhaps to add a detail. The "corner of the mantle," he seems to think, was an error: the fact was (according to Herbert) that Thomas got a grip on Tracy by his hauberk, and, with that aid, hurled him backward and almost dashed him on the pavement.

§ 6. *Hugh of Morville*

[212] The grounds on which Stanley elsewhere, and Tennyson here, represent Hugh of Morville as gentler than the rest are probably these:

Benedict, in describing the Palace interview, says that when the knights left the Archbishop's room with threats, "he followed them as far as the chamber-door, repeatedly calling to Hugh of Morville—who ought (debebat) to have been better than the rest in reasonableness as he was in birth—to return to speak to him."

[213] This however does not say that Hugh *was* better, but only that he *ought* to have been. Stanley, it is true (p. 80), refers to Benedict and Garnier as justifying his statement that the Archbishop "implored Moreville, as more courteous than the others, to return and repeat their message." But this misrepresents the facts. (1) "Repeatedly calling, or shouting (inclamitans)" is not "imploring." (2) By saying that Hugh "*ought to have* been better," Benedict implies, in this context, that he *was not* better. (3) Benedict himself represents John of Salisbury as remonstrating with the Archbishop for *following the knights to the door and provoking them* (*Mat.* ii. 9), "What need was there for a man of your

position to get up [from your seat] [simply] *to exasperate these rascals and to follow them even to the door?*" So far from "imploring," then, Becket seemed to John to be irritating Morville. And this is borne out by Garnier, who tells us that, although the Archbishop perfectly well heard what the knights had said when they proclaimed him a traitor, he rose up and followed them to the door, *challenging them to repeat it* (l. 5268): "And he cried aloud after them, Hugh, *What is that you said? Say [it again].* (Et cria après els, Huges, k'as tu dit? di!)" And so, too, Anon. I. (*Mat.* iv. 74), "Hearing their threats, the holy man got up and followed them right up to the door of the chamber: and [there], to a knight joining in these threats, he said, *What do you say? Say [it again]! Say [it again]!*"

[214] William devotes more space to Morville than to the other three murderers all together. He tells a frightful tale about Morville's mother, how she first attempted to gain the love of young Litulf, one of her husband's vassals, and then, as he refused, contrived a plot that resulted in his being boiled to death. All this is intended to shew that from Morville himself, being "the offspring of vipers," nothing but venom could be expected. This bears on the present question so far as it indicates no belief among the Canterbury monks that he was gentler than the rest.

§ 7. *Stanley and Tennyson*

[215] The modern writers have been led by William's error (supported by Garnier) to insert touches of softness and personal appeal that distort the whole scene.

[216] Tennyson has gone so far as to make the Archbishop say to one of the knights, that he has "but half a heart" for his foul work, and even "God pardon thee and these!" We may be sure that if St. Thomas had thus imitated St. Stephen, the whole of the ecclesiastical world

would have heard, marked, believed, and inculcated the historical fact, in such a way that it should never be forgotten. It is a real mischief that the poet should have done the Saint this injustice—for an injustice it is, because it does not appreciate his kind of saintliness; that of a knight.[1]

[217] Stanley, beside making the Saint speak of "my church," misses the sequence of cause and effect in leading up to the first blow. It was not the "sight of Fitzurse's drawn sword" that "kindled afresh the Archbishop's anger." The "drawn sword"—which will not come in its place till the next chapter—warned the Martyr of his imminent death, and he prepared himself accordingly. There were no "coarse" words after that. The "coarse epithet" addressed to Fitzurse, and the rebuff that almost dashed him to the ground, were the results of Thomas's knightly loathing at being dragged and hauled about by men whom he despised as his inferiors and detested as brutal instruments of despotism. These words and these acts of the Saint were not saintly according to the ordinary standard. They sprang from the defects of his qualities. But, had it not been for them, he might never have died a Martyr's death. The word "pander," and the sharp thrust backward, goaded Fitzurse to strike the first blow, and thereby brought England a step nearer to Magna Charta.

---

[1] The italicized words must have some force, but it is difficult to find, in "Come; *as he said*, thou art our prisoner." Also, while the single rebuff of Fitzurse, leading, as it does, to the Martyr's death, is dramatically necessary, the second rebuff (which the poet supposes Tracy to have received) makes the martyrdom too much like a melée. Here Tennyson is misled by following Herbert.

CHAPTER IX

THE FIRST BLOW

§ 1. *The different accounts*

[218] (1) (Grim) At this rebuff, the knight, all in a blaze of terrible fury, replied, " I owe you no fealty nor obedience against my loyalty to my lord the King." At the same time he brandished his sword [for a blow] against that consecrated head. So the Martyr, unconquered [to the last], discerned that the hour was imminent that was to end the miseries of mortality, and that the crown of immortality, prepared for him and promised by the Lord, was now close at hand. Accordingly, bending his neck as though for prayer, he joined together and raised his hands upward,[1] and commended his cause and the Church's cause to God and St.

---

[218] (1) (Grim) Miles vero, pro repulsione, furore terribili totus incanduit, ensemque vibrans contra sacrum verticem, "Non fidem," ait, "non tibi subjectionem debeo contra fidelitatem domini mei regis." Cernens igitur martyr invictus horam imminere quae miserae mortalitati finem imponeret, paratam sibi et promissam a Domino coronam immortalitatis jam proximam fieri, inclinata in modum orantis cervice, junctis pariter et elevatis sursum manibus,[1] Deo et sanctae

---

[1] "Upward." This is the view taken by Grim, who was clasping him (Garnier) "from behind." Perhaps Robert of Merton, who seems to have inspired Anon. I., may have been a little in front, at this moment, where a spectator would have received the impression that he (Anon. I.) "covered his eyes with his hands." Or Grim's words might possibly mean "raising his folded hands in prayer" so as to be *before* his *eyes*, not, *above* his *head*. In that case, the two agree : and Anon. I. may be describing inferentially in one way the same fact that Grim describes inferentially in another. The latter says, in effect, "he raised his hands *in prayer*," the former, "he placed his hands before his eyes so as to cover them while he committed himself to God in the moment before death."

Mary, and the Martyr St. Denis. Scarcely had he uttered the words when the execrable knight, fearing lest he might be rescued by the people and escape alive, leapt suddenly on him, and, shearing away the top of the crown,[2] consecrated to God by holy unction, wounded in the head the sacrificial lamb of God. The same stroke [almost] cut off the arm of the writer of this relation : for he, in the universal flight of monks and clerks,[3] steadfastly kept by the Archbishop, and held him fast, embracing him in his arms, until the very [arm] that he opposed to [the stroke] was [almost] cut off.

[219] (2) (Fitzstephen) The monks, too, held him back. With them[4] there was also Master Edward Grim, and he, interposing his arm, received the first sword-stroke aimed by William de Traci at the Archbishop's head. This same stroke wounded the Archbishop on the head, slantwise, and Grim on the arm, severely . . .

Mariae et beato martyri Dionysio suam et ecclesiae causam commendavit. Vix verbum implevit, et metuens nefandus miles ne raperetur a populo et vivus evaderet, insiliit in eum subito, et summitate coronae,[2] quam sancti chrismatis unctio dicaverat Deo, abrasa, agnum Deo immolandum vulneravit in capite, eodem ictu praeciso brachio haec referentis. Is etenim, fugientibus tam monachis[3] quam clericis universis, sancto archiepiscopo constanter adhaesit, et inter ulnas complexum tenuit, donec ipsa quam opposuit praecisa est.

[219] (2) (Fitzstephen) Et monachi eum retinebant : cum quibus[4] et magister Edwardus Grim, qui et primum a Willelmo de Traci in caput ejus vibratum gladii ictum brachio objecto excepit ; eodemque ictu et archiepiscopus in capite inclinato, et ipse in brachio graviter est vulneratus . . .

---

[2] "Crown," see 224. Here the context makes it more easy to see that the meaning is "crown of the head."

[3] Contrast Fitzstephen's "et monachi eum retinebant." But we may perhaps partly reconcile the two by supposing that the monks kept their hold until now, and only fled when they saw Fitzurse advancing to strike the first blow. The Archbishop's "clerks" had fled before. If so, the meaning here is, "when all the monks fled, as they now did, and as the clerks had done some time before."

[4] This can hardly be exactly reconciled with Grim's account. But Fitzstephen's error may be one of omission. Grim *was* with the monks *then*. But he was *not* with them a moment or two afterwards, when they ran away. It is not clear whether Fitzstephen, by not again mentioning himself as present (as he did above), implies that, by this time, he himself had fled. If he had fled, that might account for some error in what follows, which he possibly did not witness.

[**220**] (3) (John) After these words, seeing his executioners with their swords drawn, he bent his head as though for prayer, uttering these last words, "To God and St. Mary, and the Patron Saints of this church, and St. Denis, do I commend myself and the cause of the Church." The rest, who could tell without sighs, sobs, and tears? Pity does not permit the enumeration of details one by one . . .

[**221**] (4) (William) Saying these words, he stretched his head forward, adjusting it to the impending blow, sounding forth these as his last words, "To God and St. Mary, and the [5] Martyr Denis, and the Patron Saints of this church, I commend my spirit and the cause of the Church." But Fitzurse, hastening to snatch a trophy by striking the first stroke, and to gain his wages by hurrying to hell, leapt forward, and with all his force inflicted a wound on the outstretched head, exclaiming, as though in triumph over a conquered enemy, "Strike! Strike!"

[**222**] (5) (Benedict) And to another[6] wearing a hauberk,

---

[**220**] (3) (John) His dictis, videns carnifices eductis gladiis, in modum orantis inclinavit caput, haec novissima proferens verba, "Deo et beatae Mariae, et sanctis hujus ecclesiae patronis, et beato Dionysio commendo me ipsum et ecclesiae causam." Caetera quis sine suspiriis, singultibus et lacrimis referat? Singula prosequi pietas non permittit . . .

[**221**] (4) (William) Dixit, caputque protensum ferientibus coaptavit, haec verba novissima psallens, "Deo et beatae Mariae, et [6] martyri Dionysio, patronisque hujus ecclesiae sanctis commendo spiritum meum et ecclesiae causam." Accelerans autem Ursides de primo ictu referre tropaeum et de festina perditione sua lucrum, prosiliit, et toto conamine suo capiti protenso vulnus incussit, exclamavitque tanquam devicto hoste triumphans "Percutite, percutite."

[**222**] (5) (Benedict) Et ad alium [6] loricatum, quem gladio nudato appro-

---

[5] William seems to copy John's version, but has dropped out "saint (beato)" before "Dionysio," by mistake. Perhaps, he thought that St. Denis, as being a martyr, ought to come before "the Patron Saints," and then felt that "*beatae Mariae et beato* Dionysio" sounded so badly that it was preferable to omit the second "beatus," supplying it from the first. "I commend *my spirit*" is a non-historical "improvement" on John's version, the former being more like Scripture, Luke xxiii. 46.

[6] "Another," *i.e.* different from the knight that "struck off the cap." But William attributes that action to "Reginald." This section of Benedict's narra-

whom he saw approaching him with a naked sword, he turned and said, " What is [this], Reginald ? I have bestowed many benefits on you ? And come you to me, into a church, in arms ? " In these words, did not the imitator of Christ seem to set forth an image of Christ, who said to the Jews " As against a robber have ye come out with swords and staves to seize me ? "[7] The King's knight, filled with a spirit of frenzy, replied, " You shall speedily know. You are a dead man."

[**223**] (6) (Herbert) So, as we briefly signified above, as soon as this our bony[8] champion of Christ seized that one of those murderous knights whose name we gave above, (as we said above), and so mightily shook him off, the man lifted his sword on high, wrath adding to his strength, and aimed a heavy blow at the head of the Lord's Christ (or Anointed). But[9] he did not as yet receive on himself the full force of the blow. For a clerk, who had lately come to

pinquare videbat, conversus dixit, "Quid est, Reginalde? Multa tibi contuli beneficia ; et ad me in ecclesiam armatus accedis ? " Nonne his verbis videbatur imitator Christi Christum exprimere, Iudaeis dicentem, " Tanquam ad latronem existis cum gladiis et fustibus comprehendere me ? "[7] Cui satelles spiritu furoris plenus, "Jam scies," inquit ; "mortuus es."

[**223**] (6) (Herbert) Igitur, ut praetetigimus, mox ut illum carnificum militum quem praenominavimus noster osseus[8] hic Christi athleta apprehendit, ut supra diximus, et tam valide excussit, ipse gladium exaltans, ira vires augente, fortiter christi Domini caput percutere nisus est : quod[9] tamen necdum vim ictus in se excepit, clerico quodam, qui proxime ad videndum pontificem venerat, et eum de

tive (if indeed it comes from his pen) seems to have been placed too late by the *Quadrilogus*. Perhaps it is really a modification of William's narrative (**174**). Note that in the words " Do you come armed against me ? " Benedict adds " into a church," which is omitted by William but inserted by Anon. X.

[**222***a*] Benedict, as reported by *Quadrilogus*, mentions no "first blow." Its place is taken by the "casting off" of "the cap." See **175**, **273**.

[7] Matth. xxvi. 55.

[8] In a digression of five pages, Herbert has likened St. Thomas to Samson (among others) conquering with the *jaw-bone* of an ass.

[9] " But he (quod)." I do not understand the construction, and have taken " quod " as though it were " qui." Herbert may have intended to write " But a certain clerk was the *cause that* (quod) he did not receive the blow," and may have strayed off into a different construction.

see the Pontiff, and who "followed" near at hand "to see the end,"[10] interposed his arm between the falling sword and the Pontiff's head; and, by exposing to danger his arm of flesh so as to make of his own body a shield fitted to protect the Pontiff, he secured for himself the protection of salvation . . . and a participatory first-fruits of the coming sacrifice. That this man's name may be remembered with blessing, I here insert it. His own proper name, then, was Edward; his surname, Grim; he was born in the town in England called Cambridge. So this clerk, struck by the heavy stroke, sustained the first brunt (lit. weight) of the blow. But on feeling himself struck and unable to bear its full weight, he straightway drew back his arm, and the rest of the blow was received by the Pontiff's head.

[224] (7) (Anon. I.) And Rainald[11] said, "I owe you neither faith nor homage against my fealty to the King." So Rainald, seeing that he could not be moved from the spot, and fearing lest he might be rescued by the people who had come together to hear vespers, drew near to smite him at last with sword unsheathed. So the holy man, seeing his

---

prope sequebatur ut videret finem,[10] bracchium suum inter gladium venientem et pontificis caput interponente, et exponente bracchium suae carnis ut de se ipso vel sic aptaret pontifici scutum protectionis, protectionem salutis . . . et inchoatae jam immolationis primus primum participium habuit. Cujus memoria ut in benedictione sit, nomen hic intersero; dictus videlicet nomine proprio Edwardus, cognomento Grim, castello illo in Anglia quod dicitur Cantebrige oriundus. Clericus itaque hic graviter caesus pondus ictus sustinere coepit. Verumtamen illo, cum se caesum sentiret et pondus ictus sustinere non posset, confestim bracchium retrahente, reliquum ictus in se pontificis caput excepit.

[224] (7) (Anon. I.) Et Rainaldus[11] ait, "Nec fidem nec hominium tibi debeo contra fidelitatem regis." Videns igitur Rainaldus quod a loco moveri non posset, timensque ne a populo, qui ad audiendas vesperas convenerat, eriperetur, evaginato gladio jam percussurus appropinquavit. Videns vero vir sanctus martyrium

---

[10] A contrast between Grim and Peter, who (Matth. xxvi. 58) "followed him *afar off* . . . to see the end."

[11] [224a] Grim has (170) "Reinalde." The dropping of the "g," dropped also by Garnier, no doubt, better represents the name as uttered by the Archbishop.

martyrdom imminent, and his executioner now standing face to face with him, joined his hands and covered his eyes, and, stooping his head towards the executioner, said, "To God, and the blessed St. Denis, and the holy St. Elphege, I commend myself." On his saying this, Rainald approached, and struck him obliquely a strong blow on the head, and lopped off the top of his crown,[12] and cast down his cap. The sword glanced on to the left shoulder, and passed on, rending[13] all his garments, so as to leave the skin bare. But Master Edward, seeing the stroke imminent, threw his arm in front as if to protect him, and it was almost completely cut off

[225] (8) (Anon. II.) When therefore he was on the point of receiving the stroke of the sword, forth leapt one of the clerks, Edward by name, surnamed Grim. He—as though rivalling St. Peter's confidence[14] in venturing to

---

suum imminere, jamque cominus stare percussorem, junctis manibus operuit oculos suos, caputque inclinans percussori, dixit, "Deo et beato Dionysio sanctoque Elfego me commendo." Haec cum dixisset, accessit Rainaldus et percussit eum ex obliquo fortiter in capite, amputavitque summitatem coronae[12] ejus, pileumque dejecit. Lapsus est ensis super laevam scapulam, insciditque[13] omnia vestimenta illius usque ad nudum. Magister vero Edwardus, qui juxta virum Dei stabat, videns ictum imminere, jecit bracchium econtra quasi eum protecturus ; quod fere penitus abscissum est.

[225] (8) (Anon. II.) Cum ergo percutiendus esset, prosiluit unus ex clericis, Edwardus nomine, cognomento Grim, ac velut aemulatus beati Petri fidentiam[14]

---

[12] "Crown (coronae)," apparently used here, as by Grim (218), for "the crown of the head." The name was also given (Stanley, p. 284, App. II.) to the circle of hair left on a priest's head by the tonsure. Fitzstephen (*Mat.* iii. 142) has, first, "corona capitis," and then (having thus defined it) "coronae," absolutely. See below (332).

[13] "Passed on, rending." "Inscindo" is not inserted by Lewis and Short. Garnier has "encisa." Forcellini gives it as = "scindo." Dufresne (ed. Favre) does not give the verb, but has "Inscindens-Ferrum, cognomen, Gall. Tranche fer."

[14] *i.e.* "self-confidence." The author regards it as "not right." He ignores the fact that Grim did not draw a sword as Peter did, and did not even "shake off" any one!

defend his Master—wrapped his arm in his cloak and boldly interposed it to meet the uplifted swords, shouting [15] to them to spare the Archbishop.

[226] Though this venturesome act was dictated by affection, yet, as being wrong, it was prohibited by the Pontiff of Christ, and (as though mindful of that inhibition . . . "Put up thy sword, etc. . . .") "Cease, brother!" said he; "not such is the defence that the Lord would have." [16] But meanwhile the murderous knight did not spare the clerk, but, turning his rage first on him, almost cut through the middle [17] the arm interposed, and laid him low on the ground confounded by the force of the blow, like one bereft of life. . . . Well may we believe that a Divine Providence secured the clerk's escape, lest the holy man, who played the main

---

ut magistrum defenderet, obvolutum pallio brachium levatis ensibus audenter objecit, ut Archiepiscopo suo parcerent clamans. [15]

[226] Cujus ausum, quamvis pium, tanquam tamen minus rectum prohibuit Christi pontifex, et (velut illius cohibitionis memor . . . "Mitte gladium tuum etc. . . .") "Desine," inquit, "frater, non hanc defensionem vult Dominus." [16] Interim autem clerico miles funestus non pepercit, sed in eum primo desaeviens, brachium quod objecerat fere per medium [17] gladio secuit, et ex ictus vehementia perturbatum velut exanimem solo stravit. . . . Sane vero creditur divinitus pro-

---

[15] "Shouting." Garnier alone mentions this.

[10] This "leaping forward," and the "folding of the cloak round the arm," and the "calling" to the knights to spare the Archbishop, and the Archbishop's words "Cease, brother," are all (with the exception of the expostulations, inserted by Garnier) traits peculiar to this writer; who records a great deal more about Grim than Grim himself does. (1) Grim could not "leap forward," for he could not afford to let go his hold from behind: (2) there was no use in shouting, and he needed all his breath for what the *Saga* calls "the tug": (3) as he was holding the Archbishop round the waist with his two arms, there was no time, or means, for taking off his cloak and wrapping it round one arm.

It is astonishing that Stanley and Tennyson should have been influenced by such a sensational unveracious writer as this. St. Thomas's rebuke to Grim is a fiction of cold-blooded, mendacious, and ungrateful ecclesiasticism.

[17] "Almost . . . through the middle" perhaps means "almost through the bone." The order of the words forbids us to render "per medium" by "interposed." The writer gives an entirely false impression, as if the knight, failing to strike the Archbishop, deliberately turned against Grim.

part in this martyr's agony, should be bereft of his due glory, and lest the perversity of the evil-minded should impute the mighty miracles that followed to the merits, not of the Master, but of the disciple alone.

[227] (9) (Anon. IV.) Then one of them stretched out his sword, and brandishing it over the Archbishop's head, almost cut off the arm of a certain clerk that stood by, and, at the same time, wounded the Lord's Christ (or Anointed) himself in the head. For the said clerk had stretched out his arm above the head of his [spiritual] Father, to receive, or rather ward off,[18] the blow.

(10) (Anon. V.) Then, inclining his head, full of the spirit of confession, he received the first stroke of death, and rendered his soul to God, while his body fell lifeless to the earth. But the first of the torturers cut off the top[19] of his head.

[228] (11) (Anon. X.) Then one of the above mentioned sons of Leviathan, raising a sword [that] he was holding, almost lopped off the arm of the aforesaid clerk, and by the same stroke smote on the head the sacrificial

---

curatum ut evaderet, ne laudis debitae gloria vir sanctus, cujus principaliter agon erat, fraudaretur, solisque discipuli meritis virtutes miraculorum secutas malevolorum perversitas deputaret.

[227] (9) (Anon. IV.) Cumque unus ex iis extendens vibraret gladium in caput archiepiscopi, brachium cujusdam qui adstabat clerici fere abscidit, et ipsum pariter in capite vulneravit christum Domini. Extenderat enim idem clericus brachium suum super caput patris, ut ferientis acciperet, vel potius illideret (? elideret)[18] ictum.

(10) (Anon. V.) Dehinc inclinato capite, plenus confessione, primum mortis ictum excepit, animamque Deo reddidit ; corpus vero exanime ad terram concidit. Primus vero tortorum verticem[19] capitis ei praecidit ;

[228] (11) (Anon. X.) Tunc quidam ex praefatis filiis Leviathan, elevato gladio [quem] tenebat, clerici praedicti brachium fere amputavit ; eodemque

---

[18] "Ward off (elideret)" should probably be read for "illideret."

[19] "Verticem" is also used by William (and without "caput") for "the crown" (324). No other writer says that the Martyr fell at the first blow.

Lamb of God,[20] destroying his own [spiritual] Father in the womb of his Mother.[21]

[229] (12) (Garnier) Now sees St. Thomas well his martyrdom at hand. His hands placed to his face, he renders himself to God's doom, To the martyr St. Denis, to whom sweet France belongs, And to the saints of the Church he commends himself at once, The cause of Holy Church and his own likewise.

[230] William came foremost ; no will has he to pray to God : To be lighter for action he will carry no hauberk ; "The traitor to the king" he begins to demand.[22] When they could not cast the Saint outside the Minster, Within it, he proceeded to give him a mighty blow upon his head ;

[231] So that it carried away the top of the crown thereof, And struck down the scalp[23] and greatly gashed it. The sword glanced thence on to his left shoulder, Sheared off his mantle and his clothes even to the skin, And cut Edward's arm almost in two.

---

ictu agnum Deo immolandum[20] in capite percussit, patrem proprium in matris utero[21] perimens.

[229] Or veit bien saint Thomas sun martire
en présent.
Les mains mist à sun vis, à Dampnedeu se rent,
Al martir saint Denis, cui dulce France apent,
E as sainz de l'Yglise se commande erraument,
La cause seinte Yglise et la sue ensement.
[230] Willames vint avant, ne volt Deu aorer.
Pur estre plus legiers, n'i volt hauberc porter.

Le traïtur le Rei commence à demander.[22]
Quant ne porent le saint hors del muster geter,
Enz el chief de l'espée grant cop li va doner ;
[231] Si ke de la corone le cupel en porta,
Et la hure[23] abati et granment entama.
Sur l'espaulle senestre l'espée li cola,
Le mantel et les dras très k'al quir encisa,
E le braz Edward près tut en dous colpa.
ll. 5486-5500.

[20] "Sacrificial Lamb of God," from Grim (218).

[21] [228a] "In the womb of his mother" means (294a) "in the church." So Herbert (*Mat.* iii. 510) "patrem suum in ipso matris suae utero decalvantes."

[22] This and the two previous lines seem out of place, belonging rather to the entrance into the Cathedral than to the present moment. Ll. 5491-5500 look like a short summary that has found its way into the text from a first draft.

[23] "Hure" is (Godefroy) "poil qui couvre la tête, et tête d'homme ou de bête." A comparison of Garnier with Anon. I. shews that they agree exactly, except that the latter substitutes "cap (pileum)" for "scalp." Did Garnier mistake "chapel" meaning "head-gear" for "chapel" meaning "skull" or "head" (253)? A friend suggests that "pileus" may be an error, from "poil."

[232] (13) (The *Saga*) Now that the man of God, Archbishop Thomas, seeth that his life-day is waning—for his enemies shake their swords over his head—he turneth to the east, towards that altar of our Lady, God's Mother, which was nearest to him, and whereat he had stood in those steps of the Holy Ghost which we mentioned before. He bendeth down on both knees before the altar [24] with these, the last words that could be heard through the loud noise of God's enemies, saying, " Into the hands of Almighty God and of His most blessed Mother, the holy Mary, and of the Patrons of this church, the holy Dionysius, and all Saints, I commit myself and the cause of the Church."

[233] Next to this, spring forward the wild wolves on the gentle herd; the degenerate sons, on their own father; the cruellest murderers, upon the innocent victim of Jesus Christ. First among them, William of Traci dealeth a blow to the Archbishop, aiming at his head: but inasmuch as the clerk Edward standeth in dauntless faith nearest to his lord in this war-storm, the blow falleth on the arm of him, cutting it nearly through, and then on the head of the Archbishop, who received the less of it that the clerk had taken off the greater weight of the wound.

[234] (i.) (Stanley, pp. 91-2) Fitzurse, glowing all over with rage, retorted—" I owe you no fealty or homage, contrary to my fealty to the King," and waving the sword over his head, cried " Strike, strike ! " (" Ferez, ferez "), but *merely dashed off his cap*.[25]

---

[24] "Before the altar." See 62, for another instance of the *Saga's* sacrifice of fact to fitness.

[25] "Merely dashed off his cap." The Archbishop at this stage appears to have stood quite still; and it is extremely unlikely that Fitzurse would miss his aim and "merely dash off his cap," unless Grim's arm intervened. Moreover, if it was a down stroke, and not a merely terrifying feint, it could hardly strike off his "cap" without doing something more. Lastly, it seems odd that a knight who has missed his aim should call on the others to strike, *till he has himself struck*. William and Garnier both agree in making the words " Strike ! Strike ! " proceed from some one *who has himself struck an effective blow first*.

[235] The Archbishop covered his eyes with his joined hands, bent his neck, and said, "I commend my cause and the cause of the Church to God, to St. Denys the martyr of France, to St. Alfege, and to *the saints of the Church.*[26]

[236] Meanwhile Tracy, who, *since his fall, had thrown off his hauberk* to move more easily, sprang forward, and struck a more decided blow.[27]

[237] Grim, who up to this moment had his arm round Becket, threw it up, *wrapped in a cloak*, to intercept the blade, Becket exclaiming, "*Spare this defence.*"[28]

[238] The sword lighted on the arm of the monk, which fell wounded or broken; and *he fled disabled to the nearest altar*, probably that of St. Benedict within the chapel.

[239] It is a proof of the confusion of the scene, that Grim the receiver of the blow, as well as most of the narrators, believed it to have been dealt by Fitzurse, while Tracy, *who is known to have been the man* from his subsequent boast, believed that the monk whom he had wounded was John of Salisbury.[29]

---

[26] "The saints of the Church." More probably, "of this church," *i.e.* St. Elphege and others, the special patron saints of Canterbury Cathedral (**255-7.**)

[27] "Since his fall." It has been shewn above that probably only Fitzurse, and not Tracy, had been rebuffed. But in any case, there was hardly time between the rebuff and the stroke to take off the hauberk. Garnier (l. 5491), to whom Stanley refers for the statement, says that Tracy "would not wear a hauberk, in order to be lighter"; but he places this *before the call for the "traitor," and before the endeavour to drag the Archbishop from the Cathedral.* It may have been taken off, in order to facilitate the attempt to place the Archbishop upon Tracy's shoulders; but Garnier gives the impression that Tracy *entered* the Cathedral with his hauberk off, and that this was the reason for his being "in front," because he was "lighter." See, however, **247.**

[28] The only authority for these statements is Anon II., a worthless and unveracious writer, who inserts what never happened in order to draw an absurd comparison between St. Peter actively smiting with the sword and Edward Grim passively interposing his arm!

[29] "Tracy, who is known to have been the man." William (**321**), who is the writer that records Tracy's boast about wounding John, merely says that they *conjectured*, from this boast, that he was the man who had wounded Grim. Against such vague hearsay evidence, we have the evidence of Grim as an *ear-witness*, as well as eye-witness. If the knights were in full armour, he might

[240] The spent force of the stroke descended on Becket's head, grazed the crown, and finally *rested* on his left shoulder, cutting through the clothes *and skin*.[30]

[241] (ii.) (Tennyson)

FITZURSE (*advances with drawn sword*). I told thee that I should remember thee!

BECKET. Profligate pander!

FITZURSE. Do you hear that? Strike, strike.

[*Strikes off the* ARCHBISHOP'S *mitre, and wounds him in the forehead.*

[242] BECKET (*covers his eyes with his hand*). I do commend my cause to God, the Virgin,

St. Denis of France and St. Alphege of England,

And all the tutelar saints of Canterbury.

[GRIM *wraps his arms about the* ARCHBISHOP.

Spare this defence, dear brother.

[TRACY *has arisen, and approaches, hesitatingly, with his sword raised.*

FITZURSE. Strike him, Tracy!

ROSAMUND (*rushing down steps from the choir*). No, No, No, No!

FITZURSE. This wanton here. De Morville, Hold her away.

DE MORVILLE. I hold her.

ROSAMUND (*held back by* DE MORVILLE, *and stretching out her arms*). Mercy, mercy,

As you would hope for mercy.

FITZURSE. Strike, I say.

---

not have known Fitzurse by *sight;* but he heard the Archbishop call him by name ("Reinalde"), and thrust him back, and then saw the same knight, after being thrust back, rush on vindictively to inflict the first stroke, by which his own arm was almost severed. Grim's evidence is worth twenty hearsay reports about confessions, or boasts, of Tracy's.

[30] "Skin." Hardly "cut through the clothes *and* skin." Nor does the blow seem to have "*rested on* the left shoulder." The sword "glided" (Garnier "cola," Anon. I. "lapsus est") "on," or "over," the left shoulder, then it "cut into," or "rent downwards or onwards" (Garnier "encisa," Anon. "inscidit") his garments, "down to the skin (ad nudum)," but apparently not so as to "cut through" the "skin." If it had, the wound would probably have been mentioned later on in the enumeration of the Martyr's wounds. Probably the sword sheared off the clothes on the left shoulder and side.

[243] GRIM. *O God, O noble knights, O sacrilege!
Strike our Archbishop in his own cathedral!
The Pope, the King will curse you—the whole world
Abhor you; ye will die the death of dogs!
Nay, nay, good Tracy.* [*Lifts his arm.*
FITZURSE. Answer not, but strike.

§ 2. *Who struck the first blow?*

[244] There is a discrepancy as to the name of the knight that struck the first blow. Grim says that it was the knight that had been just irritated by his rebuff, whom the Archbishop had addressed as "Reinald." Anon I., who surpasses the rest in clearness as well as in vivid brevity—says distinctly that it was "Rainald." William also, in the *present* passage (but see below, 321), speaks of Fitzurse as the striker, and as "desiring to gain a trophy from *the first blow.*" On the other hand, Fitzstephen says that it was Tracy; and Herbert, after mentioning Tracy as the man whom the Archbishop shook off, now declares that it was "the above-named" that aimed the first blow, which almost severed Grim's arm, and wounded the Archbishop's head.

William appears to be inconsistent with himself. For, whereas he here represents Reginald as striking the first blow, and makes no mention of Grim, he says, later on, that (1) Grim did not know who had wounded him, but (2) "we conjecture" the name "from the fact that William de Tracy afterwards boasted of having cut off John of Salisbury's arm." If Grim's narrative is genuine, the first of these two statements is false. The second is a mere conjecture, based on hearsay.

[245] The discrepancy may possibly in part be explained by the fact that those writers who described Fitzurse as simply striking off the Archbishop's cap, were near the altar of Benedict, *on his right*, where they could

not perceive that the sword, besides striking off the Archbishop's cap, really inflicted a wound on the *left side* of his head. That this was the fact, is clearly stated by Anon. I.: " As he said this, Rainald came up and struck a heavy blow sideways on his head, and sheared off the top of his crown and *cast down his cap*. The sword glanced on the left shoulder, and passed on into his vestments, rending them even to the skin."[1] It is scarcely possible to doubt that these clear details are a statement of what actually occurred.

[246] Fitzstephen, who has told us that *the visors of the knights were down*,[2] might well be unable to recognize them ; and it will be observed that up to this point he does not attempt to distinguish them by name: it is " quidam," " aliquis," " aliquis," " unus grassator," " aliquis," " quidam." Possibly, therefore, Fitzstephen may here be recording what had been "conjectured" (as William tells us) from the report of Tracy's boast. A much surer guide would be the Archbishop's " Reinald " addressed to Fitzurse, *audible to Grim, and certain not to have been invented by him*. Fitzstephen's omission of " Reginald," in any words uttered by the Archbishop, suggests that he was by no means so close to the Archbishop as Grim was. It may be added that, if Fitzstephen was *at some distance*, and saw the Archbishop's " cap " fall off and the sword glance from his head to his shoulder, while he stood erect, he might mistake this for " a blow with the flat of the sword *on the shoulder.*" To

---

[1] " Passed on into . . . rending," an attempt to render "'inscindens." Did Garnier ("encisa") take "inscindens" as "incidens"? The fragments of Benedict's narrative, after describing the cap struck off with the edge of the sword, speak of the Archbishop as "awaiting a *second blow*." If, therefore, we had the whole of Benedict's narrative, we might find that he agreed with Grim and Anon. I. in regarding the stroke that struck off the cap as a real blow and not as a feint.

[2] Ancient pictures may be quite untrustworthy. The one given in Knight's *Pictorial History*, vol. i. p. 456, from a painting hung at the tomb of Henry IV., represents the murder as taking place before the altar, where it did not take place : and the murderers have visors up and surcoats on.

him, then, the first *real blow would seem to be the one that followed*, which was inflicted by *Tracy*.

§ 3. *Garnier's testimony*

[247] Garnier, it must be admitted, distinctly affirms that the striker was Tracy. But, in a point of this kind, his evidence is not on the same footing as that of an eye-witness. His narrative shews that he had taken great pains to piece together evidence that could hardly harmonize, and, with all his pains, he has left traces of failure. It has been shewn above that his introduction of Tracy, here, reads as though he were describing the knight's first entrance into the Cathedral, when they called out for the "traitor":—

> "William came in front, he had no will to pray to God,
> In order to be the lighter, he would not carry a hauberk.
> He *begins to call for the traitor to the King.*
> When they could not cast the Saint out of the Minster,
> He proceeded to give him a great blow on the head."

All this seems quite out of place.

[248] Again, Garnier omits all mention of the striking off of the "cap." He also represents Tracy, and not Fitz-urse, as saying "Strike! strike!" And that his evidence was based on Tracy's boast he confesses almost in the same words (**287**) as William uses. At the beginning of his description of the entry of the knights into the Cathedral, he says that they wore hauberks, and this is the unanimous testimony of those who describe their arms at all. Not a single writer says that Tracy was an exception. Yet, later on (**288**), Garnier describes the "green coat and variegated cloak" of Tracy, and says that he was "well known by sight and voice." Contrast this (1) with the silence of all the rest, (2) with the express statement of Fitzstephen that the knights were in full armour, "covered except for the eyes," and (3) with the fact that even William, when trying to

shew that Tracy was the striker, merely puts forward his view as a "conjecture," based on Tracy's confession, and says nothing about any tokens by which he could be distinguished.

[249] Lastly, add (4) the fact that the *tendency exhibited by pictures* in early times was to discard the monotony of four visored knights in complete panoply by diversifying them in various ways. Thus, in one of the earliest—perhaps, as Stanley suggests, painted about February 1173 [1]—Fitzurse and Tracy have coats of mail up to their eyes, but Morville is without helmet or armour. In another, painted on a board at the head of the tomb of Henry IV., Bret has boars' heads on his surcoat, and Fitzurse bears: Tracy also has what (in the engravings) appears to be a mantle over his surcoat. The faces of all are clearly visible.

[250] All these considerations lead to the conclusion that, when Garnier came to Canterbury in 1172, he found existing already some difference of opinion as to the circumstances of the first blow inflicted on St. Thomas. In his poem, as well as in William's narrative, there are indications of a tendency to combine parts of one tradition, which assigned the first blow, rightly, to Fitzurse, with parts of another, which assigned it, wrongly, to Tracy. If Fitzurse's blow left the Archbishop standing still erect, it is quite possible that Tracy—who struck the second and third blows and brought the Martyr to the ground—may have himself believed, and may have said in confession, that the first blow was his.

[251] If Grim was thrown to the ground by the shock of Fitzurse's blow, and had not time to arise from the ground before Tracy struck, it was quite natural that Tracy,

---

[1] Stanley, p. 113 "A much more faithful representation is given in an illuminated Psalter in the British Museum (Harl. 1502), undoubtedly of the period, and, as Becket is depicted without the nimbus, probably soon after, if not before, the canonization." See frontispiece.

in the excitement of the moment, should suppose Grim's fall (as well as the Archbishop's) was due to his sword; and so, returning that night to Saltwood, he might boast that he had "cut off the arm of Becket's faithful companion —of course, John of Salisbury." Thus Tracy would naturally originate a second error.

[252] As regards Garnier's omission of "the striking off of the cap," the question cannot be satisfactorily settled till some one gives us a full analytic comparison of the Latin of Anon. I. and the French of Garnier, so as to shew whether, either borrowed directly from the other, or from some original of the other.[2] Meantime, there are two reasonable explanations. (1) He may have omitted it because nothing came of the act, and because it was difficult to gather whether it was the result of a feint to terrify, or of a blow intended to kill. (2) The early picture (of 1173) above described is said by Stanley to represent St. Thomas's "grey cap dropping to the ground," but in the picture at the tomb of Henry IV.—according to Stanley again—"on the ground lies the bloody scalp, or cap, *it is difficult to determine which.*"

[253] If that is so in the second picture, may it not have been so in other and earlier pictures? A "grey cap" does not lend itself to picturesque martyrology. If it was to be retained at all, the most poetic shape for it was that given in the *Saga*, "his mitre." But might it not be no "cap" or "mitre" at all, but the scalp shorn off with a small portion of the skull?[3] If the French original of

---

[2] Garnier, for example, may have borrowed from some French early original draft of Anon. I. And it is quite possible that, in some passages, Garnier may have rendered the meaning of the original correctly, and the Latin translator incorrectly. Thus where Anon. I. describes Becket as "*tutus* et capucciatus (*safe* and hooded)," Garnier (l. 217) may be right in his "*tut* enchaperunez (*wholly* hooded)." See **25***a*.

[3] This represents what Garnier may have thought, but not the fact. The fact was that the scalp remained attached to the head, so that it could not fall to the ground.

Anon. I. described the "cap" as "chapel," might not "chapel" be there used in its sense of "dome of the skull," *i.e.*, as Garnier calls it here, "cupule," but later on (292*a*) "chapel"?

[254] On the whole, it is probable that Garnier is here wrong, and that Anon. I. represents the truth. The "cap" was struck off, and a portion of the skull was shaved off at the same time. Grim, falling to the ground with his arm nearly broken, and perhaps stunned by the shock, noticed nothing except that the Archbishop (thanks to him) still stood erect. Robert of Merton perhaps—or whoever else inspired Anon. I.—standing a little behind Grim, and having opportunity for seeing, records what he saw, and records it for this reason, that some, from a greater distance, thought the falling of the cap was caused by a feint of Fitzurse. It was not so. It was the accompaniment of the first wound, which had been intended to be fatal.

§ 4. *The Archbishop's words*

[255] In Grim's narrative, St. Thomas commends himself "to God, and St. Mary (sanctae Mariae), and the blessed Martyr Denis (Dionysius)." Anon. I. omits "St. Mary," and adds "St. Elphege." Garnier has, "To the doom of God, to the Martyr St. Denis to whom sweet France belongs, and to the Saints of the Church," where there is nothing to shew that "the Saints" are the Patron Saints of the Cathedral.

[256] In favour of the insertion of "St. Elphege" is Fitzstephen's statement that, at an earlier point in the narrative, "he commended himself to the Lord, and used the names of the holy archbishops and martyrs St. Denis and St. Elphege."[1] Perhaps the commendation included

---

[1] This was just after (171) the "blow on the shoulders with the flat of the sword," which has been shewn to be probably a confused representation

all these. St. Thomas was, from his youth, devoted to St. Mary, and could hardly have omitted her name. But Fitzstephen mentions an earlier commendation, at the moment when he received the threat of death: "I receive death in the name of the Lord, and I commend my soul and the cause of the Church to God and the blessed Mary and the holy patrons of the Church" (here closely agreeing with John of Salisbury). If the Archbishop had quite recently mentioned the name of the Virgin, it is conceivable that afterwards the names of the Martyr St. Denis, and the English Archbishop and Martyr, St. Elphege, may have come to his lips, next to the name of God.

[257] Herbert of Bosham, though omitting St. Elphege, mentions "the sainted Advocates (advocatis) of the Church of Canterbury and the blessed Dionysius, apostle of the Franks." Antecedently, it seems probable that Anon. I. and Fitzstephen are right, and that the English-born Martyr did mention the earlier English martyr St. Elphege, whose outlandish name some may have concealed under the term "patronis," or "advocatis, Cantuariensis ecclesiae."

The only difficulty is, to explain why the name was omitted by Grim, who was "English by birth." Could it be that Grim was sensitive to the fact that French readers would not know who St. Elphege was? Above (**44**), Grim describes the Archbishop as mentioning that saint in his Christmas sermon "as is asserted."

Herbert's "apostle of the Franks" and Garnier's "to whom sweet France belongs" are, of course, the explanatory comments of the writers, not the words of the Martyr. It is possible that Anon. I. may have inserted "St. Elphege" as representing the spirit of St. Thomas's words, as much as to say, "He did not mean *all* the saints of Holy Church,

---

of Fitzurse's first blow that "glided on the shoulder." Hence the words are probably placed too early by Fitzstephen, and ought to come here.

he meant the Patron Saints of the Minster, and especially the Martyr Archbishop, St. Elphege."

§ 5. *Stanley and Tennyson*

[258] (i.) Stanley appears to have been misled by attaching too much importance to the evidence of William's Appendix,[1] and of the latest of all the authoritative writers, Herbert—and that, though the latter warns us that his authority is simply the confession of Tracy. Herbert's knowledge of this may have been derived from mere hearsay: and Stanley himself has convincingly shewn that such a cloud of legend enveloped the history of the four knights within a very few years from the murder, that any tradition about what they said or did—especially in so late a writer as Herbert—must be regarded with very great suspicion.

[259] The consequences of assigning the first blow to Tracy are these. We must then suppose that Fitzurse's intended blow was a failure, and that it merely dashed off "the cap," although it was meant to kill. What followed then? A pause, during which Fitzurse does nothing, but calls "Strike! strike!" Meanwhile the Archbishop has time to commend himself to God. But could the commendation have been heard while a bloodthirsty knight was shouting at the top of his voice "Strike! strike!" almost over the head of the commender? And what were the other knights doing? It is supposed by Stanley that Tracy "since his fall, had thrown off his hauberk"; and it may be alleged that he was rising and disencumbering himself while the Martyr was praying and Fitzurse shouting. But we have shewn above that Tracy did not "fall." It is expressly said, by those who describe his rebuff, that he "*almost* fell," and a man does not take long to recover from "almost falling." Probably he was not even "rebuffed." And that

---

[1] See 320-4.

he took off his hauberk now (if at any time) is attested by no evidence, and is highly improbable.

[260] Beside these consequences, we have to suppose, according to Stanley, that Grim was wrong in saying that his arm was wounded by the "Reinald" whom he heard addressed by the Archbishop, and that the most accurate of all our writers (Anon. I.) is wrong in his exact description of Fitzurse's blow as striking off the cap, wounding the head, shearing off the clothes, and almost breaking Grim's arm.

[261] (ii.) Tennyson represents the Archbishop as uttering his commendation of his cause to God and the Saints *after* he has received his first wound from Fitzurse. This, beside going against all the best authorities, seems improbable in itself. After a blow that had removed a portion of his skull, it might be possible for the Archbishop, physically, still to stand erect, and even to repeat a few familiar words in a low tone, but it seems unlikely that he could utter a prayer mentioning a number of names, and requiring some faculty of mind and memory. Moreover, would he have had time for it? In order to give him time, Tennyson, like Stanley, represents Tracy as actually thrown on the ground (which was not the fact according to *any* accounts), and as "rising and approaching hesitatingly"; and in the meantime, during the minute or two that elapse while no blow is struck, we have to suppose the infuriated Fitzurse, after tasting blood, to be doing nothing! Surely Tracy, or some one else, would rush in at once after Fitzurse's ineffectual blow. The work was one of hot blood and speed, when it had once begun.

[262] Moreover, the acts and words of Grim, in Tennyson's drama, are not suited to the real circumstances. Grim certainly "wrapped his arms about the Archbishop": but that took place before, when the knights were trying to drag him out of the Cathedral. Grim probably kept his arms wrapped round him till he saw Fitzurse's sword descending

on the Martyr's head. Then he unwrapped them, or one of them, and raised it to avert the stroke. But according to the drama, what was Grim doing when Fitzurse struck? Seemingly nothing. He "wraps his arms round him" after the stroke, when there is no use in it. Grim is behind, not before, so that there is no "defence" in the act. Yet the Martyr is supposed to address him in the words "Spare this *defence*, dear brother"! In the untrustworthy narrative (226) from which these words are taken, the word "defence" had, at all events, some meaning, since it referred to the previously described uplifting and interposition of Grim's arm; but in the drama, coming *before* that uplifting and interposition, the word has no meaning at all.

[263] To represent Grim, at this crisis, as telling the knights that they were committing sacrilege, is justified by Garnier; and that other untrustworthy writer just mentioned describes Grim as expostulating. But does not this make Grim talk unnecessarily when a man of action would not talk at all? Even if he must talk, ought he to be condemned to say that "the King" (about whom what could the poor clerk from Cambridge know?) would "curse" them? And ought he to call Tracy "good"? Was he likely to know Tracy? Even if he did, how could he discern him if in armour? And again, if he did, would a clerk exasperate a King's knight by accosting him in that familiar style? Surely, he would (as in Garnier) address all the knights collectively; or if he addressed any one of them singly by any appellation, it would have been "my lord."

As for the introduction of Rosamund, that, of course, is a purely dramatic question. But to many it will seem that the scene is one for men alone, and that she is even more out of place than Calphurnia at the foot of Pompey's statue when "great Caesar fell."

CHAPTER X

THE DEATH AND OUTRAGE

§ 1. *The different accounts*

[264] (1) (Grim) . . . Afterwards, on receiving another blow on the head, even then he still remained immovable. But on being struck a third time, the Martyr bent his knees and arms, in the act of offering himself as a living victim, saying in a low voice: "For the name of Jesus and the protection of the Church I am prepared to embrace death." But a third knight,[1] when he had thus[2] fallen,[3] inflicted a severe wound on him, and, in the stroke, not only dashed his sword against the stone [pavement], but also separated the crown, which was [unusually] large, in such a way from the head that the blood, whitening from the brain, and the brain no less reddening from the blood, empurpled the face with the colours at once of the lily and

---

[264] (1) (Grim) Deinde, alio ictu in capite recepto, adhuc quoque permansit immobilis. Tertio vero percussus, martyr genua flexit et cubitos, seipsum hostiam viventem offerendo, dicens summissa voce, "Pro nomine Jesu et ecclesiae tuitione mortem amplecti paratus sum." At tertius miles[1] ita[2] procumbenti[3] grave vulnus inflixit, quo ictu et gladium collisit lapidi, et coronam, quae ampla fuit, ita a capite separavit ut sanguis albens ex cerebro, cerebrum nihilominus rubens ex

---

[1] "A third knight": this is Brito. The two strokes described before ("alio," "tertio") were inflicted by Tracy. Grim would naturally know none of the four names except the one that he *heard* ("Reinalde") from the Archbishop addressing the striker of the first blow.

[2] Instead of "ita . . . ut" with subjunctive, the writer uses "ita . . . quo ictu" with indicative: but it has been taken differently by Anon. X. (285).

[3] "Procumbenti" ought to mean "while falling," but it probably means "when he had fallen," as it certainly does later on (270a). If he had not fallen, the sword could not so easily have been broken against the pavement.

the rose, [the colours] of the Church as Virgin and as Mother, [the colours that represent] the life and the death[4] of a Confessor and a Martyr.

[265] A fourth knight kept off those who pressed thronging in, in order that the rest might with more freedom and licence perpetrate the murder. But a fifth (no knight, he, but that clerk who had entered with the knights)—to the intent that a fifth wound [like Christ's] might not be wanting to one who in other points had imitated Christ—placed his foot on the neck of the holy Priest and precious Martyr, and (horrible to relate!) scattered the brains and blood about the pavement, exclaiming to the rest, "Let us go hence, knights. This fellow will not rise again any more."

[266] (2) (Fitzstephen) The Archbishop, wiping off with his arm, and beholding, the blood that streamed from his head,[5] gave thanks to God, saying, "Into thy hands, O Lord, I commend my spirit."[6]

---

sanguine, lilii et rosae coloribus virginis et matris ecclesiae faciem confessoris et martyris vita et morte[4] purpuraret.

[265] Quartus miles supervenientes abegit, ut caeteri liberius ac licentius homičidium perpetrarent. Quintus vero, non miles, sed clericus ille qui cum militibus intraverat, ne martyri quinta plaga deesset, qui in aliis Christum fuerat imitatus, posito pede super collum sancti sacerdotis et martyris pretiosi (horrendum dictu), cerebrum cum sanguine per pavimentum spargens, caeteris exclamavit, "Abeamus hinc, milites, iste ulterius non resurget."

[266] (2) (Fitzstephen) Archiepiscopus a capite defluum cum brachio detergens et videns cruorem,[5] gratias Deo agebat, dicens, "In manus tuas, Domine, commendo spiritum meum."[6]

---

[4] It seems to have been a tradition with writers of the "Passion of St. Thomas" to liken the white and red to the white of an innocent life and the purple of a martyr's death, so that "vita et morte" probably means "with life and death [as it were, represented by their colours, white and red]" (331, 334).

[5] "Cum" appears to be used for "with" signifying instrumentality (as perhaps also at the end of this passage "cum mucrone"). The author can hardly mean "flowing from his head together with his [left] arm," for he has made no mention of the "arm" as being wounded, and he says, a little later, that all the wounds were on the head. "And beholding" seems to mean "and beholding [from the stains on his sleeve, what a copious stream it was]": that is to say, "beholding that it was the prelude to death."

[6] "Lord, etc." These are the words (from Ps. xxxi. 5) assigned by Luke

[267] A second stroke was dealt on his head, whereat also he fell flat on his face, first having knelt, clasping and stretching out his hands to God, near an altar, which was there, belonging to Saint Benedict. And he took pains, or [rather received] grace, that he might fall in honourable fashion,[7] covering himself down to the ancles with his pallium, as though to adore and pray. He fell on the right, on his way to God's right hand.

[268] When he was fallen (or "falling"),[8] Richard Brito struck him with such force that even the sword was broken against his head and against the pavement of the church: "Take this," said he, "for love of my lord, William, the King's brother...."[9]

[269] Four[10] wounds, in all, had the holy Archbishop, all in the head: and the whole of the crown of his head was lopped away. Then might we see how his limbs did

[267] Datur in caput ejus ictus secundus, quo et ille in faciem concidit, positis primo genibus, conjunctis et extensis ad Deum manibus, secus aram, quae ibi erat, sancti Benedicti; et curam habuit,[7] vel gratiam, ut honeste caderet, pallio suo coopertus usque ad talos, quasi adoraturus et oraturus. Super dextram cecidit, ad dextram Dei iturus.

[268] Eum procumbentem[8] Ricardus Brito percussit tanta vi ut et gladius ad caput ejus et ad ecclesiae pavimentum frangeretur: et ait "Hoc habeas pro amore domini mei Willelmi, fratris regis...."[9]

[269] Quatuor[10] omnino habuit ictus sanctus archiepiscopus, omnes in capite; et corona capitis tota ei amputata est. Tunc videre erat, quomodo artus spiritui

---

xxiii. 46 to Jesus, as His last utterance, where Matthew and Mark mention merely a "cry."

[7] Fitzstephen (who is full of allusions to the Latin poets) probably borrowed this point from Ovid's description of the death of Lucretia, *Fast.* ii. 833 "Tunc quoque, jam moriens, ne non procumbat *honeste* Respicit. Haec etiam *cura* cadentis erat."

[8] Probably means "when he had fallen," as in 270*a*. See also 264.

[9] The writer here adds that the Archbishop had interdicted William's marriage with a lady whose former husband had been a cousin of William's.

[10] "Four" probably includes Tracy's second blow, which, with one from Fitzurse, would make three: and Brito's would make the fourth. Possibly Fitzstephen abstains from details as he is not certain about them. It seems improbable that he would call Mauclerc's extraction of the brains, after death, a "wound."

obedient service to his spirit. For as in mind, so too in body, it was seen that he made no resistance to death either by parrying or avoidance.¹¹ For his death was voluntary, welcomed out of his desire to be with God—not a mere violent death from the swords of the knights.

[270] A certain Hugh of Horsea, known as Mauclerc, after the holy Martyr had fallen,¹² set his foot on his neck, and drew forth from the hollow of the amputated crown blood and brains with the point of his sword. . . .¹³

[271] (3) (John) For it did not suffice them to profane the church with the blood and slaughter of a priest, and to violate a most sacred day, unless they also lopped off that crown which had been dedicated to God by the anointing of the sacred chrism, and—horrible even to speak of!—drew forth with their murderous swords the brains of the Martyr when he had breathed his last, and most cruelly scattered them on the pavement with his blood and bones.¹⁴

---

famulabantur. Nam sicut nec mente, ita nec membrorum objectu vel dejectu¹¹ morti visus est depugnare ; qui mortem excepit magis ex Dei desiderio voluntariam, quam de gladiis militum violentam.

[270] Quidam Hugo de Horsea, cognomento Malus Clericus, sancti martyris procumbentis¹² collum pede comprimens, a concavitate coronae amputatae cum mucrone cruorem et cerebrum extrahebat. . . . "¹³

[271] (3) (John) Non enim suffecit iis sanguine sacerdotis et nece profanare ecclesiam et diem sacratissimum incestare, nisi, corona capitis, quam sacri chrismatis unctio Deo dicaverat, amputata (quod et dictu horribile est) funestis gladiis jam defuncti ejicerent cerebrum et per pavimentum cum cruore et ossibus crudelissime spargerent ; . . .¹⁴

---

¹¹ "Objectu etc." seems to mean "by putting an arm in front, to *parry*, or casting his body down, to *avoid*."

¹² [270a] "Fallen" (not "falling") must be the meaning of "procumbentis" here, as it probably is in 264. This sentence is inserted rather abruptly, as though it were an afterthought.

¹³ In a passage somewhat later on (omitted by J.) the writer likens the white and red visible in the martyr's wounds to the lilies and roses of the church.

¹⁴ Contrast Grim's words (265) "*not a knight*, but a clerk." John might be excused for writing thus in a letter on the night of the Martyrdom, but hardly for repeating the statement in a biography.

[272] (4) (William) At this word,[15] I, who speak, thinking (even as the rest) that I likewise was to be "struck" with the sword,—as being conscious of sins and unfit for martyrdom [16]—turning my back in rapid flight, ascended the steps,[17] beating my hands together [for horror].[18] Forthwith some that were still standing to pray dispersed [or, "dispersed to pray"]. For no slight fear was cast on all by the Lord, but a great fear indeed, and one that might befall even the most steadfast. . . . So the murderers, instigated by the minister of confusion, accumulating wounds on the [original] wound, dashed out his brains.[19]

[272] (4) (William) Ego qui loquor, hoc verbo,[16] sicut et caeteri, arbitrans me gladio pariter percutiendum, tanquam peccatorum conscius et minus idoneus martyrio,[16] celeri tergiversatione gradus [17] ascendi, complodens manus.[18] Protinus quidam stantes adhuc ad orationem dispersi sunt. Non enim levem omnibus timorem Dominus incussit, sed magnum, et qui posset cadere in quemvis constantissimum. . . . Itaque ministro confusionis instigati carnifices, in vulnere vulnera conferentes, cerebrum excusserunt.[19]

---

[15] At Fitzurse's cry, "Strike! Strike!"
[16] Comp. what John of Salisbury says to the Archbishop in the palace (*Mat.* iv. 74), "We are sinners and not yet prepared to die: and I see no one (except you) that wants to die for nothing."
[17] "Steps." As he does not say "certain steps" or tell us what "steps" are meant, it is probable that the writer means the same "steps" that are frequently mentioned by the other writers, as leading to the choir. The same cause that induced the monks to lead the Archbishop up these steps, would induce William to run up them, namely, the fact that they led to the High Altar, which even the knights would probably respect.
[18] "Beating my hands together," an action recognized by classical writers as indicative of extreme agitation. Quintilian calls it "theatrical (scenicum)." Stanley translates it "with clasped hands": but that does not quite express the extremity of fear and despair.
[19] This bald, abrupt, and inaccurate sentence was probably written by William (like the corresponding narrative of John) immediately after the Martyrdom; perhaps on the same night, in his diary. It will be seen that he adds an Appendix in which, apparently, he relieves the knights collectively from the charge of "dashing out the brains" (324).
What William says about "accumulating wounds on the wound" is confirmed by the rest, *e.g.* by Benedict, "enlarged the preceding wound."
[272a] Who is "the minister of confusion"? Fitzurse, or Mauclerc? It can hardly be a term for Satan, who would rather be "the *author* of confusion."

[273] (5) (Benedict) And with head inclined he awaited the arrival of a second wound.[20] And, when the second wound was inflicted on his head, with body straightened, as though prostrating himself for prayer, he fell flat on the earth. But a third [knight],[21] lopping off a great portion of the skull, horribly enlarged the preceding wound.

[274] But the fourth, being chidden by one of them because he delayed to strike, directing his sword with great force at the same wound, broke the weapon to pieces on the marble pavement, and left to the church both the blade and the hilt. . . .[22]

[275] . . . Nor did it seem to suffice the same son of Satan to have perpetrated such an outrage against God's Priest unless also—horrible to speak of!—he plunged his sword into the Martyr's most holy head, and drew out the brains after he had now breathed his last, scattering them most cruelly about the pavement, and calling aloud to his partners in that crime "He is dead. Let us go hence with all speed." Hence it may be conjectured that they feared lest. . . .[23]

[273] (5) (Benedict) Et inclinato capite secundi vulneris praestolabatur adventum.[20] Secundo vero vulnere capiti ejus inflicto, recto corpore quasi ad orationem prostratus in terram corruit. Tertius [21] autem plurimam testae portionem amputando vulnus praecedens horribiliter ampliavit.

[274] Quartus autem, ab uno eorum quod ferire tardaret correptus, in idem vulnus vi magna gladium vibravit, gladioque in pavimento marmoreo confracto, tam cuspidem quam gladii sui capulum reliquit ecclesiae. . . .[22]

[275] Nec sufficere videbatur eidem filio Sathanae in Dei sacerdotem tantum perpetrasse flagitium, nisi etiam, quod dictu horribile est, injecto in sanctissimum caput ejus gladio, jam defuncto cerebrum ejiceret, et per pavimentum crudelissime spargeret, sceleris ejusdem participibus clamans, "Mortuus est, quantocius eamus hinc." Unde timuisse illos conjici potest. . . .[23]

---

[20] No "first wound" has been mentioned in the extant fragments of Benedict: see 175, 222a.

[21] The writer passes from the "second *wound*" to the "third (*knight*)," assuming that each knight inflicted one wound. But this was not the case. Tracy struck twice, Morville not at all. "Tertium," a third (wound), would have been correct.

[22] [274a] This, Benedict proceeds to say, portended the breaking in pieces of the sword of oppression directed against the Church.

[23] [275a] The language very closely resembles that of John of Salisbury (271),

[276] (6) (Herbert) And by this time that sacred blood began to trickle forth along the face. So, perceiving [this], the Priest of the Most High, sacrificing himself to the Most High—straightway casting away the cap [24] that he had been wont to wear on his head, raising up his eyes to heaven, bending his knee, and clasping his hands before his face, after the manner of one praying [25]—in the temple [and] before the altar,[26] [as a true] priest, offered himself up a living sacrifice to God. ... And so he extends his neck,

---

[276] (6) (Herbert) Et jam sacer ille sanguis coepit emanare per faciem. Sentiens itaque sacerdos ille Altissimi, semet ipsum Altissimo immolans, immolationem jam inchoatam, confestim quod (*sic*) supra caput gestare consueverat abjecto [24] pileo, attollens in caelum oculos, genu flexo et, orantis modo, junctis ante se [25] manibus, in templo ante altare [26] sacerdos obtulit se ipsum hostiam vivam Deo. ... Extendit itaque collum, exponit caput, se et ecclesiae causam

---

which Benedict had probably read. But what John attributed to all the murderers, Benedict attributes to one, "the same son of Satan," whom he *seems* to call previously "the fourth (knight)."

Now what had this "fourth (knight)" done? He had—after being chidden for delay—aimed a great blow at the fallen body, but it is not said that he outraged the body of the Martyr *when dead*, but merely that he shattered his sword.

There is probably some error in the text. It seems to have been originally applied to *all* the knights: for this is the most natural way of explaining the "conjecture" that "*they*" were "afraid" of the people; in consequence of which *they* would say "Let *us* depart with all speed."

Or possibly Benedict may have here inserted (what the *Quadrilogus* omits) a description of Hugh Mauclerc as the instigator of the knights (comp. William (272*a*) "instigati ministro confusionis") and may then have proceeded thus: "It did not seem enough for *this son of Satan* that *they* (*i.e.* the knights) should have perpetrated. ... unless *he* also. ..."

[24] "Casting away (abjecto)." Herbert seems to regard the cap, not as being "struck down" or "cast down" ("decussus, dejectus," etc.) by the sword of Fitzurse, but as "cast away" by the Archbishop himself, in the act of preparing himself for his sacrificial death. This indicates that Herbert found a difficulty in the divergent traditions about "the cap."

[25] See 218-24, where Grim and Anon. I. say that he (1) lifted up his hands, or (2) placed his hands before his eyes. Herbert combines facts connected with the *first* wound—*i.e.* the casting off of the cap, and the raising of the hands, and the commendation of the Martyr's soul—with the "bending of the knees" which Grim places after the third wound.

[26] "Before the altar," inaccurately added in order to enhance the sacrificial aspect of the death (232).

exposes his head, commending himself and the cause of the Church, to God, and to Mary the blessed Mother of God, and to the Advocatory Saints of Canterbury church, and to St. Denis the Apostle of the French : [to St. Denis, I say] in order that the cause of the Church might, through the inspiration of God, be commended more especially to that one martyr in particular to whom he himself, in the church, by a similar martyrdom, was destined to be presently assimilated in respect of the kind of his death : this Martyr, like that, being (?) deprived of the scalp.[27]

[277] So after exposing himself [to the stroke],[28] he presently commended the cause of the Church, which he had pleaded, to its Patrons,[29] and prayed for his [people]. But why say I " prayed " ? Nay rather, although, in these butchers' hands, he had already begun to welter in his own blood, yet over his butchers still exercising the authority

Deo et beatae Dei genetrici Mariae et sanctis Cantuariensis ecclesiae advocatis, et beato Dionysio Francorum apostolo commendans, ut illi inter martyres potissimum Deo inspirante sic commendaretur ecclesiae causa, cui ipse in ecclesia per martyrium simile jam assimilabitur in poena, isto, sicut et illo, decalvato.[27]

[277] Se itaque exposito,[28] mox causam ecclesiae, quam egerat, patronis[29] commendavit, et pro suis oravit. Sed quid dico "oravit"? Quin potius, etsi inter lanistarum manus jam etiam in sanguine suo volutari inciperet, tamen super

---

[27] [276a] (?) " Deprived of the scalp." " Decalvare " means " make bald." Apparently Herbert uses it here to mean " being scalped," or " having a part of the skull sliced off." It is similarly used in a letter (*Mat.* vii. 431) written (ostensibly by the Archbishop of Sens) to the Pope immediately after the Martyrdom. In one MS., the actual authorship is claimed for Herbert, writing in the Archbishop's name. The style indicates that the claim is just.

But the legend says that St. Denis was "*beheaded*," and that he *carried his* "*head*" *after death.* St. Chrysolius is said to have walked carrying " his *cranium*, which had been cleft from his scull by the executioner " (Brewer's *Dictionary of Miracles*, p. 169). I do not know whether there was any similar tradition about St. Denis.

[28] " Exposing " refers to " exposes his head," above.

[29] This is a confused repetition of what Herbert had said above about "the Advocatory Saints of Canterbury Cathedral." There were two versions : the first mentioned the Patron Saints of *the Cathedral;* the second mentioned the Patron Saints of *the Church.* Herbert gives the first above, and the second here.

of a priest, on the part of Almighty God, and under penalty of anathema, he imperiously inhibited[30] them from touching any one, or harming any one, of his [people]. . . . For indeed he did not so much pray to them to spare, as anathematize them if they did not spare. . . . So (as we have already said above) extending his neck, exposing his head, like unto one praying, he clasped his hands and bent his knees, while the lictors[31] (I can hardly write this . . . without an exuberant fountain of tears) the lictors (I say) on this side, and on that, strike and strike again, strike (I say) and strike again (*sic*), until they separated the crown of his head from the head.

[278] And so the Lord's Christ, the Lord's Anointed, was immolated precisely in that spot [of his body] in which he was anointed, while the sword of slaughter first took the place of, and then gave place to, the sacred oil of unction.[32] For that holy flesh, remaining elsewhere untouched and unharmed, suffered that unprecedented sacrilege merely in that small portion of the flesh where the priestly and

---

lanistas suos sacerdotalis officii auctoritate fungens adhuc, ex parte omnipotentis Dei et sub anathemate imperiose inhibuit[30] ne quem suorum tangerent, ne quem laederent. . . . Nec enim tam orabat ut parcerent, quam anathematizabat eos, si non parcerent. . . . Itaque (ut jam supra diximus) collo extento, capite exposito, orantis instar junctis manibus et flexis genibus, lictores[31] (quod sine exuberante lacrymarum fonte . . . vix dicere valeo) lictores (inquam) hinc inde feriunt et referiunt, feriunt (inquam) et referiunt, donec coronam capitis separarunt a capite.

[278] Et ita christus Domini, unctus Domini, ibi est immolatus ubi unctus, sacro oleo unctionis succedente et cedente gladio occisionis.[32] Nam sancto illo corpore in reliquis intacto et illaeso, in sola illa corporis particula qua sacerdotii

---

[30] Herbert places here, with tedious repetition, the anathema placed much earlier by the other writers. Here follow some seven pages of ejaculatory writing, containing no facts. A few specimens are given above, to show the style.

[31] See 129.

[32] The sword, for the moment, *usurped the place* of the chrism, filling it with blood. But soon the sword, subdued by the Martyr's miracles, had to *give place*. The shattering of Brito's sword was a type of this (274*a*).

pontifical privilege was conspicuous.³³ And so by the lictors he was bereft of scalp and crown:—and that, too, not by a blow from behind. But, as one who (even to the end) had always "stretched forwards to those things that are before ³⁴"—always a Patron of what was right and straight—so now with body straight he fell forward on his face in death upon the pavement of the church.

[279] And this is the end of his consummation. And these things were done by the four knights, together with a cohort, in this Passion of the Lord's Christ, as also in the Passion of Christ Himself. And one of the cohort, turning back, approached and drew near: who also, in order that he might carry certain news of the Martyr's death—though he had already died—pierced him with the point of his sword, and drew forth the brains of that holy head, and poured them forth upon the pavement of the church: [he was] as was said, [sprung] from that above-mentioned offspring of vipers,³⁵ namely Robert de Broc.³⁶

[280] (7) (Anon. I.) Then approached William de Traci and with a great blow smote him on the head. But

et pontificii eminebat privilegium,³³ inauditum illud sacrilegium admissum est. Et ita a lictoribus decalvatus decoronatus est, ut quidem non a tergo, sed qui usque in finem in anteriora se semper extenderat,³⁴ patronus semper recti, recto corpore super ecclesiae pavimentum jam moriens ante faciem cecidit.

[279] Et hic est consummationis viri finis. Et milites quidem haec fecerunt quatuor cum cohorte in hac passione christi Domini, sicut et in passione ipsius Christi. Et unus de cohorte revertens accessit propius. Qui et, ut certissime nuntiaret mortuum, qui tamen jam mortuus erat, cuspide gladii fixit et sancti capitis cerebrum extraxit, et super ecclesiae pavimentum effudit; ut dicebatur, de praefata illa viperarum progenie,³⁵ videlicet Robertus de Broc hic erat. . . .³⁶

[280] (7) (Anon. I.) Tunc accessit Guillelmus de Traci, grandique ictu

---

³³ "Privilege," the anointing on the crown.
³⁴ Philipp. iii. 13.
³⁵ "Offspring of vipers." Comp. Herbert's previous words (*Mat.* iii. 483) "And especially that offspring of vipers called the De Brocs (progenies illa viperarum quae dicitur de Brocheis) kept insulting and wronging him (the Archbishop)."
³⁶ An error. It was Hugh Mauclerc.

as yet he showed no signs of falling. Then the said William smote him again still more mightily, and at that blow the holy man fell flat forward on the pavement. But Richard Brito smote him, when he was prostrated on the pavement, and broke his sword in the middle, by contact with the stone. While this was doing, Hugh of Maureville was occupied in driving away the common people, who were pressing in; and so it came to pass that he did not smite him with his own hand. But Hugh Mauclerc, wickedest of all mankind, approaching the Archbishop where he lay, set his foot on his neck, and fixing his sword deep in the head, scattered the brains upon the pavement, saying in a loud voice, "Let us go; for the traitor is dead."

[281] (8) (Anon. II.) Then the brave champion said to the murderers, "If ye would have my life, on the part of God, by anathema, I prohibit you from touching any of my [people], because nothing that I may have done is to be imputed to them . . .:" Then, fortifying himself with the sign of the cross,[37] and joining his hands after the manner of one praying to God, inclining his head to meet the impending swords, he stood unmoved, uttering these as his last words, "To God, and St. Mary, and the Saints of this

percussit in capite; qui tamen adhuc minime cecidit. Item percussit isdem Guillelmus enixius, et ad illum ictum corruit vir sanctus pronus in pavimento. Ricardus vero Brito jam in pavimento prostratum percussit, fregitque ensem suum per medium ad lapidem oppositum. Dum haec aguntur, Hugo de Maurevilla in abigendo populo qui imminebat occupatus erat; et ita contigit quod manu sua non percussit eum. Hugo vero Malus-clericus, omnium hominum sceleratissimus, accedens ad jacentem posuit pedem super collum ejus, gladiumque defigens in capite spargebat cerebrum ejus super pavimentum, clamans et dicens "Eamus, mortuus est enim proditor."

[281] (8) (Anon. II.) Tunc athleta fortis ad carnifices "Si caput," inquit, "meum vultis, ex parte Dei per anathema prohibeo ne quenquam meorum tangatis, quia nihil imputandum est illis quod egerim;" . . . Deinde signo crucis [37] se muniens, et junctis in modum orantis ad Deum manibus, contra gladios imminentes caput inclinans, stetit immotus, haec ultima verba proferens, "Deo et sanctae Mariae et hujus ecclesiae sanctis beatoque Dionysio commendo me et

[37] Not mentioned by any other writer.

Church, and St. Denis, I commend myself and my Church." But, under the headlong impulse of the devil, these madmen presently rushed furiously upon him and attacked him with their swords—all the more villainously because he was unarmed and unprepared [38] and neither legally judged nor legally examined, yet steadfast and free from all sign of perturbation. For not even in that last moment was his fixed purpose turned aside; [39] but with neck in that instant stretched out he bravely received great blows on the crown that had been blessed and consecrated with chrism.

[282] What need of words? Ah, sorrow! The Lord's Christ, the Blessed of God, before the altar of St. Benedict,[40] on the fourth [41] day after Christ's birth,—after the top of his head, with the brains, had been cut off—was mutilated and laid low by the monstrous act of cruel men; to the intent that, under the wonderful providence of God, he might receive death in front of the sepulchres of his dead co-archbishops, neither resisting, nor uttering complaint, or

ecclesiam meam." Diabolico vero praecipitatus impulsu furentium impetus mox eum gladiis apetiit tanto nequius quanto minus praemunitum et improvisum,[38] et nec judicatum nec discussum, constantem tamen et velut in nullo turbatum. Nec enim vel adhuc aversus [39] est rigor ejus, sed collo tunc extento grandes super benedictam et chrismate sacratam coronam fortiter ictus excepit.

[282] Quid multa? Proh dolor! christum Domini, benedictum Dei, ante altare sancti Benedicti,[40] die quinto [41] natalis Christi crudelium immanitas—capitis, cum cerebro, summitate praecisa—truncavit et stravit, ut, mira Dei providentia, mortem ante mortuorum coarchiepiscoporum sepulturas exceperit, nec resistens nec conquerens nec obmurmurans nec ingemiscens, sed se post ictus aliquot velut ad

---

[38] " Unprepared " seems contrary, not only to fact, but to the writer's narrative. Could it mean "unprovided (with means of defence)"? "Improvisum," in classical Latin, means "unexpected."

[39] See note 43. The meaning is that his body was as straight, stiff, and erect, as his mind.

[40] There is a play on the name, "the *Blessed* of God before the altar of *St. Blessed.*"

[41] "Fourth" (29 Dec.). The Latin language, reckoning 25 Dec. as one of the days, says "fifth."

murmur, or groan, but (after some blows) stretching (?)[42] himself out as though for prayer on the pavement, so that even here, too, his fixed purpose was not turned aside,[43] but, from that time forward, his soul, altogether intent on heaven, left behind it [on earth] a just fear of a more terrible vengeance.

[283] Then one of the knights [44]—himself too a son of Belial, made by his wickedness conspicuously wicked among the wicked for all ages—searched with the point of his sword for the remnant of the brain in the remnant of the skull of the now lifeless head, and cast it out, and scattered it on the ground, not so much to remove lingering doubts about death (in the case of one who had already died) as rather to allow his frenzied cruelty to satiate itself (or, to satisfy himself with a frenzy of cruelty).

[284] (9) (Anon. IV.) Even then he stood . . . without murmur, without complaint, and, while offering himself as a holocaust to the Lord, implored the advocacy of the Saints. And, lest any of these murderous knights of the King should possibly be maintained to be guiltless on the ground that he had not touched the Archbishop, the second . . . and the third cruelly dashed their swords against the top [of the

---

orationem in pavimento distendens,[42] ut et hic quoque non fuerit aversus [43] rigor ejus, sed ex tunc anima ipsius, caelo prorsus intenta, terribilioris vindictae metum juste reliquerit. . . .

[283] Tunc unus ex militibus,[44] et ipse filius Belial, inter scelestos caeteros saeculis omnibus scelere detestabilior, in residua capitis jam exanimis testa cerebri residuum cum ensis mucrone scrutatus ejecit et solo sparsit, non tam ne mortis in jam mortuo dubitatio resideret, quam ut sibi saevitiae dementia satisfaceret.

[284] (9) (Anon. IV.) Stabat adhuc . . . sine murmure, sine querimonia, et se ipsum holocaustum offerens Domino sanctorum patrocinia implorabat. Et ne quis funestorum satellitum intacto praesule inscelestus argui posset, secundus . . . et tertius gladios suos vertici constantis athletae atrociter illiserunt, con-

---

[42] "Distending," the editor makes no remark. It is perhaps an error for "extendens."

[43] This seems a repetition of the thought above, "nec enim vel adhuc aversus est rigor ejus." Probably the writer has in view the refrain in Is. ix. 12, 17, 21, "For all this, his anger is not *turned away*, but his hand is *stretched out* still."

[44] [283a] An error. It was the "clerk," Hugh of Horsea.

head] of the steadfast Champion, [and] shattered [them], and precipitated to the ground the [sacrificial] victim of the Holy Spirit. The fourth,[45] in a frenzy of cruelty worse than that of beasts, nay, [worse than that][46] of madmen, when he was now prostrated, when he was now breathing his last,[47] lopped off the shaven[48] crown, scattered the [bones of] the skull,[49] and after inserting the sword's point in the top [of the head] poured forth the brains with the blood upon the stone pavement. . . .[50] Thus our holy Saint . . . Thomas, . . . a precious stone in the celestial building [of the Church], being [as it were] carved foursquare[51] by the blows of their swords, was joined to the corner-stone, namely, Christ, in the heavens.

(10) (Anon. V.) While two others were smiting him on the head, the fourth, plunging his sword deep into the head,[52] dug out the brains and scattered them along the pavement.

---

fregerunt, et Spiritus Sancti victimam solo tenus praecipitaverunt. Quartus,[45] plusquam ferali, immo furiali,[46] crudelitate debacchatus, jam prostrato, jam exspiranti,[47] coronam rasilem[48] abscidit, testam capitis dissipavit,[49] et mucrone vertici intruso cerebrum cum sanguine super pavimentum lapideum effudit. . . .[50] Sic noster beatissimus . . . Thomas, . . . caelestis aedificii lapis pretiosus, gladiorum conquadratus[51] ictibus angulari lapidi Christo in caelis est conjunctus.

(10) (Anon. V.) Aliis duobus ipsum in caput ferientibus, quartus[52] gladio in caput profundius injecto cerebrum illius effossum per pavimentum sparsit.

---

[45] "The fourth." An error (283*a*). The best authorities agree that Hugh of Morville did not strike the Archbishop.

[46] If "plusquam" is not repeated before "furiali," the meaning will be, "nay, worthy of madmen."

[47] No other writer suggests that this outrage was inflicted while life remained.

[48] This writer, alone, inserts the epithet "shaven," so as to define "crown." He speaks of the "tonsure," whereas Herbert speaks of the chrism, as (apparently) consecrating the head.

[49] Gervase (396) mentions "bony pieces of the head (testulas)"; and perhaps this is the meaning here. "Testa" can hardly mean "the brains," as they are mentioned in the next clause.

[50] Here the writer compares the white and red of the wounds to the white linen of innocence and the purple of martyrdom (264).

[51] "Conquadratus" refers to the *four* blows, as if it meant "carved so as to be four-square."

[52] Beside committing the error of imputing this outrage to one of the knights, this writer takes the curious view depicted in the picture on Henry IV.'s tomb

[285] (11) (Anon. X.) Afterwards, on receiving another blow on the head,[53] the Martyr bent his knees and arms. But a third [blow] inflicted a severe wound on him when thus fallen on the ground.[54] A fourth [blow], in the crown, which was of [unusually] large width, so enlarged the wound [55] that the blood whitening from the brain, and the brain reddening from the blood, decorate the face of the Martyr and Confessor at once with lilies and roses, the colours of the Church as Virgin and as Mother.[56] But this is worthy of special wonder that they did not inflict different wounds on him but enlarged one and the same wound. The crown, just as it was, they almost lopped off.[57]

---

[285] (11) (Anon. X.) Deinde alio [53] ictu in capite recepto martyr genua flexit et cubitos. At tertius ita solo procumbenti grave vulnus impressit.[54] Quartus in corona, quae amplae latitudinis erat, ita vulnus ampliavit [55] ut sanguis albens ex cerebro, et cerebrum rubens ex sanguine, liliis et rosis, coloribus virginis et matris ecclesiae, faciem confessoris et martyris decoret.[56] Hoc admiratione vero non minima dignum, quod non ei diversa vulnera inflixerunt, sed unum et idem vulnus ampliaverunt. Coronam, sicut fuit, fere absciderunt.[57]

---

(249), where one knight has struck off the cap, or scalp (which is lying on the ground), two (Brito and Tracy) are striking at the head with their sword-blades, while a fourth (Fitzurse) is holding his sword vertically in two hands above the kneeling Martyr, and plunging the point into the wound.

[53] This is a version of Grim, falsified by omitting (between "head" and "the Martyr") the words, "Even then he still remained immoveable. But on being struck a third time."

[54] The writer (apparently substituting "third [blow]" for "third knight") has appropriated the first part of Grim's sentence *ita procumbenti grave vulnus inflixit*, quo ictu" etc. In the next sentence he applies to the "fourth [blow]" what Grim applies to "a third knight." "Procumbenti" (270*a*), "fallen," not "falling."

[55] Comp. Benedict, "horribly enlarged the preceding wound."

[56] The words "that the blood . . . Mother" are from Grim, omitting all that is difficult.

[57] It would be possible to render thus, "the crown, almost as it was, they lopped off." "As it was" means that the crown was not gashed or mangled by a diversity of strokes. The writer defers the account of the scattering of the brains till the next section.

[286] (12) (Garnier) Then did Master Edward abandon him at this blow. "Strike," said then William, But then there struck him Lord Renald Fitzurse, but smote him not down. Then struck him again William de Traci Who smote his brains quite out, and St. Thomas fell.

[287][58] To Saltwood returned those felons. Of their great felony that night they boasted. William de Traci said and affirmed That he had gashed the arm of John of Salisbury:[59] For this cause know we that he wounded Master Edward.

[288] Because he was without armour he was quite the first to follow him,[60] And was well known by face and voice: A coat green and mantle parti-coloured. When he saw that Renald Fitzurse recoiled, Twice, as I have said, did he smite the Saint on the head.

[289] But when Richard le Bret saw him thus struck down, And on the pavement lying all stretched out, Somewhat in haste,[60a] he smote him with other blows, So that on

---

[286] Dunc l'aveit à cel colp mestre Edward guerpi.
"Ferez," fet dunc Willames. Mès idunc le féri
Danz Renalz, le fils Hurs, mès pa ne l'abati.
Idunc le referi Willames de Traci
Qui tut l'escervela, et saint Thomas chaï.
[287][58] A Saltewoode sunt li felun returné.
De lur grant felunie se sunt la noit vanté.
Willames de Traci a dit et afermé
Johan de Salesbire aveit le bras colpé:[59]
Pur ço savum qu'il ot mestre Edward nafré.

[288] Pur ço k'iert desarmez tut primiers le siwi,[60]
Et bien fu conéuz et al vis et al cri;
Une cote vert ot et mantel mi-parti.
Quant il vit ke Renalz li filz Urs resorti,
Dous feiz, si cum j'ai dit, le saint al chief feri.
[289] Mès quant Richarz li Brez le vit si abatu,
E sur le pavement gesir tut estendu,
Un poi en bescoz là des autres cops feru,[60a]

---

[58] The next ten lines state, as a digression, what William of Canterbury states in an Appendix (320).

[59] These words appear capable of meaning "John of Salisbury had his arm wounded": but Garnier regards them as meaning "he had wounded the arm of John of Salisbury," and this is William's view (321).

[60] Garnier has said above (l. 5491), "William came in front. . . . In order to be lighter, he would not wear a hauberk." He now seems to say that on this account William de Traci was *the first to follow the Archbishop into the Cathedral.* He did not mention this above, where the four knights (seemingly) enter simultaneously.

[60a] "Bescoz." Godefroy gives "bescousse (bescosse)" = "secousse," "agitation." Perhaps it means "excitement."

the stone he broke in two his sharp sword. —At the Martyr's tomb the piece, quite bare, is kissed [by pilgrims].

[290] When those felons smote him and wounded him, And roughly put forth all their strength to smite him, He struggled [60b] not, nor groaned, nor cried, nor called aloud, Nor hand, nor foot, did he draw in, or stretch out, For on God throughout did his courage lean. And even as in Calvary God was crucified By Jews who were His sons, and [that, too,] for human sin, [So] there, where their trespasses were set right by righteousness, Did his own sons [61] make martyr of this man for the clergy, [Even] there, where their misdeeds are taken away and made naught.[62]

[291] Hugo of Moreville had run beyond, And checked [and drove] back the people who had come up; [He] feared lest the Archbishop might then be taken from them:— This may be because he came to himself; And thus was he kept from [working] his felonious intent.

[292] When in Jerusalem this son of Rachel was thus murdered, These knights of Herod (that seed of Ishmael) Severed not the crown [63] from his head, But he retained it by the flesh of the forehead and by the skin, So that all bare to view you might have seen the brain.

K'à la pière a brisié en dous sun brant molu.
—Al martir beise l'un la pièce tut à nu.
[290] Kan ke li felun l'unt feru et detrenchié
E del ferir se sunt durement esforcié,
N'aveit bret, ne gruni, ne crié, ne huchié; [60b]
Ne pié ne main n'aveit à sei tret he sachié,
Car à Deu ot del tut sun corage apuié.
Et si cum en Calvaire unt Deu crucifié
Geiu, ki si fil èrent, et pur l'umain pecchié,
Là où li forfet èrent par justise adrescié,
Unt pur les clers cestui si fil [61] martirié;
Là où li mesfet sunt osté et esneié.[62]

[291] Huge de Moreville esteit ultre coruz;
Chachout le pueple arère, ki esteit survenuz;
Cremi ke l'arcevesques ne lur fust dunc toluz.
Puet cel estre qu'il s'est en sei reconeūz;
E de sa felonie s'est issi defenduz.
[292] Quant en Jerusalem fu ociz li filz Rachel,
Li chevalier Herode, la lignée Ismael,
Ne li serrèrent pas del chief le chapel: [63]
Mès al charnail del frunt retint et à la pel,
Que tut à descovert véissiez le cervel.

[60b] "Bret." Is this from "brester"="se débattre," "se démener"?

[61] "His own sons." The knights were, technically, the "sons" of their Archbishop, their "father in God."

[62] "Even there." That is, in the church, where the sacrifice of the Mass was offered up for the sins of men.

[63] [292a] "Crown (chapel)." The French word also means "cap."

[293] And the above-named Hugo Malclers, who entered after them, On the neck of St. Thomas set his foot and pierced [him]; The brain with his sword out of the head did he cast, Upon the pavement, and cried out to them: "Let us go hence," said he, "never will he rise again."

[294] (13) (The *Saga*) Yet the wound was so great that the blood flowed over the eyes and face of the Archbishop. After this, William called in a grim voice on his fellows, saying, "Cut ye, cut ye!" says he. But at this call there came such fear upon the Archbishop's men that each fled his own way. But at this first wound the holy lamb-offering of the living God, lord Archbishop Thomas, lifteth his hands and eyes up to heaven, and thus awaiteth the second blow with a bared head. And next another knight dealeth a blow down upon the head, and at that blow the Archbishop falleth forward, his body being stretched on the floor so sweetly as if he were offering himself in prayer a living sacrifice, as one who died in order to redeem the human race. As was said even now, the limb of the foe felleth and layeth low on earth his own father[64] in the womb of his mother.[65]

[295] After this the third knight setteth upon the Archbishop, lying on the floor, in such manner that he brandisheth the sword and cutteth away nearly the whole of the crown, so that only a little held it to the forehead... But as the fourth knight is egged on by his comrades to get him a share of this mighty deed, he dealeth a blow into the wound of his lifeless father with such force that the

---

[293] E cil Huge Malclers, qui après els entra,
Sur le col saint Thomas mist sun pié et ficha;

Le cervel od l'espée hors del chief li geta,
De sur le pavement, et à cels s'escria:
"Alun-nus en," fet-il, "jà-mès ne resurdra."
ll. 5501-45.

---

[64] *i.e.* his "father in God." See 290.

[65] [294a] *i.e.* inside the church. Comp. Herbert (228a), and also the letter to the Pope written ostensibly by the Archbishop of Sens, but probably (276a) by Herbert (*Mat.* vii. 432), "in visceribus propriae matris proprium peremit patrem."

point of the sword dasheth against the marble, and the sword itself breaketh into two parts. And so he departeth therefrom that both fragments of the sword lie behind as memorials for the church. . . .[66]

[296] Now as the two kinsmen, Ranulf and Robert, were the first to join the warfare of the two knights, so they desire to get their share in the wicked deeds. Ranulf therefore . . . this devil's limb thrusteth the point of the sword into the opened skull and stirreth the blood together with the brain, scattering it afterwards about. . . . But when his kinsman Robert seeth this mighty deed, he . . . driveth the sword into the empty skull of the Archbishop, crying at the same time to his accursed followers, "Away hence, away hence!"

[297] (i.) (Stanley, pp. 92-4) The next blow, whether struck by Tracy or Fitzurse, *was only with the flat of the sword*,[67] and again on the bleeding head, which Becket drew back as if stunned, and then raised his clasped hands above it.

[298] The blood from the first blow was trickling down his face in a thin streak; he wiped it with his arm, and

---

[66] This prefigured, he adds, the breaking of worldly power. Then he asks who could possibly be the men that would wreak on the dead body unprecedented deeds of shame? They could be none other than "the vipers of Broc." So he makes them *both* do this deed. Herbert makes Robert de Broc do it. Both are misled by the fallacy of *the Fitness of Things* (379). Possibly they may have been also misled by a tradition assigning this deed to "a limb of Satan," or "son of perdition"—a name given by Becket to Ranulf de Broc (460).

[67] "The flat of the sword." The only writer that mentions a blow inflicted on the Archbishop with the flat of the sword is Fitzstephen (171), and he places it much earlier, during the attempt to frighten or force the Archbishop out of the Cathedral. Concerning this blow, Stanley has said above, that it was "perhaps in kindness."

Stanley refers for this statement to "Will. Cant., 32; Grim, 66." Will. Cant. chap. 39 (*Mat*. i. 134-5) describes a blow with the flat of the sword inflicted, *not on the Archbishop, but on* "*one of the brethren*." Grim, chap. 82 (*Mat*. ii. 437), describes all the blows in detail, but mentions none as dealt with "the flat of the sword."

when he saw the stain, *he said—" Into thy hands, O Lord, I commend my spirit."* [68]

[299] At the third blow, which was also [69] from Tracy, he sank on his knees—his arms falling—but his hands still joined as if in prayer. With his face turned towards the altar of St. Benedict, he murmured in a low voice, which might just have been caught by the wounded Grim, who was crouching close by,[70] and who alone reports the words —" For the name of Jesus, and the defence of the church, I am willing to die."

[300] Without moving hand or foot, he fell flat on his face as he spoke, in front of the corner wall of the chapel,[71] and with such dignity that *his mantle*, which extended from head to foot, *was not disarranged*.[72]

---

[68] "I commend my spirit." These words, which are placed by Stanley after the *second* blow, are placed by Fitzstephen (the only writer that mentions them) after the *first*. As will be shewn below (310-14), they were probably not uttered at all.

[69] "At the third blow, which was also from Tracy." But (1) the first line of this passage speaks of the *second* blow, " whether struck by Tracy or Fitzurse," and (2) the last extract from Stanley assigned the *first* blow unhesitatingly to Tracy. Thus the question left open in (1) leaves it open to suppose that Tracy struck the first *three* blows—a view contrary to all evidence, and supported by no writer, even the most inaccurate.

[70] "Grim, who was crouching by." This is very likely. But Stanley has said above (quoting from William) that Grim " fled disabled to the nearest altar, probably that of St. Benedict within the chapel."

The two statements are incompatible. If William is telling the truth, "several of the brethren" were sheltering at that altar to which Grim "fled"; and these would have heard what Grim heard. But no other tradition has preserved these words. Probably William is not telling the truth, and Grim is. If so, we may keep the words "crouching by." But we must cancel "fled," above.

[71] "In front, etc." A more explicit tradition is that preserved by Garnier (332) and Herbert, quoted in *Quadrilogus* (*Mat.* iv. 398), that he fell "toward the north." If the altar of St. Benedict was to the east, the Martyr would fall not so as to front it, but having it on his right hand.

[72] "His mantle . . . not disarranged." The only authority for this is Fitzstephen. Even Herbert, who is diffuse about the grace and quietude of the body, says nothing about the mantle. Fitzstephen appears to be borrowing from Ovid's account of the becoming death of a chaste woman a detail inapplicable to the fall of a man and a martyr (267).

[301] In this posture he received from Richard the Breton a tremendous blow, accompanied with the exclamation (in allusion to a quarrel of Becket with Prince William) "Take this for love of my lord William, brother of the King." The stroke was aimed with such violence that the scalp or crown of the head—which, it was remarked, was of unusual size—was severed from the skull, and the sword snapt in two on the marble pavement. The fracture of the murderous weapon was reported by one of the eye-witnesses as a presage of the ultimate discomfiture of the Archbishop's enemies.

[302] Hugh of Horsea, the subdeacon who had joined them as they entered the church, *taunted*[73] *by the others with having taken no share in the deed*, planted his foot on the neck of the corpse, thrust his sword into the ghastly wound, and scattered the brains over the pavement— "Let us go—let us go," he said in conclusion. "The traitor is dead; he will rise no more."

[303] This was the final act. One only of the four knights had struck no blow. *Hugh de Morville throughout retained the gentler disposition*[74] *for which he was distinguished*, and contented himself with holding back at the entrance of the transept the crowds who were pouring in through the nave.

[304] (ii.) (Tennyson)

DE TRACY. There is my answer then.
               [*Sword falls on* GRIM'S *arm, and glances
                from it, wounding* BECKET.
GRIM.   Mine arm is sever'd.

---

[73] No one says that the knights taunted the clerk, Hugh of Horsea. Those who mention any "taunting," or chiding, regard it as addressed by the knights *to one of their own number*, the striker of the last stroke. None regard the outrage on the dead body as the result of "taunting."

[74] "Gentler disposition." On the origin of this error, see **212**. To what is there said may be added the Archbishop's rejoinder to Morville, in the Palace interview, recorded by the authoritative Anon. I. (*Mat.* iv. 73): "How high you hold your head!"

I can no more—fight out the good fight—die
Conqueror.   [*Staggers into the chapel of St. Benedict.*[75]
BECKET (*falling on his knees*). At the right hand of Power—
Power and great glory—for thy Church, O Lord—
Into thy hands, O Lord—into Thy hands![76]——   [*Sinks prone.*
DE BRITO. This last to rid thee of a world of brawls!
                                                          [*Kills him.*
The traitor's dead, and will arise no more.[77]
FITZURSE. Nay, have we still'd him? What! the great Archbishop!
Does he breathe? No?
[**305**] DE TRACY. No, Reginald, he is dead.
                                                                 [*Storm bursts.*[78]
DE MORVILLE. Will the earth gape and swallow us?[79]
DE BRITO.   The deed's done—
Away!
  [DE BRITO, DE TRACY, FITZURSE, *rush out, crying* "*King's men!*"
  DE MORVILLE *follows slowly. Flashes of lightning thro' the
  Cathedral.* ROSAMUND *seen kneeling by the body of* BECKET.

§ 2. *Details of the death*

[**306**] Grim, Anon. I., and Garnier agree that the Archbishop did not fall till the third blow. Others say that he

---

[75] See 299.

[76] "Into thy hands." See 298.

[77] "Will arise no more." Tennyson assigns to one of the *knights* the words uttered by the *clerk*, who commits the outrage. But some such change is dramatically necessary. The clerk, in any case, could not have been exhibited on the stage as doing what he did. It is perhaps, however, a defect that the words "will arise no more" follow immediately on the last blow, dispensing with the interval that really occurred. Afterwards, Tracy's "he is dead" comes somewhat as a bathos. The last words of these instruments of Satan were, according to the best authorities, negative—a denial of St. Thomas's resurrection: and for retaining them in that position there is much to be said historically, theologically, and, perhaps, dramatically.

[78] "Storm." Fitzstephen is the only authority for this "storm." It probably springs from the fallacy of the *Fitness of Things* (see 341-5).

[79] "Gape and swallow." Tracy is asserted by Herbert to have said in confession to the Bishop of Exeter that when the knights left the Cathedral they felt as though the earth would swallow them. As a fact they left shouting "King's men!" And Tracy is said to have been very free that night in Saltwood Castle, boasting of his achievements.

fell at the second, and one (Anon. V.) at the first. Grim, a stranger, mentions none of the visored knights by name, except 'Reinald," whose name he heard pronounced by Becket. The rest he mentions by number, "the third," "the fourth." Of the fifth, however, who was not in knight's armour, he says, "no knight, but that clerk who had entered with the knights." This, as Fitzstephen and Anon. I. tell us, was Hugh of Horsea, or Mauclerc. Herbert (probably confusing the "entering" into *the Cathedral* with the "entering" into *the Palace*, where *Robert de Broc* was the leader) says, "This was *Robert de Broc*"—an error adopted by *Quadrilogus*. The text of Benedict, as preserved by *Quadrilogus*, states that the fifth, the man who pushed out the brains with his sword, was "the same child of Satan" that inflicted the fourth blow: but there may have been omitted some passage of Benedict's mentioning Hugh Mauclerc as coming with the knights into the Cathedral. Possibly, therefore, Benedict is not in error.

[307] Anon. IV. and Anon. V., perhaps because they found no part in the actual murder assigned to the fourth knight, ascribe this vile action to him. Perhaps they were also misled by a similarity of names, the fourth knight being Hugh of Morville, while the "wicked clerk" was Hugh of Horsea. Grim, Anon. I., and Garnier explain that Hugh of Morville (whom the last two mention by name) was engaged in keeping off the people from attempting a rescue.

[308] William tells us frankly that at this point he had fled. So had John of Salisbury. These two[1] seem to assign to *all* the knights the scattering of the Martyr's brains. At all events they describe it as done by "*them*"; but perhaps they use the pronoun indefinitely. Here, then, the earliest writer (John) goes wrong; and the corrections made by Grim, Anon. I., Garnier, and (in some respects) Herbert, are

---

[1] On Benedict's assignment of the act to "the above-mentioned (idem) child of Satan," see 275*a*.

signs of later narratives correcting an earlier one that had been too hastily published.

[**309**] The act of Hugh of Horsea, outrageous though it was, appears to have been at all events dictated mainly, if not entirely, by the desire to ascertain that the victim was quite dead : and this is, perhaps too positively, asserted by Herbert. He likens the act to that of Longinus (the soldier that pierced Christ on the Cross), but descants on the man's wickedness as compared with that of the Roman soldier. Anon. II. protests against this too lenient view. The man did it, he says, "*not* so much to ascertain the Martyr's death as for the satisfaction of his insane cruelty."

§ 3. *The Archbishop's last words*

[**310**] These are recorded by Grim alone, as follows : "For the name of Jesus and the protection of the Church I am prepared to embrace death."

Why do Stanley and Tennyson reject these words ? Apparently, because (1) no other writer records them, (2) they may seem to be a repetition of what (according to Grim) the Martyr had already twice said before,[1] (3) they are not so attractive to the modern reader as the familiar words "Into thy hands I commend my spirit."

(1) But if no other writer recorded them, one reason is

---

[1] *Mat.* ii. 436 "I am ready to die in the name of Him who redeemed me by His blood," "I am prepared to die for my Lord, that in my blood the Church may obtain liberty and peace." Comp. an anonymous letter *written to the Pope by one who* "*came to Canterbury on the day*" *of the Martyrdom.* It compresses all the sayings into one, and makes *one* "executioner." To the question, "Where is the Archbishop?" he replies (*Mat.* vii. 436) "taliter, *demisso* quidem sed *audibili* valde sermone," " Ego sum ; et tu, O Reginalde, *cum complicibus tuis* vade retro, quia nescitis quid facitis. Verumtamen si me quaeritis occidendum, ne ceteros contingatis. *In nomine ejus mortem excipere paratus sum qui pro me servo suo mori dignatus est.*" In the italicized words, the writer closely resembles Grim as well as in what follows : and the similarity suggests that *he may have borrowed* (*not quite accurately*) *from Grim an oral account of the Archbishop's last sayings.* See **315a** for further similarities.

that some of those who were the earliest to write, viz. John of Salisbury, William, Benedict, and Fitzstephen, were in the Cathedral, and *did not hear them;* and *these would naturally record, as far as possible, what they heard; and their records would preoccupy history.*

[311] (2) That they were a repetition of what the Martyr had twice said, ought not to make them improbable, regard being had to the special circumstances. When a man is nearly stunned, or on the point of death—or both—his mind, if it works at all, naturally goes back to ruling thoughts and fundamental convictions: and those of the dying man might well be "death," "Lord," "liberty of the Church." His "Lord" suffered "death" for him and he was prepared to suffer "death" for his "Lord," a feudal as well as natural gratitude. "Liberty" must come through the shedding of blood:—that was a knightly as well as a priestly thought: For "the Church," for Christ's body, for the oppressed everywhere, but especially in England, and most especially (as he might think) in Canterbury—for the protection of the Church against brute force and greed such as he identified with De Broc, that "son of perdition"—he was "prepared to die." This preparation had been coming on him during years of conflict and exile; now it had come, and was consummated. Mechanically, when the battered brain was almost refusing to act, the tongue might be just able to repeat—"in a low tone," as Grim says—the resolution of the heart of this true "knight" of Christ: "for Him and His Church I am prepared to die."[2]

[312] (3) The fact that these really uttered words are not apparently so saintly as the words ascribed to St. Thomas by Fitzstephen alone, is in reality *a condemnation of the historical accuracy of the latter.* We have seen, at every

---

[2] Note Grim's distinction between what was said before, "in quite audible words," and this, which is "in a low tone." No other writer makes this distinction between the Archbishop's various utterances: and it has a savour of veracity.

stage of our narrative, that *many of the narrators cannot be trusted as to any detail that tends to assimilate the Martyr to the Saviour*. Now the words assigned by Fitzstephen to the Archbishop are precisely those assigned by Luke to Jesus as His last utterance on the cross. Had they been historical, would they not have been eagerly caught at and repeated by the other historians?

[313] It might also be justly urged (as has been suggested above) that these words, alone, without some words implying death for *a cause*—death for *liberty* to the enslaved, death for *peace* to the harassed, death for *protection* to the oppressed—are not true to the Martyr's nature, because they do not represent the active, aggressive, and knightly kind of sanctity to which alone he can lay claim. But the importance of this consideration must not be allowed to overshadow the other, which is quite distinct, and which is based on a fundamental rule of historical criticism :—*When a plausible statement, attractive to contemporary readers and to posterity, is made by one alone of a number of writers, it is to be rejected.*

[314] In the present instance, beside these excellent reasons for not preferring Fitzstephen's statement to Grim's, we have others also, namely that (4) Grim was present and distinctly affirms that the Archbishop uttered the words "in a low tone," (5) that his narrative of the Martyrdom is generally, as far as we can judge, veracious, admitting little or nothing of inaccurate detail under the bias of inference, or the Fitness of Things.

CHAPTER XI

AFTER DEATH

§ 1. *The different accounts*

[315] (1) (Grim) But in all this the illustrious martyr exhibited an incredible steadfastness. Neither with hand nor with cloak did he attempt—as human frailty might attempt—to arrest the fatal stroke. Moreover, when struck, he uttered no word, gave forth no cry, or groan, or any sound that might betoken any pain whatever. But he held immovable the head that he had inclined to meet the unsheathed swords —until, besprinkled with a confused mass of brain and blood, as though stooping forward to pray, he laid his body on the pavement, and his spirit safe in Abraham's bosom.[1] . . . And

---

[315] (1) (Grim) Sed in his omnibus incredibilis constantiae virtutem exhibens martyr insignis nec manum nec vestem, ut est infirmitatis humanae, opposuit percussori, nec percussus verbum protulit, nec clamorem edidit, non gemitum, non sonum cujuscunque doloris indicem ; sed caput quod inclinaverat gladiis evaginatis immobile tenuit, donec confusus sanguine et cerebro, tanquam ad orandum pronus, in pavimento corpus, in sinum Abrahae spiritum, collocavit.[1]

---

[1] [315*a*] The first part of this (" Sed in his omnibus . . . immobile tenuit donec ") closely resembles John's account below ("in his omnibus cruciatibus . . . donec consummaretur tenebat immobile ").

The second part resembles a passage in an anonymous letter written to the Pope immediately (as it appears) after the Martyrdom by one who (*Mat.* vii. 437) " came to Canterbury that day." After giving the Archbishop's last words it says : " et porrectum caput spiculatori porrexit feriundum, qui mox, amputata ad modum coronae cervice (ed. suggests " amputato . . . vertice ") *confusis sanguine commixtum et cerebro, tanquam ad orandum pronus in pavimento corpus, in sinum Abrahae spiritum collocavit.*"

The question arises, (1) Did Grim borrow from both these writers, or (2) did

thus the Priest of God, migrating from this world, was born in heaven, on the fourth day before the Kalends of January, in the year from the Incarnation of our Lord and Saviour 1171.[2]

[316] (2) (Fitzstephen) And indeed—as formerly, when Christ was suffering in His own body, so too when He was again suffering in the person of His soldier Thomas—the sun averted its eyes, and veiled the day with darkness, not to behold this crime; and "a dreadful storm-cloud knit the brow of heaven"; sudden and swift fell the sleet; there was thunder from heaven. After this, there shot forth a great redness of the air, in token of the blood just shed, and in horror of the outrage. . . .

[317] [The sons slew their father in the womb of their mother. Verily in the flowers of the Church neither lilies nor roses are wanting; and in the Passion of St. Thomas there is drawn forth, along with the cruel sword's point, both the brain shining white and the blood blushing red. . . . Archbishop and Contender in the lists [of God's soldiers], Confessor and Martyr, about to receive from the Lord a stole

---

. . . Itaque Dei sacerdos, a saeculo migrans, coelis nascitur, quarto calendas Januarii, anno ab incarnatione Domini ac Salvatoris nostri MCLXXI.[2]

[316] (2) (Fitzstephen) Et quidem, sicut quondam Christo patiente in proprio corpore, ita et eodem patiente in milite suo Thoma, avertit sol oculos, obtenebravit diem, ne videret scelus hoc, et "horrida tempestas caelum contraxit," subitae ruerunt imbres, intonuit de caelo. Postea rubor aeris magnus emicuit, in effusi sanguinis signum, in flagitii horrorem. . . .

[317] [Occiderunt filii patrem in utero matris suae. Equidem floribus ecclesiae nec lilia desunt nec rosae, et in beati Thomae Passione cum saevo extrahitur mucrone et cerebrum candens et sanguis rubens. . . . Archiepiscopus et Agonista, Confessor et Martyr, duplicem stolam a Domino percepturus, et de

---

they come to him for the facts—which they embodied, in their several letters, nearly in the words in which Grim related them?

The latter is the more probable supposition. But it is also possible that Grim, publishing his record long after John's had become authoritative, may have been influenced *verbally* by John, although he had himself supplied the *facts* to John.

[2] 29th Dec. 1171 (an error for 1170).

of twofold colour—white and bright because of his pure administration of his archiepiscopate, and purple because of the happy consummation of his martyrdom. . . .³]

[318] Concerning the time of the Passion of St. Thomas the Martyr, some one has published this couplet :—

"The year was the one thousand one hundred and seventy
First,⁴ when the First [in our Church], Thomas, fell by the sword."

[319] (3) (John) But in all these tortures,⁵ the Martyr —such was his unconquerable spirit and admirable steadfastness—sent forth no word or cry; uttered no groan; neither with arm nor with garment attempted to arrest a blow, but held his head, which he had inclined and exposed to their swords, immovable till his consummation. Finally, falling forward to the earth, with body straight, he moved neither hand nor foot, when the assassins insultingly declared that by the destruction of a traitor they had restored peace to their country.⁶

---

archiepiscopio fideliter administrato candidam, et de martyrio feliciter consummato purpuream. . . .³]

[318] De tempore passionis sancti Thomae martyris quidam hoc distichon edidit :
"Annus millenus centenus septuagenus
Et primus,⁴ Primas quo cadit ense Thomas."

[319] (3) (John) Sed in his omnibus ⁵ cruciatibus invicti animi et admirandae constantiae martyr non verbum vel clamorem emisit, non edidit gemitum, nec brachium aut vestem opposuit ferienti, sed caput, quod inclinatum gladiis exposuerat, donec consummaretur, tenebat immobile. Denique in terram procidens recto corpore, non pedem movit aut manum, sicariis insultantibus se in strage proditoris pacem patriae reddidisse." ⁶

---

³ The bracketed words are omitted by the MS. called J. They are probably an addition made by the author or editor. The whole passage is highly poetical. The words "horrida . . . contraxit" are from Horace, *Epodes* xiii. 1. For the passage about "roses and lilies," see 264, 285, 331, 334. For the "womb of the mother," see 228*a*, 294*a*.

For Fitzstephen's description of the Archbishop's calmness in meeting death, see 269.

⁴ An error for 1170. "Primas" is "Primate": there is a play on the two similar words. "Primus" is perhaps intentionally emphasized. See 346.

⁵ "But in all these . . . till his." See note on Grim's account, with which this closely agrees (315*a*).

⁶ This writer mentions no date for the martyrdom.

[**320**] (4) (William)[7] But a clerk, sharing the suffering of his father [in God] out of affection, one that was by birth an Englishman, Edward by name, throwing his arm in the way, among the strokes [8] [that fell on the Archbishop] received a stroke; and, fearing for himself wounds following on wound, and worse following on bad, he turned aside [9] to the nearest altar (or, to an altar that was very near), whither many of the brethren had taken refuge together, fearing for their lives.

[**321**] He did not [then] know from whom he had suffered the blow.[10] But concerning the author of the wound, we form a conjecture on these grounds, namely, that William [de Traci]—when his partners were relating at Saltwood Castle their several exploits against the Martyr and boasting

---

[320] (4) (William)[7] Clericus autem, pro affectu patri compatiens, Anglicus natu Edwardus nomine, brachio suo objecto ictum inter ictus [8] excepit; timensque sibi post vulnus vulnera, post gravia graviora, ad altare proximum divertit,[9] quo plures ex fratribus vitae metuentes confugerant.

[321] Nesciens a quo pertulisset ictum.[10] Sed de auctore vulneris inde conjicimus, quod Willelmus, cooperatoribus suis apud castrum Saltwede quantum

---

[7] This appears to be of the nature of an Appendix. The writer's narrative, up to this point, has described (1) the first blow (which it assigns to Fitzurse), mentions (2) Fitzurse's cry "Strike! Strike!" then (3) the general flight, and (4) the "dashing out (excusserunt)" of the brains. But it has made no mention of Tracy and the rest, or of any blows but the first: and it was also silent about Grim. These omissions the Appendix supplies.

[8] "Ictum inter ictus (?)," "one blow among (many) blows (?)," or is "inter ictus" a mistake for "interjectus," *i.e.* "interposing"? It could hardly be intended to mean "stroke on stroke," since that is expressed, later on, by "post vulnus vulnera."

[9] "Turns aside, etc." This is probably not true. (1) Grim does not mention it: (2) Grim mentions the successive blows and the last words of the Archbishop, ("uttered in a low tone") with a minuteness and apparent accuracy that suggest that he was close to the Archbishop (see 314).

[10] "He did not know." Perhaps William means "not knowing at the time," which is the natural meaning of "nesciens." But, in any case, Grim (contradicting William) says that the knight who cut off his arm was the one addressed by the Archbishop as "Reinald."

of their villainy—said also that he had cut off the arm of John of Salisbury.[11]

[322] But moreover one of the brethren, standing by his father [in God], face to face with [his enemies], suffered a blow. But the prayer of the good Shepherd—imitating the true Shepherd who said, "If ye seek me, let these go their way," brought it to pass that he alone fell, and the flock suffered no loss. Consequently, he was [but] smitten with the flat of the sword and brought back [from it nothing worse than] a stunned head.[12]

[323] By this time the wearied knees of the Martyr were tottering; by this time his house of clay was verging to its fall. In the midst of the smiting, his mind prays in silence; he sings psalms with his mind, psalms with his spirit also; the voice was not audible to the outer ear. But he is smitten with their swords like sheep; no murmur is

---

quisque saevisset in martyrem referentibus, scelusque suum jactantibus, dixerit etiam se brachium Joannis Saresberiensis praecidisse.[11]

[322] Sed et unus ex fratribus circa patrem studio compassionis obversatus, ictum pertulit. Verum oratio boni pastoris verum Pastorem imitantis dicentem, "Si me quaeritis, sinite hos abire," obtinuit ut grege non diminuto ipse solus occumberet. Unde plano gladio percussus caput attonitum reportavit.[12]

[323] Jam genua martyris effoeta lababant, jam domus lutea vergebat in casum. Inter caedendum mens in silentio orat; psallit mente, psallit et spiritu; vox exterius non auditur. Sed caeditur gladiis more bidentium; non murmur resonat,

---

[11] This report of a boast of Tracy's depends on hearsay, and probably late hearsay, and counts for very little against Grim's evidence that Fitzurse was the man. See 245. Note also that Garnier's words on the subject (287) might mean that Tracy exultingly said that "John of Salisbury *had his arm cut off*," not that *Tracy cut it off*. Such a saying might be quoted, originally, simply to shew that one of the knights had confused Grim with John. It would be an easy transition to quote it as shewing that this knight had also *done the deed*.

William himself speaks of this as only a "conjecture."

[12] The only mention of a blow with "the flat of the sword," in the other writers, is made by Fitzstephen. But he says that it was *the Archbishop* who was thus struck.

It is possible that William's story about "the flat of the sword" is a confused (or perverted) account of what happened to Grim. William is singularly reticent about Grim even in the Appendix in which he makes mention of him. The other writers generally say that Grim's *arm was* "*nearly severed.*" William does not. He *implies* a wound; but he does not mention even that.

heard, no complaining; but in his silent heart his mind, conscious of right, preserves its patience.¹³ But when the Martyr was at last falling, or rather lying,¹⁴ on the stone pavement, one of the murderers, continuing the assault, dashed his sword's point against him : but the blade leapt apart [broken], the Lord thereby presignifying that in the Martyr's blood the Church was triumphing, and overcoming malice. . . .

[324] Not even yet was [? their] impiety satisfied, for as [? the] other four rushed in [? out]¹⁵, one, repeating the

---

non querimonia ; sed corde tacito mens bene conscia conservat patientiam.¹³ Unus autem ex carnificibus jam cadentem vel jacentem ¹⁴ martyrem prosecutus lapideo pavimento mucronem incussit ; sed acie dissiliente praesignabat Dominus in sanguine martyris ecclesiam triumphare, malitiam superare. . . .

[324] Necdum saturabatur impietas, nam quatuor aliis irrumpentibus,¹⁵ unus,

---

¹³ [323*a*] The words "more bidentium | *Non murmur resonat, non querimonia*," are in the Asclepiad metre. The italicized line will be found in Herbert below. The insertion of "in" would reduce to Asclepiad metre the words : " Sed corde (in) tacito mens bene conscia | Conservat patientiam." In 128 Fitzstephen has " Non murmur edidit, non querimoniam."

¹⁴ The phrase suggests that William was familiar with the traditional and ambiguous "procumbens" above mentioned (270*a*), and that he is here correcting it : "falling, or rather, lying."

¹⁵ [324*a*] " Rushed in." The Editor suggests "erumpentibus, rushed *out*." Then the meaning will be, " When *the other four* murderers rushed *out*, one of them (*i.e.* one of the five murderers, the clerk, Hugh) proceeded to outrage the body."

But if we are to retain "irrumpentibus," the meaning must be, " Not even yet was Impiety satisfied ; for *four others rushed in*, and one, repeating the crime [*of the first four*] pierced the brains with his sword's point. But the Martyr— [being now in Paradise] triumphing over the sword's point of the *former* murderers, [and consequently unmoved by this outrage from the *later* group of murderers] — lay still. . . ." This represents a tradition that finds some support in Garnier, viz. that " four other knights waited outside in the cloisters." Stanley gives Foss's *Judges*, i. 243 as his authority for the statement that one of these four was called Fitzranulph.

But neither Garnier nor any one else of our authorities asserts that these four knights entered the Cathedral. Possibly William has misinterpreted some words such as (Garnier, 5641) " And that Hugh Malclerc who entered after them [*i.e.* after the first four knights]." This might be confused with "And that Hugh Malclerc *and those* who entered after them," *i.e.* the second group of knights whom he brought into the Cathedral.

crime, and assailing the dead in hostile fashion with threats,[16] fixed his sword's point deep in the empty top [17] [of the head]. But the Martyr, triumphing [in Paradise] over the sword's point of the former murderers, [now] after the manner of one prostrated in prayer, lay still unmoved.

Now the Passion of the Primate [18] and Legate in the church and for the Church took place on the fourth day before the Kalends of January. . . .

[325] (5) (Benedict). . . . Now the Passion of the excellent Champion of God, Thomas, Archbishop of Canterbury, Primate of all England, and Legate of the Apostolic See, took place in the one thousand eleven hundred and seventieth year from the Incarnation of the Lord, in the fifty-third year of his own age, on the fourth day before the Kalends of January, the third day of the week, about the eleventh hour.[19]

---

scelus renovans, et minis [16] hostiliter funus infestans, vacuo vertice [17] mucronem infixit. Verum martyr, de priorum carnificum mucrone triumphans, ad modum prostrati in oratione jacebat immotus. . . .

Passus est autem quarto Kalendas Januarii Primas [18] et Legatus, in ecclesia et pro ecclesia. . . .

[325] (5) (Benedict). . . . Passus est autem egregius Dei athleta Thomas, Cantuariensis archiepiscopus, totius Angliae Primas, et apostolicae sedis Legatus, anno ab incarnatione Domini millesimo centesimo septuagesimo, vitae vero ipsius anno quinquagesimo tertio, quarto calendas Januarii, feria tertia, hora quasi undecima.[19]

---

[16] "With threats." But "minis" is probably a mistake for "nimis," *i.e.* "with cruelty unpardonable even in an enemy." The *Quadrilogus* has "nimis," and the Editor's note there is (*Mat.* iv. 399) "This is printed *minis* in vol. i. p. 135, perhaps wrongly."

[17] "Vertex," in poetry, means sometimes "head." But here it seems to mean "top (of the head)."

[18] [324*b*] "Primate." Why does William, only here, use this word, elsewhere using "archiepiscopus," etc. ? Probably because tradition connected *the date of the death with the punning distich quoted above* (*about* "*Primas*" *and* "*primo*") *by Fitzstephen.* In that distich the year was given (wrongly) as 1171. William gives no year.

[19] This date is correct, 1170. "The eleventh hour" is 5 P.M. On "Primas" see 324*b*.

[326] (6) (Herbert). . . . For in this severing of the top of the head,[20] in this severing of the crown, . . . when the concavity [21] of the head, with the crown of unction, was being separated from the head . . . there was neither murmur nor complaining. . . . [22] And when these gladiators, on this side and on that, struck and struck again, hastening his death, the sword of one of these gladiators was broken on the concavity of the head. . . . [23] For, until the whole consummation was made and the oblation entirely completed, he remained immovable, in one set form, with composure of body corresponding to the calm of his mind ; and, with knees bent and hands joined (as we said above)—so steadfastly did he keep his neck stretched out and his head exposed [to the stroke], that the very arrangement of his body was in itself a prayer to the Lord. . . . Against the violence of the strokes of those who fell upon him he opposed nothing, interposed nothing ; not one of his limbs did he draw down, not one did he draw,[24] or draw back ; his clasped hands he does not loose asunder, neither this way nor that way does he incline his head. . . .

[326] (6) (Herbert). . . . Nam . . . in hac decalvatione,[20] in decoronatione hac . . . ubi testa [21] capitis cum corona unctionis separatur a capite . . . nec murmur resonat nec querimonia. . . . [22] Et cum gladiatores hinc inde percuterent et repercuterent, mortem viri accelerantes, super testam capitis unius gladiatorum gladius frangitur. . . . [23] Nam donec consummaretur totum et inchoata perficeretur oblatio, sic immobiliter, sic uniformiter, et sicut aequanimiter, sic aequaliter, flexis genibus, junctis (ut diximus) manibus, collum semper extendit et caput exposuit, ut ipsa corporis compositio oraret Dominum. . . . Contra ictuum super se venientium vim nil opponit, nil objicit, de membris suis nullum subtrahit, nullum trahit [24] vel retrahit, non manus conjunctas dissolvit, non hac vel illac inclinat caput. . . .

[20] "Severing, etc." See 276a.
[21] "Concavity (testa)" seems used here for "brain-pan."
[22] "Nec . . . querimonia," an Asclepiad line, see 323a.
[23] No other writer makes this extraordinary statement. Herbert proceeds to enlarge on the strength of this " bone " of " the second Adam," against which the sword of Satan is broken.
[24] The style is so astonishingly diffuse, even for Herbert, that possibly there is some corruption.

[327] So, after it (*i.e.* the body) had been unclothed, after they received the body of Thomas [duly] washed....[25] Now there was in the crypt of the church a new tomb, hewn out of a rock [26] many days before, ... in which no man as yet had been placed.[27] And ... they placed the body of Thomas in this new tomb which had been hewn out of the rock, in the year after the Incarnation of the Lord one thousand one hundred and seventy-one,[28] but about the fifty-third of his own life.

[328] (7) (Anon. I.) Now his Passion took place in the one thousand one hundred and seventy-first [year] after the Incarnation of the Lord, on the fifth day from the birthday of the Lord, and on the third day of the week.[29]

(8) (Anon. II.) Omits this, and adds a long discourse on the Archbishop's virtues, and on his eminence as a martyr.

---

[327] Igitur postquam exutum fuit, postquam lotum [25] acceperunt corpus Thomae. . . . Erat autem in crypta ecclesiae monumentum novum, excisum de petra [26] a multis diebus, . . . in quo nondum quisquam positus fuerat.[27] Et . . . posuerunt corpus Thomae in hoc monumeuto novo quod erat excisum de petra, anno ab incarnatione Domini millesimo centesimo septuagesimo primo,[28] vitae vero ipsius anno circiter quinquagesimo tertio.

[328] (7) (Anon. I.) Passus est autem ab incarnatione Domini millesimo centesimo septuagesimo primo, quinto die a nativitate Domini, feria vero tertia.[29]
(8) (Anon. II.) Omits this.

---

[25] "Washed." It was not washed (407).

[26] Matth. xxvii. 60. No other writer describes the sarcophagus in these terms. But Herbert wishes to conform his language to that of Scripture. For the same reason, perhaps, he drops the terms "athleta," "praesul," "Martyr," etc., and uses "Thomas" to correspond to the Scriptural "Jesus."

[27] John xix. 41.

[28] An error, as above, 1171 for 1170.

[29] An error, as above, 1171 for 1170. We should call 29 Dec. the *fourth* day after Christmas day, but Anon. I. follows the Latin or inclusive method of reckoning. The writer proceeds to enumerate the memorable Tuesdays (feria tertia) in the Archbishop's life, describes the burial in three sentences, mentions miracles in one, and so concludes.

But the Paris MS. adds "The following is found in another legend (legenda)" and proceeds to quote "Quis quod sequitur," (220) John of Salisbury's acco of what followed the death. Then comes a collection of miraculous stories f Benedict.

(9) (Anon. IV.) Omits this, and adds a brief exhortation to imitate the Martyr.

[**329**] (10) (Anon. V.) Omits this, and—after describing the binding up of the head, and the collecting of the blood and brains by the monks—continues thus:—

"Moreover, as I have heard from the veracious report of men, the body, lifting itself up [after being] long dead, signed both itself and them that stood by with the sign of the cross, and again fell flat to the ground. Then the monks, taking off his garments . . . found haircloth. . . . There was also found . . . a letter . . . about his imminent death. Meanwhile, as we have again heard on true report, a blind man, who had been of his household, running up, received sight in the blood of the murdered man, by touching his eyes [with it]."[30]

[**330**] (11) (Anon. X.) In all [this], the Martyr—such was his unconquerable spirit[31] and admirable steadfastness, neither uttered word nor gave forth groan; neither arm nor garment did he oppose to the smiter: but he held immovable his head (which he had inclined and exposed to the sword's stroke), and at length, falling forward on the ground, with body straightened, as though prostrated in prayer, he

---

(9) (Anon. IV.) Omits this.

[329] (10) (Anon. V.) Etiam, sicut veridica hominum relatione didici, corpus diu mortuum se levans, signo crucis vivificae et se et astantes consignavit, rursusque ad terram concidit. Dehinc monachi vestes ejusdem auferentes . . . cilicium invenerunt. . . . ˙ Inventae sunt etiam sub eo litterae . . . de instante ejus morte. Interea sicut iterum veraciter percepimus, caecus quidam, qui de sua familia fuerat, accurrens, in sanguine occisi, oculos proprios tangens, visum recepit."[30]

[330] (11) (Anon. X.) In omnibus, invictus[31] animi et admirabilis constantiae martyr nec verbum protulit nec edidit gemitum, non brachium aut vestem opposuit ferienti, sed caput (quod inclinatum gladio exposuerat) tenebat immobile, et tandem in terra procidens, recto corpore, quasi in oratione prostratus, non pedem

---

[30] I have altered the editor's punctuation. The author proceeds to relate a ⁻aculous cure of a dumb man (**433**) and other marvels.

[31] This closely resembles John of Salisbury and Grim, but with omissions and ⁻tions. For example, "In omnibus" (Grim "in *his* omnibus," John "in *his* bus *cruciatibus*") is hardly Latin.

moved neither hand nor foot.³² And thus the Champion of God, migrating from this world, entered heaven as a conqueror on the fourth day before the Kalends of January.³³ Nor did it suffice to the assassins to perpetrate this shameful sin unless besides—horrible to relate—they cast forth the brains of the deceased Archbishop with their deadly swords.³⁴

[331] (12) (Garnier) Whoso might then have seen the blood and the brain fall, And lie, one with the other, on the pavement, Might have bethought him of the rose and the lily : For then would he have seen the blood keeping its red colour in the white brain, The brain likewise keeping its white colour in the red blood ³⁵ (ll. 5546-50). . . .

[332] For the Church of the North, and in the aisle of the North,³⁶ And facing the North did St. Thomas suffer death (ll. 5561-2). . . . For the good crowned [Martyr], in behalf of his crowned people (?), Gave his own crown, unarmed against the armed. Full of the spirit on his side was

---

movit nec manum ;³² et sic Dei athleta, a saeculo migrans, quarto kalendas Januarii ³³ caelos victor introivit. Nec suffecit percussoribus tantum flagitium perpetrasse, nisi etiam—quod dictu horribile est —funestis gladiis jam defuncti praesulis [cerebrum] ejicerent.³⁴

[331] Qui dunc véist le sanc et le cervel chaïr,
Et sur le pavement l'un od l'autre gesir,
De rose et de lilie l'i poïst sovenir :
Car dunc véist le sanc el blanc cervel rogir,
Le cervel ensement el vermeil sanc blanchir.³⁵
. . . . .

[332] Pur l'iglise del Nort, et el èle del Nort,³⁶
E vers le Nort turnez, suffri sainz Thomas mort :
. . . . .
Kar li buens coronez pur sa gent coronée,
Sa corone en dona, as armez desarmée,
Mult fu esperitals de sa part la meslée

---

³² The words "in terra procidens—nec manum" are in John (319), with the exception of "quasi in oratione prostratus." Benedict has (273) "recto corpore quasi ad orationem prostratus in terram corruit."

³³ Comp. Grim (315) "Itaque Dei sacerdos, *a saeculo migrans*, coelis nascitur, quarto, etc." But, whereas Grim inserts the year of the martyrdom (1171, wrongly), this author omits it here. He mentions 1170, a little before, rightly, as the year of the Archbishop's return from exile.

³⁴ The words "nec suffecit . .. . ejicerent" are (substantially and more fully) in John and Benedict. The author concludes with accounts of miracles mostly taken from Benedict's book (see 439).

³⁵ Garnier describes a *contrast*, "red *in* white, white *in* red" : Grim and ! Saga, a *blending*, "the brain reddening *from* the blood, the blood whiten *from* the brain."   ³⁶ "The North." See 149.

the conflict, When he made of his crown a shield against the sword [37] (ll. 5611-14). . . .

[333] Since now in these late times a new martyr is given you, Garnier the clerk, native of Pont Saint Maxence, Would have you certified of the time of the martyrdom : It was one thousand one hundred and seventy years Reckoned from the time when God was incarnate in the Virgin (ll. 5781-5).

[334] (13) (The *Saga*) In such manner is beautified the bright countenance of this martyr and confessor—that the blood brightened from the brain and the brain reddened from the blood, as if rose and lily were beautifully blended together.

[335] (i.) (Stanley) " As the murderers left the cathedral, *a tremendous storm of thunder and rain burst over Canterbury*, and *the night fell in thick darkness* upon the scene of the dreadful deed. The crowd was every instant increased by the multitudes flocking in from the town. . . . At last, however, the cathedral was cleared, and the gates shut ; and for a time *the body lay entirely deserted.* It was not till the night had quite closed in, that Osbert, the chamberlain of the Archbishop, *entering with a light*, found the corpse lying on its face. . . .

[336] (ii.) (Tennyson) [*Storm bursts. Flashes of lightning thro' the Cathedral*. . . . ROSAMUND *seen kneeling by the body of* BECKET.

Quant fist de sa corone escu cuntre l'espée.[37]
. . .
[333] Pur ço k'or tart vus est novels martirs donez,
Guarniers li clerc, del Punt sainte mescence nez,

Vus voelt fère del tens del martire acertez :
Mil anz cent et seissante et dis tut untez
I out, dès que Deus fu en Virgine encharnez.
ll. 5546·50 . . . 5561-2 . . . 5611·4 . . . 5781·5.

---

[37] This play on "the crown" (which might be paralleled by others from Herbert, etc.) is inserted to show how early a misunderstanding might arise as to the word. It has been questioned in modern times whether " Becket's Crown " means sometimes a part of Canterbury Cathedral or the bone relic. Stanley 285, Note F, ii.) refers to Eadmer's *Hist. Nov.* ii. p. 92 as saying that selm, having had a place assigned to him in a Roman Council, was given *a \ in the crown: "in corona sedes illi posita est*, qui locus non obscuri honoris \li conventu solet haberi."

§ 2. *Was the body "entirely deserted" ?*

[337] Stanley's words about the night falling "in thick darkness," about the body being "entirely deserted," and the Chamberlain "entering with a light," give the reader the impression that, when the Archbishop fell, he was left quite alone, and in absolute darkness, till Osbert arrived.

But the facts are these. Benedict (325) says that the martyrdom took place "about the eleventh hour," *i.e.* 5 P.M., of 29 Dec. Suppose 29 Dec. to correspond to our 3 or 4 Jan.: yet, even then, the sun would have set by 4 P.M., so that it would be as dark as night by 5 P.M., at all events inside a cathedral. Lights must have been kindled there long before. What Fitzstephen says is, "diu quidem ibi jacuit *fere* solus, et derelictus a clericis, et monachis, et caeteris cunctis, nec etiam adhuc ablato (Ed. suggests, no doubt rightly, adlato) *lumine ad sanctas ejus exsequias.*"

[338] In other words, the body was *not left "entirely alone,"* but probably under the charge of the servants of the Minster in St. Benedict's chapel,—lighted, as it had been for the last hour or more, dimly, no doubt, but in the usual way—while the monks took counsel, under the presidency of Prior Odo (who was not perhaps at that time a strong partisan of the Archbishop), as to what should be done. Meantime there was delay in sending "[a] *light for the holy exsequies,*" *i.e.* a taper, or tapers, to be lighted and placed round the body.

[339] This paragraph is omitted by the MS. called J. No doubt the Editor, or Author, when inserting it, intended to blame the monks for not detaching some of their own number to remain at once with the body. But even he does not say that the body was left "entirely alone." It was lef "*almost* alone," perhaps guarded by some half dozen me armed.

[340] As regards Osbert the Chamberlain, Fitzstep'

says simply that "he cut a strip from his shirt with a small knife in order to bind up the remnant of the half-severed head." This leaves it open to suppose that Osbert was one of those who remained from the beginning with the body. Stanley quotes "Grandison iv. 1" for his statement about "Osbert ... entering with a light." Grandison's name seldom occurs elsewhere among Stanley's references, and then only to support doubtful or unimportant statements. It is natural to ask whether Grandison, a writer of the 14th century, has not derived his information from Fitzstephen, and amplified it by his own inference.

§ 3. *Was there "a tremendous storm"?*

[341] Almost certainly there was no storm, or, at all events, no tremendous storm. This conclusion is based on the following reasons.

(1) The only evidence for it is Fitzstephen. Yet it was a phenomenon that all present must have noted, and all the Archbishop's friends must have regarded as a sign of the wrath of heaven. If "flashes of lightning" played, as Tennyson's stage-direction says, "thro' the Cathedral," why did not Grim, Benedict, and William see them, and take note of them? The omission of all notice of the storm by the other writers is, under the circumstances (**313**), fatal to its historical truth. Even the poet Garnier says nothing about it.

[342] (2) Fitzstephen introduces his statement with the words, "As, when our Lord was suffering in His own body," referring to the miraculous darkness alleged to have happened during the Crucifixion "from the sixth to the ninth hour." That, in itself, is enough to throw suspicion on his historical accuracy; for it exhibits a mind ready to catch up any loose exaggeration, or poetic metaphor, and to interpret it as fact because it would assimilate St. Thomas's Passion to Christ's Crucifixion.

[**343**] (3) Fitzstephen's words "the sun turned his eyes away" are manifest poetry, and flagrantly opposed to fact. If the sun sets at 4 P.M., how can he "turn his eyes away" at 5 P.M.? As his words "A horrid storm-cloud veils the brow of heaven" are taken from Horace, so the notion of the averted eyes of the sun may possibly be taken from Virgil's words about the sun's behaviour at the death of Caesar,[1] or from some similar personification (for there are many) in Latin poetry.

It is very natural that statements of this kind originating in hyperbole should be interpreted as fact.

[**344**] (4) The *Flores Historiarum* (vol. ii. p. 84) asserts that in 1172 there were storms throughout the world, which shewed that the blood of St. Thomas "cried in thunder to the Lord." It is quite possible that a few years after the Martyrdom a statement that "this happened *after* St. Thomas's death" was changed into a tradition that "it happened *immediately after*." Such confusion is all the more likely because instances of chronological error at this date are found in the *Flores Historiarum* (**347**), and our own authors are divided between 1170 and 1171 as the date of the Martyrdom.

[**345**] (5) It may be added that when a tremendous storm *does* occur, three or four months afterwards, just at a time when the Archbishop's enemies were supposed to be plotting the removal of his body, Benedict chronicles it as a Providential interposition.[2] This gives point to the first of the above-mentioned considerations, which, in accordance with the rule previously (**313**) laid down, alone suffices to demonstrate that there was no such "tremendous storm" as is described by the two modern authors.[3]

---

[1] *Georg.* i. 465-6.

[2] **484.**

[3] Stanley explains the "redness of the air," which (according to Fitzstephen) followed the storm, as "the red glare of an aurora borealis which, after the

§ 4. *The date*

[346] Why do all our authorities, except Benedict and Garnier, either omit the date, or give it incorrectly, as 1171 instead of 1170? Perhaps the fact that, in most parts of England and Europe, the death (occurring on 29 Dec. 1170) would not be known till 1171, and would be associated with 1171, may have contributed to the error. But Fitzstephen (318) quotes a distich making the date 1171; and a short saying of that kind in verse might be more easily remembered and more widely circulated in England than Garnier's French quintet or Benedict's tradition in prose. If the author of the distich was a Canterbury monk, it would naturally be supposed to have the authority of Canterbury. It is true that Benedict was subsequently Prior of Canterbury, and had an inclination for chronological order, as may be seen from his Book of Miracles. On the other hand, the Preface to William's Book of Miracles expressly disclaims chronological order as superfluous; and this, though probably written under William's influence, is nominally written in the name of the whole body of monks. Putting these facts together with indications that Benedict, as Prior, was not very popular with the monks, and that his Book of Miracles did not commend itself to them, we may conjecture that the consensus of monkish tradition might be biassed against Benedict's statement (though confirmed by the Frenchman Garnier) and in favour of "the Canterbury distich," if it may be so called.

[347] Another instance of confusion of date, as regards

---

stormy evening, lighted up the midnight sky." I am not aware at what hours of the night, and in what circumstances, the aurora borealis may have appeared in the south of England. But, even though that explanation may be physically possible, the considerations above-mentioned require that the "redness" should be rejected along with the "storm."

[345*a*] The laws of nature may allow us to believe in it. The laws of evidence do not.

events occurring in the years 1171-3, may be found in the text of Matthew Paris, retained by his editor (commonly called Matthew of Westminster), but supplemented in the following extraordinary way: (1) (Editor) "In the year of Grace, 1173. *Those who were rising in arms against the King were taken, the King of Scotland.* . . . The King came to Canterbury. In a Chapter, he was absolved by the Convent of Canterbury. He also gave up, over the High Altar, those Customs[1] for which St. Thomas contended even to death"; (2) (Matthew Paris) "In the year of Grace, 1174 . . . The King, invoking the aid of St. Thomas the Martyr, bestowed on Canterbury Cathedral, for the finding of lights (*i.e.* for the providing of wax tapers) forty pounds of annual rent. On that very day, the day of the Sabbath, God delivered William King of Scotland into his hands."[2] If it were not for the mention of the taking of the "King of Scotland," how easily might historians be induced to suppose that the chronicle relates *two* visits of King Henry to the tomb! The full explanation of these errors must be left to chronological experts. But the obstacles in the way of eliciting exact historical truth from ancient records are vividly illustrated by the fact that, among all those of our Latin authorities who mention the date of Becket's Martyrdom, only one gives it correctly.

---

[1] "Those Customs," *i.e.* the "customs" of Henry's predecessors on the throne, as set forth by him in the Constitutions of Clarendon, against which the Archbishop contended. "*For* which (pro quibus)," therefore, means "*to prevent* which," as in "a remedy *for* fever."

[2] *Anno gratiae MCLXXIII. Capti sunt rebelles regi, rex Scotiae . . . Rex venit Cantuariam. In capitulo absolvitur a conventu Cantuariae. Resignat etiam illas consuetudines, super majus altare, pro quibus beatus Thomas decertavit usque ad mortem.*

Anno gratiae MCLXXIV. . . . Rex, invocans auxilium beati Thomae martiris, contulit ecclesiae Cantuariensi ad luminaria invenienda annui census xl. libras. Ipsa die scilicet sabbati tradidit Deus regem Scotiae Willelmum in manus suas. . . .

CHAPTER XII

INFERENCES

§ 1. *A general inference*

[348] From a comparison of the narratives above given the first and most general conclusion is one that must be most unsatisfactory to all those who desire short cuts to truth. For it is this: that no general rule can be laid down as to the value of an early account as compared with a late one. An early account sometimes teems with falsehoods. A late account sometimes corrects falsehoods; sometimes makes them falser and adds to their number. The value of a writing depends upon facts that are often very difficult to ascertain—namely, the position and character of the writer, his opportunities for observation, or for collecting evidence from those who have observed, and his power of setting down what he has observed or collected, either without inferences of his own, or, at all events, in such a way as to allow the reader clearly to distinguish facts observed from facts inferred.

§ 2. *An early narrative, if not from an eye-witness, mostly contains " lies "*

[349] The word "lies" is printed as a quotation, being quoted from Garnier's criticism of his own early poem on the Martyrdom, written within two years from its occurrence (36). He composed it, he says without time to insert and

to omit, and to temper the sweet with the bitter; and hence he says that he "often lied (suvent i menti)." No doubt, he was honest, and he does not intend to deny his own honesty: still, he calls the result, in part, "lying."

[350] The same tendency to honest, zealous, and affectionate "lying" may be illustrated from a letter written immediately after the murder by the Archbishop of Sens to the Pope.[1] Regarding the Martyr as a sacrifice, the writer speaks of him as "standing before the altar," "embracing with his hands the cross that he had been wont to bear before him,"[2] offering himself up "between the horns of the altar and the cross," and lastly as " praying for his persecutors, adding also and most passionately (affectuosissime) supplicating that at least his household might be preserved unhurt." Moreover, as to what preceded, instead of saying that Becket refused at first to take any notice of the knights when they entered his presence, the writer says that "immediately on their entering they were saluted by the holy man but did not salute him in return."

[351] This letter is a tissue of small inaccuracies, all dictated by the best of motives, affection for the dead, and a desire to honour his name, but still very misleading. Because the first martyr, Stephen, prayed for the dead, therefore the writer assumes that the last martyr *must* have done the same. Because the Saviour bore His cross, therefore

---

[1] *Mat.* vii. 429, footnote "The authorship of this letter is claimed for Herbert of Bosham by the C. C. C. MS. . . . and the same writer's later narrative (*Mat.* iii. 487 *sq.*) has much in common with the letter." Herbert, having been sent abroad by Becket just before his death, might naturally be resorted to by the earliest messengers who were sent from the monks to carry the news to France that it might be forwarded to the Pope.

[2] When the Archbishop "fought with wild beasts" at Northampton, he had actually insisted on carrying the cross himself instead of letting it be carried, as usual, by his cross-bearer. The bishops remonstrated with him on his strange conduct, and one even tried to wrest it out of his hands. Herbert was present then. Did he suppose (inferring it from the messengers who reported the death) that the Archbishop did the same thing on the day of the Martyrdom?

also did the Martyr. Because St. Thomas "sacrificed" his life, therefore he must have died "before the altar."

[352] Yet the same volume that contains this letter of "lies," gives another, written about the same time, which—though making no mention of the four knights except under the general phrase "the executioner"—represents the words of the Archbishop with very fair accuracy. But why? Because the writer "came that evening to Canterbury," and, though not an ear-witness himself, appears from internal evidence (315*a*) to have had conversation with the most faithful of the ear-witnesses, Edward Grim.

Far less pardonable than the errors of the Archbishop of Sens, or Herbert his scribe, are those of John of Salisbury. He was an eye-witness up to the point where he ran away; nor had he the excuse of haste, since he did not write till three or four months after the event.[3] Yet he repeatedly describes the Archbishop as dying "before the altar," and, once, as dying "amid his fellow priests and in the hands of the clergy who had been caused by the uproar of armed murderers to *flock to* that stupendous and pitiable spectacle[4]"—where accuracy would substitute, for "flock *to*," "run away *from*." He also imputes the outrage on the dead body, not to Hugh the clerk, but to the four knights.

§ 3. *The evidence of one eye-witness is of more value than the concurrent testimony of many non-eye-witnesses*

[353] An admirable illustration of this is afforded by the evidence of Grim as to the circumstances attending the first of the wounds inflicted on the Archbishop. A great number say that the striker was Tracy, and have (for the

---

[3] His letter (*Mat.* vii. 463) speaks of "many" miracles in England and France. There were not "many," even in England, till Easter 1171.

[4] *Mat.* vii. 464 "inter consacerdotes et manus religiosorum quos armatorum carnificum tumultus fecerat ad stupendum et miserabile spectaculum convenire."

present) carried the day with posterity: but Grim tells us that he heard the Archbishop address the striker as "Reinald [Fitzurse]," and his testimony is supported by Anon. I., a writer whom, from internal evidence, there is very strong reason for supposing to have been himself an eye-witness, or to have derived his facts from eye-witnesses.

[354] On the supposition that Anon. I. was an eye-witness, another illustration may be derived from his details of "the striking off of the cap." He, alone of all our authorities, records it as part of the result of the first blow which inflicted a slight scalp wound. The others, if they mention it at all, speak of it as the result of a feigned sword-blow, or they describe the cap as struck off with the hand, or, vaguely, as cast away: Anon. I. alone gives a clear and definite account, putting the incident in its right place, and enabling us to discern how he saw, as an eye-witness, what others, at a distance, took to be a mere feint or else a blow with the flat of the sword on the shoulder.

[355] Note that Grim is valuable to us because he is here recording what he saw and heard. When he ceases to be an eye-witness, his evidence (though he remains honest) may be expected to cease to be trustworthy, except so far as he reproduces the testimony of an eye-witness. That this expectation is realized will appear in the following section.

§ 4. *The evidence of non-eye-witnesses is only so far valuable as it preserves the evidence of eye-witnesses, distinct from inferences and corrections made by the former*

[356] This ought to be a truism. But it is far from being so. Many readers suppose that an early account (and still more, a number of concurrent accounts, early or late) introducing a new detail, must always be of importance. But this will not be the case, if we have reason for thinking

that the detail is a mere inference of the writer copied by other writers. Thus, Herbert tells us that Robert de Broc was the man that outraged the Archbishop's dead body; and a statement coming from so authoritative a writer,— one intimate with the Archbishop and with his friends, and one who took pains to collect facts while residing in England, —might naturally seem entitled to great weight. But in reality it is of no weight at all, because it can be shown that this author frequently bases statements on inference. He may have confused the guide of the knights into the Cathedral with the guide of the knights into the Palace, who really was Robert de Broc. Or he may have been influenced by the motive that actuates the writer of the *Saga*, who naively attributes the act to the two brothers De Broc, on the ground (in effect) that the action is diabolical and that these two are pre-eminently children of the devil.

[357] Even Grim, so accurate and trustworthy here, ceases sometimes to be accurate and trustworthy when he describes events beyond the range of his own observation. For example, in telling how Thomas Becket, in his youth, while hawking, was saved from drowning, he says that the falcon, catching a wild duck as it dived, was drawn under water by the latter, and that Thomas dismounted and leapt into the stream for pity of the falcon. Then, just when he was in danger of being drawn under a mill-wheel, the wheel stopped and did not move till he was drawn out.

[358] Compare this with the account of Garnier (who says he heard the story from Thomas himself), and with the similar account of Anon. I.: Grim will be found to have given to the story a dignified and miraculous tinge. The truth was, that Thomas wished, not to save a drowning falcon, but to bring one back that had flown after its prey, some distance beyond a river, so that he was in danger of losing it. To recover the falcon, he rather rashly crossed a foot-bridge with a horse. In crossing, he *tumbled in*. He did not *leap in*.

The mill-wheel stood still because the miller just in time *happened to turn off the water*, not knowing that any one was in danger.[1]

Thus Grim himself accentuates the lessons, most important for the students of evidence, 1st, that documents must be weighed, not counted, 2nd, that, even in the same document, the weight of this or that statement must vary with the author's access to means of observation. Garnier (**39a** and l. 5836) tells us that he received information about St. Thomas from his sister and from those who had attended him from infancy. We do not know that Grim possessed any such information, and the facts above stated lead us to suppose that he did not possess it.

§ 5. *The evidence of a late non-eye-witness is particularly liable to the inferential taint.*

[359] This is antecedently natural in proportion to the lateness of the writer. Early non-eye-witnesses are not so strongly tempted as late ones to remove difficulties arising from discrepancies, and to interpolate or alter for purposes of edification. It is in later times, after controversies, that such temptations arise, or increase. As for eye-witnesses, though they are not exempt from error of inference—as when Fitzstephen and William, from a distance, infer, as they seem to do, that the first blow was a mere feint—yet it is comparatively rare (except where imposture is practised, or where ignorant people record scientific marvels). Often, they are too full of what they have seen to supplant sight by inference, though they may most tediously supplement it by moral comments.

[360] But a late non-eye-witness, such as Herbert of Bosham for example, can hardly justify his writing unless he infers. He has to collect divergent accounts, to weigh

---

[1] See **397-401** for the accounts of Grim, Garnier, Anon. I., and the *Saga*.

their authority, to compare and contrast their statements, sometimes combining this with that, at other times rejecting this while accepting that. If he gives reasons in each case, he is almost sure to be tedious; if he does not, he is quite sure to be misleading. Not seldom he contrives to be both. But throughout the whole of his narrative, so far as it is not a mere repetition of the words of eyewitnesses, he must be, with or without warning, inferential.

His inferences may deal with (1) the writing and interpretation of words; (2) the order, and (3) application, of statements; (4) the truth or falsehood of statements; (5) the necessity of supplying omissions.

§ 6. *Errors of Word*

[361] In our narrative, these are of slight importance. The narrators wrote too near the time of the action described to allow the intervention of oral tradition, or the frequent succession of new MSS. replacing old ones,—both of which processes cause great perversions of words. Nevertheless, such errors have been shown to exist, as when Anon. X. represents Grim's "murderers *of the flesh (carnis)*" in the phrase "murderous *dogs (canes)*." We have also seen that possibly William, by writing "irr-" for "er-," converts a statement about "*the* four others rushing *out*" of the Cathedral, into a statement about "*four* others rushing *into* the Cathedral," which may explain a tradition found in Garnier, but in none of our Latin authorities, about "four other knights" following the first four in the cloisters, but not entering the Cathedral.[1]

---

[1] An amusing verbal corruption is mentioned by Stanley (p. 91). "The words in which this act [the wounding of Grim's arm] is described in almost all the chronicles have given rise to a curious mistake: 'Brachium Edwardi *Grim fere* abscidit.' By running together these two words, later writers have produced the name of 'Grimfere.'" Stanley does not give references for this very interesting statement.

[362] It is in the process of translation, however, that verbal errors are most to be expected. If Garnier had not obtained evidence from eye-witnesses, coming to Canterbury within two or three years after the facts, we might have expected to find a good many corruptions arising from his rendering of Latin (or English) into French, and then, in later times, from the rendering of his French into Latin (or English). Even as it is, there are perhaps signs of such confusion. We have above noted his use of "cupel" and "chapel" to denote the scalp or upper part of the skull, and his silence about the "cap" which might also be called "chapel"; and the ambiguity of the latter word may explain his silence. There has also been noted his use of the rather commonplace "bad man (hum malveis)," where Anon. I. has "my man (homo meus)." But these are slight matters. Garnier can be corrected by an abundance of other witnesses, so that he does not afford adequate illustration of the serious difficulties that may sometimes arise from an early verbal ambiguity in a writer who is the sole authority for what he records.

[363] An amusing instance of divergence arising from verbal obscurity occurs in the interpretation of the well-known story of Queen Philippa's intercession for the burgesses of Calais, recorded by Froissart alone. Lingard contends that King Edward was not in earnest, and never really intended to execute the burgesses; which is proved, he thinks, by the fact that (Johnes' Transl.) "*the King gave a wink*," when Sir Walter de Manny interceded. Every one will think that, if the King was getting up a scene (to intimidate the French and at the same time spare the burgesses), it was extremely foolish of him to spoil it all by that "wink." In the next place, the student will be puzzled by finding that the "wink," in some translators and later writers, makes way for various substitutes: (Berners) "the King *wryed away* from him," (Holinshed) "regarded them

with a fell countenance," while modern writers vary between "*winked*," "*ground his teeth*," "*changed the aspect of his countenance*," "*grinned*," etc.

[364] The facts are these. The Editio Princeps of Froissart (? 1495) has "Adonc *guigna* (1513 guygna) le roy," "the king *made a sign*," which suits with what follows, viz. "and ordered the executioner to come in." This would mean that he "'*made a sign*' for the executioner to be sent for." But Simeon Luce (1873) and Lettenhove read "se grigna," which would mean "grincer," "gnash," or "grin"; and it is said that some MSS. add "les dens"; others have "se renga." Perhaps Lingard, or Johnes, or both, read "cligner," "wink."

§ 7. *Misarrangement of statements*

[365] Many instances will occur to the reader of variations in the order of statements, and particularly as to the words of the Archbishop. Almost all, for example, differ from Grim in placing the words in which the Archbishop commends his soul to God after, whereas Grim and Anon. I. place them before, the first wound. A more important instance relates to the order of the words recorded by William, "Reginald, I have bestowed many benefits on you, and do you come to me in arms?" Why do Grim and Anon. I. omit them? In substance, they resemble words said by Fitzstephen to have been uttered in the Palace. Ought they to be transposed to the Palace? Or were they uttered in the Cathedral, only in a different form, better represented by Anon. I. ("you are my man")? Or is William wrong in omitting the words "into a church," and Benedict right in inserting them ("come to me *into a church* in arms"), so that the charge is, not one of *ingratitude*, but one of *sacrilege*?

[366] Again, Herbert, contradicting all the rest, repre-

sents the doors of the Cathedral as shut long enough for the knights to knock violently at them. Is that a misstatement, or a transposition to the Cathedral of a statement about the Palace? It is probably the latter. So, perhaps, is his statement that De Broc was with the four knights in the Cathedral.

[367] Transpositions of this kind may often result in inferences that the same event happened twice. For example, the *Flores Historiarum* describes (**347**) one visit of Henry II. to the Martyr's tomb in which he resigns the Customs of Clarendon, and another in the following year in which he gives the monks a large annual sum "to provide lights." Both these entries are known (by abundant evidence) to refer to the same visit (in 1174). But, if such evidence had been wanting, we might easily have inferred that two visits had been paid in two consecutive years.

[368] Again, William records the dashing out of the Martyr's brains, first, as the act of all the knights in killing him, and then, in an Appendix, as a detailed outrage on the part of one person. His confused account leaves it doubtful whether he regards the "dashing out" as the mere result of the four wounds, or as a separate and deliberate mutilation: but in any case the *Quadrilogus* is misled into describing it, first (Benedict) as an act of malice perpetrated by a "child of Satan," and then as an act (William) "hostile even to excess (nimis hostiliter)," yet performed by one who (Herbert) "wondered whether he were already dead." This is a good instance of a very frequent error, which may be conveniently called *The Error of Duplication*.

§ 8. *Misapplication of statements*

[369] Sometimes a statement is misapplied through carelessness, and especially through neglect of context. A hasty writer will hardly let his witness finish his sentence

before he catches up one or two striking words, and makes a note of these alone, which he will afterwards expand into something that takes his own fancy. Thus, for example, when the first blow inflicted on the Archbishop had been erroneously supposed by Fitzstephen, and perhaps by others, to be a blow with the flat of the sword, William, adding his Appendix, in which he for the first time mentions Grim, gives one the impression of having said to himself, "There certainly was something about a blow with the flat of the sword. To whom could it refer? Not to Grim, for his arm was nearly cut off. Not certainly to the Archbishop, because that would be undignified. It must have referred to one of the monks, and I shall put it down so."

[370] Again, with reference to the ascending and descending of "steps," William, if he happened to have run away before that took place, or if he thought that the doing and, as it were, undoing of an action was not to the purpose, might take the view that the tradition referred not to the "steps" of a staircase, but to the "steps" of the Archbishop, either as having come several steps to meet his murderers, or as planting his footsteps to meet his death at their hands.

[371] Again, with reference to the "shaking off" by the Archbishop—certainly he did "shake off," or "shake out," something: but—so William and others seem to have argued—"it could hardly be one of the knights. That would be too secular an act for a Saint. The knight, if he recoiled, may have done so through remorse, or through reverence, or to give force to his impending stroke. But what the Archbishop did was 'to shake the corner of his pallium out of the man's hand.'" Other instances have been given above (**366**), where the misapplication was one of place, so that what had been said or done in the Palace was described as having been said or done in the Cathedral.

[372] One very important class of errors of this kind

springs from misapplying metaphor to fact. But this seldom occurs except in passing from oral tradition, or poetic tradition, to prose history; and it requires more time than is allowed by the short interval between the Martyrdom and the composition of most of the narratives quoted above.

[373] However, it is quite possible that a metaphorical statement about "the sun turning away his eyes" and "darkening the day" may have, in part, led Fitzstephen (and him alone) to mention a storm as immediately following the Archbishop's murder; and the "redness in the skies" (which he also, almost alone, mentions) may have originated (in part) from some poetic phrase about the Archbishop's blood "going up to heaven to call down flames of vengeance." Still more probably may we explain thus the legend, recorded by only one of our authorities, that the Martyr's dead body arose before the High Altar, and blessed, and signed with the Cross, both itself and the monks that stood by. Such a legend was not unlikely to arise, expressive of the fact that the Martyr's death was blessed both to him and to others, bringing to himself the crown of Martyrdom and to the church of Canterbury peace and prosperity.

[374] The statement made by some that the Martyr died while embracing his cross, may be in part due to the Fallacy of the Fitness of Things; but it may also be an extension of the tradition of Herbert, who described him as hastening *to* the Cross *with* the Cross, and of phrases about his being "crucified," or "carrying his Cross." Moreover a tradition (146) describing the Archbishop as having seen himself in a vision, crucified in the very spot where he suffered, appears to have been confused with a vision of "a Man crucified," which probably meant at first "Christ crucified"—whence it was inferred that, since Christ is crucified afresh in the sufferings of His martyrs, the vision

really amounted to one of the crucifixion of the Martyr himself.

[375] The *Saga*, as being later than our other authorities, and also as being poetry, might be expected to afford instances of the misapplication of metaphor. Accordingly it describes a well as miraculously springing up in the crypt to supply the pilgrims with St. Thomas's Water. Another of its legends, that the stone pavement became soft as snow so as to receive the imprints of the Martyr's feet, is difficult to explain thus. To most modern minds it may seem hardly serious: but there seems no beauty in the story if the poet told it believing it to be false; and the circumstantial manner in which he refers to it afterwards indicates that the origin was not linguistic. " His blood did not flow over the floor of the church, as might seem likely it would, but had run together on the marble into small cups so that it might be easily taken up. And it is seen ever since, how the marble departed from its nature, whereas it grew soft and sank in for to receive the blood. But where blood and brain mingled together, it stood on the flat stone which remained unchanged in its nature." The Fallacy, here, is that of the *Fitness of Things*, which makes the writer believe that, in order to preserve the blood of St. Thomas, it was fit that the stone should change its nature, as it had done also to preserve his footprints.

§ 9. *Misjudgment of statements*

[376] In deciding the truth or falsehood of a statement, the right criterion as to fact is the credibility of the witness. If an all but perfectly credible witness asserts that he heard the Archbishop of Canterbury say, " There is no God," it is reasonable to believe the former as to the fact, though not necessarily as to such inferences as he may draw from the fact. The witness may have omitted to add that, before

those words, the Archbishop uttered others, *e.g.* " The fool hath said in his heart."

[377] But this method—of going back in the first place to the credibility of the witness, and of accepting one credible eye-witness against masses of hearsay, and of "antecedent probability "—is not the popular method. In dealing with the lives of the great, we are often more influenced than we should be by the Fallacy of the Fitness of Things, which leads us, sometimes to hasty negations, such as, " He never could have said this," " This never could have happened," sometimes to hasty assertions, " The words uttered must have been these," " The affair must have happened thus." Hence, for example, although Benedict expressly declares that the body of the Martyr was *not* washed, owing to the need of haste in the burial, Herbert insists that it *was* washed (probably being dissatisfied with Benedict's explanation, that the washing in the Martyr's blood sufficed for the Martyr). Hence, also, one of the authorities quoted above represents the four knights as each striking one blow, four in all, because of the symmetry in this division of the four blows.

[378] So we have seen that the *Saga* openly states its reason for assigning to the De Brocs the outrage on the Martyr's body to be, that the action, being devilish, was peculiarly suitable for these children of the devil. But this Fallacy is best exemplified in details assimilating St. Thomas to Christ. These are frequent, *e.g.* the " tomb hewn out of the rock " (mentioned by Herbert alone); the sun " turning away its eyes " and " darkening the day " (mentioned by Fitzstephen alone);[1] the recoil of Fitzurse (or others) from

---

[1] [378*a*] Above (344), it was shown that the writer (or the writer's informant) may also have transferred to 1170 an account of a later storm. This, then, is a good exemplification of a most important rule, viz. *A legend may have several contributory causes.* This legend may have begun in (1) poetry. Then (2) the memory of an *actual* storm may have suggested that the metaphor *might be* literally true. Then (3) the Fitness of Things led people to conclude

the mere presence of the Archbishop (as the Roman cohort recoiled and fell to the ground before Jesus). To these may be added, as indications of Herbert's general tendency, that he actually calls the retinue of the knights a "cohort," and describes them as armed "with swords and staves." Moreover, the later *Quadrilogus*, after describing the knights as meeting "under a certain tree" in order to slay "the Lord's Christ," goes on to say that "the tree withered away (as we read in the Gospels)."[2]

§ 10. *Omissions or alterations for edification*

[379] The Fallacy of the Fitness of Things has induced several of our narrators to omit words and acts that appeared unseemly, unedifying, or impossible.

Almost all omit Garnier's graphic statement that Fitzurse seized and shook the Archbishop, and that the knights tried to place him on Tracy's shoulders. Several writers omit the statement that the Archbishop "shook off" one of the knights and nearly threw him to the ground. This last fact could not, indeed, be suppressed; for it so happened that Herbert, one of the latest and most authoritative writers, being himself of a militant disposition, emphasized this detail. But had it not been for Herbert, the Harmony of the Four Lives might have altogether omitted it. Not one, except Grim, who was by the Archbishop's side, tells us that he called Fitzurse "pander (leno)." Also, describing the interview in the Palace, John of Salisbury omits his own remonstrance with the Archbishop on his exasperating manner toward the knights, and in particular on his following them to the door with (apparently) provoking words. Others even

---

that it *must be* literally true because the Martyrdom must needs have been like the Crucifixion.

[2] This takes place (*Mat.* iv. 385) when they "go out from the face of the King." William describes them as preparing for the slaughter under a mulberry-tree after they have gone out from the presence of the Archbishop.

change these provoking words into words of "temperate request," and we have seen that Stanley himself, misled by these writers, describes them as expressive of "entreaty" and "despair."

[380] This last instance is one in which a tradition, too firmly rooted to be eradicated, is modified instead of being omitted. Similarly, we have seen that the "shaking off" of a knight appears in some writers simply as the "shaking free" of a cloak from the knight's hands; and the recoil of the knight is attributed, not to the Archbishop's push but either to the knight's own act, stepping back for the next stroke, or else to motives of reverence, or remorse.

[381] Hence is seen the fallacy of the common canons, that "later accounts always add," and that "additional picturesque details are always to be suspected." No such sweeping rules can be laid down. Later accounts sometimes condense for brevity, sometimes omit for edification. In each case, the nature of the writer, and the nature of the detail, must be considered. If the writer bears the stamp of first hand knowledge (or access to it), honesty, accuracy, and absorption in his subject, and if there are few or no signs of a desire to write up to controversial ends, and of a desire to edify the reader by pointing morals and inculcating analogies, then a picturesque detail, though found in only that one writer, may freely be accepted. Nay, more, if the addition be of the nature of a stumbling-block or scandal to hero-worshippers, then (provided that the writer is a lover of the hero) it may be accepted as almost demonstrably true, and as confirming the previously formed favourable opinion of the writer's honesty.

§ 11. *Floating Tradition*

[382] No reader can have even glanced at the thirteen accounts of the outrage inflicted on the Martyr's body

without perceiving that from a very early period there were current certain poetic moralizations on the subject that constituted a kind of common stock from which any writer of a Passion might borrow. The breaking of the sword against the pavement, typifying the breaking of secular oppression against the rock of the Church, is one of these. But the most striking is the comparison of the blood and the brains of the Martyr to the roses and lilies of the Church (who is both Mother and Virgin), and to the white robe of the Saint with the empurpled garment of the Martyr. It will be observed that the writers who use these metaphors never acknowledge from whom they have borrowed them, and it would be a matter of great difficulty to determine which, if any, of our writers originated them. The differences between Garnier and Grim indicate that both these writers borrowed from some common tradition, the former (like Fitzstephen) taking the metaphor to be strictly that of a nosegay ("white in red, and red in white") while Grim, having seen the actual fact, that one was *mixed with* the other, uses language that is slightly incongruous with the metaphor of flowers, describing the brains as reddened *from* the blood and the blood as whitened *from* the brains.

[383] We are on safer ground when we come to such a passage as this, found in several of our narratives, "*Nor did it suffice to these murderers*, etc. etc., to profane, etc. etc., *unless they also*, etc. etc., and cast out the brains, scattering them on the pavement." Bearing in mind (1) the rhetorical turn of this sentence, (2) the fact that many of the writers who insert it are indifferent composers, (3) that John of Salisbury had a very high reputation among all his contemporaries for literary composition, (4) that his biography is mentioned with praise by many of the later biographers of St. Thomas, (5) that he used a sentence very similar to the above, in a letter written to a French Bishop in 1171 and subsequently embodied in his biography, which is believed

also to be very early—we are almost certainly justified in saying that the writers who use that or a similar sentence took it from John's narrative.

[384] In all these cases, the reader will find no sense of literary copyright. The writers are absorbed in their subject. They often write anonymously and borrow indiscriminately from named and anonymous authors, from oral and written tradition. If William or Grim borrows from John of Salisbury, the borrower seems to regard himself as borrowing, not from John, but from "The Passion according to John": for John himself must have borrowed from others his information as to facts that he did not witness. Hence great caution is needed before asserting that one author borrowed from another. Grim's work was almost certainly not written till after 1171, yet we have found words in it closely agreeing (315*a*) with a letter to the Pope written early in 1171. Yet it is not likely that Grim is the borrower. More probably he is the lender.

§ 12. *The importance of internal evidence*

[385] The last section shows the importance of verbal and textual criticism, and the value of internal evidence, in eliciting historical truth from a number of parallel narratives.

In the present instance we have a great advantage, because Grim tells us that he was with the Martyr in his last moments. But suppose he had omitted that sentence. His narrative, being then anonymous, would probably have been pushed into the background, like that of Anon. I. Yet, as a fact, Anon. I. is the most valuable of all our authors (except Garnier), and in some cases more valuable than all the rest put together: and the value of Anon. I. is known, not from external evidence as to the author, but from internal evidence alone.

[386] It appears, then, that in the comparison of

documents we must begin by trying to put ourselves into the position of each writer, in order that we may ascertain whether he is to be trusted, or distrusted, or put aside as worthless.

[387] Those who are to be put aside as worthless are writers like Anon. X. who merely borrow scraps from earlier writers, and contribute nothing of their own; so that their only value consists in their occasionally throwing light on the text of some one earlier than themselves.

[388] The man who is to be distrusted is the man whom one must always suspect of wanting to infer, and to rearrange in chronological order where there are no data for so doing, and to insert what is edifying, and to omit or modify what is non-edifying, and to clear up what is obscure by slightly altering the words—and, worst of all, to do all this in such a way as not to allow us to distinguish what belongs to him from what belongs to his originals. In proportion to this man's ingenuity he will often be all the more dangerous, as he will be more open to the temptation of cleverly emending the text or drawing some subtle conclusion;—as, for example, that because the Teacher makes a reference to "the inside of the cup and platter," therefore the utterance must have taken place at a meal. Goodness of purpose, and zeal, are no protections for such historians as these. Of all the writers about St. Thomas, none probably loved him better than Herbert of Bosham; none cares less about the miraculous, or is more jealous for his hero's character and individuality, lest it should be lost and forgotten in the Saint. Well may we believe the tedious, prolix old man, when he says that he cannot write about the Martyrdom for tears, and yet cannot desist from writing because he cannot tear himself away from his old friend and patron. Yet, in spite of all this, we have seen above that he makes repeated mistakes, where he ceases to be an eye-witness, and that these are largely caused by the Fallacy

of the Fitness of Things and the desire to assimilate the Martyr to the Saviour.

[389] It is the plain prose writer who is to be trusted, when he writes about what he has seen and heard :—the man who is not a classical student, not given to allusions, not a fastidious composer, softening facts for style's sake ; not a historical student, given to the finding of analogies, or correspondences between cause and effect ; not a theologian, bound to find sermons in facts and good everywhere. The simple, matter-of-fact reporter, losing himself in his subject, will often insert what is characteristic of his hero, even though it may be non-edifying or even a little scandalous. He feels, perhaps, an admiration too deep to be touched by the thought of "scandal." He will often, if he writes as an eye-witness, be artistically guilty of disproportion, emphasizing what struck him at the time, and not consulting the feelings of posterity. Hence he is sure to be neglected when the hero, becoming far-famed, attains to the distinction of having his life recorded by writers of ability. If he happens, as Grim did, to be connected with the hero by some picturesque personal link, his book may remain ; but it will not exercise the influence attained by more artistic and discreet compositions. And if his book happens to be anonymous, and not to indicate, by internal evidence, any such striking relation between the author and the hero as Edward Grim was able to allege, then his work may be relegated for many generations to the background. Such has been the fate of the work called Anon. I., of which the author, if not Robert of Merton, was inspired either by Robert, or by one who had many opportunities (either as an eye-witness or as one who had access to testimony, written or oral, from an eye-witness) for ascertaining the exact truth.

[390] After internal evidence has been combined with external to help us to discriminate between the three

classes above mentioned, the worthless must be resolutely cast aside. The temptation must be rejected to "give some weight" to this or that statement, because "it is supported by no less than — authorities within — years from the event," etc. Mere repetitions should have no more evidential "weight" than those of parrots or starlings.

[**391**] The untrustworthy are not to be thus cast aside, but they are to be most suspiciously criticized, with a rigid determination to reject any detail — not contained in a trustworthy writer—that either tends to edification, or shews signs of harmonizing.

[**392**] The small remnant of trustworthy witnesses must be treated with the care and reverence due to their honesty and painstaking accuracy. One such witness must be for us a Samson against multitudes of adversaries of the two former kinds. Yet even here we must use discrimination. Samson is not Samson when he has cast away his strength; and Grim is no longer the trustworthy Grim of the Martyrdom when he passes out of the sphere of an eye-witness to record the saving of young Thomas from drowning (**399**).

APPENDICES

APPENDIX I

GERVASE OF CANTERBURY

[393] GERVASE, who was perhaps born about 1141, was made a monk of Canterbury on 16 Feb. 1163.[1] He does not say that he was present at the Martyrdom. But neither does John of Salisbury, who was unquestionably present; nor Benedict, who (for many reasons) might be supposed likely to be present.[2] Even Grim gives us no reason for supposing that he was present till he comes to mention Reginald's sword as "wounding the arm of the author of this narrative." Consequently we cannot infer from the silence of Gervase that he was absent. He had been a monk from 1163, whereas William did not enter the monastery till after the Archbishop's exile, which began in Nov. 1164.[3] Gervase, therefore, must have been senior to William, who was not invested by the Archbishop with the monastic habit till 1170. If he was in residence, and not prevented by illness, he might naturally be expected to attend vespers, in which case he would be in the Cathedral when the knights broke in. Then he may have fled. Or he may have remained in the Choir, till all was over.

[394] Probably he did thus fly, or was absent. He is extremely vague as to all that concerns the attack on the Palace, and the Martyrdom, while he is definite and diffuse on the state of the body immediately after death, when he may be supposed to have emerged from his hiding-place.

The Editor tells us that Gervase probably began to write his chronicle in 1188: "for the period 1163-70," he adds, "with very

---

[1] *The Historical Works of Gervase of Canterbury*, vol. i. ed. W. Stubbs, D.D., 1879, pp. 226-228.   [2] See **18**.   [3] *Mat.* i. p. xxix.

minute exceptions, the whole of the materials which he has used are borrowed from the biographies of William of Canterbury, John of Salisbury, Alan of Tewkesbury, and Herbert of Bosham." The following narrative confirms these words, but also indicates in Gervase a general preference for William. He appears to make no use of Grim.

There is scarcely a suggestion of the writer's own except as to Fitzurse's recoil, in the struggle with the Archbishop. Here he suggests a not very likely hypothesis, that *he "went back a little" till he "saw his companions now close at hand."* This adds one more to the ingenious interpretations and alterations (206) by which non-militant monks endeavoured to hold fast the belief that St. Thomas, in the moment of his martyrdom, acted in all respects like the ancient saints and martyrs.

[395] His testimony, in one respect, differs from William's to confirm Anon. I., viz. in asserting that the first blow, struck by Fitzurse, *wounded the Archbishop besides striking off his cap.*

The words "Let us go: he is dead," he assigns, not to Hugh of Horsea, the clerk, the perpetrator of the outrage on the body, but to "one of them," *i.e.* one of the four knights.

As Gervase's account is much later than the rest, and devoid of individual information, it has not been thought worth while to translate it into English, but the Latin is given below, arranged in eleven sections corresponding to those of the narratives given above.

(i.) *The Knights prepare to attack the Palace*

[396] Exeuntes itaque de palatio, introduxerunt in curiam archiepiscopi quos prae foribus reliquerant satellites dum cum archiepiscopo loquerentur. Exeuntes autem se cappis et tunicis, apparuerunt loricati.

(ii.) *The breaking open of the Palace*

Gervase omits this.

(iii.) *The conveyance of the Archbishop to the Cathedral*

Dum igitur hii (*sic*) et alii se armis induerunt, et monachi in ecclesia vesperas cantarent, vix tandem archiepiscopo persuasum est ut vesperas auditurus ecclesiam introiret.

(iv.) *The entrance of the Archbishop into the Cathedral*

Cum autem a monachis impulsus magis quam ductus ecclesiam fuisset ingressus, et jam in ecclesia aliquot gradus ascendisset,

(v. and vi.) *The approach, and the entrance, of the Knights*

ecce a tergo quatuor illi armati per claustrum exertis gladiis ecclesiam cum impetu ingrediuntur.

(vii.) *The meeting of the Archbishop and the Knights*

Quorum cum primus exclamasset, "Ubi est traditor ille?" et nemo responderet, subjunxit, "Ubi est archiepiscopus?" Ipse autem omnium voces praeveniens, de gradibus quos ascenderat descendens ait, "En ego."

(viii.) *The struggle*

Et adjecit, "Reginalde, Reginalde, multa tibi contuli beneficia, nunc ingrederis armatus ad me?" At ille pallium archiepiscopi apprehendens ait, "Hoc scies jam. Egredere, jam morieris." Archiepiscopus autem de manu illius pallium excutiens, "Non egrediar," ait. At ille dixit, "Fuge ergo." "Non," inquit, "fugiam, sed, si me quaeritis, prohibeo ex parte Dei et sub anathemate, ne alicui ex meis quicquam mali faciatis." Ille autem, paululum retrocedens, et socios suos jam adesse conspiciens,

(ix.) *The first blow*

in caput archiepiscopi gladium vibravit, quo brachium clerici, magistri scilicet Edwardi, fere amputavit, ipsumque archiepiscopum in capite, excusso pilleo, vulneravit, et exclamavit, "Percutite, percutite." Extenderat enim clericus ille brachium suum super caput archiepiscopi ut ictum elideret ferientis.

(x.) *The death and outrage*

Videns autem jam de caetero Sanctus vocandus horam suae passionis adesse, inclinato contra lictorum gladios nudato capite, haec ultima verba dixit : "Deo et Sanctae Mariae et Sancto Dionisio et sanctis hujus ecclesiae patronis commendo me ipsum et causam ecclesiae." Accurrens autem alter ex eis, et is loricatus, cum magno impetu gladium suum in testam sancti martyris profundius incussit, et cerebrum violavit. Jam labare coepit in corpore hostia Christi, sed mente firmior ; et, ferientibus caeteris, quasi ad orationem in pavimento prostratus est, omnibus membris decenter compositis, ac si manibus dirigerentur humanis. Quidam autem ex eis immanior caeteris et inhumanior, jam jacentis, jam expirantis testulas capitis quas alii inciderant abscidit, et ex facili transitu pavimentum offendens gladii cuspidem fregit. Plaga autem a cono capitis usque ad cellam memorialem descendens, partem illam occipitii patulam fecit. Accessit postremo quidam Hugo, re et nomine Malus-clericus appellatus, ensis cuspidem patenti capiti crudeliter inpressit, cerebrum penitus dissipavit, extraxit, et in pavimentum cum testulis et sanguine sparsit. Unus autem ex eis, "Eamus," inquit, "mortuus est." Et redeuntes per claustrum, in signum dampnatae (*sic*) militiae suae clamabant, "Regales milites, regales." . . .

(xi.) *After death*

. . . Accurrens autem populus civitatis patrem patriae suumque pastorem tam dire in ecclesia Dei interemtum videre cupiebant.

O admirabilis viri sancti constantia ! Non regis insania, non episcoporum vel principum malitia, non exilium, non amicorum vel parentum suorum proscriptio, non gladius, sed nec ipsa mors eum a via veritatis avellere potuerunt. Et, quod mirabilius est, militi percutienti non caput avertit, non vestem vel manum interposuit, sed percutienti caput inclinavit, in pedibus stans donec consummaretur. In terram corruens membra quasi ad orandum composuit. Jacens non pedem, non manum movit vel caput, nisi quantum expiranti conceditur. Sed, ut aestimo, Deum habuit dispositorem et angelos cooperatores. Necdum animam expiraverat, et ecce ab omnibus fere Sanctus Thomas appellatus est. Vix aliquem in tanta videres multitudine qui ejus sanguine non vellet esse intinctus ; nam in ejus sanguine digitos imprimebant, et ipsius sancti nomen invocantes in frontibus suis vel oculis signum crucis faciebant. Collectus est ille sacrosanctus sanguis cum cerebro et testulis, et diligenter repositus est, post modicum toti mundo propinandus. Delatum est autem corpus exanime ante altare Christi, ubi tota nocte illa clausis oculis, compressis labiis, membrisque decenter compositis, adeo vividus intuentibus apparuit ac si vivens in corpore carperet sompnum (*sic*).

APPENDIX II

HOW THOMAS WAS SAVED FROM DROWNING

In the following condensed paraphrases, the italicized words represent the principal differences between the several accounts.

§ 1. *Garnier* (ll. 206-30) (non-miraculous)

[397] For a good half year together, as I have heard him say, Thomas was wont to go with a friend of his father, Richers de l'Aigle by name, through woods and by streams. Then began he to love hawk and hound. One day, Thomas went with his friend on the river-bank to learn the ways and manners of birds (*i.e.* hawking). They came to a mill-stream spanned by naught save a plank. Richers, who went first, passed across the plank. Thomas came afterwards *all hooded. But one of his horse's feet slipped. He and the horse were plunged in the stream.* Down he floated, drawn fast towards the

---

[397] En la maisun sum père soleit dunc osteler
Richers de l'egle ; od lui soleit Tomas aler
En bois et en rivère, et od lui converser
3en demi an ensemble, si cum l'oï conter.
Dunc komencha mult chiens et oiseus à amer.
  Od lui ala un jur Tomas en la rivère.
Des oiseus volt aprendre les gez et la manère ;
Vindrent à un grant duit ; n'i out punt ni charère,

K'une planche, ù passa celes genz poïnnère.
Li bier ala devaunt et li enfes derère.
Par desus la plaunche est li chevalers passez,
Tomas ala après, tut enchaperunez.
Mès à sun cheval est un des peiz eschapiez,
Il et li chevaus est enz el duit reversez.
Il a vuidé la sèle. Aval esteit flotez.

mill-wheel. Just when he was bound to be dragged under the wheel, *the miller turned off the water*. Thus God, for that time, guarded the youth from death.

§ 2. *Anon. I.* (*Mat.* iv. 6-7) (non-miraculous)

[398] For a year and a half Thomas lived with Richer de l'Aigle, his father's friend, who was fond of hawking and hunting, and Thomas learned the same liking, which he afterwards indulged sometimes, in hours of leisure. One day, the two went out hawking and came to a rapid stream crossed by nothing but a footbridge. The knight, despising the danger, went over first. Thomas, *safe and hooded*, inasmuch as he anticipated no disaster, followed in his steps. *The horse's foot slipped, and the youth, with the horse as well, fell into the stream.* Torn from his horse, he was hurried down to the mill-wheel, when suddenly *the miller turned off the water*. The knight and his retinue followed the boy with cries along the river-side. Hearing their voices the miller came out, and dragged Thomas out half dead.

De de juste la plaunche out un mulin mulaunt,	Ke il deveit par lui si granz bens acumplir !
De grant ravine ala ; Tomas i vint flotaunt.	Les asquanz soffre Deus à vivre et à guarir,
Quant il dut en la roue chair, le chef avaunt	Pur ço que mult granz maus deit par eus avenir ;
Li muners out mulu, mit l'escloture à taunt :	Et li asquanz redeivent mult granz biens par-
Si guarist Deus de mort, à cele feiz, l'enfaunt.	furnir. II. 206-30
Kar Deus le volt por ço guarder et guarauntir,	

[398] Hospitabatur in domo patris sui miles quidam nomine Richerius de Aquila, vir quidem secundum saeculum nobilis et honorabilis, canum tamen et avium exercitationi fere semper intentus. Hunc Thomas adhuc puer, cum per dimidium annum a scholis vacaret, ad talia negotia procedentem libenter frequenterque sequebatur, plurimumque talibus occupationibus delectabatur, indeque hujusmodi traxisse creditur consuetudinem, cui etiam in majori postea aetate, quotiens vacabat, operam impendebat. Contigit autem ut memoratus miles quadam die ad simile negotium more solito exiret, et Thomas eum equo sedens sequeretur; eratque iis transitus per quendam fluvium rapidissimum, in quo erat pons parvus et arctus, qui tantum pedestres transmittere posset. Erat quoque non longe inferius molendinum, ad quod iste fluvius, ripis hinc inde congestis ne efflueret, magno cum impetu praeceps vergebat. Miles autem, compendii causa periculum contemnens, transivit pontem prior ; quem Thomas, tutus et capuciatus, quippe qui nihil infortunii suspicabatur, e vestigio subsequitur. Et ecce, cum ad pontis medium venisset, subito pes equo labitur, et puer cum ipso equo in medium fluminis prolabitur. Excipitur igitur ab aquis, et violento undarum impetu ab equo disjunctus ad inferiora rapitur ; jamque molendino, tam a rota conterendus quam ab aquis suffocandus, approximabat. Dum haec agerentur, et Thomas in confinio mortis constitutus videretur, homo qui molendinum curabat, nihil penitus de his quae agebantur sciens, aquam subito a rota exclusit. Miles autem et qui eum comitabantur magnis et miserandis clamoribus puerum secus ripam sequebantur ; quorum

Both these writers comment on the result as providential. Garnier adds that God suffers the bad to live and recover because many great evils must needs come to pass through them; and some He saves to do great good.

Neither sees a miracle. But the next narrative, besides quite altering the circumstances relating to the loss and the rescue of the falcon, apparently sees a miracle in the standing still of the mill-wheel.

§ 3. *Grim* (*Mat.* ii. 360-1) (miraculous)

[399] One day, while Thomas was hawking with his rich [friend], a falcon, following a wild duck and *just catching it as it dived, was itself drawn under water*. For pity of the *perishing* falcon, the youth *dismounted*, and *leapt into the stream*. But he was in danger of drowning, and his friends could give him no help. Presently he drifted down towards a mill-wheel. Just as he drew close to the outrush of the mill-stream, the wheel stood, and did not move once till he was drawn out, alive, but terribly bruised. But his bruises were healed by the healing hand of the Saviour, who protected him when despaired of in the waters.

§ 4. *The Saga* (i. 33) (miraculous)

[400] One day, Thomas, with many companions, flieth his hawk at a certain bird; and in such way they parted that the hawk

vocibus, molendino jam quieto et a strepitu cessante, auditis, homo praefatus tandem de molendino admirans quid vellet egreditur, et Thomam in mediis fluctibus conspicatus, injecta celeriter manu semivivum eum et vix palpitantem ad terram extraxit. Quis hoc casu contigisse crediderit, et non potius divinam providentiam tam subitam et inopinatam subventionem periclitanti puero et futuro ecclesiae suae antistiti misericorditer procurasse?

[399] Die vero quadam accidit ut, ad ripas eunte Thoma simul cum divite, motam de flumine anam accipiter insequeretur, secutusque divertentem in flumen cum ipsa pariter mergebatur. Quod videns adolescens, miseratus accipitrem jam periturum, equo desiliit, seque in gurgitem, ut avem eriperet, praecipitavit; sed priusquam avem contingeret, raptus ipse intra alveum fluminis, et nunc mersus sub aquis, nunc undarum vi impellente levatus, periclitari coepit, et penitus periisse putabatur ab intuentibus, dum nullus adesse potuit qui manum porrigeret pereunti. Denique ad molendinum, quod tunc forte molebat, aquae tractu perlatus, ubi primo aquae exitibus propinquavit, stetit rota nec se movit semel, quousque vivus quidem, sed vehementer afflictus, adolescens extractus est. Sed fovit afflictum medica manus Salvatoris, quem inter undas desperatum protexit ne exstingueretur lucerna futurus in Israel, cujus morte pretiosa tanta cernimus beneficia provenisse.

pursued the prey *across a certain river, where it alighted far away. Thomas being minded to fetch the hawk, rideth forth unto the river; but soon, coming to the slight bridge, got off his horse and walked on the bridge.* Then *his foot slipped and he tumbled into the river.* [For the rest the writer quotes Robert of Cricklade.] "Straightway, as he was hurried into the madly rushing torrent, the mill-wheel stopped, and the river became, in the twinkle of an eye, like the calmest river-pool"; and the Prior averreth that the current did not move again to turn the mill-wheel, ere all the limbs of St. Thomas had been lifted out of the water unto the dry land.

[401] Garnier gives the correct account. But the *Saga's* supplement may very well be true, viz. that the hawk had flown *across the stream a long way*, so that Thomas (and perhaps the knight, too) wanted to recover it quickly. This explains why they were so foolhardy as to cross a footbridge with their horses.

Anon. I. may have mistranslated the French "tut," "all," taking it to mean "tutus"; and his addition, "suspecting no danger," may shew that he felt it difficult to make sense out of his error. Perhaps he took "tutus" to mean "feeling safe." See, however, 25a.

Grim's account can hardly have come from the French, but may well have sprung from some Latin not very different from that of Anon. I., "pes equo labitur." This he may have interpreted as meaning "ex equo," or "de equo, labitur," "he got nimbly off his horse."[1] So, too, Grim may have taken "he hastily went to recover a falcon that had lighted *across* the stream, and was in danger of being *lost*" as meaning "that had lighted *on* the stream, and was in danger *of being lost in the stream.*" The next step was to invent a diving duck as a cause for this "danger of *being lost*"!

It should be noted that, in the *Saga*, Robert of Cricklade, and not the poet, is responsible for the miraculous part of the story.

---

[1] In Virg. *Aeneid*, xi. 596 "curru delapsus" means "slipping nimbly from the chariot," a voluntary act.

PART II
ST. THOMAS'S MIRACLES

SECTION I

THE BEGINNING OF THE MIRACLES

§ 1. *Miracles, at first, unfashionable, and even dangerous*

[402] THE miracles at Becket's tomb, or in connection with Becket's name, seem to have begun almost immediately after the night of his death. It became necessary to appoint a special monk to sit near the tomb and to receive offerings: and on him it naturally devolved to hear the accounts of these marvels and to report them to the Chapter of the brethren, before whom, says Fitzstephen,[1] they were publicly read.

[403] But the publicity was at first confined to the chapter-house. In the spring of 1171 no one dared to mention the miracles abroad. The De Brocs beset the bridges and roads leading to Canterbury, and stationed men outside the hospices to intimidate or arrest any who spoke well of the Martyr or magnified his miracles. The higher clergy, as well as the knights and nobles, followed the King in setting themselves against the Archbishop's memory and the marvels that redounded to his glory. It was the poor, and at first mainly the poor of Canterbury and the neighbourhood, whose imaginations and affections went out towards the Martyr as their champion and father, and who persisted, so to speak, in being cured, at a time when such cure was unfashionable or even dangerous. Women of a higher class, and priests, formed also a large element in

---

[1] *Mat.* i i. 151. For the meaning of this and other references, see 1*a*.

the patients healed. But it was, for the most part, the lowest class who in the earliest days reverenced St. Thomas as a martyr and prepared the way for the conversion of the prelates, the barons, and ultimately the King himself. Hence, in those first days, when any imposture, detected by the De Brocs or other enemies of Becket's fame, might have been used effectively against the monks of Canterbury, they were naturally forced to be careful in testing the evidence for each miracle reported to the Chapter.

§ 2. *The nature of the first miracles*

[404] Benedict, who was the first appointed to report the miracles, seems to have been well adapted for the task, a man of (comparatively) simple and unaffected style,[1] peculiarly accurate (for those times) in matters of chronology, free from exaggeration, and disposed to suspect exaggeration and imposture in others. Hence, great weight must be attached to his accounts of the early miracles. The diseases healed by them were for the most part (as might have been anticipated) nervous disorders, such as might be cured by a strong emotional shock. In some cases, Benedict frankly tells us that the cure was not at first perfect; in others, that it was followed by relapse. In one case he informs us that the reputed water of St. Thomas was not St. Thomas's at all. It was a fraudulent imitation; yet it performed the desired cure.[2] Let the reader compare, in the following extracts, Benedict's (or Fitzstephen's) account of the healing of one William, a London priest, four or five days after the Martyrdom, with the corresponding account given by an anonymous writer (Anon. V.), who probably

---

[1] [404a] Compare *Mat.* ii. 27, where Benedict says that when he questioned St. Thomas (who had appeared to him in a vision) in French, the saint replied to him in Latin: this may possibly imply that Benedict was rather more proficient in the former language than in the latter.

[2] *Mat.* ii. 216.

wrote less than five years after the event. The latter makes two visions instead of one, and makes the priest come to Canterbury, not in consequence of, but in anticipation of, the Archbishop's death (**433**)!

[**405**] Further remarks may be deferred till we come to the comparison of Benedict's and William's accounts of the individual miracles. The following extracts describe generally how the miracles began amid persecution and discouragement. No details will be given except as to the one or two mentioned as occurring first of all.

§ 3. *Benedict's description of the night and day after the Martyrdom*

[**406**] (1) Benedict (*Mat.* ii. 15) declares that when the body was raised from the earth there appeared a ring of blood round the head, but none on the face except a thin streak from the right temple down to the left cheek across the nose, "with which sign he afterwards appeared in visions to many that knew nothing of the matter; and these described it in relation precisely as though they had seen it with their bodily eyes." Even while it was still lying on the pavement, some smeared their eyes with blood; others brought little vessels and took by stealth what they could; others dipped strips from their garments in it. In the general confusion each did as he would. But as much of the blood as they had left to the church was placed, "with all care of cleanliness, in a clean vessel," and stored up for keeping in the church.

[**407**] The night passed in lamentation. Next morning, there was again a large force of armed men gathered outside the city walls; "and it was noised abroad on all sides that they had collected for the purpose of forcibly carrying away the body of the holy Martyr. They therefore proceeded in haste to bury him, even leaving the body unwashed

(except in the blood of martyrdom, which was better than any anointing). When taking off the outer garments in order to array him in pontifical robes, they found not only the shirt, but even the drawers, of haircloth, and the monk's habit above that.

[408] Almost all our writers lay great stress on the unexpected contrast between this inward self-mortification (especially in the use of haircloth for drawers as well as shirt) and the outward pomp of the deceased Archbishop. "Looking at one another," says Benedict, "and astounded at the sight of such a secret religious practice beyond belief," they wept more bitterly than ever. He then digresses to describe the Archbishop's foreknowledge of his death, and concludes the Passion with its date (correctly given) and the doxology.

§ 4. *Benedict's account of the first miracle*

[409] At this point begins the Prologue of Benedict's Chronicle of Miracles (*Mat.* ii. 21), describing first of all the sorrow of the bereaved Church, and then the consolation springing from the marvels that immediately followed, and the moral effect of these marvels on the whole nation and in foreign parts, particularly as confirming the title of Pope Alexander. The Prologue concludes with an enumeration of the different kinds of miracles to be related.

[410] The first book of the treatise begins with an account of three visions, in which the Martyr appears on three consecutive nights to Benedict, holding a lantern and saying, " I carry a lantern, but it cannot be seen because of an intervening cloud"; which meant that the Saint's good actions were prevented by the cloud of persecution from shining before men. Then follow other visions connected with, or predictive of, the Martyrdom, and then the writer passes from visions to miracles, of which the first is as follows.

On the third day, the news of the murder came to the wife of a knight in Sussex, who suffered from a weakness ("infirmitas") accompanied with blindness ("excaecaverat eam ipsius infirmitatis vehementia"). "'St. Thomas,' she cried, 'precious martyr of Christ, I devote myself to thee. If thou wilt restore me the blessing of my lost sight and recall me to health, I will visit thy resting-place to pay vows and offerings . . .' Immediately—as though the Archbishop had said to her, 'O woman, great is thy faith, be it unto thee even as thou wilt'—in about half an hour . . . she received her sight and within the sixth day rose from her bed." Her delay to perform her vow was visited with a still more severe weakness ("gravioris flagello infirmitatis"). "She renewed her vow. At once she recovered, and hastened to Canterbury with her husband and household to render thanks to the saint for his double blessing." Benedict applies to the miracle the words used in the Fourth Gospel concerning the sign at Cana: "This beginning of signs did Jesus in Sussex of England, and manifested the glory of his martyr before the faces of us his disciples who ate and drank with him before . . . he was slain."

§ 5. *John of Salisbury*

[411] (2) John of Salisbury (*Mat.* ii. 322), after describing the burial in a marble sarcophagus, continues thus : "And there . . . great miracles are wrought . . . For in the place of his passion, and in the place where he lay before the great altar previous to burial, and in the place where he was at last buried, paralytics are cured, the blind see, the deaf hear, the dumb speak, the lame walk, lepers are cured . . . and (a thing unheard of from the days of our fathers) the dead are raised."

[412] No instance is mentioned by Benedict or William of "the dead being raised" *at the tomb*, and therefore John

is probably referring to instances of revivification by means of the "water of St. Thomas," away from the tomb. But the fact that he makes no special mention of the vast number of miracles wrought at a distance, is indicative of a very early date.

§ 6. *William's Preface*

[413] (3) William's (*Mat.* i. 137-8) Book of Miracles is introduced by a prefatory letter of the monks of Canterbury to King Henry: "We *have thought fit* to bring to the notice of your serene highness . . . the works wrought by the Martyr Thomas through various places *in your realm*.[1] But further, if you have leisure (though your ears be wearied with a vast multitude of affairs) . . . we will proceed to relate (prosequemur) the signs whereof we receive report *from other regions*. . . . For this cause, we have sent our beloved brother William, with a book on which he has laboured for some time, according to your request."

§ 7. *Apparent allusions to Benedict*

[414] In the preface to his own book on the miracles, Benedict says that St. Thomas appeared to him on the night of his martyrdom and again on the second or[1] third night, signifying that his light was to be manifested on earth by miracles. Similarly William relates that, when he was requested by the monks to set forth for the purpose of transcription the miracles which he was concealing uncorrected and incompleted in separate leaflets (in schedulis occultabat incorrecta et imperfecta), he also received a vision in which St. Thomas said to him, "Choose what thou wilt."[2]

[415] The letter of the monks to King Henry suggests

---

[1] Apparently the monks are here referring to Benedict's work which, in its first shape, probably contained none but English miracles. William's, from the first, included a large number of foreign ones.

[1] Probably " vel " is a mistake for " et." [2] *Mat.* i. 2.

a comparison between Benedict and William. If Benedict received three nightly visions of St. Thomas, so did William, too; and one of these (like Benedict's) dated from the beginning of the Passion. In the first two visions, a "book" was "cast" by St. Thomas toward William, who could not then understand what the "book" might mean. But there came a time when the brother whose business it was to hear and record the miracles found himself no longer equal to the multitude of wonders. And now a third vision indicated the meaning of the "book." William heard in the night the command "Give thine aid (operam adhibe)." Next morning, "when the brethren were in full assembly, and complaint was freely made that sufficient diligence and pains were not given to the hearing of the reports of the miracles, which were so gloriously manifested in the church at Canterbury, and which were related by the concourse of folk coming to pray [at the tomb], it was unanimously enjoined on the brother now in question" [William] "that he was to take his part in the task. In his writing, therefore, he touches briefly on only a few points, *following the truth, not the order, of the miraculous facts. For as to what came earlier and what came later, there is neither leisure to attend to* [*such questions*], *nor does it make much difference.*"

There can be little doubt that Benedict is the unnamed "brother" here alluded to as unequal to the task of recording the miracles, and whose care (at the commencement of his task) to distinguish "what came earlier and what came later" seemed to the Canterbury monks so superfluous.

§ 8. *William acts on the principle "Choose what thou wilt"*

[416] The Easter of 1171 saw the first public outburst of miraculous efficacy. This would certainly recur more vehemently than ever in the Easter and Whitsuntide of 1172. In that year the younger king Henry began a war

against his father—in which many might recognize (as the so-called Matthew of Westminster does) a retribution for the murder of the late Archbishop. In the same year, King Henry "purged himself" before the papal legates at Avranches. By this time, then, miracles at the tomb and pilgrimages to the tomb would be quite safe for all; and soon, if not already, they would become in fashion among the "middle classes (mediae manus homines)," respected, if not yet much practised, by the knights and nobles, and profitable for beggars and impostors. This was the date (May 1172) when William was called by a vision and by the monks of Canterbury to Benedict's aid. In the early days of miracles, the chronicler could not afford to be a chooser; but now, with so vast a multitude of instances, William was well able to select those that were best authenticated, or most edifying, or most interesting—in some cases, we may say, most amusing—acting on the convenient principle revealed to him in his vision, "Choose what thou wilt."

[417] Concerning the rise and development of miracles, William gives no information at all, not even so much as is found in small works on the Passion. Disclaiming chronological order, he gives the first place to a miracle that does not occur in Benedict's work till the beginning of his Fourth Book and was possibly absent from Benedict's work in its earliest edition.

§ 9. *Grim's account of the first miracle, and of the burial*

[418] (4) Grim (*Mat.* ii. 439 *sq.*) says that on the night of the Martyrdom few dared at first to lament openly. Partly they feared the King's servants who were everywhere busy about the precincts, partly, "not even the majority of the monks, and no one at all of the rest," felt any special regard for the *person* of the deceased, any more than for the death of one of the common people, "except that such an

unprecedented act (perpetrated in a *church*) caused universal horror. I say 'for the *person*': for in our hearing one of our own habit and tonsure slanderously said that he ought certainly not to be regarded as a martyr, having been slain as the reward of his own obstinacy." But his fame was speedily vindicated by miracles, since "on the third day" after the Martyrdom "a new light sent from above restored the light of [this] world to one who invoked the Martyr's name."

[419] These words prepare the way for an accurate abridgment of Benedict's miracle of the restoration of sight (" the light of this world ") to the Sussex knight's wife, who " invoked the Martyr's name." General terms of time are used : " *She scarcely finished these words*, when she regained her much-desired sight *in the selfsame hour* [B. " half an hour "], and in *a short time* [B. " a week "] completely recovered from the rest of her disease." This cannot be called exaggerated. Grim adds that this and several other miracles were kept quiet for the time as though they were not believed, until the opposition of the impious gave way by reason of the multitude of the marvellous acts.

[420] On the morrow, in order to anticipate outrage on the Martyr's body threatened by one of the King's courtiers, it was buried that night; and the unexpected discovery of haircloth round his limbs so infested with worms "that any one would deem yesterday's martyrdom lighter than that," completely converted the brethren: "See, see," they cried, "he was indeed a monk, and we knew it not." No one of them now doubted that he deserved to be called a martyr.

[421] When the body was laid in the crypt, "they collected the blood by heaven-sent inspiration . . . and, by drinking this, so many benefits were speedily bestowed that, if they were written singly, they would be beyond the belief of the weak. For he it is who is the lover of the brethren and of the people of Israel . . . by whose merits and intervention

the blind see, the lame walk, lepers are cleansed, the dead rise. . . ." Here the narrative of the Passion concludes, with a doxology.[1]

§ 10. *Anon. I. on the burial*

[422] (5) Anon. I. (*Mat.* iv. 78-9), after describing the closing of the Cathedral and the placing of the body before the high altar, says, "They also placed vessels beneath, to catch the blood that streamed from the body; not being ignorant of the very great preciousness of the blood of the Martyr, which had been poured out for the love of God and the church." Next morning, he continues, came Robert de Broc sent by Randulph de Broc, who, with threats of outrage, bade the monks bury the body at once. Unclothing it for burial, the monks found haircloth next the flesh, and all the vestments so adjusted as to admit of frequent "discipline; for indeed he frequently had himself scourged. On the very day on which he suffered, he is asserted[1] to have been thrice scourged.[2] . . . Then indeed the monks, seeing that this saintly man had in his secret life all the tokens of sanctity and religion, rejoiced inexpressibly, and said to one another, Behold one that was indeed a monk and indeed a hermit, who endured torments not only

---

[1] The author passes to describe the desolation of the Cathedral for nearly a year, and the King's penitential visit (1174) to Canterbury accompanied by an improvement in his fortunes. He concludes abruptly with a dream of the King in which Henry sees Benedict the Prior of Canterbury sent by St. Thomas to rescue him from falling into an abyss.

[1] On this point, see Grim (*Mat.* ii. 417-8), who says that he received his account of the daily scourgings of the Archbishop from his chaplain Robert of Merton. Hence it must be admitted that the words "it is asserted" are rather against the hypothesis that Robert was the author of Anon. I. However, the first person is avoided throughout that biography.

[2] Anon. I. (as also Fitzstephen) makes no mention of the "worms" described by Benedict and Grim. But Anon. I. may include them in the following words, "*omnia* sanctitatis et religionis *insignia* in occultis suis habentem." The *Saga*, also (446), omits the "worms."

in death but also in life." Then, full of consolation, they laid him in the crypt, " where blessed gifts of healing and of miracles, numerous and indeed past numbering, are through his merits conferred on the faithful, bestowed by our Lord Jesus Christ, who, with the Father and the Holy Spirit, reigneth for ever. Amen."

§ 11. *Fitzstephen's account of the burial*

[423] (6) Fitzstephen says (*Mat.* iii. 146) that for a long time the dead Martyr lay almost alone, deserted by clerks, monks, and all the rest; not even light was brought for the performance of the obsequies.[1] Osbert his Chamberlain cut a strip off his shirt to cover the remnant of his half-severed head. Then, amid general lamentation, the parts of the wounded head were adjusted, and the body was placed before the high altar. Robert of Merton, the Archbishop's chaplain and confessor, shewed the monks the haircloth next the skin, and the monk's habit above it. Then there was great rejoicing. Perceiving with their own eyes this "double martyrdom, voluntary during life, and violent in death, they fell down and kissed his hands and feet," invoking him as Saint and Martyr. "Soon a monk of the church, Ernold the Goldsmith, and certain with him, return to the place of martyrdom, and with all cleanliness collect in a basin the blood and brains scattered on the pavement of the church." "Next morning it was loudly rumoured (perstrepit rumor) in the church that the house of de Broc and their accomplices had prepared to drag him out of the church, regretting that they had killed him in a church."[2] The monks therefore determined to bury

---

[1] "Nec etiam ablato (? adlato) lumine ad sanctas ejus exsequias." This paragraph is omitted by J (15*a*).

[2] "Regretting." This differs greatly from Garnier, Benedict, Grim, and Anon. I., who mention threats made by De Broc, or others, to cast the body into a cesspool.

him at once, deciding that he "should not even be washed except as he was already, in his own blood."

There follows a full description of (1) his burial clothing, (2) the younger Henry's sorrow on hearing of the murder, and (3) the placing of the body "in a new sarcophagus of marble, before two altars."

§ 12. *Fitzstephen's account of the first miracles*

[424] Then comes an account of the first miracles: "Immediately after the burial, in the same [night and in the same] week the action of the divine virtue manifested its presence."[1] A citizen of Canterbury, who had beheld the martyrdom, returned home to his paralytic wife with a garment dipped in the Martyr's blood. On hearing his story, "she begged that the blood might be washed off and caught in water so that she might drink its healing draught. It was done, and she was at once cured. This, the first of the signs, God wrought for his Martyr the same night. Hence, as I suppose, came the custom (through divine inspiration) of infusing a portion of the blood of St. Thomas in water, and of distributing this mixture of blood and water (illud sanguinis et aqua mixtum) to the pilgrims of St. Thomas in tin phials to carry home for the healing of their sick folk. . . . And indeed that mixture with water (illud aqua mixtum) besides availing sick folk innumerable for healing, has also availed some that were dying for the averting of death ; nay, I assert something more, [a thing difficult] but healthful to believe—it has availed some that were dead, so that they have risen to life."

[425] "*On the fourth night from his passion* (a passione ejus nocte quarta) . . . it was revealed to a clerk of London that a priest of London, William de Capella, who had become

---

[1] "In ipsa [nocte et in ipsa] hebdomade divinae virtutis affuit operatio." J. omits the bracketed words; and they look like an insertion made for the sake of definiteness.

dumb, should go to the tomb of St. Thomas, and there be cured. And so it was.² . . ."

[426] Another saw "a nightly vision of Jesus Christ crucified in that part of the crypt where the earthly remains of St. Thomas were laid. And rightly; for He Himself suffers in each of His martyrs."³ Further, a woman leading the life of an anchorite, ignorant of letters, and not knowing how to speak any Latin except some Psalms, the Lord's

---

² [425a] This miracle is told in greater detail by Benedict (*Mat*. ii. 42-3), who places it fifth in order, following others which occurred, severally, on the 3rd, 5th, 6th, and subsequent days after the Martyrdom. It is introduced by him with the preface "Et post dies *octo*," and must therefore be supposed to have occurred on the 8th day from the Martyrdom, *i.e.* on 5th Jan. So far, the accounts are compatible. But Benedict adds another detail, viz. that *the priest's paralytic attack began on the fourth day before the Martyrdom.*

This has caused a curious exaggeration in a later writer (Anon. V.), who has confused this, the date of the *attack*, with the date of the *vision* (which was "on the fourth day *from*, i.e. *after*, the Martyrdom "). Hence Anon. V. (433), placing the vision on the fourth day *before* the Martyrdom, represents it as *predictive*, so that, when the two men come to Canterbury, they have their faith confirmed by finding the Archbishop slain that very day!

[425b] Benedict says that this priest was "the first of all" to taste the water hallowed by the saint's blood, and that he received the gift of speaking, though imperfectly, while at Canterbury; on his returning home, it was perfected.

It is quite possible that the miracle performed (424) on the citizen's wife may not have come to Benedict's knowledge till long after its occurrence, and then may have been passed over by him as not sufficiently attested, or not important enough, to take the first place in his list (427a). Fitzstephen may have derived his information, as he often apparently does, from the servants of the Minster and from Canterbury people.

³ [426a] Comp. *Mat*. i. 132, where it is said by William that *St. Thomas*, while living, had seen ("as it is asserted") a vision of *himself* crucified in the place where he fell. See 146, 162a.

There seem to have been many versions of this tradition. William (*Mat*. i. 144) says that Fermin, a physician of Canterbury, before the Martyr's Passion, saw "a man (or, the man) crucified in the place where he was buried." But (*Mat*. i. 142) a clerk of Coutances (also before the Passion) saw " the Crucified (crucifixus) " bearing His cross and leaning toward the north as if on the point of leaping towards England—which prefigured the Martyrdom, because Christ is crucified afresh in His martyrs. The clerk (like Fitzstephen) quoted the story about Jesus going to Rome to be crucified in the place of St. Peter. There was probably some confusion between (1) "the Crucified," (2) "a man, or the man, crucified," (3) "himself crucified." Of these, (1) seems the original.

Prayer, and the Creed, wrote these Latin words in an ecstasy soon after the Martyrdom, " Noli flere pro Archiepiscopo. Caput ejus in gremio Filii mei requiescit."

§ 13. *Fitzstephen on the hostility to the miracles*

[427] Fitzstephen goes on to describe the emissaries of de Broc as standing by night near the hospices in Canterbury, ready to arrest any that spoke well of the Archbishop, and watching at the bridges and cross-roads to take the names of any that came on pilgrimage to him—" until the grace of the acts of healing and the concourse of the people so prevailed that even the Archbishop's enemies cried ' We labour in vain : there is no counsel against the Lord.[1] Lo, all England goeth after him.'" Then he enumerates the diseases healed, and particularly seven cases of leprosy healed in the first year. After describing the increase in devotion to God resulting from the reverence for St. Thomas, he concludes with a prayer that the Saint may intercede for all with God, who is glorified in His martyrs for ever and ever.

§ 14. *Herbert on the burial*

[428] (7) Herbert of Bosham (*Mat.* iii. 518 *sq.*) very lengthily, but with little or no addition of fact, describes how the crowd—but "the poor, and only the poor"—rushed into the Cathedral after the Martyrdom, to tinge their napkins and garments in the Archbishop's blood. The

---

[1] [427a] So Benedict says of the London priest that he praised God in secret, for fear of persecution : for "no one as yet spoke openly concerning him, or confessed his mighty works in public, but much was murmured in secret about them among the people." This also would explain, in part, why the wife of the Sussex knight for some time delayed her promised pilgrimage, and why the cure of the citizen's wife above mentioned (425b) did not come at all (or only after a long interval) to Benedict's ears. By Easter 1171, the miracles were so numerous that Benedict might naturally decline to insert in his records all the miracles that now began to put forward claims to be the first, especially when dealing with paralysis, and performed on a woman of the citizen class.

body is then placed before the high altar, beautiful in death, in spite of the continued dropping of blood all through the night. The threat of the "vipers" (*i.e.* the house of Broc)[1] is then mentioned, that, if the body is not speedily buried out of sight, it shall be "dragged by horses (distrahendum equis) through the whole city, or hanged on a gibbet." Then comes the hasty burial, and the unclothing of the body, and the contrast between the outward and inward garments, and the consequent exultation of the monks; "and whereas most, even of them (inter ipsos plerique), as also the men of this world, had doubted his sanctity, now, seeing this, they were smitten with a terrible astonishment and a wholesome contrition, and thus were immovably strengthened [in their faith] . . . saying, 'Truly this was a son of God.'"[2] He concludes thus, "And on account of their fear, hiding away as it were the body of Thomas in the crypt of the church, they placed it in this new tomb, which was hewn out of the rock, in the year of the incarnation of the Lord, one thousand one hundred and seventy-one, and about the fifty-third year of his life."

§ 15. *Herbert's silence on the miracles*

[429] Herbert's silence about miracles does not imply that he disbelieved in them. But it probably does imply that he, writing some twenty years after the Archbishop's death, felt that the miracles tended to overshadow the man. Dedicating his book to Baldwin, Archbishop of Canterbury, he disparages Becket's miraculous "signs," in comparison with *the "signs of his works" during life*, holding up for

---

[1] Comp. Benedict (*Mat.* ii. 46) "cujusdam . . . quem B. Thomas in scriptis suis *perditionis filium* appellare consueverat," where the editor's marginal note is "Ranulf de Broc, Ep. v. 73, p. 848, ed. Lupus."

[2] This agrees with Grim, where Benedict and others are silent. Grim, as a new-comer, would be especially shocked by the lukewarmness or disaffection of the majority of the monks towards the Archbishop, until the discovery of his asceticism.

imitation, as the true sign, his championship of the Church: "I desire, as it were by benefit of pen, to restore to you an example snatched from the world; an example of true purity by which you should regulate your own life and government, and which you should also daily peruse. For to you especially has this exemplary man given an example, that, as he did, ye also should do likewise. For this cause, also, throughout this history, I have set forth this man as an example, *not to be wondered at for his signs, but to be imitated for his works*. For as for his signs—given for unbelievers—which others have seen and written, I say nothing; I pass them over in the whole of this historical work of mine. I give my attention solely to those signs of this exemplary man which consist in works, signs given to believers not only to wonder at but also to imitate—and especially for you to imitate, called as you are by God—and (unless I am mistaken) somewhat fearing, though venturing—to wage the battle, and to bear the burden, and to fill the chair, of this great champion."

§ 16. *Anon. II. on the miracles*

[430] (8) Anon. II. (MS. Lambeth, *Mat.* iv. 134 *sq.*) throws little light on the origin of the miracles. It lays stress on the proof of sanctity afforded by the clothing, and especially on the "multitude of vermin." Then, defending the Archbishop against the charge of pride, and appealing to his miracles as a proof that he was a true martyr, the author adds that "beginning from his tomb they spread through the world."

§ 17. *Anon. III. and Anon. IV. on the miracles*

[431] (9) A MS. of very early date (*Mat.* iv. 145, where it is called Anon. III.) says that at first none but the poor and lowly crept to the tomb; then "the middle class

(mediae manus homines)." Afterwards, "when the fear of the king was at last removed," clerks, barons, soldiers, and the whole people of England and neighbouring islands and realms, came in crowds to Canterbury. Another MS. says (*ib.* p. 160) that the King, when he first heard of the miracles, did not believe them, and took steps to discourage them :[1] (p. 161) he was actually said—but the writer trusts it is not true—to have threatened vengeance against the body of the Martyr ; even afterwards, he insisted on a share of the offerings, but he receded from this position some time before his submission and act of penitence.

(10) Anon. IV. (*Mat.* iv. 195) merely speaks of miracles marvellously manifested not only at the Martyr's tomb but also in divers nations and realms.

§ 18. *Anon. V. reports legends*

[432] (11) Anon. V. (*Mat.* iv. 199) asserts that the Archbishop's body, long dead, arose, and signed itself and the bystanders with the sign of the cross (signo crucis consignavit), after which it fell to the ground.[1] Then the monks unclothed it and discovered the haircloth teeming with worms. Seeing this, "certain of the malefactors *beat their breasts*."[2] There were also found on him letters which

---

[1] "Suos qui ierant corripuit." Benedict (*Mat.* ii. 186) speaks of having seen Odo of Falaise, the king's accountant, near the tomb, disguised as a beggar, in the summer of 1171.

[1] Possibly this legend may have arisen, (1) from the statement, suggested by the Fitness of Things, that, when the Martyr fell to the ground, he signed himself with the sign of the cross, (2) from a saying, originally metaphorical, that when the body was raised from the ground it brought down on itself and on all around it the blessing of heaven. These two may have been confused together.

One MS. inserts a version of this in a letter from the Archbishop of Sens to the Pope written immediately after the murder (*Mat.* vii. 432), "when he was lying in the choir on the bier, about dawn, he raised his right hand and gave the blessing."

[2] Comp. Herbert concerning the finding of two hair-shirts *in the plunder of the palace* after the Archbishop's death : (*Mat.* iii. 513) "On finding two hair-shirts . . . they did not divide them or cast lots for them, but cast them

he had received on the preceding Sunday from some of the King's courtiers, warning him of his approaching death.

[433] "Meanwhile," the author continues, "as we have received on truthful testimony (veraciter), a blind man, who had once been of his household, received his sight in the blood of the slaughtered Martyr, touching his eyes [with it].[3] We have also heard (audivimus) that, while the Archbishop was still living, a London priest, who had long[4] lost the use of his tongue, saw in a vision[5] that, if his tongue were touched with the Archbishop's blood, it would be forthwith loosed. The same vision concerning the aforesaid dumb man was also frequently[6] revealed to a friend of his." Accordingly, they come to Canterbury. Presently, approaching the city, they hear that the Archbishop has just been slain. "So they were the more strengthened in faith, and, entering the city, besought that some of the blood of the murdered man might be given them; and thereupon (indeque) the tongue of the dumb man, on being touched,

---

aside . . . ; yet were exceedingly amazed . . . at such a token of religion. Wherefore also presently most of the band said to themselves with the centurion in the gospel (but silently by reason of their fear) 'Truly this was a just man.' And *beating their breasts* they accordingly returned " (Luke xxiii. 48). If the writer took this from Herbert, he would be shewn to be of a very late date. But both he and Herbert appear to be recounting *confused traditions that attempted to assimilate the Martyrdom to the Crucifixion.*

[3] [433a] We have seen (406) that Benedict describes a multitude of common people as crowding round the Archbishop's bleeding body some of whom smeared their eyes with blood—a striking testimony to the prevalence of ophthalmia. It is quite possible that one of these may have ultimately recovered his sight : the writer does not here say that he received it immediately. But his story must be rejected, (1) because it is not recorded by any other of our numerous witnesses, (2) because Benedict, mentioning the "eye-smearing," almost obliges himself to mention this cure, if he knew of it, (3) because Anon. V. is guilty of inserting a legend above, and of perverting facts in the story that immediately follows.

[4] "*Long* (multo tempore)." Benedict says that the paralytic attack was only "*four days* before " the Martyrdom (425a).

[5] Benedict and Fitzstephen (425) say that the vision appeared, not to the priest, but to *his friend alone.*

[6] Benedict and Fitzstephen do not mention it as occurring more than once.

was loosed.[7] This was reported to our acquaintance by very many, who afterwards heard the man celebrate mass."

[434] The author proceeds to describe a nightly vision in which a monk in the crypt sees one of the ancient martyrs celebrating mass near the tomb and censing it: the brethren open the tomb and find a wonderful fragrance. He concludes thus: "They say that very many other miracles are being wrought (fieri) in the same place: but I have taken pains to commit to writing [merely] what I have been able to ascertain with special certainty (quod verius scire potui). While I was writing the above, there came in one asserting that one of the Archbishop's murderers had turned mad and killed his own son." The last sentence indicates that the author wrote before, or not much after, the end of three or four years from the Martyrdom: for within that time (30) the four murderers were all believed to be dead.

[435] This testimony is peculiarly instructive. For it exhibits a man of learning, apparently writing in good faith, *and probably within four or five years from the Martyr's death*, yet (1) assigning to the dead body a stupendous miracle not found in any of the numerous descriptions of his death that proceeded, about the same time, from competent witnesses; (2) describing a miracle, wrought by the blood of the Martyr while still lying on the pavement—a miracle, whether manifested then or afterwards, at all events unrecorded by any other witness; and (3) greatly exaggerating a miracle correctly described by an eye-witness (Benedict) and by one who was intimate with the Archbishop (Fitzstephen).

[436] (12) The *Early Quadrilogus* (*Mat.* iv. 412), after quoting from Herbert, adds a passage not in Herbert, in which it refers the reader to the book of miracles written by Benedict. The passage is somewhat similar to one by

---

[7] Benedict says the cure was partial at Canterbury but perfected in London.

Anon. I., but calls Benedict " Abbot of Peterborough " instead of " Prior of Canterbury."[8]

§ 19. *Anon. X. on the burial and miracles, " redness in the sky "*

[437] (13) Anon. X. (*Mat.* iv. 438-9) says that on the morning after the murder, word was brought to the monks that an armed force had been gathered outside the city walls to drag the Archbishop's body out of the church with outrage. The monks, in fear, buried it, without the customary washing, in the crypt before the altars of St. John the Baptist and St. Augustine. The outer garments, when taken off, disclosed the hair clothing, beneath the monastic habit, covering all parts of the body, and caused general lamentations. " When buried," the author continues, " Thomas, the Martyr of God, began so suddenly to reveal his glory in (coruscare) miracles that no man could suffice to write or tell them. But a few, which are selected from many, and which (having had their truth tested) no one will be able to refute, are here briefly and truthfully noted down."

[438] Then follows an account of a redness in the sky (on the night of the murder) which, at the time, the monks thought wonderful, but not miraculous : but afterwards they ascertained that a redness had been seen in the north from Rouen.[1]

[439] After this follow some miracles taken (with some alterations of language) from the first two books of Bene-

---

[8] The *Late Quadrilogus* says that when the four knights left the presence of King Henry, they took an oath under a tree to slay the Archbishop, which tree presently withered. This may be a legend based on the statement of William of Canterbury (*Mat.* i. 130) that when the four knights went out from the *Archbishop's* presence, they threw off their surcoats under "a mulberry tree," preparing to slay him.

[1] [438*a*] This writer says that some monks thought the city was on fire : but the servants rushed out and brought back word that the redness was in the sky. Fitzstephen omits this, but mentions a storm and heavy rain (341-5).

dict's treatise, beginning with his first miracle, the one performed on the wife of the knight of Sussex. Only one has been reprinted by the editor of the *Materials* as differing essentially from Benedict. It describes the cure of one William, son of a citizen of Canterbury. The boy had seen in a dream St. Thomas looking on him and bidding a monk to take the boy a cup of his blood. The father, says Benedict, attempted next day, and the day following, but in vain, to procure the water tinctured with blood: on the third day, when the illness was worse than ever, the blood was obtained and the boy was healed.

According to this, nothing happens on "the next day." Anon. X. inserts something. The boy had a second dream, in which he saw St. Thomas requesting the Virgin to succour and heal him; but she refused, saying, "He has offended me"; then he awoke, suffering increased pains. The rest (except for a slight addition) agrees with Benedict's version.

§ 20. *Garnier on the burial and miracles*

[440] (14) Garnier says that the monks laid the body before the high altar after gathering up the blood and the brains, and that they watched it through the night, receiving the blood that flowed from it. Next morning, Robert, nephew of Randolph de Broc, bade the monks hide the body somewhere unless they wished it to be dragged out by horses, or torn in pieces, or cast into a cesspool and to dogs and swine.[1] The outer clothes of the Archbishop were taken off for the purpose of the burial, and all his garments are most minutely described, and the joy of the monks, exclaiming

---

[1] Garnier's words (l. 5669) "Geté en un *putel et en greignur puur*" are rendered by Benedict (*Mat.* ii. 16) "in paludem, vel quemlibet locum viliorem quem nec nominari decet," by John (*ib.* 322) "in paludem viliorem," by Grim (*ib.* 441) "in foetentem puteum." Anon. I. omits it. Fitzstephen (423) takes a much milder view. Some might omit the details owing to their revolting nature. Others, and especially the monks of Canterbury, might emphasize them as an excuse for the hasty burial.

when they see the proofs of his piety, "Behold the good monk: here you may find him." The vermin are also described as constituting a second martyrdom.

[441] After mentioning the date of the death he continues, as follows: "There was never heard, since the first age, That God shewed greater love to a dead man; Many great miracles did He for him by night and day. On earth is God with us, for love of the Martyr, And makes the dead to live, the dumb to speak, the deaf to hear, The deformed well-formed; He causes gout and fever to be cured; Dropsied and leprous folk He restores; The blind He makes to see, and the mad to return to their senses. Many Kings[2] come straight to seek him in pilgrimage, Princes and nobles, and dukes with their barons. . . .

[442] In semblance of wine and water did God cause His own blood to be used by the world, in order to save souls: In water and in phials did God cause to be carried by the world The blood of the Martyr to heal the sick, By healing and by sign He doubled the honour for him" (5806-10).

§ 21. *The Saga; St. Thomas's Well*

[443] (15) The *Saga*, immediately after likening the appearance of the Martyr's body to "the rose and the lily," proceeds thus: "Now the heavenly King revealeth at once this miracle for a beginning . . . that at the time when the

---

[441] Ne fu unques oï, dès le siecle primur,
Que Deus à home mort mustrast greignur amur;
Mult granz miracles fet pur lui, et nuit et jur.
 En terre est Deus od nus, pur amur al martir,
E les morz fet revivre, muz parler, surz oïr,
Les contrez redrescier, gutus, févrus guarir,
Idropikes, liéprus, en santé restablir,
Cius véer, en lur sens les desvez revenir.
 Plusur Rei[2] le requièrent en dreit pelerinage,

Li prince, li barun, li duc od lur barnage,
. . . . .
[442] En semblance de vin et d'ève fet user
Deus sun sanc par le mund, pur les anmes sauver;
En ève et en ampules fet par le mund porter
Deus le sanc al martir pur les enferms saner,
En santé et en signe i fet l'onur dubler.
   5788-97, 5806-10.

---

[2] "Kings" may include Prince Henry, who had been formally crowned. He visited the Martyr's tomb before his father's visit. The latter took place in 1174. Garnier cannot include the visit of Lewis VII., which took place in 1179.

learned men had gathered together into one large chalice the brains with the blood, and were carrying it unto the altar, the Holy Ghost descendeth down upon it in the likeness of a dove. . . .

[444] Hereby also goeth another wonder, inasmuch as the great wound which the clerk Edward received was whole and healed before the body of the Archbishop was cold on the floor. . . . Thus the monks and the clerks spend this dread night in sorrow and weeping and much wailing, as God alone knoweth.

[445] But . . . , that same night, there sprang up through a stone in the crypt a fair and desirable spring which sithence is called St. Thomas's Well. . . . By divine providence also things were so ordained this night, too, that they had no need to go out on any errands; for now cometh a true news by rumour flying unto the church, that the murderers of the Archbishop are minded to take his body with force away, and to drag it through the town or to hang it to the gallows."

[446] The *Saga*, in describing the unclothing of the Martyr, makes no mention of vermin, but speaks of " the worry of the itching and the smarting of the cloth " as being a permanent martyrdom. It does not expressly say that the body was not " washed," but after stating that the body was " not embalmed," adds, " He had no need to receive the anointment of this world who was already reddened in the blood of so glorious a passion."

§ 22. *Origin of the Saga's legends*

[447] The miracles here described by the *Saga* are such as might easily have sprung up in a very few years through poetic transmission. Nothing was more natural than that, within five years from the Martyrdom, the pilgrims of St. Thomas should say that the Holy Ghost had blessed his

blood to the healing of the world and had descended on it from that first moment when the monks began to collect it. Moreover, to say that "virtue went out from the crypt in which he was laid for the healing of all the world" might easily be expressed—with allusion to the Water of St. Thomas carried about through all the world—by saying that "From the crypt of St. Thomas, on the night when he was there first laid, there came forth a fountain to heal disease and sin." The miraculous healing of Edward Grim is of quite a different character. No metaphor can explain that story. But it arose naturally in the minds of men unable to distinguish marvellous and instantaneous cures of nervous and muscular diseases, which can be explained by natural causes, from other cures or restorations, which cannot be thus explained. Men believed that the Saint could heal all bodily unsoundness. They assumed that he must have had the will to heal the wound of the man who had stood valiantly by him at the last. How then could they fail (unless acquainted with Grim, and confronted with the obstinate fact of his continued disablement) to infer that St. Thomas must have exercised his undoubted power for his faithful clerk?[1]

§ 23. *Contrast between the Saga and a contemporary letter*

[448] (16) In contrast with the last may be placed a brief extract from the letter from the Archbishop of Sens to the Pope written immediately after hearing of the murder:[1] "And since, after the departure of the holy man, through the operation of the Lord, we have heard (on the frequent testimony of many) that certain things worthy of note have come to pass, they ought not to be passed over in utter silence. For it is said and constantly asserted that after his

---

[1] For the *Saga's* legend about the miraculous impression of the Martyr's last footprints on the pavement where he stood and fell, see **192**. For another version of the healing of Grim, see **810**.

[1] *Mat.* vii. 431. It was probably written by Herbert (**350**).

Passion he appeared in a vision to many to whom he declared that he was not dead but alive, showing no wounds but only the scars of wounds." This probably refers to Benedict's vision on the night after the murder. It makes no mention of any acts of healing.[2]

§ 24. *The singular value of Benedict's testimony*

[449] Confining ourselves to the very earliest of the acts of healing, we may say that very rarely have so-called miracles been recorded in circumstances more favourable for ascertaining the truth. No doubt, the monks who recorded them desired to believe they were miraculous. But they wrote amid a multitude of watchful enemies, able to detect, and on the alert to detect, imposture, to whom such detection would have afforded a delightful triumph. For their own sakes, therefore, the monks would be bound to confine themselves to facts.

And Benedict's testimony has this singular value that, in the early days of the miracles, it appears to have been set down in writing at the time, as each miracle occurred or came to the knowledge of the monks. Moreover, the contrast between his frank and moderate accounts and the exaggerations of others who were not eye-witnesses, should deepen our faith in the former, since it shows how strong the current set in favour of exaggerations (among the lower clergy and the poorer laymen) and leads us to infer that Benedict must have been a man of exact and temperate mind, to state his facts so fairly. In some cases, where the cure was wrought in the Cathedral, he was an eye-witness of

---

[2] One MS. of the letter, besides inserting "visions to an ancient monk named Neel," adds a recovery of sight by a blind man "by anointing his eyes with the blood while it was still fresh (crudo)." This is "omnino auditum." A relighting of candles round the tomb is "non infida multorum relatio." The scribe adds, as a greater miracle, the blessing given by the dead Saint to those round the bier when he lay before the high altar "about dawn." See 432-3.

the alleged miracle itself, and, in others, of the consequences of the miracle—attested by the patient afterwards coming to the Martyr's tomb, accompanied by witnesses corroborating the patient's statement and offering themselves for examination by the monk whose business it was to test the evidence.

[450] On the supposition that Benedict's account of the beginning and growth of the miracles is substantially true, we are enabled to understand many phenomena, before hardly intelligible, in the early Christian Church; and, in particular, the effect exercised on the minds and imaginations of vast numbers of the poor, the afflicted, and the diseased, by a faith in some Champion of the oppressed and miserable, himself destroyed by the oppressor, yet conceived as still living and acting, with hand stretched out to heal and bless those who invoke his aid. The incredulity of the comfortable and intellectual classes, and the active discouragement, or persecution, practised by the classes possessing political power, instead of quenching, tend to augment the flames of such a faith. Noised abroad through the land, the story of the Martyr brings home to thousands of sufferers in far distant hovels the very form of his body, the garments that he wore, and the wounds that he received in his last moments, so that when he appears in a vision or ecstasy to the sick and sorrowful, they see the red blood-line " stretching from the right temple down to the left cheek," and can describe him, says Benedict, "just as if they had actually seen him." Such a record ought to make it easy to believe St. Paul's account of the miracle-working habitual among the early Christians.

SECTION II

THE GROWTH OF THE MIRACLES, OR BENEDICT'S EARLIEST RECORDS

§ 1. *Benedict's list compared with William's*[1]

[451] It was not till Easter 1171 that miracles came in crowds. At first each single one was a great event, eagerly welcomed by the monks, and not to be despised though performed on women and poor folk. Hence Benedict's list of patients contains, in the first thirty, about an equal proportion of males and females, whereas William, in the same number, gives little more than a seventh to the latter. As might be expected, also, the earliest patients are from Canterbury, London, and the Home Counties.

[452] Here are the first thirty cases recorded severally by Benedict and William. It will be seen that the latter gives a larger proportion of priests or clergy, and a good many foreigners. William gives the first place to a miracle of a very remarkable nature (see below 596) authenticated by the burgesses of Bedford. Then he places one performed on a woman of the same village. William's fourth, sixth, seventh, and eighth cases are of epilepsy, or "falling sickness." This illustrates his principles—if they can be so called—of arrangement. He is influenced sometimes (1) by strength of testimony, at others (2) by similarity of disease (or even of name of patient), (3) by identity of locality, either of the

---

[1] In the following section, Roman followed by Arabic numbers mean a volume and page of the *Materials* (1a).

miracle, or of the testifier to the miracle. Benedict's work also, in its later parts—some of which do not proceed from his pen—adopts occasionally these irregular classifications.

BENEDICT (ii. 37-66).	WILLIAM [2] (i. 155-187).
[453] (1) Emma, wife of a knight in Sussex (Blindness).	(1) Ailward of Westoning (Blinding and Mutilation).
(2) Huelina, daughter of Aaliza of London: cured at Gloucester (Complaint in head).	(2) Levive of Westoning (Dropsy).
(3) William Belet, knight, of Enborne in Berkshire (Swelling in arm).	(3) Son of a knight of Pontefract (Death).
(4) Brithiva of Canterbury (Blindness).	(4) Petronilla, a nun of Polesworth (Epilepsy).
(5) William, priest, of London (Paralysis).	(5) A monk (A severe cough).
(6) Stephen, knight, of Hoyland ("Nocturnal terrors").	(6) An Italian and his son (Epilepsy).
(7) William Patrick, servant of William of Warbleton (Pains in the jaw).	(7) William of St. Albans (Epilepsy).
(8) Robert, son of a knight of Surrey (Disease of Liver).	(8) Emma, wife of the Bishop of Winchester's steward (Epilepsy).
(9) Alditha of Worth, near Sandwich (Saved in child bearing).	(9) Nicholas, the little son of Nicholas of the neighbourhood of Glastonbury (Lameness).
(10) Miracle concerning the Saint's blood (Ulviva).	(10) A baby, six months old (Internal obstruction).
(11) Miracle concerning the Saint's blood (At Colchester: Radulf, a monk of Canterbury).	(11) Robert, priest near Lincoln (Ill health).
(12) Miracle concerning the Saint's blood (Near Colchester).	(12) Alan of Lindsey, priest (Grievous infirmity).
(13) Miracle concerning the Saint's blood (William, priest of Bourne).	(13) Richard of Coventry, and his wife and grandson (Various ailments).
(14) Miracle concerning the Saint's blood (A "pardoner").	(14) Robert, son of Guy of Chichester ("extreme sickness").
(15) Daughter of Ralph of Bourne (Condition approaching death).	(15) Robert of Marton, clerk (Bleeding to death).

---

[2] This list does not include the visions or miracles of chastisement which William prefixes to these.

(16) Audrey, living at Canterbury (Fever).

(16) Baldwin of Fontenelle, in Flanders (Contraction of muscles), and Heiliff of (?) Cherneside (Bedridden).

(17) William, son of a citizen of Canterbury (? Tumour).

(17) Symon, Canon of Beverley (State resembling death).

(18) Goditha, wife of Matthew of Canterbury (Swelling in legs).

(18) Ralph, a clerk, of (?) Chingford (Ulcers).

(19) Samson, from Oxfordshire (Dumbness).

(19) Richard, Canon' of Chichester (Fistula).

(20) Geldwin, son of a baker of Canterbury (Long sickness).

(20) Odo of Aldrington (Ulcer).

(21) Two other sons of the baker (Fever).

(21) William, a clerk, of Lincoln (Ulcers).

(22) Manwin, a poor man of Canterbury (Blindness).

(22) Adelicia of Lincoln (Disease in breast).

(23) Emmeline of Canterbury (Lameness).

(23) Ralph de la Saussaie (Dysentery).

(24) Edilda of Canterbury (Lameness: a partial cure).

(24) A young man "de villa Dyena" (A festering wound).

(25) Wlviva of Canterbury (Lameness).

(25) A young man of (?) Marcham, Berks (A festering wound).

(26) Edmund of Çanterbury (Partial blindness, and an internal obstruction).

(26) Adam, a knight, near Winchester (Piles).

(27) Muriel, on the point of death, brings up fruit-stones, acorns, etc., and is cured.

(27) Thomas of Beverley (Swelling of neck and jaw).

(28) Ethelburga (Gouty pain in arm).

(28) Paul of Rouen, a vinedresser (Weatherbound).

(29) Robert, a smith, of Thanet (Blindness).

(29) Roger of Middleton (Dropsy).

(30) Henry of Fordwych (Madness).

(30) Robert of Bromton, a knight (Dropsy).

§ 2. *Miracles of January*, 1171

[454] It is a remarkable testimony to the rapidity with which news travelled in those days, that the second miracle occurred at Gloucester on the fifth day after the Martyrdom (2 Jan.). Huelina, daughter of Aaliza of London,[1] had been liable, from her fifth to her sixteenth year, to a monthly

---

[1] ii. 39.

swelling of the head which, while it lasted, rendered the whole body almost immoveable, and made rest and sleep impossible. Potions, caustic, and other remedies had been tried in vain. The girl happened to be suffering as usual, when the mother, hearing of the Martyr's death, and believing that England "had gained rather than lost a champion," invoked St. Thomas, promising a pilgrimage in her daughter's name, should she be cured. Scarcely had she uttered the words when the girl turned on her side and fell asleep, and the disease was from that moment eradicated. "We afterwards heard," says Benedict, "both [mother and daughter], and examined the matter with our own eyes; and we came to the conclusion that credit must be given to this miracle."

[455] No other witnesses are mentioned, so that the evidence is rather below that of many other miracles in Benedict's book; and he himself seems to imply that they had some scruples about it, and might perhaps not have accepted it but for another miracle wrought on the following day (3 Jan.) on a knight in Berkshire. This would of course reach their ears some time before the Gloucester miracle. Moreover a poor woman of Canterbury recovered her sight on 4 Jan. Hence the monks might naturally argue that the same power that worked miracles on the third and fourth of January might very well work one on the second.[2] However, they did their best, he says, to ascertain the truth by a rigid cross-examination "for the sake of others and especially because of the slanders of maligners." Taken in

---

[2] He speaks of the miracle as "approved by a decision of irrefragible testimony (miraculo huic . . . irrefragibilis testimonii *sententia* comprobato)"; and he adds that, if they had rejected it, they would have been convicted of want of faith by the marvel of *the following day* (3 Jan.), which seemed by its unshaken testimony to support the sign that preceded it. Does "sententia" mean the decision of the monks in Chapter, or of some ecclesiastical authority at Gloucester? If the latter, would it not have been mentioned? In "Alioquin argueret nos incredulitatis diei sequentis prodigium, quod praecedenti signo inconcusso videbatur testimonio suffragari," the sense seems to demand that "inconcusso" should qualify "testimonio."

conjunction with the circumstances, the facts thus recorded by Benedict may reasonably be accepted as being substantially correct, and, if they are, many will believe that the cure was not a mere sequence but a consequence of an emotional shock, probably conveyed through the mother to the daughter, who may be supposed to have been present when the vow was made to St. Thomas.

[456] The third miracle was wrought on a venerable knight William Belet, widely known and of good repute, in a town of Berkshire ("quae Anglice Aeinesburna vocatur").[3] For three months he had been confined to his bed by a terrible pain in his left arm, which had swollen to the thickness of his thigh. Coming home from church, in tears, his wife told him the news of the murder, and he besought the Martyr to deliver him, promising a pilgrimage if he were healed. "When he ended his prayer, his pain found the beginning of its end": he was refreshed by an unusually sweet sleep on the night that followed; and, when he awoke, his pain was gone, and his left arm no bigger than the right. Benedict does not say that the knight's promised pilgrimage was fulfilled; but elsewhere he mentions vows, if unfulfilled. So we may infer here that the knight came to Canterbury, and that Benedict records the facts from his testimony.

[457] The next day (4 Jan.) a poor woman of Canterbury miraculously recovered her sight.[4] Going to the house of a neighbour, she besought her to lend her any relic of the Martyr that she might touch her eyes with it. We have seen above that many people in Canterbury had dipped strips from their garments in the Martyr's blood at the time of the murder. Accordingly, the neighbour produced a rag thus stained. "The blind woman touched her eyes and wiped away her darkness. She had come guided. She returned without guidance."

---

[3] ii. 40-41.   [4] ii. 41.

[458] On the eighth day[5] occurred the healing of the paralytic Priest, William of London, mentioned above. This was the first instance in which the blood of the Martyr, mingled with water, was given to any patient by the monks: and the practice "was not begun," says Benedict, "without great fear: but when it was seen that the sick benefited thereby, fear gave way, and by degrees was succeeded by confidence." By "fear," he means fear of profanity: for the fear of persecution did not disappear till several months afterwards. The Priest, says Benedict, "returned rejoicing, and magnifying the Lord in His Martyr, yet secretly for fear of the Jew-like persecutors—Jew-like, I say, because, even as the Jews were fain to blot out the name of Christ whom they had slain, so were these desirous of extinguishing the glory of the Martyr whom they had destroyed. . . . But in vain did they attempt to hide the rays of the sun."

[459] This prepares the way for the next miracle, performed on Stephen, a knight of Hoyland,[6] who had been for thirty years liable to a nightly oppression or suffocation, which so afflicted him that he would beg the servants who watched near his couch to pull him up by the hair of his head, when what he called "the demon" leaped upon him. Twice, even during the banishment of the Archbishop, he had been temporarily benefited by an appeal to God "for the love of" His exile; but when, on hearing of his death, he had caused mass to be celebrated for him, he was entirely delivered. True, the demon still sometimes appeared to him in the form of a dwarf[7] running round and round him as though trying to get at him. But the knight defied him in the name of the blessed Martyr: and from that hour the phantom troubled him no more. After waiting to satisfy

---

[5] ii. 42.   [6] ii. 44.
[7] [459a] The Editor justly remarks that the unfamiliar word "nani (dwarf)" is more likely to be correct than the readings "navi (ship)," "avis (bird)." "Nani" was probably first corrupted to "navi," and then "navi" was altered to "avis," for sense.

himself that his deliverance was complete and permanent, he came on foot to the Martyr's memorial: "His humility was clearly proved by the despicable garb[8] he had assumed. His discourse, as he told his story, savoured of a marvellous joy: in our presence he extolled with a wonderful passionateness the Martyr who, while living, had once, nay twice, rescued him from extreme misery, and now, after death, had given him permanent deliverance."

§ 3. *Lent*, 1171

[460] The miracle next recorded took place about the middle of February. William Patrick, servant of William of Warbleton,[1] was delivered from pain in the jaw, which had caused him such paroxysms that he had been almost put under restraint as a madman. The man saw, in a vision, one who declared that he was a clerk of my lord of Canterbury. "Do not say that to any one," replied he. "It is not safe." The figure replied, "I am not afraid of them; it is for them, not for me, to tremble. See, I have a letter from my lord the Pope that all concerned in the Martyr's death must be punished." Then, mentioning by name some one whom St. Thomas had been wont to call in his letters the son of perdition,[2] he said, "As for him, he goes straight to the pit of hell: but what ails you?" On being informed, he bade the man open his mouth, and waving the air into it with his mantle, applied the border to the patient's cheek. "He awoke, and found himself freed from all pain." Benedict adds that the young man described exactly, to the astonishment of those who heard him, the pallium of the Archbishop. But, as this miracle happened at the beginning of Lent, and was not reported by Patrick before Whitsunday, by which

---

[8] Odo of Falaise (**547**) assumed the garb of a beggar as a disguise, to avoid the displeasure of the King.

[1] ii. 46. [2] Ranulf de Broc.

time the tide of miracles was flowing strongly and the person and clothing of the Martyr must have been known by talk and pictures in almost every poor household in England, we may be unable to share in Benedict's astonishment about this detail, and may even suspect that the young man had, consciously or unconsciously, elaborated the circumstances of his vision.

[461] Another miracle performed about the middle of Lent on one Robert, son of a knight in Surrey,[3] was—like the last—not reported till Whitsuntide. This was an acute case of disease of the liver, which none of the London physicians could cure. Not till they had despaired of the patient and sent him back to his Surrey home where he lay in bed for eleven weeks, did he "return to himself and flee to St. Thomas." The same hour that witnessed his prayer witnessed his amendment. Grateful for his recovery, he had "a vehement desire to come in haste to Canterbury: but seeing the wind of persecution as yet strong, he feared to go thither, and put off the fulfilment of his desire to a less dangerous time." This implies that, by Whitsuntide 1171, a change had taken place in the attitude, or at least the action, of the authorities toward the Canterbury pilgrims.

[462] Aliditha of Worth, near Sandwich,[4] is next recorded (without date) to have been saved from death in child-bearing by faith and by the application of a handkerchief that had been blessed by the Martyr. No witnesses are mentioned: but the priest from whom she had received the sacrament in expectation of death, and by whose advice the handkerchief was applied, might naturally attest the case.

[463] Then follows an instance of the miraculous multiplication of the Saint's blood in a wooden vessel, attested on oath by Ulviva, the lady principal of a leper-house. This is accepted by Benedict, partly on her testimony, partly

---

[3] ii. 47.   [4] ii. 48.

because of a second instance [5] attested by the monks of Colchester Abbey. The former may be an error of malobservation. In the latter, the most obvious conclusion is that the blood had been diluted by some zealous monk at Colchester before the glass vial was publicly opened there. The Colchester monks also told another similar tale.[6] After washing the wax stopper of their vial, they enclosed in a pyx the water in which the wax had been washed, as a present to a neighbouring church. The priest first placed it on the altar, but afterwards transferred it to his own house. Next morning the pyx was found split, and not a drop remained. "Thus," says Benedict, "the blood was given and multiplied for those for whom the Divine Ordinance so willed it: and from him to whom it was not given, even that which he seemed to have was taken away."

[464] We need not suspect the Colchester monks of deliberately neutralizing their present by giving it in a leaky pyx: for something similar is recorded soon afterwards. William of Bourne, a venerable priest,[7] gave some of the blood in a pyx of boxwood to a travelling preacher or Pardoner, whom Benedict seems not to rate highly. The pyx was immediately broken when it touched the holy Water,[8] but the wax prevented the spilling of the blood. Yet next morning the Pardoner, who had taken it to his home, found not a trace of blood. The reason for this was much discussed: "but not a few conjectured, and with some probability, that the man's intentions were open to the charge of avarice." Subsequently, however, such cases became so common that tin vials were invented and completely displaced the wooden vessels.

---

[5] ii. 50.   [6] ii. 52.   [7] ii. 53.
[8] "Ad contactum sanctuarii": comp. ii. 70 "illa . . . *sanctuarii* non ferens virtutem," "the pyx . . . not enduring the divine force of *the holy Water*," *i.e.* the Water of Canterbury, which was water containing a small portion of the Saint's blood.

[465] This same William of Bourne [9] also saved a little child at the point of death by wrapping it in the Martyr's pall (which was in his possession): and along with this miracle is mentioned one [10] described above, in which William, the son of a Canterbury citizen, was healed—when he had lost his speech and had so swollen that he seemed near bursting—by drinking of the blood in accordance with a vision. The last miracle recorded as happening before Easter is the cure of Goditha, wife of Matthew of Canterbury,[11] who could not walk by reason of horrible swellings in her legs. Two women carried her secretly to the tomb, and the tinctured water was applied. The swelling abated; but apparently not at once, for she departed secretly. However, she improved every day, and speedily regained perfect vigour.

Benedict concludes his first book by saying, "These, and several more were the great acts that the Lord wrought before Easter:—but these are small and almost to be despised in comparison with those which follow."

§ 4. *Easter*, 1171

[466] On Easter day there could be no service in the Cathedral because it had not yet been purified from the murder. But a vast crowd suddenly rushed into it, drawn by a report of the extraordinary contortions of a dumb man, who [1] wallowed foaming, and kept falling and bruising himself. At last, settling down, in a scarcely intelligible voice, he asked for something to drink. His speech could hardly be understood; but he said that he had been born in Oxfordshire, and had lost his speech five years before, sleeping out in a meadow; he had fallen asleep a healthy man; he woke up, dumb.

Recently, two figures of reverend aspect had appeared to him in a dream, saying that the Martyr's tomb was the only place in the world where he could be cured. He called himself Samson. A good many believed, but some doubted. He brought no witnesses, but the monks had this strong proof of his veracity, that, although he stayed some time with them and made some progress, he could not attain to perfect clearness of speech. He had been lately living in Rochester, and the monks made inquiries there, but elicited nothing contrary to the man's statements. Moreover, says Benedict, "I often conversed with the host with whom he had stayed for several days. He told me he had over and over again made the lad drunk, but could never extract from him a single word [to contradict his story], though it is an old and true proverb that through lads and liquor one can extract the truth. We therefore exclaimed . . . 'This is the day that the Lord hath made, let us rejoice and be glad therein.'"

Taking into consideration the fact that this "mute," as soon as he spoke, "asked for something to drink," that his host found no difficulty in making him "over and over again drunk," and that no testimony from any clerk or priest is alleged proving that the man had ever been dumb, we can hardly feel surprised that about this miracle "some doubted." And Benedict himself seems to have had some difficulty in working himself up to such a state of mind that he could "rejoice and be glad therein."

[467] On the same Easter Sunday[2] a child in Canterbury who had lain for three days voiceless and speechless without food or drink was restored by drinking the Water, and afterwards[3] two brothers of this child were healed of fever. Thus, as miracles became gradually numerous, "the rest of the sick folk of Canterbury by degrees resorted to the Martyr. Among these one Manwin,[4] poor but well known in the city, had lost his sight for almost two years. Obtaining a drop of the blood from a neighbour, he had been led home

---

[2] ii. 58.   [3] ii. 59.   [4] Ib.

as usual. Scarcely had he bathed his eyes when one of his little children fell and began to cry. Stooping to lift the little one, he brushed the moisture off and saw the child before he lifted it: "The city of Canterbury, which knows that he was blind before, knows equally that he afterwards regained his sight."

[468] Emeline of Canterbury[5] was cured in the Cathedral on the same Easter Sunday. She had been lamed by a fall four years before, and could not walk a step without a crutch. Drawn by the reports about the miracles, she came to the Cathedral to invoke the Martyr. Presently her soul was stirred within her and she fell down (conturbata corruit) in the exact place where the dumb man above mentioned had fallen. There, in agony and convulsion (volutatione), she spent the whole day. When night came on, "she departed, wearied, but healed. Still, we advised her to support her wearied frame on her crutch. But she despised it."

[469] During all this time the multitude had not been admitted publicly or freely to the Martyr's tomb. The doors of the crypt had been kept closed and barred. If any one was admitted it was in secret. But now the people began to murmur. The monks were warned that they might seem to be hiding the talent entrusted to them by God, and to be envying the Martyr his glory and the sick the blessing of health. Moved by these reproaches, they threw open the crypt to the people on Friday in Easter week. From that time, says Benedict, the scene of the pool of Bethesda was being continually renewed in the Cathedral, and great and wonderful miracles were of daily occurrence. Incidentally, in a previous passage, he describes himself as attending to the sick folk who were "lying in pain all about the church."[6]

---

[5] ii. 60.
[6] ii. 47 "per totam ecclesiam laborantibus." This was about Whitsuntide.

[470] Among these were two lame women,[7] Edilda (or Elditha) and Wlviva, both of Canterbury. Benedict's temperate account of their cure commends itself to belief. The latter, who had been for three years bowed down by Satan and could not walk without a crutch, arose erect after a short prayer and "refused now to bear the staff that had once borne her." The former, who had not set foot to ground for a year and a half, was brought into the church by three women, leaning on a staff and with her left knee suffering from the least touch. She returned with her pain assuaged: "In token of her cure, she violently struck her knee with her clenched fist in presence of us all: and the people saw her walking and praising God. . . . But why she remained lame and did not obtain a complete recovery we omit to discuss, judging it safer to keep entire silence concerning the hidden judgments of God than rashly to infer anything from them (inde temere diffinire)."

[471] Edmund of Canterbury[8] was blind of one eye and had been for two years troubled by something that seemed to shift its place in his left side, causing him strange prickings and wonderful tortures. When a drop of the Martyr's blood was applied to his eye (and he also drank it), "he threw himself on his face, then on his side, struggling and shrieking: often he would try to get up, but could not stand steady; down he fell on his face, dashed on the stones; his visit seemed to be doing him nothing but mischief, and you would have thought him mad. . . . At last, he found relief in slumber, and fell fast asleep on his back. The Saint of God stood by the sleeper, and took him by the shoulder and shook him, saying, 'Arise, go forth.' Immediately awaking, he felt that the shifting thing that caused him such internal torture was being driven to the lower part of his throat. To save himself from suffocation he reached his

---

[7] ii. 61-2.   [8] ii. 62.

hand down to touch and see what it was. Suddenly, as though a bladder had burst, the thing was driven out of his mouth by some power of God, and he felt a taste like gall. Forthwith he rose up, threw off his cloak and went to the Martyr's tomb to give thanks : and, in return for the restoration of his eye and his health, he took the cross with a pledge to go to Jerusalem for the love of the Martyr. And all the people, when they saw it, gave praise unto God."

[472] In the case of Muriel [9] (apparently of Canterbury), diseased for two years, the tinctured water at first seemed to fail, and indeed to make her, for three days, worse than before. On the third day, she was so ill that she was taken out of bed, "lest, contrary to the custom of the Christian religion, she should die on a feather bed (plumis)." The Priest came in haste to administer extreme unction. But unexpectedly she threw up a mass of cherry-stones, plum-stones, and acorns, some of which were sprouting and "were shewn to us. . . . Nor can there be a doubt that they would have speedily effected the sick woman's death, but for the aid of the holy draught." On the next day, the woman came on foot to the Martyr's tomb : "and all the people rejoiced because of all the things that were gloriously wrought by him."

[473] This miracle may be a mere coincidence, or rather a mere sequence. The vomiting may have followed the drinking of the potion but not have been caused by it. But it raises an interesting question, suggested also by several other miracles where the drinking of the potion was followed by vomiting, or the application of the lotion by grievous pain. While the monks were mixing the blood with water might they not think themselves justified in blending the water with some medicinal drug? This could not well be done in the instances where water was sent to places at a

---

[9] ii. 63.

distance, no special disease being in view : but it might be done at the tomb. And might it not be compatible with the faith of the monks in the Martyr's blood that it should be combined with some remedy to strengthen the weaker faith of the recipient? It is quite conceivable that, in many diseases, a faith-cure might be made more easy and more rapid if the patient first found the Martyr's potion producing some definite and powerful effect on him.

[474] To return to the sick people of Canterbury and the neighbourhood. Ethelburga,[10] a matron known to the monks for her good works, was cured of a pain in her left shoulder from the moment when she measured her arm with a thread with the view of offering a wax candle of that size to the Saint. Robert, a smith, of Thanet, blind for two years, had been ordered in a vision of the preceding December to go to Canterbury and to have "milk" put on his eyes by one of the monks.[11] But not till the Easter outburst of miracles did he recognize that a Martyr's blood is the sweetest "milk." Then he came with his wife and daughter, and, says the chronicler, after anointing his eyes, he prostrated himself for prayer, and felt "a thunder-clap" go off in his head : "receiving his sight, he arose, and gave public thanks to God."

[475] About the same time, the mad Henry of Fordwich[12] was dragged by his friends to the tomb, with his hands tied behind him, struggling and shouting, and there remained all day, but began to recover as the sun went down, and, after a night spent in the church, returned home in perfect sanity. From the same neighbourhood[13] came a woman, whose name is not mentioned (perhaps owing to the multitude of cases at this time). She was deaf and troubled with pain in the head. The mixture above mentioned was poured into her ears, and also given her as a potion : then she devoted

---

[10] ii. 64.   [11] ii. 65, "milk," see 771 (6).   [12] ii. 66.   [13] Ib.

herself to prayer. As she prayed, "she was tortured worse than ever and thought a number of little twigs were being broken to pieces inside her, asking the bystanders whether they heard the sound in her head. So while she was in this trouble she cried unto the Lord and He heard her. For, while she cried, there was a breakage as it were of an apostheme and a flow of matter from her ears, followed by a flow of blood, and this, in turn, followed by the blessing of restored hearing."

§ 5. *Two disappointments*

[476] On two occasions, however, the Saint expressly told the patients not to expect a cure.[1] Both were boys. The former, lame, while resting his head on the tomb, unfortunately fell asleep. "Why do you lie on me?" said the holy Father, suddenly appearing, "You shall certainly not recover. Go hence, I will do nothing for you." The boy awoke, and, relating his vision to his mother and the monks, caused himself to be removed to another place. "We bade him," says Benedict, "still devote himself to prayer." But though the poor boy consented, he was hopeless of changing the Saint's decision: and no benefit in the way of recovery resulted.

[477] The second case was still harder. Some one appeared to the boy as he slept, and said, "Why do you lie here? The Archbishop sends you word you shall certainly not be healed. Sin, committed before your birth, deprives you of recovery." "This," says Benedict, "does not lead us to believe that the son bore the iniquity of his parents, but rather that the Lord desired to scourge the parents in the son in order that the bodily loss of the son might be a punishment of sorrow for the parents. Accordingly, a few days afterwards the boy departed this life. I confess, we

---

[1] ii. 67.

grieved and sympathised sorely with both these lads . . . but we were gladdened by the Martyr in other cases."

§ 6. *The Water of Canterbury*

[478] Of the "cases" above mentioned, the first that occurs to Benedict is one of the successful use of "the Water of St. Thomas" or "the Water of Canterbury," as the tincture had now come to be called in districts round the city. Agnes of Canterbury[1] suffered five weeks from a horrible putrefying tumour in the face and a flow of phlegm. After she had drunk the Water, there fell from her mouth into the basin of phlegm a four-footed worm, one and a half inches long, so agile that some said it came from the Enemy[2]: yet when plunged in the phlegm (so it was thought) and placed in an upper window, it disappeared.

[479] At this point[3] Benedict inserts a number of instances in which the Water was lost owing to the splitting of the pyx containing it. How the sacred Water slipped this way and that, and bubbled as though boiling, and finally vanished; how one person was consequently impelled to confess "every sin he could think of, and that, not to one, but to thirteen priests"; how another, having been induced to carry her pyx into the house of a friendly Jewess—whom she had been in the habit of obliging with an occasional charm or incantation as an antidote against pains in the feet —was warned to leave "the accursed house" by the splitting of her pyx from top to bottom; and how persistently the Water that remained in the pyx of the pious refused to

---

[1] ii. 68.

[2] "cursuque suo tantae se vivacitatis esse ostendit ut a nonnullis de adversa parte esse diceretur; in phlegmate tamen, ut putabatur, submersus, et in editiori fenestra positus, non comparuit." A similar experience was told to Dr. Gray by the present (1898) Ameer of Afghanistan as having occurred to himself, with manifest expectation of being believed. Here the narrator is very candid in admitting that the worm could not afterwards be found.

[3] ii. 69-73.

remain when poured into that of the impious—all these "mirthful miracles (jucunditatis miracula)" are here related by Benedict in a digression from which he speedily returns to "the facts that preceded in chronological order."[4]

[480] William, an old knight, of Dene[5] in the neighbourhood of Canterbury, long paralysed in his legs and feet, was brought on horseback to the Cathedral, held on by a servant on each side lest he should fall. Leaning on them and a staff he was brought to the tomb: "There, on fervently invoking God, and His Martyr, he felt his legs and feet regaining their sensibility, his muscles becoming warm, and his whole body receiving as it were a gift of easy motion." He threw off his cloak, leapt forward amid a crowd of spectators, and felt that he was healed. Then he sat down, took off his shoes, and with bare feet prostrated himself before the Saint. Finally, he returned on foot without help, and mounted his horse amid general rejoicing, leaving his crutch behind as a sign of his restoration.

[481] Saxeva, of Dover,[6] suffering from intestinal disease (incisione viscerum) and continual pain in the arm, from Christmas to Easter, was weary of living. She fled for aid to the Martyr, and prayed and slept near his tomb. The Martyr appeared to her. "'Rise,' he said, 'offer thy candle.' She leapt up, and found herself healed. Then she obeyed the command, and shewed herself so agile that she hyperbolically declared she could fly like a bird."

[482] A scholar (scholasticus) of Northampton, Richard son of Walter,[7] had suffered for nine years, first from diarrhœa,

---

[4] Benedict does not seem to take a severe view of those who are thus eluded by the Saint (ii. 71): "Nonne lusisse videtur hic martyr cum homine . . .? Ludus martyris dicendus est an reprehensio?" Still he implies that the men are in fault, not the pyx. It would be interesting to know whether the pyx was generally supplied by the monks. In one case the pyx belonged to the pilgrim Ralph of Sheppey, who (ii. 69) "pyxidem ligneam ad aquam suscipiendam protulit"; Ralph emptied the water into another, apparently supplied by himself. Then, says Benedict, "we obliged him with a third, keeping the two (ourselves)."

[5] ii. 73.   [6] ii. 74.   [7] Ib.

then from liver-complaint. His illness had begun with a nightly vision of a terrible figure, which had commanded him to choose between death in nine days, or a living death for nine years. He chose the latter.

[483] The phantom struck him with his fist, and he awoke, unable to walk, and suffering from continual dysentery. No physicians had been able to help him. Towards the end of the ninth year, a little brother of his saw in a dream a beautiful man who said that the sick man was to go to Canterbury, and to Canterbury he went. To walk or ride was impossible, so he was drawn in a carriage. The nearer he came to the city the more he felt that his disease was departing. " He left his carriage and approached the Martyr on foot. I never remember," writes the chronicler, " to have seen a man so lifeless-looking and pale. His skin scarce cleaved to his bones. His face was marred with, I cannot call it pallor, say rather dusky colour suggestive of putrefaction. Never was man more like a resuscitated corpse three or four days old. I must give up description. It would seem past belief. Such as he was, when he tasted the holy Water, he prostrated himself on the ground and prayed. Suddenly, as though in anguish, he began to howl and cry aloud, wallowing and writhing this way and that. Then, tired out, he fell asleep. He awoke restored to health. For some days after his recovery he stayed on at Canterbury, partly to ensure that his recovery was permanent, partly for devotion's sake." During this period the monks asked him whether his mental condition had corresponded to his bodily state when his gesture and action seemed to proclaim him mad (arreptitius). "He replied that he had been as it were in an ecstasy, but that at first he had felt that his stomach (which had been inflated) was being reduced and greatly compressed; and that *the church was too narrow for him* (angustam sibi exstitisse ecclesiam). He could recollect no more." It is interesting to know that Benedict

had received similar answers from many other ecstatic patients.

§ 7. *Danger from the enemies of St. Thomas*

[484] It was at this time, soon after Easter, that the Archbishop's enemies—irritated, and perhaps alarmed, by the general and public outburst of miracles—were suspected by the monks of planning to carry off the body. It was accordingly taken from its marble tomb and hidden behind the altar of the Virgin Mary. The monks had also prepared a force to resist the attempt,[1] and "that night there were as many watchers as monks in the church." But, adds Benedict, "the Lord also watched for us—He who neither sleepeth nor slumbereth—and scattered them by His power, as also was shewn to one of our brethren in a vision." This brother happened to be sick, apart from the rest, and ignorant of what was going on. But he saw a vision which was interpreted to him as meaning that a terror from God should avert some danger impending on the Cathedral. Hearing the interpretation the brother awoke and besought the Lord for the defence of the Cathedral; and there was suddenly a sound from heaven, and a horrible roaring of thunder and flaming of fire and lightnings and floods of rain and such a tempest as had not been known for years.

[485] On the following day, Richard, son of Einold,[2] was delivered from a contortion of the legs and feet which prevented him from walking in the usual way. It had come upon him nearly thirty-four years before, when, during the civil wars, he had taken the harvest of a poor woman, who had "cursed him in the name of the Lord." When he approached the Virgin's altar, behind which the Martyr's body was secreted, this strong man shook all over. Then he prostrated himself before the altar, "repeatedly falling

---

[1] ii. 77 "Parantur a nobis vires contrariae."   [2] ii. 79.

and rising, rising and falling again, and leapt forward above the altar (super altare) with a quickness and agility that even the healthiest and nimblest could scarcely equal; and then again, as though in an agony, dashed himself headlong from the altar. We were wondering whether he had not broken his neck; but after a long fit he arose from the ground, and from that time forward was able to stand like others on the soles of his feet." To the question why he had thus leapt on the altar he replied that he could do nothing but that which he was constrained to do by the power of the Mother of God and the Martyr of the Lord.

[486] Mentioning another similar cure,[3] which however was followed by a temporary lameness, Benedict tells us[4] that the number of miracles now became so numerous that the monks feared more than ever some attempt of the Archbishop's enemies to carry away the body. They accordingly determined to surround the tomb with a wall, leaving small apertures through which pilgrims could reach their heads to kiss the stone. This leads him to recount two or three instances—extraordinary indications of the effect of imagination—in which some found themselves able, while others, less large and stout, were unable, to put their heads through the apertures. In one case[5] a madman, full-grown and tall, thinking himself pursued by Satan, leapt headforemost into the hole, and there, uncurling his body, placed his head near the Martyr's feet and his feet near the head. There he remained stretched out. The monks began to think they would have to destroy the structure, if they were ever to get him out again, when suddenly he emerged by another aperture. When he was cured, the monks asked him to repeat the action: but it could not be done either by him or by a lithe youth whom they caused to make the attempt.

[487] On the day of the Finding of the Cross (3 May)

---

[3] ii. 80.   [4] ii. 81.   [5] ii. 82.

there was to be seen lying in the Cathedral a great multitude of feeble folk, blind, lame, and withered, awaiting the Martyr's help. They were mostly from the southern or eastern counties, and if there had been impostors among them, the danger of detection would have been great in so large a concourse of pilgrims from their several neighbourhoods. The pains, contortions, and diseases of several are described in painful detail, and it is said that as many as ten were cured on that day: "but some," says the chronicler, "we are unable to recall as they have slipped [from our memory];[6] some we rejected because they had no witness [to the truth of the story of their ailment]." In several of these cases Benedict records the gradualness or incompleteness of the cure. In one,[7] a miserly old woman from London, at death's door and insensible, was scarcely laid before the tomb when she received sense and speech, and, sitting up, besought the Martyr that she might either die at once on the spot or depart on her feet in health. The monks wondered at her presumption. But suddenly, "as though the Spirit of the Lord had fallen on her," she leapt up, went repeatedly round and round the tomb with a quick firm step, and returned to her lodging on foot. Next day, however, she had a relapse into weakness, and lost her wits besides: and this was attributed to her having abused the name of the Martyr in a false oath to her husband about the possession of some money. Presently, she became quiet and confessed her guilt. On this, she was carried back to the tomb, where she offered fervent prayer and penitence: "by the pity of heaven she again returned on her own feet, with her body whole, but her mind bordering on insanity. In course of time she completely recovered."

---

[6] ii. 86 "Sed quosdam elapsos revocare nequimus." If the text had "nequiimus," the meaning might be, "some slipped away, and we *were* unable to call them back [and ascertain their names]." This is a more natural way of rendering "elabi" and "revocare." [7] ii. 90.

[488] In spite of all these wonders, slander still raised its voice, asserting that the monks of Canterbury, by magic charms, first caused pilgrims to be possessed with devils and then cast the devils out. But this charge, says Benedict, was met by so vast and sudden a display of prodigies all over the country that, in order to make their words good, these slanderers would have had "to accuse all England of the aforesaid crime (of magic)."[8]

[489] At this point Benedict inserts a miracle bearing on these slanders. A knight of the province of York, Thomas of Etton, having slandered the Martyr, was immediately punished by an attack of quinsy. Ascribing his illness to his fault, he repented, and was at once healed. As soon as possible, he hastened to the Martyr's tomb, where "he also testified that, subsequently, by invocation of the Martyr's name, he had been delivered from acute attacks of fever."[9]

§ 8. *Increase of Miracles after Easter*, 1171

There follow a number of cures, some of which might be explained as coincidences, some as the results of sympathetic faith, some as the results of faith on the part of the patient, and in most there might be exaggeration; but there is little probability of imposture.

[490] A knight's lady, in Essex, as honourable as beautiful,[1] and known to the chronicler, was saved from death (after childbirth) when she was speechless and awaiting extreme unction, by a nurse who persuaded the knight to offer to St. Thomas in her behalf a candle as long and thick as the lady's body. Ralph Fitz Ralph of Lincolnshire,[2] in a decline, after two days' hemorrhage, having vainly tried charms, herbs, and stones, was being prepared for death by

---

[8] ii. 91. [9] See Parallel Miracles (709).
[1] ii. 92 "non minus moribus honesta quam facie." [2] ii. 93.

the last sacramental rites when his friends invoked the Martyr in his behalf, and, rising from their knees, found that the flow of blood had ceased. Diet soon restored his health and his parents accompanied him to Canterbury. Poor folk from London are next mentioned — Matilda and Roger,[3] whose illegitimate infant is saved by St. Thomas as soon as he is "measured for a candle"; and Gilbert a shoemaker,[4] suffering from fistula. The latter had a terrible journey to Canterbury on foot; but, taking back the Water to London, he presently so recovered that he walked the whole fifty miles in one day to thank St. Thomas for his cure. There he stripped himself to shew that he was sound, and even challenged others to run him a race.[5] The same disease was cured for Hugh of Bourne,[6] after the physicians had given him up. He fell ill again on returning to work in the fields. So he went back to Canterbury, washed in the Water, and departed. There was no longer any issue of matter, and in eight days the flesh was completely sound.

[491] The next miracle recorded is of a festive nature. An Essex farmer, Richard by name,[7] was dining with friends when his shepherd entered with a pyx. "What have you there, shepherd?" He replied that it was the Canterbury Water. "Well," said Richard, "let this be a sign between us. If the Saint has let you bring the Water, then let us agree that you have served me faithfully. But if he has not left you a drop, then let us agree that he has proved you a thief." They both agreed. The pyx was opened and found absolutely dry. "Confess, my son," said the farmer, "give glory to God." The shepherd at first denied any kind of dishonesty, but as he could not deny that the pyx was remarkably solid and that he had brought the Water from his house, which was close by, he ultimately

---

[3] ii. 94.   [4] Ib.
[5] ii. 95 "Et se ipsum nobis nudum et perfecte curatum ostendens, etiam alios ad cursum invitare non timuit."   [6] ii. 95.   [7] ii. 96.

admitted that he had not been perfectly honest in making up his accounts of cheese and butter: "The fault was pardoned for love of the Saint, and became a general joke, redounding to the glory of the Martyr, and, as a monument and memorial of this festive miracle, the pyx was hung up in the church."

[492] At St. Frideswide's, in Oxford, there appears to have been doubt about St. Thomas up to this time. One of their Canons[8] being so grievously ill that he could not so much as pronounce the Martyr's name, a brother ran to fetch the Water. Returning, he found him speechless and his eyes closed. He poured a drop down his throat. At once the Canon called out, "St. Thomas, have mercy," and sat up. Next day he returned to the regular conventual discipline. Then the Prior summoned two of the Canons who had been hitherto unconvinced, and asked them whether they were still waverers. They replied that they had no longer a particle of doubt. The Prior himself communicated these facts to Benedict together with a very long account of his own cure partly during, and partly following on, a pilgrimage to Canterbury. Another narrative[9] tells how a knight, suffering in the same way, was bidden in a vision to go on a pilgrimage: "Fail not to do this, whether it please thy wife or displease her." He could not walk; and, even on horseback, could go only a mile the first day. But the further he went the more he improved. Reaching Canterbury he spent the night in the Cathedral. There his pains were worse than ever; but this increased his hopes of recovery, and he offered two waxen legs of the same size as his own. Next morning, says Benedict, he confessed that all pain had vanished: and so it had, leaving no trace. Afterwards the knight's wife herself came on pilgrimage to give thanks for her child's deliverance from fits of terror

---

[8] ii. 96-7.   [9] ii. 101-2.

during which he would cry out, "See where they come!" "See where they come!" The knight cured the first attack by hanging round the child's neck a shred of the Martyr's clothing. When they went to bed, they took the relic off; but the child began again, "See where they come!" "So we jumped out of bed," said the mother, "and ran to him and repeated the remedy. We also made a vow to the Martyr in our son's name. Presently he was restored to his senses. So I have come here to pay the Martyr what I promised him."

§ 9. *Influence of neighbourhood; the worm; the cherry-stone*

[493] One cure provoked others in the same neighbourhood. A clerk of Lincoln of wide repute, being cured of fever by the Water, preached to the people the glory of St. Thomas, and many sick folk came to his house and were cured in the same way. A London clerk was even cured (also of fever) by merely sleeping "in some place where he had heard that the Martyr had slept."[1] Solomon of London,[2] who was nearly a hundred years old, had been blind for six years and now recovered his sight in the morning after he had prayed at the tomb: and his cure gathered a great number of Londoners, who returned more devoted than ever to the Martyr.

[494] The miracle of the ejection of a worm (478), in an instance above mentioned, could not be substantiated by the production of the worm. But this objection cannot be brought against the cure of Henry, a boy of ten, the only son of a knight in Essex,[3] who had suffered, from his second year, "as though his intestines were being cut up with razors." The Water of Canterbury seemed at first to increase this poor child's malady, when suddenly he threw up a worm of half a cubit long ("semicubitalem"): "the boy

---

[1] ii. 103-4.   [2] ii. 104.   [3] ii. 105.

presently fell asleep, perspired, and awoke in perfect health. The worm was hung up in the church."

[495] The next pilgrim mentioned is a venerable knight of Rokesley.[4] He was healed after four years of weary sickness, during the last two years of which he had been "face to face with death confessing himself, not once, but seven times, a week." Another,[5] Hugh de Beauchamp by name, could not find a physician to undertake the cure of Nicolas his son suffering from dropsy, so "their prayers were directed to the Physician of Canterbury." They measured the boy for a candle for St. Thomas. The thread, casually breaking, proved to be just of the right length! "They all wondered concerning the thread, but were still more gladdened by the boy's recovery. For without any carnal medicine he felt his swelling subside, and in a short time presented himself to his Physician [*i.e.* St. Thomas] healed." A third, Adam of Hadleigh,[6] was cured of the same disease, without invocation, by a spontaneous apparition of the Martyr, who, in vanishing, cried "Come, come!" The patient immediately recovered. But he did not know where to "come." Some days afterwards, warned by a second vision not to delay, he consulted a priest, who told him he must go to Canterbury: and to Canterbury accordingly he went and told the monks his story.

[496] A fourth, John, chaplain to the arch-deacon of Salop,[7] suffering from a polypus in the nose, which subsequently affected his head and finally his whole body, seems to have given Benedict a most graphic account of the effect of the Canterbury Water. For five or six days he had remained without eating or drinking, unable to move hand or foot or any member except the tongue, with which he confessed his sins and vowed a pilgrimage to Canterbury, and, in course

---

[4] ii. 106. Ed. marg. adds "since united with North Cray."
[5] ii. 106.   [6] ii. 107, or "Headley" (Lat. "Hethlega").
[7] ii. 108.

of time, an altar to the Martyr: "Wonderful to relate and scarce credible even to believers! As soon as he swallowed the Water, he felt it penetrate into every limb and every joint, first going down as cold as ice and then mounting up again through his whole body and (as though it were chasing his disease) almost freezing his brain. The trouble in his head was even greater than usual, and he was in such agony that he thought that the medicine of life was going to end in his sudden death. But in the midst of these agonizing tortures, he happened to sneeze. Feeling as if something had slipped down into his brain, he put his fingers into his mouth and pulled out a cherry-stone. Straightway he regained the use of all his limbs. Up he got, called for his shoes, put them on, and without delay began to walk up and down in the courtyard. When he came to us, he was quite restored to health, though much weakened by continuous fasting. He shewed us the cherry-stone, but could not be persuaded to leave it with us."

§ 10. *Two peaceful deaths*

Few chroniclers of miracles record instances where the miraculous power bestows, not life, but the blessing of a peaceful death. Two such instances are placed next by Benedict.[1]

[497] Robert Fitz-Jocelin, a knight of Springfield in Essex, when seriously ill, received the Water of St. Thomas, and was exhorted to demand, in faith, the blessing of health. But he replied, "Far be it from me to ask for a cure in this absolute way. The Lord grant unto me, for the merits of His saint and the virtue of this holy draught, the health of my soul, or such health as He knoweth to be expedient for me." After spending the rest of that day and the earlier portion of the night in peace and quiet, he awoke in the

---

[1] ii. 109-111.

very early morning with more than usual cheerfulness, and asked for the " viaticum." In reply to the expostulations of his friends, he said that the blessed Martyr, appearing to him splendidly clothed in a beautiful orchard, had said to him, " Fear not, neither be sad. With all speed shalt thou enter into fellowship with me." So he received the viaticum, and commending his soul to God " breathed forth his spirit rather like one sleeping than one dying."

[498] No less pathetic and pious was the end of Roger, son of Herbert of Bisley,[2] "a knight, but a knight of God rather than of this world." By the advice of his friends, he sent to Canterbury for the Water; and he received it after the sacrament, but with these words, "Give me the Water of the blessed Martyr, but with this condition, that, by the intercession of this glorious friend of God, I may either regain my bodily strength in three days, or this day obtain the everlasting health of the soul." At once, after drinking the mixture, he bade his servants carry him into the outer hall. It was Ascension-tide, and the usual procession was passing with the clergy chanting. Hearing their voices, he ordered himself to be laid on the ground, as a dying man, in sackcloth and ashes, and besought the Lord Jesus, who had that day ascended bodily to heaven with His ineffable procession, to take his soul also that day (for the merits of His glorious Martyr and friend) that he might be counted worthy to be found in that heavenly procession and in the fellowship of the Martyr. Scarcely had he finished the words when he breathed forth his spirit, in the presence of several of the clergy, knights, and very many of the common people. These facts, says Benedict, the monks heard from the knight's son, who had himself been delivered from death's door by invoking the Martyr.

---

[2] ii. 110.

§ 11. *A boy blind from birth*

[499] Benedict's second book concludes[1] with a few miscellaneous miracles (presumably reported about Ascensiontide) describing cures of partial blindness, stone, tumour, violent rheumatism, decline, etc., performed on patients from the home counties. Among these, two[2] concern sailors, or pilgrims, who are saved from shipwreck, or brought into port after being becalmed. Godiva, of Chelmsford,[3] who had been five years blind, "falling before the Martyr's tomb, saw the sunlight, and could discern bodies and colours, but she did not receive her sight perfectly."

[500] Last but one in the book (the last place being given to a case of contortion of the foot) comes the case of a boy from Chalgrave,[4] blind from his birth, fourteen years old. When his eyes were touched with the Water, "they swelled up incredibly in the following night, and such a flood of matter gushed from them that any one who mentioned the amount would perhaps seem to be exceeding the bounds of truth." Three days afterwards, the swelling went down, and when he opened his eyes still red with the clotted blood, he shewed by manifest tokens that he could see whatever lay before him. But although he could discern things with his eyes he could not distinguish by name any colours except white.

[501] The candour with which in these last two cases, as in others, Benedict mentions incompleteness in the cure, combines with the truth to nature of his facts and dialogues, to make it extremely improbable that he is ever deliberately deceiving, or that he is frequently (in his own person) exaggerating. Even where he seems to accept a miracle on doubtful evidence, as in the case of dumb Samson (**466**), he

---

[1] ii. 117. In the Paris MS. it ends above, just before the pious deaths of the two knights.
[2] ii. 112-3.   [3] ii. 115.   [4] ii. 116.

tells his readers that "some doubted," and gives them fair reasons for doubting. With all reasonable deductions, his narratives, so far, afford remarkable instances of the general power of human imagination, and noteworthy testimony to the intensity of the reverence and affection with which the minds of the poor folk in England had already canonized the murdered Archbishop before the formal canonization had taken place.

§ 12. *Whitsuntide; candle-miracles*

[502] The miraculous relighting of candles is a frequent theme in books of the lives of the Saints. Scientifically regarded, the phenomenon is often easily explained. "What so likely," says a popular writer on miracles,[1] "as the draught of an ill-built cell to blow out a candle?—and if the wick is long and incandescent, another puff of wind would relight it. When candles were in common use it was a game of fun with children to blow out a candle, and by a sudden jerk upwards, or a puff of the breath, to relight it. I have done it many a time."

[503] This is quite a different phenomenon from the miracle imputed to St. Severin in which the *unlit* candles of Christians burst into a flame while those of the Pagans remained as they were. In order to receive a natural explanation, the story must describe, or at least allow of, a wind or draught, which may first puff the candle out and then puff it in again, as in the case of St. Dunstan's mother and several others recorded by the writer just quoted. Such circumstances are distinctly mentioned in the so-called miracle next described by Benedict: and it is a noteworthy testimony to the want of observation in those days that the physical explanation seems not to have so much as suggested itself. Had the monks known of it, they might have easily

---

[1] *Dictionary of Miracles*, by the Rev. E. C. Brewer, LL.D., 1884, p. 378.

used it for the production of marvellous relightings (caused by bellows placed in secret places) which might have effectively imposed on the multitude. But the Bishop of Poitiers thinks it worth while to write to the monks of Canterbury to relate the relighting of two candles in an open air procession meeting him on his return from St. Thomas,[2] and William, a priest of York, solemnly describes his finding a candle relighted on the altar, followed by the restoration of sight to his blind son.[3] It would be against nature that impostors should thus describe impostures to fellow impostors. Possibly in later times the monks may have played tricks in this matter, but there is no suspicion of trickery here.

[504] Benedict begins the narrative with which he opens his third book by descanting on the appropriateness of the Whitsun season, when the Lord sent down the Spirit with tongues of fire. Then, he passes to facts,[4] of which we will give two. The daughter of Aylward of Canterbury, after two days of convulsions and shrieks in the Cathedral, had been freed from the fits to which she was subject. But she had nothing to offer to St. Thomas. A motherly woman had compassion on her. Taking out of her pocket a great lump of wax and a thin thread, she doubled the thread for a wick, and folded the wax liberally round it, so as to make something between a rush-light and a candle, which she then gave the girl to place in the middle of the tomb.

[505] What follows must be described in the words of Benedict, who was probably the monk in charge at the time: "Presently from the opposite window a slight draught blew in, and—amid a number of candles burning all around —extinguished only this girl's, the wax being too thick and the wick too thin. . . . Seeing the wick smoking, the monk called a servant, 'You see that girl's candle out? Light

---

[2] William (i. 438).   [3] Ib. 449.   [4] ii. 118 sq.

it!' While he was hurrying to the spot, putting down what he held in his hands, the candle was beheld rekindled without human aid. The whole of the people were spectators of this glorious sight, for they had seen the candle so effectively put out that it sent up quite a column of smoke: and now they saw it so effectively rekindled that it produced quite a long stream of flame. And although, as I said above, the wick was thin, and the wax unusually thick, yet so speedily did the flame consume it that hardly any of the wax could be saved [as a relic]." "Now," continues Benedict in triumph, "now let those traitors and parricides who called the Saint a traitor and destroyed him —now let them say where they have heard or read of a traitor or criminal vindicated and cleared by such a miracle!" He proceeds to enlarge on inferior precedents such as those of Nadab and Abihu destroyed by fire, and Saul of Tarsus merely encompassed by fire, concluding thus with allusion to subsequent repetitions of this miracle: "St. Martin was but once thus glorified; Elijah twice; Thomas was specially privileged with a fourfold repetition of it."

[506] On the next day, Goditha, daughter of Baldwin of Wye,[5] after lighting two candles, fell down and overturned one of them herself, and then, when the poor weak girl rose trembling all over to relight it, she struck down the other. Seeing both her offerings thus as it were rejected by the Martyr, she waved the extinguished candles in her hands despairingly calling to the people "Woe is me! Both my candles are put out." Not one had a light to give her; even her own sister, whom she caught sight of at a distance, refused to help her—afraid, she said, to touch or come near her. So the poor girl appealed to heaven: "O sweet lady Virgin Mary, O holy lord Thomas, Martyr of Jesus Christ, what am I to do? See, both my candles are

---

[5] ii. 120.

out!" Benedict proceeds graphically to describe the agitation of the girl—probably accompanied by motion that naturally granted her prayer. "While the girl looked this way and that way [for help], and with lamentable wailings kept casting back her eyes to her [extinguished] candles, both blazed forth freshly lighted!"

From a sinner she had now become well-nigh a saint. "Ye see, my masters," she cried, calling to the vast multitude that had gathered for the festival, "the blessed Martyr Thomas has lit my candles." Benedict concludes thus, "It would be difficult to relate the universal exultation, the floods of tears, the abundance of thanksgivings. With bent knees and uplifted hands, they all gave glory to God, and after manifold utterances of thanks, they dispersed through the whole city of Canterbury to impart their joy to the rest. From that flame all the lights of the church were kindled. The [girl's] candles were in part preserved [by us], in part given away [as relics] to those who begged for them. Blessed be the Lord throughout all things, whose fire is in the Sion of Canterbury, and whose hearth is in the heavenly Jerusalem!"

§ 13. *The moral effect of the miracles*

[507] There follow other cures of the usual kind, at which Benedict himself was present. Gunnilda of Elvaston (?),[1] after two years and a half of weakness, found herself unable to put her feet to the ground, and spent six months "in a kind of continuous death." Being brought by her servants to the place where the Martyr fell, she suddenly stood on her feet. They flew to support her, but she said, "Depart. Leave me to myself. I will try to walk on foot to my lord's sepulchre." Thither she came, though with slow and feeble steps. "She produced witnesses of her

---

[1] ii. 122. Text, Elfiestun, other MSS. Elfsiestun or Elfiesimine.

disease to us there sitting, and said her prayer, and returned to her lodging (which was at a considerable distance) with firmer steps. So she completely recovered, and went her way."

[508] The cure of the paralytic Aylmer[2] is especially interesting because we are incidentally informed that he had been brought "for several days to the Saint." It was only by degrees that he recovered the power of moving and using his limbs. Even then, at first he used crutches: "Soon, however, being made quite strong, he left them [as offerings] to him that had made him strong." Such a case as this must have encouraged many of the sick folk of Canterbury (of which Aylmer was a native) to persevere in attendance at the Cathedral. This must have largely added to the daily concourse. Perhaps, too, in the eyes of strangers, it may have indicated a larger average of pilgrims than really existed. Eilwin and Walter,[3] both of Berkhampstead, are next brought to our notice. The former had used crutches for sixteen years; the latter, with darkened eyesight (oculis caligantibus), and suffering from tumour, had lived for ten years in a kind of death. Both of them were in sore need as they could not work: both "simultaneously came to the tomb, simultaneously fell on the ground, simultaneously arose, were simultaneously cured, and simultaneously departed in great joy, leaving all of us who were present, and who are now witnesses of the fact (nos qui aderamus et rei hujus testes existimus) rejoicing with them, nay, weeping with them for joy. I afterwards saw both of them, not, as before, in rags, but men of great respectability (validae virtutis) and well clothed."

[509] After recording the cure of a little girl[4] whose father had first "confessed and given satisfaction, lest by his own sins he should hinder his daughter's recovery,"

---

[2] ii. 123.   [3] ii. 124-5.   [4] ii. 125-6.

Benedict digresses to remark that this was but one of several instances showing the moral benefit exercised by these miracles; and he solemnly declares that many who had spent years in sin without confession, now repented and confessed because they did not dare to approach the Martyr's tomb with an impure conscience.[5]

[510] A great triumph was gained at this time in the case of William de Broc—brother of Robert de Broc, an attendant of the King and former enemy of St. Thomas. After four years of suffering from fever and intestinal disease, attracted by the certain accounts of the Martyr's miracles, he hastened to Canterbury. There, after thrice drinking of the Water, and twice vomiting freely, he obtained a complete restoration, and "promised that he would not deny it to any of the [Saint's] maligners.[6]"

§ 14. *Dream ? self-deception ? or lie ?*

[511] Next[1] comes a narrative—which Benedict says he ought to have placed earlier as it happened on the Sunday before Ascension day—well illustrating the powerful imaginations (or were they sometimes romancings?) of the simple people in those days. Early in that morning a boy started from Salisbury for Marlborough to carry tidings of the death of his mother. Issuing from the city, he met an old woman, to whom he gave the half of one of his two loaves. Then, on Salisbury plain, he encountered three tall men clothed like hermits. Of these the midmost and tallest carried a

---

[5] At this point (ii. 127) he records two cases in which blind men recovered the sight of one eye only. In these (one from London, the other from "the Marshes," *i.e.* prob. Romney) no witnesses are mentioned: yet in describing the cure of the next patient, a lame girl—Avice, daughter of Ordgar of Goshall (in Ash, next Sandwich)—he says, "On our requiring witnesses to the genuineness of her infirmity we found two trustworthy ones, and, as seeing is more trustworthy than hearing, she was told to walk about in a courtyard. Then she left no doubt in our minds." He seems to have suspected at first that (in hysterical excitement) she said she was cured when she was not.

[6] ii. 128.   [1] ii. 129-30.

bowl of blood, and asked him for "the other half of that which thou didst give to the old woman to-day." He also reminded the youth of a dream that he had had the night before, and bade him go back to Salisbury to tell the dean and canons to make a procession round the city: else, a great storm would fall on it. After the boy had turned and gone a furlong, he looked round: but, "though even a dwarf, miles away, could not escape notice on that expanse, no one was to be seen." Did the boy dream this, or feign it in order to shirk his long journey? In any case, "he returned and told his story to the Salisbury Chapter, and they believed him." This miracle seems to Benedict to have pre-signified the circulation of the blood and water of St. Thomas, which, at that time, had not yet been carried to distant regions.

[512] This leads the chronicler to relate, in a somewhat lighter strain, stories about the monks themselves, in relation to the Water; how it persisted in boiling or bubbling when in certain hands, and how one who wished to appropriate a vessel of it was disappointed by a miracle which "was no less generally laughable and amusing than it was wonderful."[2] "I shall be tedious to my readers," he says, "if I give a chapter to each breakage of a pyx." So he proceeds to say that the cases were so numerous that something had to be done: "At last it came into the mind of a young man to make phials of lead and tin by casting, and then the miracle of breaking ceased." Still, however, it occasionally happened that phials were found unexpectedly empty (or, more rarely, unexpectedly full).

§ 15. *Benedict is scolded for scepticism*

[513] In the great multitude of pilgrims that now daily resorted to St. Thomas, many, of course, went away uncured;

---

[2] ii. 134.

but it is only fair to accept also Benedict's statement on the other side, that many went away cured but not recorded: "We believe," he says,[1] "that the cases we have described above are slight and few in comparison with those that have not come to our knowledge. For the number of simple and obscure persons (idiotarum) who received the blessing of health and departed unknown to us, is known to God alone." A carriage-driver of Canterbury humorously complained that St. Thomas took heavy tolls from him; for, said he, "I bring him a whole carriage-load of sick folk and carry back two!" And here Benedict describes the diversities of cure in respect of time :—how some received it at the time of their vow; others on the way to Canterbury, but a long way off; others on coming into the city; others in the Cathedral or at the tomb. Some were healed in the moment of departure; some, not till they had returned to their homes.

[514] A cure performed at a distance required attestation. Not seeing the need of this, Beatrice of Woodstock made grievous complaints against Benedict himself for his incredulity. He was in charge of the tomb when she arrived, cured of blindness on the way to Canterbury. One of her eyes had not seen for seven years, another for four; the sight of one was restored entirely before she arrived, and that of the other after a night spent in the Cathedral. She was of a mean appearance, says Benedict, both in person and garments, and had no witness except that of the girl who accompanied her. "I confess," he adds, "my incredulity, if incredulity is a fair name for hesitation felt not on my own account but for others." She would not endure his cross-examination, and at last, he says, "gave me bad words, calling me hardhearted, wicked, and unbelieving, unfit and unworthy to attend at the tomb of such a martyr, inasmuch

---

[1] ii. 138.

as I envied his glory and detracted from his miracles in my excessive anxiety to track out the truth."[2]

[515] Godwin, of Brithwell[3] in Yorkshire, after spending some days at Canterbury, was going back as lame as ever, when he received a vision bidding him return to the tomb and pray more earnestly. He was not disposed to obey; but was persuaded to do so by two knights of his own county whom he met next day. In their company, he had no sooner placed his head near the Martyr's feet than he recovered, to the astonishment and delight of the knights.

§ 16. *Welsh miracles*

[516] No date has been specified later than the candle-miracles at Whitsuntide. But Benedict at this point reports that miracles had been wrought on the borders of Wales by certain relics of the Martyr which the monks had given to a nobleman of Cheshire, William Fitzralph by name, to deposit in Whitchurch with the special view of keeping the Welsh in order. In the course of a few days, toward the end of June, they had effected no less than twenty-two cures.[1]

[517] It was perhaps to be expected that, by this time, animals would be included in the miraculous efficacy: and, just before the Welsh miracles, comes a story about one. Emeline[2] (domicile unmentioned), beside being herself cured, bore witness also to the cure of her horse. It had been so severely wounded in the eye that every one who saw it thought the sight was gone for ever: but she had the eye imitated in wax, signed it [with the cross] in the Martyr's name, and, next day, contrary to the general expectation, found it perfectly cured. But Benedict is careful not to commit himself to this miracle. "She informed us (indicavit)," he says, and he remarks that "she had promised to lead a

---

[2] ii. 140.   [3] ii. 141, Breithwella (? Bridewell).
[1] ii. 145.   [2] ii. 144.

more respectable life for the future (studiosiorem honestatis se futuram esse)," which perhaps may imply that she had not formed habits of exact veracity.

[518] The relics and early miracles in Wales naturally produce further results. Some of these exhibit interesting touches of the native sentiment and imagination. One Griffin,[3] suffering from a swollen and ulcerated leg, after three days of prayer and vigil at Whitchurch, returned with his lameness lessened but not removed. In a vision, he sees a beautiful bird, whiter than snow, and shoots at it. The bird flies off to a distance, and he takes a second shot. "Why, Griffin, dost thou shoot at me?" cries the bird. "Take this lance, and keep it carefully." Unable to interpret the mystery, he is told by a person of reverend countenance, who appears to him in a second apparition, that the snow-white bird is the Martyr of the English, that the first shot is the visit to Whitchurch; the second and longer one means a pilgrimage to Canterbury: the lance means perfect health. Straightway he set out on foot, though he knew he could not in his present condition walk a mile a day. Yet he walked five miles, the first day; twenty, the next; then, forty miles, or more, daily. "Afterwards," says Benedict, "when he came to Canterbury, we found him so improved that the wound was skinned over and there was scarcely a vestige of his ailment."

[519] One Welsh boy, so the monks were informed, had been dumb from his birth, and he left Canterbury dumb; but by the time he had passed Rochester, "his tongue was loosed and he began to speak in Welsh and in English too," but more fluently in the former, as being more accustomed to hear it. This the monks heard, not from the Welsh people, but from the Abbot of Welsford,[4] who met them on

---

[3] ii. 145-7.

[4] ii. 147. The Editor adds " or Sulby, Northamptonshire." The text is "Wellesfordensis," one MS. "Veldefordensis."

the road, shouting for joy and leaping so that tongue could scarce describe it. Their delight was increased by the fact that one of their companions had similarly received her sight while on her journey back. They could not afford the expense of returning to Canterbury; so they asked the Abbot to report how they had prospered on their way.

[520] Along with these startling miracles, the Abbot described one of his own experience. A vessel in his bosom, containing the Water, slipped into a horizontal position, and was found by him, with the stopper out, yet with not a drop lost. On this Benedict comments: "We confess that it is in our judgment incontestable [5] that He who caused vessels to be broken by the power of the holy Water in the case of the unworthy, or caused the Water to disappear suddenly in the vessels, was able invisibly to close the open mouth of this vessel for this man of God, that he might not lose the Water."

§ 17. *St. Thomas or St. Ithamar? An enemy convinced*

[521] A nice point is raised by the next miracle, the cure of a blind man from Gloucester.[1] Returning from Canterbury *without a cure*, he had entered Rochester Cathedral, on his way back. There, suddenly, he burst out into horrible cries and shrieks, and called for a priest to confess him. Being taken by the monks to the shrine of St. Ithamar, he there offered up prayers and received his sight. The Rochester monks naturally claimed this miracle, and Benedict replies, "Although we believe it was caused by the power of our Water, yet we do not contradict those servants of God, when they ascribe it to St. Ithamar: though we positively know that in the middle of the highway a similar miracle occurred, which no one by fraud or force could wrest from our glorious Martyr."

---

[5] ii. 148 "inconcussa veritate nobis constare."   [1] ii. 148.

[522] He proceeds to describe how one Gilbert Foliot[2] —kinsman and namesake and steward of one of Becket's former enemies, Gilbert Foliot, Bishop of London—meeting a blind man returning from Canterbury with his eyes bandaged, asked him what he had gained from his pilgrimage. The poor fellow replied that he had brought back nothing but loss. Blind he had been from his birth, and blind he was still. Moreover, whereas his eyes had not pained him before, now they were swollen, and running with matter, and torturing him beyond expression. Moved by curiosity, Foliot raised the bandage, upon which the blind man called out, as though in the height of his pain, "Holy Mary, our Lady! Holy Mary, our Lady!" The steward anxiously asked whether he had hurt him; but he answered, "Not at all, sir; I am not hurt at all. But I can see. And, Lord God, how beautiful a thing is man (forma humana)! This is the first day in which I have seen the beauty of a human face (vultus humani decor)." Amid the general joy and congratulations, the kinsman of the Martyr's enemy remained alone doubtful. Cross-examining the man, he found that he could distinguish forms and colours, though he could not give them their right names; and he was compelled to be satisfied that the case was genuine.

It was not to be expected that the steward of the Saint's notorious enemy would testify publicly in the year 1171 to a miracle of St. Thomas: but his private attestations were conveyed to Benedict by a veracious and religious hearer for the purpose of being set down in writing: "No one," says Benedict in conclusion, "ought to doubt about the glory of a martyr, when even a rival is compelled to proclaim it."[3]

---

[2] ii. 149-50.
[3] Later on, William (i. 251) tells us that the Bishop of London himself, seeming at the point of death, allowed himself to be pledged to a pilgrimage to St. Thomas, and redeemed the pledge on being healed. The fact that Benedict lays so much stress on the mere testimony of the Bishop's steward, and makes no

[523] To this, Benedict attaches another cure of blindness,[4] attested by the Prior of Folkestone who had met a Cornishman near Winchester returning from Canterbury, where he had received his sight after a stay of two weeks there. Possibly, by this time, some pretended to be pilgrims, and even to have been delivered from diseases, in order to extract alms from wayfarers: but the Abbot satisfied himself by cross-examination that the man had seen the neighbourhood, and Benedict accepts this as one of many instances recalling the old words "Were there not ten cleansed? But where are the nine?"

§ 18. *Offerings of money*

[524] Here for the first time, I believe, occurs the mention of an offering of money for the recovery of the sick.

The daughter of Wivelina of Littlebourne ties a *denarius* to the head of her dying mother to be offered to St. Thomas in case of a recovery.[1] The daughter of Radulph the Fleming[2] has a *quadrans* tied to her broken leg, with the vow of an annual payment of the same sum in case the treatment should prosper. It is recorded with manifest satisfaction that "the silver plaster" answered, and that the cure was inexpensive: "the girl was brought by her parents to Canterbury, and she paid to her Physician for her cure the medicine with which she had been healed. Thus one and

---

allusion to the more important event, indicates that his work was published *before* the Bishop's *conversion*.

It should be noted that Benedict did not witness this miracle, and only ascertained indirectly the words uttered by the blind man, which may have been inaccurately reported. As the story says, the man could not call things by their right names. Then, how could he call by their right names "the human form" and "the human countenance"? Did he call them right by a guess? or did he use the terms perhaps wrongly, looking at something else?

One would have anticipated that his immediate condition would have been one of complete bewilderment, and that until he had touched it, he could have called nothing "by its right name."

[4] ii. 150.   [1] ii. 151.   [2] ii. 157.

the same *quadrans* served both for medicine and for oblation." These small and innocent beginnings introduce into St. Thomas' miracles a new element, which becomes much more prominent later on.

[525] Perhaps, too, we may already perceive that the increasing vogue or fashionableness of the Martyr was beginning to deteriorate some of the wonders connected with his name. We have seen above that Emeline's horse's eye was supposed to have been cured by the Martyr after the offering of an eye moulded in wax: now a Fleming[3] (the Radulph above-mentioned), after vainly attempting for eight days to catch a hawk, vows a *denarius* to the Martyr if he will bring it to him : " At once," says the chronicler, " it came to him as though it had been tamed to his hand : and we have seen the hawk and we have received the offered *denarius*."

[526] At another time,[4] a rascally servant of the monks, who had been constantly pestering them for a *denarius*, was found devoutly offering that very coin at the tomb. Knowing the fellow's avaricious nature, they cross-examined him as to his motives, and elicited that he had had an attack of fever followed by an apparition of St. Thomas, who said to him, " Arise quickly and offer a *denarius* on my tomb lest the fever catch you again." Thus, says Benedict, the Martyr simultaneously cured both fever and avarice.

§ 19. *The stories of Edric*

[527] Edric, priest of Ramsholt in Suffolk,[1] would appear by his name to be " English by birth," and—as he had a baby daughter—not up to the mark of Roman ecclesiastical rule : but the Martyr took pity on his little daughter after he had tried charms and medicines in vain. At four o'clock they measured the little one's head for a candle in the

---

[3] ii. 157.   [4] ii. 156.   [1] ii. 153.

Martyr's honour, and by the time the sun had gone down the child's sore had begun to heal. In three days she had not a spot on her.

[528] The same Edric tells of the sorrows and consolations of two little Ramsholt children. The elder, a girl, had mislaid a cheese presented to her mother and entrusted to her keeping. Searching high and low and not finding it, and sadly fearing a whipping, she proposed to her brother to go and get another of the same sort from the man who had given the first. But it was a long way off, and he demurred —probably not exactly in the following words, but we must tell the tale as it is told to us: "By no means will we do this. By God's help we shall do much better. I have heard, and it is now noised abroad everywhere, that St. Thomas, the Martyr of God, manifests himself in innumerable miracles. Verily, if we flee to him for succour with all devotion, we shall not have to regret the rejection of our prayer. Let us therefore beseech his clemency that he may cause us to dream where the cheese is." They agreed. After saying the Lord's prayer, they went to bed, and both had a dream. The girl was directed by the Martyr to an old disused churn where she had put the cheese and forgotten it. Running to her brother, she said, "Hugh, I have found the cheese." "I know," replied he, "where you have found it." They compared dreams and found them to be the same. They told their mother. Their mother told Edric the priest. The priest "examined the brother and sister separately and heard from each precisely the same story without the slightest discrepancy, and coming to Canterbury he amused almost every one who heard him relate it."[2]

[529] Other miracles follow, not certified by Benedict himself: the setting of the dislocated arm of Edric[3] of Worcestershire, which leapt back of itself into its place,

---

[2] ii. 153-5.   [3] ii. 158.

when a vow was made to St. Thomas, after the surgeon had vainly attempted to set it for five weeks; the healing of Constance daughter of Robert Fitzgilbert, a nun of Stixwold, by the Saint's glove, and of her sister-in-law Matilda. The latter recovered from tumour (by drinking the Water) "so rapidly that she could put on her tightest dress, and wonderfully recovered her figure in less time than it would have taken her to gallop a mile on horseback."[4] Then come three miracles attested by the Abbot of Jorvaux, who tells how he restored a monk of Byland,[5] after he had received extreme unction, by causing him to drink of water in which he had dipped a portion of the Saint's hair-shirt.

§ 20. *The testimony of Henry of Houghton*

[530] The next witness is Henry of Houghton, one of Becket's former clerks. Near St. Alban's, he met a Berkshire knight returning from Canterbury, who expressed thanks for his own restoration to vigorous health, but still more for the partial cure of a blind servant, who accompanied him with a bandage round his eyes. The youth had a protuberance on one of his eyeballs as large as an acorn, caused by sleeping in the open air while looking after his sheep. For two years he had not closed his eyelids. Having failed at Canterbury, he had returned to Rochester, and was sleeping there,[1] when he saw the Martyr, in a vision, touching his eye and signing it with the sign of the cross. On awaking, he found a stream of matter issuing from the tumour. Such was the knight's story about his servant.

---

[4] ii. 158-9 "equo transvolare potuisset."
[5] ii. 160 "Locum ab accolis *Belelande* appellatum, quod Latine *speciosum saltum* resonare videtur."
[1] ii. 161-2. Possibly he stopped at Rochester to try the efficacy of St. Ithamar, see above, 521.

Henry dismounted, took off the bandage, and finding the eyelids now closed, separated them, and having cleared away (sullevasset) the empty tumour with a thorn, found the eye-ball quite intact and healthy. The boy cried out that he could see capitally. The other two cried out in thanksgiving. "These things," says Benedict, "though our eyes have not beheld, yet being certified by the eyes and tongue of the above mentioned Henry, which are as good as our own, we do not hesitate to insert."

[531] For several pages Benedict has mentioned no dates, and given us no means of inferring the times of the miracles recently recounted. Probably they almost all belong to the first year, 1171 : but, in his desire to break the monotony of cure after cure wrought at the Martyr's tomb, he may have inserted some cases that occurred later and at a distance. A little above,[2] he tells us that one Curbaran, a shoemaker of Dover—"who was absolutely and incredibly simple enough to repeat the Lord's prayer daily for the soul of the holy Martyr, not knowing that he who prays for a martyr wrongs the martyr"—was visited in a dream by St. Thomas, who told him that it was but fair that his service should be rewarded, and directed him to a place under a mill where he was to take what he would find. He found "a very thick and rusty *denarius*," which some one, "a good deal sharper than he was," tried with his teeth and found to be gold. It turned out to be a coin of the Emperor Diocletian, worth forty pieces of silver.

[532] Now, towards the end of his book, Benedict introduces a dialogue between the above mentioned Henry of Houghton and a nobleman, probably Richard de Luci, formerly one of Becket's enemies. At a meeting of some English lords (regni optimatibus), when the conversation

---

[2] ii. 156.

fell on the miracles, De Luci declared that the reports of them surpassed belief, and that he should decline to believe all of them,[3] had he not received ocular proof of one. In a certain manor of his[4] there was a priest, whose right arm he knew to have been for some years paralysed, so that he could not celebrate the sacrament, or raise his hand to his mouth: "Now he has come back from Canterbury; and besides doing the office of a priest at the altar with perfect ease, he hurls the stone with my squires and serving-men, and beats them all." Then, turning to Henry, he said, "What sort of justice or reason is there, Henry, in this paradox? That the very man who was harder on the Church than any of us when he was Chancellor, should now surpass any single saint that the Church reads or sings of, in the number and wonder of his miracles!"

Henry, instead of appealing at once to Becket's sanctity of life, prudently argued that, if St. Peter was not prevented from becoming a saint by his denial, neither ought St. Thomas to be prevented by the alleged severity, which, if true, had been expiated by seven years of banishment and hardship. This satisfied De Luci, who thanked Henry for delivering him from a scruple which, said he, "I would not have had take root in my soul for forty pounds." Probably this nobleman would have felt no "scruple," after King Henry had done penance at Canterbury (1174) — and perhaps not after the King had purged himself before the Papal legates (1172). It is therefore quite possible that this dialogue may have taken place about the end of 1171.

---

[3] ii. 163 "Ab omnium eorum credulitate mens mea relapsa deficeret." This probably means "I should reject them all." But it might mean "I should fail to accept them all [though accepting some]."

[4] "Apud quoddam *praesidium* meum": Ed. suggests "praedium." It must have contained several "armigeri."

§ 21. *Miracles at Newington*

[533] Benedict tells us that he inserts this dialogue of Henry's in order to show how graciously St. Thomas led his old enemies to repent of their injuries towards him lest they should add sin to sin. He goes on [1] to narrate other miracles worked in a manor of the above-named nobleman, "which is called in English Niwentona (*i.e.* Newington) but in Latin Nova Villa." In the midst of the town a cross had been set up, no one knew by whom, "dating from the first days of the miracles." It was the place where the Archbishop had confirmed a number of children, a few days before his death, on a journey from Canterbury to London. Most bishops were in the habit of confirming from horse-back, but he, " out of reverence for the sacrament, was wont to dismount and place his hands on the children, while standing." Hence, says Benedict, was fulfilled at Newington the saying " There shall come unto thee they that reviled thee and they shall worship the prints of thy feet (Ps. cxxxii. 7, Vulgate)."

[534] From Newington, then, come almost all the rest of the miracles recounted in this section of Benedict's work, about fourteen in number. In some of these cases the pilgrim came on to Canterbury, but not in all; so that they are briefly described and not attested, except in general terms implying that the facts had been examined into. Six of these are cases of blindness: one, of a child three years old, born blind, who is briefly said [2] to have received its sight "in the presence of many witnesses." Goditha, of Hayes (?),[3] was cured partly at Newington, partly at Canterbury. The case of Walter Torel of Warwickshire [4] is peculiarly pathetic, besides

---

[1] ii. 164 sq.   [2] ii. 166.
[3] ii. 166, text, "Heisa"; other MSS., "Hesa" or "Heysa."
[4] ii. 167-8.

throwing light on the general fashionableness, so to speak, of miracles, and reminding us that English people were all this time being cured at other shrines than that of St. Thomas. It seems that in the previous year, Walter, returning from church on St. Cecilia's day and finding his daughter sewing, had called down a curse on her profanity. Straightway her right side withered up and her tongue was paralysed. Horrified at his own act, the father took the half-dead girl on his shoulders and carried her about to different shrines to seek a cure; which she received, so far as the tongue was concerned, at a church of St. Edith; and the rest at Newington, whither he had turned aside on his way to the Martyr. The grateful pilgrim continued his journey to Canterbury, and, when he left it, "rejoiced to have his burden exchanged for a companion." Benedict contrasts this case, where the pilgrim was cured at Newington, on the way *to* Canterbury, with the next,[5] in which a man was cured at the same place, but on his way back *from* Canterbury. Again, Robert of Essex,[6] on his way to the Martyr to be recovered from blindness of ten years' standing, had passed Rochester when another blind man on horseback rode on him and hurt his ankle. While the two pilgrims were exchanging sympathies, Robert, passionately prostrating himself and appealing to the Lord in the name of the Martyr, saw a stone on the road. He caught it up, kissed it in ecstasy, and then, scorning his wife's guidance henceforth, flew on before his companions, running incessantly the whole of the seven miles to Newington: "afterwards, with indescribable joy, he proceeded to Canterbury."

[535] In the same place was cured a remarkable contortion in a child three years old (son of Roger of Northampton) whose right foot had been fixed to his left,

---

[5] ii. 168-9.   [6] ii. 169.

cross-like, from the day of his birth.[7] But Benedict begins to feel that his readers will be wearied by the monotony of these cures of monstrous deformities, or disgusted by their revolting details. "What avails prolixity?" he asks, "it does but create and increase disgust." So he gives us no description of the manner of healing beyond this: "The boy whom she had set down in the holy place in this pitiable condition she took up with his feet divided and his body straight (separatis ab invicem pedibus suscepit erectum)." Most pathetic in the whole group of the Newington stories is the last, which tells how the two daughters of Godebold of Boxley,[8] lame from birth, were brought to Newington Cross, and how the elder, after receiving a promise of cure from St. Thomas in a dream, felt her muscles stretch and strengthen amid the exultation of the clerks and common folk, and the bells were set ringing, and she was led into the Cathedral in triumph, leaving her younger sister still expectant under the holy cross.

The desolate girl began to accuse the Saint because he had taken her sister and left her, crying, like Esau, "Hast thou but one blessing, O my Father? I beseech thee, bless me also." On the morrow, says Benedict, "the pious Father, moved by her tears and lamentations, visited her as she slept and restored her to health, like her sister, thereby repeating his miracle and doubling the people's joy and the praises that went up to God. In the same place, others innumerable were seen freed from divers sicknesses. But inasmuch as these have not produced witnesses, and the truth has not been perfectly sifted by us (nec ad purum veritas a nobis eliquata), we let their stories pass out of our

---

[7] I am not sure that I understand the italicized words in (ii. 170) "ossa tibiarum vel nulla fuerunt vel nimis exilia ; mater enim eas, *ut inde certificaretur*, saepenumero durius attrectavit." If the subjunctive is a mistake for the indicative, they appear to imply that a certificate of this miracle (and possibly of the rest) was sent from the priest of Newington to Canterbury.

[8] ii. 170.

ears as fast as we let them come in. For we had no wish to mingle grain and chaff, truth and falsehood."

§ 22. *The thirteen "candles"*

[536] Yet Benedict cannot forbear telling us of one more place where the Saint's feet had stood—a place celebrated by the appearance of "an immense light," before the erection of the cross there. The story is attested by four witnesses, two of whom he mentions by name, Henry of Topindenne,[1] and Samuel the clerk. The other two were equally truthful and honourable. It wanted still some time to sunset,[2] when they were riding not far from the place in question, and they all saw at one and the same time (una et eadem hora) thirteen lighted candles. They leapt off their horses, and approached.the sight step by step, and side by side, in order to examine it near at hand. When they had gone about half a stone's-throw nearer to them,[3] the "candles" were suddenly withdrawn from their eyes. Filled with astonishment, they retraced their steps. Looking back again, they again see the lighted "candles" and count them over.

It might perhaps have occurred to modern travellers to leave two of their number to keep an eye on the "candles," while the other two went up again to ascertain whether some rock or group of stones, reflecting the western sun, might not have produced the effect of "thirteen candles." However, these four act differently. "Mounting their horses they began to ask one another what it could possibly be,

---

[1] ii. 171. Editor suggests "Tappington" near Canterbury. Two other MSS. have "Tropindenne," and "Trobindenne."

[2] "Supererat adhuc diei pars nonnulla."

[3] "Quumque quasi *ad* dimidium lapidis jactum cereis appropinquassent." "Ad" seems to mean "usque ad," *i.e.* "as much as." If so, we do not know how far off the "candles" still were. Presumably, the "candles" were off the high-road, and this was their reason for dismounting.

while the sun was setting (occidente sole), to cause so great a light to irradiate that place, (contending) against the darkness of night. Then the aforesaid Henry, calling to mind that the Champion of God had passed by that way, turned aside to a cottage that was in view, where he was informed by a poor woman that the Saint had stood on the very spot in question, while holding a confirmation. This explained the matter. The sanctity of the place was also afterwards manifested more palpably by the gift of many acts of healing and a host of miracles. Hence a memorial cross was set up there by the faithful. A third place, too, wherein his feet stood, was similarly made venerable by prodigies of equal glory : but of these I must not now speak singly. Not that I condemn them by silence. I merely defer them : for in such a multitude of miracles I feel considerable hesitation as to what is to be produced first and what last :—

'. . . plenty hath made me poor.'"

[537] With this quotation from Ovid's *Metamorphoses* ends the Third Book of Benedict's treatise on the Miracles of St. Thomas.[4] Manifestly we are no longer to expect the order of "first" and "last" to be rigidly observed. The author will also, as seems probable, begin to pay more attention to variety of incident and style. When he recorded the first miracle that gladdened the Canterbury monks on "the third day" after the Martyrdom, he was too much occupied with the parallel between Thomas and Jesus to think of style, or to quote Ovid, or any writer except the Evangelists. All that is now changed, and a new period begins. Possibly, indeed, the new period may have already begun, and this very conclusion and some of the pages that precede it may be due to William, or to some other assistant.

[4] ii. 172.

SECTION III

THE LATER MIRACLES, OR BENEDICT ASSISTED BY WILLIAM

§ 1. *William's attitude to Benedict*

[538] WE have seen above (415) that William was called by the monks to aid Benedict in reporting miracles about May 1172. But this implies that for some time previously there had been dissatisfaction with the reports. Benedict's words quoted at the end of the last chapter shew that the work was now too much for him. Not improbably, too, Benedict's style did not satisfy the brethren of Canterbury. It is mostly simple and straightforward, seldom aiming (at least in the earlier narratives) at any *facetiae*, or indulging in those classical allusions which might charm the Chapter on the occasions when they met to hear the new miracles read out of "the great volume" of which Fitzstephen speaks.

[539] William's style is different and was probably more to the brethren's taste. Without being uncharitable to him, we might naturally suppose that he would feel a certain sense of superiority in being publicly called to Benedict's aid. There are also signs that he felt towards the latter something of jealousy or dislike. We have seen that Benedict tried at first to adhere to chronological order. But the preface to William's book—written, it is true, in the name of the whole convent, but hardly likely to be written

without William's influence, if not by his hand—expressly depreciates such order as being useless. Compare too Grim's and William's accounts of Benedict's relations with King Henry. Grim says [1] that Benedict had been slandered to the King, who had hence conceived a dislike for him, caused, before Benedict had been made Prior of Canterbury, by "some who make it their business to sow *discord between brethren.*"

[540] This points to monkish jealousies and rivalries about the election of the new Prior in 1175, when Prior Odo, under guise of being promoted, was removed to be Abbot of Battle. There was at that time in the Abbey a monk, Alan by name, who—afterwards, in 1179—was almost forced [2] on Archbishop Richard by his brother monks on account of his high character. William appears to be referring to Alan when he tells us that, on Odo's removal, the monks unanimously strove for the appointment of a worthy brother "of commendable life," whereas Archbishop Richard wished to force on them a nominee of his own.[3] Now the context tells us that this nominee was not appointed in 1175, but it does not tell us that the brother "of commendable life" was appointed. Benedict, who succeeded, seems to have been *appointed in* 1175 *as a compromise*, when the monks wanted *some one else*. Not till two years after Benedict had been removed by "promotion" to Peterborough (in 1177), was Alan, the candidate of the monks, at last

---

[1] ii. 448-50 : for explanation of references, see 1*a*.
[2] ii. p. xliii., referring to "Gervase 1456."
[3] i. 542. This nominee was (no doubt) Herlwin, Archbishop Richard's Chaplain, who became Prior in 1177. The Pope directed Bulls to this Prior by name, commanding that *the offerings of the church should be disposed of for the repair of the church*, etc.—which does not look well for Herlwin. It is added that, *extreme age having indisposed him for government, he gave over his place* in 1179. "Extreme age" does not usually come on in two years. Probably the monks gave Herlwin, as he perhaps deserved, a great deal of trouble. For these facts about Herlwin (taken from Battely's *Somner*, pp. 141-142, part i.) I am indebted to Dean Farrar.

successful (1179). Apparently, then, Benedict was not very much liked by the monks, and probably not by William. At all events, it could hardly be pleasant for Benedict that William should suggest that, at the time of his election to be Prior, the monks wanted some one else.

[541] And now, to return to the evidence above-mentioned, afforded by a comparison of Grim's and William's narratives. Grim says that Benedict had been slandered and was disliked by the King, who would not give him an audience when he came to press for the fulfilment of the royal promises to the Abbey. William says that [4] "the King put off answering his petition, as being much occupied and not accustomed to do important business without circumspection," and again, "when the King's *prudence* put off the fulfilment of his promise, and *monkish importunity*,[5] though it was daily insistent, could obtain no result." There is here no suggestion from William that the King insulted Benedict or treated him badly. He makes the King say simply, " I began to fear you (Benedict) might have returned home wearied with *waiting and travelling up and down*, following my court." But Grim says that "the King's *fury*, but for his reverence for St. Thomas, *would have passed the bounds of royal behaviour against Benedict*," and that, until moved by a vision from the Martyr, he had "*publicly assailed him with contumelious words*, and had allowed his servants to do the same."

[542] Grim's account bears marks of truth, coming probably from Benedict himself, whereas William seems to write with a courtier-like softening and suppression. Perhaps, when Benedict was removed from Canterbury in 1177,

---

[4] i. 493.
[5] "Monachilis *improbitas*." Elsewhere, when William uses this ambiguous word, he thinks it necessary to explain (at some length) that he does not use it in a bad sense (i. 331): " Tandem vincit *improbitas* ('labor *improbus* omnia vincit') —non *improbitas*, sed fides et longanimitas instanter petentis."

and before Alan succeeded in 1179, there was a period when many of the monks felt desirous to dissociate themselves from their former Prior, who had not been a *grata persona* with the King. And even in 1172, before Benedict was Prior, there may have been a party against him, besides those who thought meanly of his official work. His book of miracles, so far, had not (according to their views) done justice to the subject. It had made too much of failures, of relapses, and imperfect cures. There were too many stories about Canterbury folk and poor obscure people, and not enough of the marvels wrought at a distance, attested by priests and prelates and knights.

It seems to follow that Benedict, though at first merely associated with William, would gradually be superseded by the latter. The forthcoming miracles, though still shewing occasional signs of Benedict's hand, are no longer arranged in order of time, no longer confined to England, and no longer so generally truthful, simple, and exact.

§ 2. *The new Prologue*

[543] The Prologue with which the Fourth Book begins is either not Benedict's, or it is Benedict's after he has been told to mend his style: "Though the Lord should multiply with manifold increase the gift of my meagre wit; though I should speak with the tongues of men and angels; though I should have bestowed on me the hands, I will not say of a swiftly-writing scribe, but even of a notary taking notes at his swiftest pace; wit would succumb, tongue would fail, fingers would be struck numb (obstupescent). If I attempt but briefly to touch on the mighty deeds of the Martyrs of Canterbury one by one (much less to set them forth fully and clearly) I am conscious of the sting conveyed by the salutary warning of the heathen poet, which I ought to have remembered at the outset—

"'Sumite materiam vestris qui scribitis aequam
Viribus, et versate diu quid ferre recusent,
Quid valeant humeri.'[1]

"But now, inasmuch as (contrary to the advice of a second wise man) I have sought things too deep for me, like one that peers into [divine] majesty, I am oppressed by its glory. Glorious indeed and inscrutable altogether are the mighty works or merits of our Martyr, and, as they attract by their sweetness, so do they oppress by their weight, the weakness of my sense. Yet, because I have begun, I will speak of my lord, though I am but dust and ashes."[2] The last sentence or two may be Benedict's. The first paragraph is probably not. Perhaps William has already "come to his aid."

The first miracle[3] is of a very remarkable kind, attested by some burgesses of Bedford and referred to elsewhere by the bishop of Durham. But the consideration of it is best deferred, as it is one of a small group of miracles described both by Benedict and by William (**710**).

§ 3. *Leprosy*

[**544**] We come, then, to the first cure of leprosy. Here Benedict's candour is still apparent. Randulf of Langton (de Longa Villa), having shewn all the signs of a leper, had made an arrangement to live in a leper house, when he heard of the miracles of the Canterbury Martyr "in whose merits he trusted as much as he felt ashamed of his own." He visited the tomb, and prayed and wept, and made vows:—a journey to Jerusalem, severe fasts, four *denarii* as an annual offering. He remained nine days at Canterbury, and, after using the Water internally and

---

[1] Horace, *Art. Poet.* 38-40.   [2] ii. 173.
[3] It is noteworthy that, whereas Benedict places it first in his Fourth Book—which begins what may be called the second (or assisted) part of his treatise—William places it absolutely first (see **596**).

externally, departed in better condition. "At the end of a month," says the reporter, probably Benedict, "we received him back, a graceful young man (elegantissimae formae juvenem). So from Whitsuntide almost to Advent abiding with us—in perfect soundness, health, and grace, and without a single spot—he went away at last, as if for the purpose of setting out for Jerusalem; and on returning home (I know not by what judgment of God) he appeared with all the signs of leprosy so manifest on him that never was leper fouler. The cause of his relapse He knows who said to the man whom He had healed, 'Behold thou hast been made whole: sin no more, lest a worse thing befall thee!'"[1]

[545] This is a very gloomy specimen to come first in a list of miracles; and it is rather startling to find, immediately after the passage last quoted, a second cure introduced with the words, "The repetition of this first miracle doubled the joy we had conceived from it." Possibly the second, occurring soon after Whitsuntide 1171, when the first cure took place, was recorded some time before the relapse, which took place after Advent in 1171 and which could hardly be recorded till Jan. 1172. And it may perhaps have been regarded by the monks as one of many instances of Benedict's excessive and inexpedient scrupulousness, that he not only inserted, but retained, and placed first in his list of such cases, a cure of leprosy that soon afterwards turned out a failure.[2]

[546] The second case is attested by the Dean of Chesterton in Warwickshire. The monks had taken pains

---

[1] ii. 183.
[2] Contrast William's method. He (i. 213) places first in his list a cure (also related by Benedict) authenticated by a bishop; and, though he mentions one case in which the cure was not perfect owing to the shortness of the patient's stay at Canterbury, others in which the evidence was incomplete, and others in which there was a relapse followed by a second recovery, he gives (I believe) *no instance* (like this of Benedict's) *where relapse, so far as the evidence goes, was final.*

to ascertain the facts. The venerable Master Edmund, Archdeacon of Coventry, had told them of a leper in his diocese who had returned from St. Thomas without a spot: "but," says the chronicler, "as the Archdeacon himself only knew of it by hearsay, and as the ear's witness is less lively than the eye's,[3] though we believed his words, we were unwilling to record it unless he sent us the leper with a letter from his Dean." Yet no details of the cure are forthcoming in the Dean's letter, except that the man, after praying and drinking the Water, "felt his disease go down from his head to his chest, from his chest to his stomach, from his stomach to his legs, from his legs to nothing." These sound like the man's own words, and perhaps the monks could get no more out of him. Possibly William was sitting at the tomb on this occasion, and did not make a great effort to elicit facts from the man himself. It is not surprising—being merely the natural effect of popular exaggeration—that—whereas the chronicler comments exultingly on this, the *second* of a long list of lepers healed—the leper himself is said to have been drawn towards Canterbury by the report that *"lepers"* were already cured there.

§ 4. *The chronicler seeks variety*

[547] To the last case the writer appends a statement —suggestive rather of William than of Benedict—that, although no Saint, in the Old Dispensation or the New, has equalled St. Thomas in the frequency of his cures of leprosy, total or partial,[1] yet he will insert a few other matters here, to avoid wearying his readers by monotony. Accordingly, he places next in order the cure of Odo of Falaise, the King's accountant. This nobleman had lost the sight of his right eye in tilting; but in the summer of 1171, while at

---

[3] ii. 183. The quotation from Horace (*Art. Poet.* 180-1) may indicate that here, as in the Prologue, there are traces of William's style.

[1] ii. 185 "emundati vel emendati."

his devotions, he happened to weep for the death of the Martyr, whom he greatly loved. On drying his tears he found that he had regained his sight. Possibly humility, but more probably the fear of the King's anger, caused Odo to come in disguise when he brought his offering to St. Thomas. The chronicler offers no explanation but merely records the fact: "We saw him coming to the Saint's Memorial with vows and offerings, but so humbly and abjectly that his mien and carriage gave one the impression that he was a beggar, and so did his clothes." [2]

[548] The next story is more like a fable than a miracle. It refers to a great fire at Rochester in 1177, in which year Benedict was removed to Peterborough. Coming as it does after a miracle of 1171, it indicates that this section was not put together under the supervision of any one who cared for chronological order. A pilgrim (name and domicile unmentioned), after many repulses at other doors, being received hospitably by the servant of one Gilbert, a baker, saves his host's house from fire, when all the rest of the city is consumed, by leaping on the roof with a phial of the Water. Placing it on the end of a pole, he thereby, as with a spear's point, drives back the flames.[3]

[549] The son of Eudes, of Parndon in Essex, when dying or dead—the writer does not know which—was restored in consequence of the prayer offered by the father, "saluting the Saint although from afar." The parents came with thanks to St. Thomas, and, in their company, the writer saw one Baldwin testifying that the Water had saved him when his life was despaired of.[4]

[550] The variety desired above is heightened by the

---

[2] ii. 186 "ut et gestus mendicum mentiretur et habitus."
[3] It may be accident that the language occasionally falls into hexameters :

". . . quisquam propriis intendere rebus.
Exsiliunt juvenes praefati cum peregrino."

In William's Book "tags" of hexameters are frequent (645).
[4] ii. 188.

marvel told by Lecarda, a nun (domicile not mentioned) who, while working a girdle for St. Thomas, refused to take shelter from a thunderstorm from which her companions fled: "I will not go in, nor move hence," said she. "Am I not working for St. Thomas? If he please, let him defend his work and workwoman from injury." And so it was. Her back was drenched, but on her front and on the girdle not a drop fell. Two of the sisters attested the miracle: "and the girdle was sent to us and hung up near the Martyr's body in memory of the miracle."

[551] Then follow two instances of the changing of the Canterbury Water into blood—the former attested by a letter from Albin, Abbot of Derby, the latter by a priest of Froyle named Ranulph—which suggest questions as to the way in which the monks of Canterbury composed their Water.

Ranulph relates two other miracles.[5] His brother, Everard, Chaplain of St. Mary's, Winchester, fell downstairs at Southwick, and then, lying senseless for seven days, was reported dead at Winchester, so that his prebend was filled up, and his books and property divided. As a last resort, Ranulph tried the Water. The patient recovered for a moment, saying, "Please God, I shall go to Canterbury." But then he relapsed, speechless and senseless as before. So Ranulph set off to Winchester to try to make some arrangement about his brother's belongings. While he was there at dinner with the monks, his brother's servant entered, saying, "My master, your brother, is close by." Ranulph, supposing that he was being brought for burial, replied, "Ought he not to have been buried with the clergy at Southwick?" "Not at all," said the man; "he is coming here." "And how 'coming'?" said the other. "Do you mean brought on a bier?" "Not on a bier," said the servant, "but on horse-

[5] ii. 193-4.

back, alive and active." "Such were the facts," continues the chronicler, "written in a rude style, as stated by the above-mentioned and oft-mentioned Ranulph. . . . As for the patient, or rather the revived, he said he could not remember his illness, or anything else, except that, when he came to himself, he ordered his horses to be brought round, and, mounting, rode about twelve miles to Winchester, where he wondered that a crowd of fools should come out to meet him."[6] Why was it left for Ranulph—who comes as a pilgrim, partly on his own account, because St. Thomas had healed him also of an acute disease—to relate this story in his brother's behalf? Why did not Everard come and offer his own gratitude? The chronicler does not tell us.

§ 5. *Foreign cures: miraculous chastisements*

[552] A large number of the cures that now follow are from foreign parts—Alelm from St. Omer who had cut his thumb at dinner, Mary of Rouen cured of fits or hysterics, Durand of Eu freed from a pebble in his ear, and others.[1] Among these stories comes one narrating how the Water compelled a man to make peace with his enemies. Meeting two men whom he disliked, he intended to pass them by without saluting them. Straightway in the phial, which he carried in his bosom, the Water began to flow out as though it were boiling over. He changed his mind, and "on the instant that his heart was at peace, the Water, to his astonishment, was at peace also."

[553] The miracle wrought on Laetitia must have been in early days, before the tomb was walled in; for she lay on the sarcophagus and even slept on it—a thing severely punished by the Saint in a miracle recorded above by Benedict. But she awoke, first with one eye restored to sight, and then with the other. This miracle is not attested.

---

[6] "turbam stupidam sibi occurrere obstupuit." [1] ii. 197-201.

As to the parents and place of residence, the writer says "of noble father but lowly mother, of a county and manor[2] whose names I suppress because of their barbarous nature." This is not like Benedict's manner.

[554] There follow some accounts of people struck with blindness for pretending to be blind, or for despising the blind, in connection with the name of St. Thomas. Geoffrey, a knight of Charlton in Gloucestershire, pretended to be blind, and obtained the Water by importunity, after the monks had declined to give it to him. Whether in consequence of this trick, or (as the context would rather indicate) because of his bad reputation in his neighbourhood, he was called "Musard (Malae Artes)."[3] In any case he was severely punished. Returning from Canterbury, he had not gone seven miles before he became blind. The visitation led him to repent. He confessed, received the sacrament, returned to Canterbury, and there, after three days of penitent blindness, regained his sight.

[555] On the other hand, a rustic of Abingdon was not equally fortunate. "Concerning his miraculously inflicted and continuous blindness," says the chronicler, "we confess that it is a fact ascertained by us;[4] and inasmuch as many have deviated from the truthful account of this miracle, and have darkened the clear sky of truth with the mist of facetious falsehood, let [my] hearers mark what truth I have ascertained in the course of a diligent investigation, that they may be able to discern light from darkness." The style is hardly Benedict's, and the language points to a comparatively late miracle recorded still later, and not until it had been widely circulated in some shape discreditable to the fame of St. Thomas or injurious to religion.

---

[2] ii. 205 "praedio."
[3] ii. 205: comp. "Mauclerc," the name given to Hugh of Horsea, who perpetrated the final outrage on the body of the Archbishop.
[4] ii. 206 "nobis constare fatemur."

[556] This man had in the first place compelled his wife and his sick brother to leave Canterbury prematurely, and, as it would seem, before the latter was perfectly cured; and then, again in spite of their objection, he had forced them to quit an inn at Rochester because some blind folk resorted to it: "I am not going to lodge with St. Thomas's blind folk," he said: "I have nothing to do with them." His punishment is described as coming by degrees,[5] but it was speedy enough:. "And the Lord covered the eyes of the countryman by degrees with the darkness of blindness: and on the morrow he was made quite blind. . . . Over and over again did he afterwards resort to the Martyr; but he was blinded once for all, and more than once did he bring back his lightless luminaries from our luminary[6] (St. Thomas); for up till this day he has life but not light."

§ 6. *The son of William of Banwell;*[1] *Matilda from the region of Cologne*

[557] The story of William of Banwell and his son is still more melancholy. When the son refused to stay any longer with his blind father at Canterbury, the old man called down vengeance on him in the name of the Martyr. Yet, as he could not remain alone among strangers, he consented to go. "If you would but wait a little," he said, "you would perhaps see me seeing;[2] but now, contrary to my hope, such as I came, such do I return." So the son led the father back; "and as he went into the next city he lost the use of his eyes. Yet he went on, lamenting, as far as the seventh milestone. There, in the utter darkness of blindness, he sat down in the midst of the highroad with his father whom he had been leading. . . Those who passed by gave them nearly

---

[5] ii. 207 "paulatim."
[6] "Sed semel excaecatus, non semel tantum a lumine nostro lumina sine lumine reportavit," a play on words, such as is frequent in this section of the treatise.
[1] ii. 207 "De Benewella."   [2] "videntem me videres."

enough to convey them both to Canterbury; but afterwards they departed without our knowledge and left us ignorant whether they ever recovered their sight."

[558] The madness of Matilda of Cologne and her tragic history are graphically told. The monks shrank from the spectacle of her violent fury: she had nothing on but a linen smock and tore that to fragments; she struck with all her might[3] a friend who wished to remove her; she would have strangled a little child, who came in her way, had he not been speedily snatched from her by the bystanders. In bonds, for four or five hours, she raved on before the Memorial, until the Martyr looked on her and drove out the evil spirit, though it still left at first foul traces behind. By degrees she returned to herself, and in the morning she became completely sane. "Her speech,"[4] says Benedict, "was scarcely intelligible to me. But she said that she had seen in her dreams the Martyr clothed in pontifical vestments, with the oblique blood-streak across his face, such as I described in the Passion,[5] and asking the nature of her disease; whereupon she had informed him of her suffering of body and mind." Then the Saint promised her recovery, and bade her go on pilgrimage to the threshold of the Apostles, or to the Church of St. James:[6] on these terms he promised her absolution.

When she was asked how she had become insane, "she said that a young man whom she dearly loved had been killed by her brother: then she, in a fit of madness, had killed with a blow of the fist her little one, christened only the day before. So she departed from the Martyr healed and rejoicing, anxious now about nothing but obtaining pardon for her sin."

---

[3] ii. 208 "non fictis viribus."   [4] "idiomate."
[5] These words shew that this narrative proceeds from Benedict himself.
[6] The latter means Compostella; the former, Rome, as containing the tombs of St. Peter and St. Paul.

§ 7. *The Saint's " merry jests "*

[**559**] " I should like," proceeds the chronicler, " to insert among these graver narratives a few stories about the Martyr's merry jests (ludis) for recreation's sake ; for even his jests are matters of gravity." So he tells us how Sibilla came into a court of law to plead for her dower, with only an obol in her purse, having just given a *denarius* away to a girl who had been delivered from madness by St. Thomas, and who had begged for that sum[1] in the Martyr's name. The monks, by the way, seem to have formed a high opinion of Sibilla's credibility : " she was ready and willing," says the writer, " to take oath on the holy sacrament that she had but an obol left, though we doubt not that her plain affirmation deserved credit." The chronicler goes on to say that, while she was waiting for the verdict, " she happened to put her hand into her purse, and found a *denarius* like the last but in remarkably good condition."[2] She whispered to one of the knights by her that the *denarius* she had given for the Martyr's sake had been returned to her. Others of the knights overheard it, and a crowd of curious people flocked round : so the woman publicly confessed it and shewed the *denarius*, which was beheld with astonishment by all. But she would not give it up to anybody. For that silver *denarius* was " more precious to her than gold."

[**560**] Similarly[3] it fared with Richard, Chaplain to the Sheriff of Devon, who, having vowed to become a pilgrim and to give alms on his way to every one that asked in the name of St. Thomas, found that his servants had forgotten to provide him with the small change that he expressly ordered, so that, having not a single *quadrans* left, he had

---

[1] ii. 209. It was a considerable sum under the circumstances. This and the following stories shew that already the profession of a pilgrim to or from St. Thomas, and especially of a pilgrim returning cured, might be very lucrative.

[2] "quantitate praestantem."   [3] ii. 210.

before him the alternative of breaking his vow or else giving every beggar a *denarius*. However, when the next beggar came, he put his hand in his pocket, and there was an obol, and so for the second, third, and all the rest, till he came to Canterbury : " Yet the venerable man asseverated to us, and that on his oath, that he was absolutely certain he had not brought a single obol with him."

[561] The chronicler adds that his faith in these two miracles is strengthened by the fact that almost the same thing happened to Ralph, Sub-prior of St. Augustine's, Canterbury. He had received five *solidi* for travelling expenses to Rochester, out of which he had paid several *denarii* for shoeing the horses, etc., and three obols for the poor. Yet on his return, on counting out his *denarii*, he found that they amounted to exactly five *solidi* and three obols, so that he had brought back more than he took away by three obols—the amount of his alms!

§ 8. *Miracles for mariners: an imposture works a cure*

[562] There follow a few miracles wrought for mariners, two or three of which, being narrated also by William, will be found below.[1] In the first of these (not given by William) Henry of London is warned by St. Thomas not to return from Norway in the vessel in which he sailed thither, as it will be wrecked ; and it is added that, if the young man takes the Saint's advice, he will have no more fevers. All happened as predicted, and Henry came to Canterbury to make an offering and give thanks.[2] Another man, dragged overboard by a rope letting the anchor down, was saved (though his leg was eaten away to the bone) by the breaking of the anchor ring consequent on his invocation of St Thomas.[3] Ivo of Lynn,[4] on a voyage to Norway, was caught in a tempest which dispersed, shattered, or sank almost all

---

[1] 721 *sq*.   [2] ii. 212.   [3] ii. 214.   [4] ii. 216.

the vessels sailing with him; but he had on board a priest, to whom St. Thomas appeared as he slept, saying, "Awake, bid thy companions say twenty Pater Nosters for my father's soul, and ye shall not perish." They obeyed, and were safely driven back to the port whence they had started. This, says the chronicler, he had from Robert of Lincoln, a clerk on board: "There are many other matters of the same kind: but one and the same sort of food cannot be continually taken without disgust."

[563] So he passes, for variety's sake, to a quite new story—brief, but one of the most instructive of all. It tells how a young man, suffering from an acute disease and being on the point of death, begged in agony for the Martyr's Water. The friends at his bedside had none of it at hand: "But one of them ran to a spring, and fetched a vessel of fresh water, saying, 'Here is the Water of the Saint which you desire.' The sick man believed and drank, and under this health-giving deception was immediately cured. For at once, abandoned by the disease, he left his bed, feeling nothing amiss except mere weakness. This same young man not only related these facts to us but also brought to Canterbury the person who drew the water from the fountain and other witnesses."

The writer seems to think his readers will scarcely credit this. Many in our days will find no difficulty in accepting it as true, and as explaining a large number of the other miracles.[5]

§ 9. *The Water: imperfect cures: Benedict's miracle*

[564] One or two of the next miracles[1] indicate that it had by this time become a general practice in churches and houses of religion to keep "the Water of St. Thomas" for

---

[5] William relates no such miracle, but has one (i. 384) of opposite tendency where a supposititious water produces no effect, and the patient is warned in a vision that she has been deceived and that she cannot recover without the genuine Water.   [1] ii. 217-19.

purposes of healing. But none of these call for special remark. A rather pathetic story about Mabel, daughter of Stephen de Aglandre, of Neen in Shropshire, describes in painful detail her sufferings from a stony tumour which had brought her into a state between death and insanity, and how, in answer to a Canterbury pilgrim suggesting prayer to St. Thomas,[2] she replied, "He cannot help me. He would have helped me if he could. For I have cried to him, oh, how many times! And he has not heard me." Then her friend begged her to persevere, and to vow a pilgrimage on foot. "She vowed," says the chronicler, "and (as far as I remember) she tasted the Water. Immediately, in a moment, the tumour broke internally . . . and in that same hour she rose from her bed, restored, though weak." One of her physicians, hearing of her recovery, said, "Whoever asserts it is a liar." However, he went in to see her, and "he was astounded with joy, and believed, though astounded."

[565] After two cures of dropsy—the second of which is despatched in six lines "lest my readers should be disgusted instead of delighted"—the narrator passes to a plain statement of facts characterized by Benedict's usual candour. A woman from Wales[3] brought to Canterbury a little boy blind from birth and a girl insane. The girl was restored on the journey: the boy was "so far improved at Canterbury that I can neither call him blind nor blessed with sight, for he could follow a lantern hither and thither when placed before his eyes, and yet could not see the way he was going. I should like to say this for fear of seeming to exaggerate, as some have done both about this same boy and also about William of Horsepool in Sherwood, a person quite unknown to us, who said he came blind and produced no witness or supporter of his assertion. I saw him using his eyes, I

---

[2] ii. 221 "ad illum preces dirigeret."
[3] ii. 223 "a finibus Gualensium, *qui se Britones appellant.*" The Welsh have been mentioned above, ii. 145, without this addition.

confess, when he departed: but I did not see him blind when he came. And when he had remained with us for several days to improve his sight, he kept, as it seemed to me, still in the same condition."[4]

[566] A cure of insanity (in Walter, a clerk of Hatcliffe, near Grimsby) is followed by a story telling how the writer himself, being attacked at night by three horribly barking dogs, silenced them with the words, "In the name of St. Thomas, hold your peace."[5] After adding that this happened to him twice in the same night, he says, "As God is my witness, I do not tell this for my own glory but for the Martyr's. For indeed the monk Roger, deputed like myself to be custodian of the sacred body, had something equally or still more wonderful befall him." This introduces the story of Eda. She was a lady from Scotland who had not put her foot to the ground for ten years. Coming to Canterbury, after three days spent near the tomb, she begged for a draught of the Water. Roger refused unless she would come to him for it. "Sir," she replied, "for ten years I have not walked a step, and how could I now come to you?" The monk answered, "In the name of the Martyr, I bid you rise and come to me." Straightway she arose; and not only came, but went thrice round the tomb. However, she could only walk on tiptoe at first. But next day she used the soles of her feet, and finally dispensed with her litter and returned on horseback to Scotland, where she "made gradual progress day by day and obtained the great blessing of a complete cure."[6]

§ 10. *Restoration after drowning*

[567] Robert, a boy of Rochester,[1] fell into the Medway about three o'clock and was not dragged out till after the

---

[4] William enters into less detail about cures of blindness. He does not, I believe, mention any cases of partial cure, or of blindness from birth.
[5] ii. 224.   [6] ii. 225 "sanitatis."   [1] ii. 226.

bell had rung for vespers. He was senseless, and blue in the face, and though he was hung up by his feet, not a drop of water came out. They rolled him about in a tub to make him vomit, but all was in vain. Night was almost coming on, and many said he was dead. The mother, who, from the moment when she heard the news, had not ceased calling on St. Thomas, now again invoked him, measuring the body with a thread and promising the Martyr a silver thread of the same length for her son's life. The boy immediately vomited the water and was restored to health. Next day he was with his playfellows as usual.

[568] The chronicler proceeds to admit that in this case life may not have been extinct ; but he invites any one who may be disinclined to believe in the miraculous nature of this restoration, to consider how it is confirmed by his next similar story about a child six months old, who had been three hours under water in a bath, Gilbert son of Ralph and Wulviva, of Sarre.[2] When the nurse brought word of the mishap, the mother in an agony snatched the body out of doors crying and shrieking so that all the women of the village came out to help. The men were away, fishing or at harvest. But one, perhaps old and decrepit, who had returned as a pilgrim from Jerusalem, bade her carry the babe in : " Why labour in vain ? The breath is long out of its body." Then said a widow, " Are not five of us widows ? Let us kneel nine times and invoke St. Thomas, and repeat the Lord's Prayer nine times in his name." They did so, but still " the boy did not arise."[3] Then one said, " Run and fetch a thread and measure the babe, and vow a candle of the same length." As soon as this was done, water and blood issued from the child's mouth, and in a very short time he moved his eyelids and burst out crying.

---

[2] ii. 227.

[3] " Non surrexit puer," a somewhat monkish expression to use about a baby of six months.

"I myself," says the writer, "went to the village of Sarre, to sift[4] the truth more carefully"; and he regards the facts as conclusive. "From nine o'clock to noon he was in the bath, so to speak, boiled;[5] at noon he was drawn out and lay without breath of life till 4 or 5 o'clock; . . . Perhaps now some carper will still dare to object, and to say that an infant half a year old could have lived half a day without breathing." He then appeals to a more remarkable case, which, as being one of the Parallel Miracles, is given below.[6] And this is followed by two other Parallel Miracles, both dealing with revivification.[7]

[569] In the half-dozen cures that follow, we may note that of Geoffrey of Lindeby, a cutler,[8] who, having lost the use of two of his fingers as penalty for working on the day of St. Peter's Chair, regained them (on consecutive days) at the Martyr's tomb; also the daughter of Edilda of Godmersham (a manor belonging to Canterbury Cathedral) recovered the use of her arm at the tomb.[9]

§ 11. *Leprosy again*

Now the chronicle returns to cases of leprosy. First comes that of Elias of Reading described below in the Parallel Miracles; then that of Gerard of Lille.[1]

[570] Gerard, when the symptoms first appeared, and even afterwards, was tolerated by his fellow-citizens as long as possible, because of his respectable position and amiable nature: but at last, receiving his sentence of banishment, he made arrangements for being taken into a leper-house, and was on the point of hastening his departure, when, one night, he saw himself in a vision prostrated at the tomb of the Martyr in Canterbury, and the sarcophagus was cleft asunder, and the Saint, through a chink, breathed into his

---

[4] "ut . . . eliquarem."   [5] "decoctus."   [6] See **732**.
[7] See **737, 741**.   [8] ii. 240.   [9] ii. 241.   [1] ii. 243.

mouth. "In this vision," remarks the chronicler, by the way, "it is especially wonderful that, just as he saw the marble tomb in his dream, just so did he find it in fact when he came to Canterbury." To return to Gerard. He sold all that he had and set out to gain "the pearl of price" —restoration to health. Confirmed by another vision, he travelled to Canterbury, where he spent nine sleepless nights, daily anointed with, and daily drinking of, the mixture of blood and water. Then, "as though cut with razors, the skin of his feet and legs (the chief seat of his leprosy) was broken so as to afford innumerable passages for the exit of his plague; the flow of matter ran down even into his shoes, and so he departed with some abatement of the pressure of his disease."[2] Having gone on board he perceived by the cessation of the prickings and burnings that he was cleansed; and—"as though the Saint were saying to him, 'Now thou hast been made whole: return and give glory to God'—a violent storm arose and drove him back to Sandwich. So, as this port was near Canterbury, he turned back and presented himself to us cleansed; and, abiding with us many days, he increased the devotion of many toward the Martyr."

[571] But against this must be set the sad case of the boy Gilbert of St. Valery, only ten years old, yet a leper, almost as diseased as Gerard, "an unbounded cause of grief and shame to his parents, who, however, faithfully supplicated the Lord that he might become the cause of praise and glory to His Martyr. And God saw that it was good; and it was so. For when he was brought to the Martyr, he was so amended, in the space of three days, that the matter, which had been flowing and hardening over the whole of his body, disappeared, and the faculty of feeling was restored to his hands and feet, and as a whole[3] he seemed (by sure

---

[2] "imminuta morbi angustia."   [3] "ipse."

tokens) fairly on the way to perfect restoration." One might almost suppose that, in its original form, the miraculous narrative stopped here, so that there was nothing to jar with the strain of triumph in "God saw that it was good." But our honest chronicler proceeds: "However, on his return home, after a very little time—by some, I know not what, inscrutable judgment of God—he became worse and a great deal worse than before."[4]

[572] After mentioning another cure of leprosy (one that convinced the Bishop of Salisbury[5]), he passes to a particularly acute case, which perhaps would have been mentioned before, had not the patient, when cured, left Canterbury without telling the monks. Richard Sunieve— son of a poor woman, but herdsman of a well-to-do knight of Edgeworth[6]—suffered, like many others mentioned in previous narratives, from sleeping out of doors. He awoke with face swelled and spotted, and for eight years the leprosy spread through his body until at last he was forced to leave not only the knight's house but even the village.[7] His mother alone "followed him lest he should perish." From head to foot he was a mass of ulcers. There was not "the space of an arrow's point" sound. So foul was his state that even his mother could only give him his food at the end of a long stick, or place it where he could find it. Now the boy heard of the Martyr's fame, and wept that he had no strength to travel to him. His tears were useless till he invoked the Saint and rose from his bed and turned towards Canterbury. He improved daily and reached his destination. "When admitted to the sepulchre, he kissed it, and a great swelling, like a small apple, which projected between his nose and lip, suddenly disappeared. He thought it must have fallen, and felt for it, but could not find it. On

---

[4] ii. 245 ("multo deterius quam ante deterioratus est." [5] See **747**.
[6] ii. 245. The text says "Cestrensi," "in Cheshire"; but the Editor suggests that it is an error for "Gloucestershire." [7] "villa."

tasting of the Water, he was affected like one intoxicated. His feet tottered, and he could scarcely make his way out of the church. Then he fell into an ecstasy.[8] Presently, arising [from the ground], he felt a new nimbleness in his body: and the skin, which, at the moment of his fall, had been distended by leprosy, was now, to his great astonishment, quite thin and wrinkled. To put off his return was not to be borne; so, in order to present himself to his friends whole, he gladdened them before us by going home at once." It is added that the knight his master, who had been doubtful about the Martyr's miracles before, "believed now with all his house; and on hearing that the lad had secretly departed, he came, with his wife and household and brothers and relations and friends, on a visit to the Martyr, and brought the lad sound and healthy. At our special request, he also allowed him to stay for a considerable time with us."

§ 12. *Trial by ordeal*

[573] The next three narratives refer to trial by ordeal.[1] No names are given, for obvious reasons in the last two. The first deals with trial by battle. The bigger and stronger combatant held the weaker in his grip, suspended in the air, and was on the point of dashing him to the ground when the latter cried, "St. Thomas, Martyr, help!" The fact is attested, says the writer, "by witnesses who were present: the stronger, just as if he were crushed by the weight of the holy name, suddenly fell in a heap under the man he was holding, and so was beaten." The next narrative is in two sentences, thus: "Two men being accused concerning the forests of the King of England and deer which they had taken, were adjudged to ordeal of water. One was thereby proved thief and hanged; the other invoked the Martyr with all his might,[2] and got off."[3] The

---

[8] The context implies that he also fell to the ground.
[1] ii. 247.   [2] "attentius."   [3] "evasit."

reason for not mentioning names is still more obvious in the following: "I suppress the number and names of others *justly accused* of the same offence, but rescued, by invoking the Martyr, from peril of death. For he stood by one of them in a vision, bidding them depart.[4] He awoke and gladdened his comrades with his dream. They were tried by ordeal of water. Every man of them got off: and all together came to the Martyr to give thanks in woollen garments and with feet bare."

[574] This narrative derives some of its force from the fact that the men were "justly accused," in other words, guilty in the eyes of the law. Are we to suppose that in the next story, Agnes, a widow from Cornwall,[5] was also legally in the wrong when she was pleading for her dower against her step-son? Possession was on the point of being adjudged to the latter, when Agnes vowed a bare-foot pilgrimage to St. Thomas. "Suddenly," says the chronicler, "her step-son's hatred was changed into affection: and without suit, prayer, or price, he gave his step-mother all that he had before refused."

[575] Facetiousness and brevity mark the next three narratives. Peter of Dennington[6] in Surrey suffered from a swelling in his head, which became as big as a bull's. He hardly breathed. The household (all but one) went to dinner just after he had received the Water, leaving him in desperate case: but scarcely had they departed when he got up, put on his shoes, washed his hands, and came down "to dine with the diners." The Latin pun cannot be translated in what follows—"Mirantur *convivae* ad *convivium* venisse, quem vix *vivum* reliquissent": perhaps it was originally a French joke. Deafness is next mentioned, an infirmity seldom found in Benedict's book: it is only in one ear, and is cured by infusion of the Water into the ear affected. After

---

[4] "Abirent." Perhaps this might mean, or might include, "on pilgrimage."
[5] ii. 248.   [6] ii. 248 "Denintona."

mentioning a cure of hernia, attested by the treasurer of the Monastery of Lisieux,[7] the writer passes to that of John of Valenciennes, blinded at Corbie in punishment of theft.

[576] This case was like that of Ailward of Westoning, of which the fame had spread through England;[8] and hence the Canterbury monks took the trouble to send a messenger to Corbie. He reported that "the executioner, finding a difficulty in cutting the eyes out, had in a fit of temper drawn a sharp-pointed knife with which he had pierced the eyes again and again so cruelly that all thought the poor fellow was worse treated in having his eyes thus lacerated than in having them torn out. They charged him with gross wickedness, in murdering the man instead of blinding him." Upon this, the messenger seems to have proceeded to the Prior of Corbie, whose letter is appended,[9] to the following effect.

When the young man had been condemned to death for theft, and taken to the place of execution, it pleased the burgesses to lighten the sentence, so that he might be merely blinded: "And presently he was blinded and severely wounded in the eyes, and then taken to the infirmary, where the keeper Radulph bathed his eyes, that night and the following, in hot water . . . and tended them [10] to assuage the pain. On the third day, when Radulph anxiously asked him whether after his blinding he had the least vestige of sight,[11] he replied that in one of his eyes

---

[7] ii. 249: the "treasurer (thesaurarius)" not only writes, but sends the patient, concluding his letter thus: "On this point, ascertain the truth from the man himself. 'He is of age; ask him.'"

[8] See "Parallel Miracles" below (710).

[9] ii. 250. It is directed to Odo, who was Prior of Canterbury up to 1175.

[10] ii. 251 "refovit (?) poulticed."

[11] "Dum ab eo sollicite percunctaretur utrum ei post excaecationem suam extremae saltem visionis aditus patuisset." This is surely very remarkable. If a man's hand was cut off, no one would "anxiously ask him whether he had a *germ of the hand still left*." Radulph's question suggests that, though rare, it was not unprecedented, that a man blinded in accordance with law should retain some faculty of seeing.

there was none, but in the other some slight brightness was admitted, but so slight that he could not walk straight without guidance. Meanwhile there came in a poor young clerk, who avowed [12] that he had a glass phial containing some of the Water of the Martyr. . . . So they took a little of the Water, and, after reverently lighting candles in honour of the Martyr, they carefully washed the man's eyes therewith. Immediately he received his sight, so that even the scars of the wounds inflicted in the blinding were also healed. Next day he returned to his home, sound and happy. And, lest any hesitation concerning this matter should linger in your mind, we testify to you that one of our brethren drinking of the same Water was freed from a flow of humour from the nostrils."

[577] This instructive letter must be borne in mind later on, when we approach two similar cases attested severally by burgesses of Bedford and by the Bishop of Durham. It shows, first, that the manager of the Monastic Infirmary was quite prepared to find some power of sight remaining in a man blinded by the public executioner; secondly, that the monks themselves made so slight a distinction between such a restoration of sight and more ordinary acts of healing, that they considered all grounds for hesitation as to the former must be removed, when it was known that the Water had cured brother so-and-so of a running cold.

§ 13. *Dropsy; beer that will not ferment*

[578] At this point, between two miracles performed on patients of the name of Geoffrey, comes another, recorded by Benedict alone, which perhaps owes its position to the fact that here, too, the name is Geoffrey.[1] Peter, Abbot of St. Remi, says, "Concerning Geoffrey a monk of

---

[12] "confessus est."   [1] See 580.

Mont Dieu,[2] I relate what I have heard as the true facts, partly from himself, but more fully from a monk of ours, who wrote on the spot and at the time. It happened that a paper of St. Thomas' Miracles had come to us from England, and from us to the brothers of Mont Dieu. The brother in question, swollen and distended all over—an unmistakeable case of dropsy—could not quit his cell. So he took the paper with faith and invocation of the Saint's name,[3] and touched his feet therewith, and his legs, and his whole body: and he recovered to such an extent that after a short interval he returned to the church and to his duty, though not completely cured." This very truthful and modest statement is principally valuable as showing how natural it was, and indeed inevitable, that the accounts of the Martyr's Miracles should appear in different versions, and at first in brief ones. Here we find mention of one of the earliest, a mere "paper." Benedict's treatise, in its first shape, was probably much later, but still both early and brief, relatively to his later edition, and as compared with William's book.

[579] Master Richard, a monk of Ely, is responsible for the next miracle, which deals with beer. Ralph of Hadfield[4] and his wife wished to visit the Martyr but had not the wherewithal. They thought they would try to make a little money by brewing some beer. But the liquor would not ferment. So the poor wife, seeing her liquor had come to naught, cast into it the string that held one of the Saint's phials: "Immediately there was such an outburst of what the brewing women call 'flowers' that it could hardly be stopped from overflowing: and thus the undrinkable was made both drinkable and saleable. These facts however I did not receive from the woman herself but from Master Richard, monk of Ely, who heard her confess this to him."

---

[2] ii. 252. The Editor adds "near Sedan."   [3] "sancti nominis."
[4] ii. 253 "Hathfeld," another MS. "Hadfeld." Editor suggests also "Hatfield" or "Heathfield.'

§ 14. *End of the Fourth Book; the Fifth Book; confusion in arrangement*

[580] Perhaps Benedict, or his assistant, found it very difficult to group miracles, now that he had given up chronological order. At all events, whereas just now we had three miracles together performed on three people called Geoffrey, so we now have, after the brewing miracle attested by a monk of Ely ("Heliensis ecclesiae"), a miracle of healing performed on "Elias (Helyae)" nephew of the dean of Sherborne.[1] Not improbably the leaflets containing some of the less important miracles were arranged at first in alphabetical order: and this was sometimes done rather mechanically. It is doubtless from the same Dean that there comes the next brief miracle, the healing of his servant Hadewisa by drinking the Water. These two are cases of intestinal disease.

[581] The next two are only worth recording as specimens of useless unattested narrative, perhaps to be explained by pressure of other miracles, and want of leisure in the monk, or monks, in charge of the tomb; (i.) "Among sufferers from stone, who more pitiable than Robert of Beverun[2]? He vowed a pilgrimage, tasted the Water, and ejected the stone in fragments, crushed by the virtue of the draught." (ii.) "Hingan, a neighbour of the above, suffered from fits. They seized him sleeping, and his agony distressed all that saw him. When he came to himself, he had no recollection of being in pain. It was supposed to be some kind of falling sickness. He too drank of the salutary Water, and, after the draught, lived in peace."[3]

[582] The two with which the Fourth Book concludes are foreign in origin and perhaps in style. William le Brun,

---

[1] ii. 254 "Decani de Siburna," another MS. "Liburna."
[2] "de Beveruno."
[3] After this comes the healing of James, son of the Earl of Clare (758).

of Caen, overwhelmed with sorrow at the approaching death of his son Gilbert, who was suffering from fever, retired to his bedroom from the crowd of friends who had come to console him, and shut his door, saying, "I will not see my son die." At last, however, hearing an outcry, and understanding that he was doubtless dying,[4] he ran to the boy's bedside and devoted him to St. Thomas. Then he approached his son, saying, "Son, for the love of God and the Martyr Thomas, if you can, speak to me." The boy, as though roused from sleep, lifted his arm and embraced his father. And he that was well-nigh dead sat up, and began to speak,[5] and in the same week he was restored to perfect health.[6]

[583] The last of all is very French. Roger, son of Savaric de Vaux an honourable knight,[7] was on the point of dying from diarrhoea, not having tasted anything but water for twenty days. His parents make a vow to the Martyr for him : " Strange, but not past the bounds of truth, is the tale I tell. After their vow they go to dinner. Among their first courses is a course of joy. For, while they were dining, up rose the boy whom they had left in his chamber half dead, and, putting on his clothes, came to them as they were at table, spinning round in a *taratantara* before their faces, as merry boys will, and full of fun. The guests present were full of wonder, and the parents rejoiced in their new guest."

[584] Here ends the Fourth Book, and the Paris MS. of Benedict's miracles contains no more. In another MS., "there is no notice that a new book begins. But the numbering of chapters is broken off, and the remaining part of the MS. appears to be written in a different hand."[8] That we have not here Benedict's own arrangement appears demonstrated by the fact that the so-called Fifth Book con-

---

[4] ii. 257 "advertens quia proculdubio moreretur."
[5] Luke vii. 15.   [6] "restitutus est incolumis."
[7] ii. 258 (?) "miles honoratus."   [8] ii. 258, Editor's note.

sists of only four miracles, all of them quite short, except the last, which is a case of leprosy, discussed below in the Parallel Miracles.[9] It ends in a style unlike that of Benedict, at least unlike that of his earlier narratives: "There are many, very many, whose skin the Martyr has smoothed and relieved from the leper's tubers : but to speak of single cases singly and collectively is incongruous.[10] For even a sweet song repeated sometimes causes weariness. Lest therefore we should make what is trite more trite to the tedium of our readers, let us await something new."

§ 15. *The Sixth Book*

The Sixth Book takes its cue from the last words of the Fifth : "We sighed," it begins, "for something new. By something new are we now kindled anew to a new love of the Martyr of the English."[1] Then the writer passes to the delivery of a man buried by a fall of earth, which will be found in the Parallel Miracles.[2] Next follows another Parallel, one of the longest and most romantic of all, about Salerna of Ifield, who throws herself into a well,[3] and then a third about John, servant of Sweyn of Roxburgh, restored after being lost in the Tweed.[4]

[585] The next relates incidentally how Geoffrey, Prior of Canterbury, went to Rouen with relics of St. Thomas, hoping to meet King Richard on his way from Palestine. The rumour of the King's arrival at Rouen was false, for he was kept prisoner by the Duke of Austria. Richard set out from Palestine in Oct. 1193, and Benedict died in 1193 or 1194.

---

[9] See **767**.
[10] ii. 260 "non congruit." Does he mean (1) "the two things are incompatible with each other"; or (2) "the combination is not compatible with my purpose"? William (i. 332-3) has a long disquisition on the nature and means of healing leprosies collectively. Does Benedict, or, more probably, Benedict's scribe, mean that he deliberately disclaims this way of treating the subject?
[1] ii. 261. The Latin play on "novus" is, of course, intentional.
[2] See **771**.   [3] See **777**.   [4] See **783**.

If, therefore, the latter was still collecting notable miracles of the Martyr to be added to his book, it is quite possible that this may have been one of the last sent to him from Canterbury. It is of a degenerate character. Geoffrey has taken with him to Rouen a bone of St. Thomas. While waiting at Eu for a passage home, he misses this precious relic. After his return, he finds it at the altar on Easter eve. Filled with grateful wonder, he bade one of the brethren record the miracle. The monk neglected to do it and was himself punished by losing a relic. But, after a vow to repair the omission, he found what he had lost.[5]

[586] If there is no error in a date mentioned in the next miracle, we should be forced to conclude that it was past Benedict's time: for it describes the Martyr's power in releasing four Christians, who were captives among the Saracens for fourteen years, dating from the triumph of Saladin in 1187.[6] If "fourteen" were not a mistake for "four," this miracle would be nearly ten years *later* than the miracle that *follows* it, which also relates the release (by St. Thomas) of a captive after three years spent among the Saracens. It is highly probable that, in the former, an original iv was taken for xiv, and that the captives came to Canterbury not in 1202 but in 1192—in time to allow of the inclusion of the miracle in Benedict's last edition of his work.

[587] There is a dramatic fitness in the juxtaposition of the last two miracles. The last but one[7] is about a bishop coming from the extreme East. The last of all[8] is about a nobleman from Ireland, the extreme West. On the very day on which the bishop from the East left Canterbury, the nobleman from the West reached it. This, says the chronicler, was ordained "in order that there might be fulfilled also in the Martyr that which the Lord says in the Gospel,

---

[5] ii. 268-70.   [6] ii. 270-3.   [7] ii. 273-9.   [8] ii. 279-81.

'Many shall come from the East and from the West and shall sit down with Abraham, Isaac, and Jacob.'"

[588] The character of these final miracles, and the style of their narratives, make it unlikely that Benedict had much if any share in the composition. But it is not improbable that when he was Abbot of Peterborough, he continued his task of collecting them, leaving to others the task of ascertaining the evidence and transcribing it: and those in the Sixth Book may be the very last sent to him.

END OF VOL. I